SETTLER GARRISON

SETTLER GARRISON

Debt Imperialism, Militarism,

and Transpacific Imaginaries

JODI KIM

DUKE UNIVERSITY PRESS
Durham and London   2022

© 2022 DUKE UNIVERSITY PRESS

All rights reserved
Printed in the United States of America on acid-free paper ∞
Typeset in Portrait Text and Quadraat Sans
by Westchester Publishing Services

Library of Congress Cataloging-in-Publication Data
Names: Kim, Jodi, [date] author.
Title: Settler garrison: debt imperialism, militarism, and transpacific
imaginaries / Jodi Kim.
Description: Durham: Duke University Press, 2022. | Includes
bibliographical references and index.
Identifiers: LCCN 2021036596 (print)
LCCN 2021036597 (ebook)
ISBN 9781478015680 (hardcover)
ISBN 9781478018315 (paperback)
ISBN 9781478022923 (ebook)
Subjects: LCSH: Military bases, American—Pacific Area. | Debts,
Public—United States. | Imperialism. | Postcolonialism—Pacific Area. |
United States—Territorial expansion. | United States—Foreign economic
relations—Pacific Area. | Pacific Area—Foreign economic relations—
United States. | BISAC: HISTORY / World | POLITICAL SCIENCE /
Colonialism & Post-Colonialism
Classification: LCC DU30. K56 2022 (print) | LCC DU30 (ebook) |
DDC 325/.32—dc23/eng/20211027
LC record available at https: //lccn.loc.gov/2021036596
LC ebook record available at https: //lccn.loc.gov/2021036597

Cover art: US Naval Base Guam on Apra Harbor. Courtesy the
Department of Defense. The appearance of US Department of
Defense (DoD) visual information does not imply or constitute DoD
endorsement.

CONTENTS

INTRODUCTION: *US Exceptionalisms, Metapolitical Authority, and the Aesthetics of Settler Imperial Failure*

Bong Joon Ho's highly lauded *Parasite* (2019) made Oscar history in 2020 by becoming the first non-English language film to win the top prize of Best Picture. The South Korean film also won Oscars for Best Original Screenplay, Best Director, and Best International Feature Film. It seemed fitting that a film with such universal resonance and appeal would be the first to win in the newly renamed category of Best International Feature Film, changed from the provincial and outdated Best Foreign Language Film. The conferral of these top Academy Awards also seemed to position *Parasite* as a partial remedy for the US film industry's lack of diversity, encapsulated in the hashtag "#OscarsSo-White."[1] By all accounts, it seemed that enduring problems of underrepresentation and English-language monolingualism (what Bong famously called the "one-inch tall barrier of subtitles") had indeed been at least partially overcome when the film achieved the trifecta of garnering prestigious awards globally, glowingly positive reviews, and high box-office receipts.[2]

Parasite's success can be attributed not only to Bong's technical prowess as an internationally recognized "genre-defying" auteur long preceding the release of the film but also to the purported universality and resonance of its critique of capitalist class dynamics and wealth inequality through a South Korean setting and cast. Indeed, analyses of the film, both in terms of reviews and scholarly articles, applaud the ways in which the "local" context of South Korea effectively serves the "universal" theme of class hierarchy. In a *New York Times* review, for example, Manohla Dargis writes, "The story takes place in South Korea but could easily unfold in Los Angeles or London. The director Bong Joon Ho creates specific spaces and faces . . . that are in service to universal ideas about human dignity, class, life itself."[3] When asked the question, "What makes *Parasite* and many of your films specific to Korean culture, yet universal?" Bong responded, "Essentially, we all live in the same country . . . called Capitalism."[4] But are Seoul, Los Angeles, and London truly so facilely interchangeable, beyond general categorization as global megalopolises? Certainly, much of the critical focus on *Parasite* has rightly praised the film's trenchant way of grappling with capitalist class inequality. Yet what if we were to widen the aperture and see alongside or beyond *Parasite*'s putatively universal "upstairs/downstairs" motif in order to apprehend something less obvious and more complex as the narrative unfolds? What would come to light is that even as the film offers a universal story of class strife that could presumably take place in any global city, it simultaneously offers a story of US-led global racial capitalism's specific modalities in South Korea.

In doing so, *Parasite* dramatizes the four interlocking concerns of *Settler Garrison*. First, the film connects the South Korean modalities of racial capitalism to what I conceptualize in this book as US militarist settler imperialism, or the conjunction of US settler colonialism and military empire heavily concentrated in Asia and the Pacific in the post–World War II era. The "Cowboys and Indians" thematic refrain in the film, what I call "Indian cosplay," allegorizes the transpacific reach and transits of US militarist settler imperialism. Introduced as innocent child's play, the climactic and gruesomely bloody reenactment of a "Cowboys and Indians" encounter in the film underscores how class dynamics in South Korea are connected to the ongoing violence of US militarist settler imperialism. Second, *Parasite* also makes visible that the United States, in particular its military, can exercise certain jurisdictional and sovereign powers in specific locales or spatial exceptions across Asia and the Pacific that it has transformed into what I call the settler garrison. Thus, although Seoul, like Los Angeles and London, is a global megacity, a crucial difference is that it is the capital city of what is effectively a militarized US neocolony. If *Parasite* is in part a ghost story, the specter of US militarist settler imperialism is embedded in the very architectural design of the wealthy Park home, which becomes apparent as a kind of garrison.

Third, *Parasite* makes visible how this exceptional spatial dynamic of US militarist settler imperialism is linked to an exceptional temporal logic. The temporal logic emerges as debt, specifically the question of debt not simply as a straight economic relation but a broader manifold cultural relation and form undergirded by asymmetries of power at multiple scales. These asymmetries of power significantly determine not only the debtor/creditor relation itself but also which debtors must conform to a strict payback schedule (what I call the homogeneous time of repayment) while others get to evade it without the threat of discipline and carceral punishment. Differential vulnerability to economic debt conditions the relationship between the Parks and the Kims in the film, the haves and the have-nots. Yet the narrative twist of triangulating the class dynamics between these two families with that of a third, Moon-gwang and her husband Geun-se, reveals how the homogeneous time of debt repayment is crushing for some but not others. It is a kind of fatal double standard. *Parasite* reveals, moreover, how the homogeneous time of repayment applies not only to financial debt but also a figurative or affective one. The way in which debt as a cultural and temporal logic, conjoined with the economic one, is imposed on material spaces of the settler garrison such as South Korea is crucial to how US militarist settler imperialism asserts and continually renovates itself. Yet as *Parasite* also dramatizes through what we might call an aesthetics of settler imperial failure, the assertions and ends of US militarist settler imperialism are never fully guaranteed or completed.[5] This is the fourth interlocking concern of *Settler Garrison*—how the transpacific imaginaries of cultural forms such as *Parasite* at once critically magnify and gesture to world-makings and relations beyond the violence of US militarist settler imperialism through an aesthetics of settler imperial failure.

Let us begin with how *Parasite*'s class critique simultaneously amplifies the ongoing story of US militarist settler imperialism in Asia and the Pacific. In the film, all four members of the impoverished Kim family land staff positions in the wealthy Park household through a series of calculated and ingenious deceptions. The stark class differences between the Kims and the Parks become more layered through the narrative twist of triangulating these two families with a third, that of the previous housekeeper, Moon-gwang, whom the Kim matriarch, Chung-sook, has displaced. The narrative twist or surprise is that Moon-gwang's husband, Geun-se, has been secretly living in the underground bunker, the basement of the basement, of the elegantly sleek Park house for multiple years in order to evade debt collectors. The very existence of this bunker is itself also a secret to the Kims and even the Parks for much of the film. What is set up as an *inter*class dynamic between the Kims and the Parks also becomes a gruesome *intra*class war between the Kims and their doppelgängers Moon-gwang and Geun-se.

As the plot unfolds, this tale of how the precariat class is compelled to survive "by any means necessary" increasingly intersects with the tale of US militarist settler imperialism. We can think along these lines by apprehending the emergence of a Native American thematic, or "Indian cosplay," in the film. This allows us to link the frontier violence of US settler colonialism to what then gets projected overseas to Asia and the Pacific in the making of a military empire and settler garrison in the post–World War II era. Viewers are introduced to a seemingly insignificant detail when Ki-woo, the son of the Kim family, goes to the house of the wealthy Parks to be interviewed as a possible English-language tutor for their high school–age daughter, Da-hye. As soon as Ki-woo enters the house, Moon-gwang, the housekeeper, notices arrows on the wall, commenting as she quickly removes them that what was once a famous architect's creation is now a "playpen." We soon learn that the arrows have been shot by the Parks' ten-year-old son, Da-song, while playing with his "Indian" (Native American) bow and arrow set. This Native American trope becomes more significant as the film progresses. We learn that Da-song has become an "Indian fanatic" just like his Cub Scout leader. His mother, Yeon-kyo, has indulged this "fanaticism" for all things Native American by ordering a plethora of stereotypical "toys" from the United States, a bow and arrow set complete with headdresses (war bonnets) and a teepee. Da-song's obsession with "playing Indian" seems to convey nothing more than a fetishism for American toys, as part and parcel of the nouveau riche Parks' fetishism of all things American. Yet his "fanaticism" draws on the long-standing trope of imperialist nostalgia for a time before the closing of the US frontier. This trope functions to recycle the myth of colonial innocence.

Parasite at once displays and shatters the myth of colonial innocence in a climactic scene. Da-song's "Indian cosplay" is indulged yet further toward the end of the film at an impromptu birthday garden party at the house that is thrown for him to make up for having to return home early from a family camping trip because of heavy rain. Meanwhile, while the Parks were gone, the Kims had indulged themselves with a night of eating and drinking at the Park house, only to be interrupted by the return of Moon-gwang, who by this point had been fired as a result of the Kims' machinations. Moon-gwang returns to feed her husband and pleads with the Kims to keep the secret and to keep him alive by feeding him surreptitiously on a regular basis. In return, they would receive ongoing payments from her. The Kims refuse and threaten to call the police, but soon Moon-gwang realizes that these four new household staff members are not strangers to one another at all but a family unit that has essentially finagled itself into the unwitting Parks' employ. Thus ensues a violent chain of events as these two impoverished families who occupy the same precarious class position within South Korea's strict capitalist hierarchy must compete to survive. By the time of Da-song's birthday party, Moon-gwang has already been injured gravely in this battle, and she and her husband Geun-se have been bound and tied up in the bunker while the Kims scramble to clean things up when Park matriarch Yeon-kyo calls to say they are returning home early from the camping trip.

The plot of the birthday party "Indian cosplay" has been worked out in advance, with the Kim and Park patriarchs each donning an Indian headdress and playing "bad Indians" against Da-song's "good Indian." The so-called bad Indians will attempt to capture Kim daughter Ki-jung ("Jessica"), Da-song's art therapist, as she presents him with his birthday cake. But the "cake princess" will ultimately be saved by Da-song as the "good Indian." This plot is thwarted, however, when Geun-se is able to free himself and emerges from the bunker to avenge Moon-gwang's death. He stabs Ki-jung ("Jessica") to death as she walks to Da-song with his cake, and Da-song has a seizure upon seeing Geun-se, the "ghost" he had encountered late at night exactly a year before when he snuck into the kitchen to devour the rest of his birthday cake. Kim patriarch Ki-taek immediately goes to his stabbed daughter, ignoring Park patriarch Dong-ik's repeated calls to him to get the car so Da-song can be taken to the hospital. Then Dong-ik asks to be thrown the car key, but Geun-se's body, mortally injured by Kim matriarch Chung-sook, falls on top of it. In turning Geun-se's body over to grab the car key, Dong-ik holds his nostrils closed. Throughout the film, he had been complaining to his wife, Yeon-kyo, that Ki-taek smells and that the odor is difficult to explain but definitely unpleasant, like a "boiled rag." Yeon-kyo then begins to notice the smell herself, and Da-song innocently notices that all four staff members basically smell the same.

This odor, which Ki-jung ("Jessica") attributes to their semibasement apartment, not only signifies class difference but also Dong-ik's class snobbery and sense of superiority. When Ki-taek sees Dong-ik hold his nose closed against what he considers to be the intolerable stench of working-class bodies, Ki-taek basically snaps. He deviates from his prescribed "Indian cosplay" role by taking off his headdress and going for Dong-ik, also taking off Dong-ik's headdress before killing him. As noted by Ju-Hyun Park in an incisive analysis of the film, given Director Bong's known reputation for storyboarding his films meticulously, this removal of the two headdresses is not insignificant. It might very well gesture to Ki-taek's, and by extension the film's, refusal to cosplay or replicate the genocidal violence of settler colonialism in an uncritical manner, and to refuse to be complicit with South Korea's aggressive allegiance to US-led global capitalism and its neocolonial status as part of the US military empire.[6]

The removal of the headdresses also signals that frontier violence is no longer metaphorical but is a real, contemporary relation. That is, the "bad Indians" transform back into the characters of Ki-taek and Dong-ik with the removal of the headdresses, suggesting at once a kind of break but also a certain continuity in the chain of violence from the settler colonial conquest of Indigenous land in what became the United States and on through the contemporary relation. That contemporary relation, as I have been suggesting, is constituted by the specific modalities of US-led global racial capitalism in South Korea and the dynamics of militarist settler imperialism.

This appearance of the Native American trope in *Parasite* doesn't simply remain at the level of innocent child's play learned in the Cub Scouts. Indeed, putatively innocent child's play as thwarted "Indian cosplay" resulting in multiple gruesome deaths reveals the distinct yet connected and imbricated dynamics of US militarism, settler colonialism, and imperialism as they make their violent transits across the Pacific. The Cub Scouts, itself a settler colonial institution through which young boys get interpellated to adopt a masculinist settler subjectivity via activities such as playing "Cowboys and Indians," gets exported overseas to South Korea as a form of US cultural imperialism, along with the necessary commodified accoutrements or "toys" and "costumes." Moreover, this form of US cultural imperialism is not only replicating as play but is also materially connected to the logics and tactics of settler colonialism on the soil of what has become the United States of America. These logics and tactics get projected overseas to pivotal parts of the US military empire such as South Korea. In turn, military empire is itself also a laboratory for configurations of rule and domination that get applied in modified form within the territory that has become the "domestic" United States through settler colonial conquest and successive seizures of Indigenous land. We thus see in *Parasite* the visible eruption of the structuring conditions of possibility of the dominant terms of order, the circuits through which US militarist settler imperialism continuously asserts and renovates itself. This is to speak of the visible eruption of the violence that is absented, invisibilized, and shunted both literally and figuratively to the bunker and the semibasement, as it were. Yet it is omnipresent. It is the ongoing violence of—and the gruesome structuring violence that undergirds—South Korea's "economic miracle" and subimperial status within Asia as part and parcel of the dominion of US militarist settler imperialism.

To speak of South Korea's "economic miracle" is to speak of its transformation into a US neocolony in the distended shadow of the division of the Korean Peninsula after World War II. To speak of this division, in turn, is to speak of the violence that is shunted, as I have observed, to the bunker. This brings us to the second interlocking concern of *Settler Garrison* that *Parasite* dramatizes—the transformation of spaces in Asia and the Pacific into America's settler garrison where US military authority and sovereignty supersede local sovereignty. We can begin to think along these lines by asking why the Park house even has a secret underground bunker, not just a basement but also a secret basement beneath that basement. The very existence of the bunker in their own house is unbeknownst to the Parks for much of the film. We learn from Moon-gwang that the house was built by a noted architect. For the architect and others of his generation, building a house with an underground bunker was not un-common given the very real and ongoing Cold War threat of possible nuclear war between North and South Korea. When selling the house to the Parks, a much younger generation for whom the threat of war is less real, the architect did not disclose the existence of the bunker out of "embarrassment." Yet his housekeeper, Moon-gwang, stayed on and continued to work in that capacity for the Parks, which would explain her knowledge of the bunker's existence and how it became a refuge or last resort for her husband to evade the aggressively persistent debt collectors.

Indeed, the "Cold War bunker" or fallout shelter is a globally ubiquitous architectural form that has been repurposed or long abandoned as one among an array of haunting Cold War ruins. The Cold War shame of this bunkered past, the shame of one's nation being divided by an external force that has then led to an existential standoff between the two divided halves, is here connected to the shame or moral economy of indebtedness. The bunker is thus a kind of return of the repressed of the Korean War, of the United States' imperial Cold War machinations in dividing the Korean Peninsula at the 38th parallel into a North and a South in the first place, and of the still formally unended Korean War (1950–53) that saw the cessation of hostilities not through a peace treaty but an armistice. The Korean War and the division of the peninsula also emerge through other details. Moon-gwang imitates famous North Korean news anchor Ri Chun-hee for fun, and Ki-taek the Kim patriarch responds that he knows quite well everything "south of the 38th parallel" when Dong-ik the Park patriarch compliments him on his good navigating skills after he shuts off the car's GPS system. The divided Korean Peninsula is a geography of milita-rism. It is a lacerated space. North of the laceration that is the 38th parallel are the lacerations of the US carpet-bombing campaign during the war, and south of it are the lacerations of US military bases and camptowns.

Moreover, *Parasite* exquisitely and excruciatingly contrasts the multilevel Park house set high in the hills of Seoul with that of the semibasement Kim apartment in the lowland areas of Seoul, which are vulnerable to flooding and

Figure I.1. Right: The exterior wall and gated front entrance of the Park house in *Parasite*. Neon

a literal "shitstorm" of sewage water. Yet this upstairs/downstairs class motif becomes complicated when we consider the specific contours of the Park house (more appropriately a compound) and how the film thematizes the issue of space and territory more broadly. It would be an understatement to say that the Park house/compound is gated, for it is surrounded and secured not simply by a gate but rather a high and thick concrete wall of dark gray. This wall completely separates the house itself from the street, affording total privacy and security. In this light, while the house includes a secret underground bunker, we could say that the house itself is a kind of bunker or garrison heavily protected and secured by not only the big wall but also multiple security cameras. The Kims thus infiltrate not only the Park family but also the Park garrison. To repeat a refrain said a few times throughout the film by Ki-woo, "It is metaphorical," or, per the English version of the screenplay, "symbolic." This house, as the metaphor or symbol of wealth, specifically nouveau riche tech wealth, is also a garrison as the metaphor or symbol of South Korea's heavily militarized status as a US neocolony. That is, South Korea is a site from which and onto which the United States projects its militarist settler imperial power.

In this sense, the garrison is more specifically a settler garrison, whose making and contours in Asia and the Pacific I will be elaborating throughout this book. In terms of South Korea, it is home to, after Germany and Japan, the third-largest number of US military bases on foreign soil. And central Seoul in particular was home to Yongsan Garrison (the headquarters of US military forces in South Korea) until its relocation to Pyeongtaek in 2017. About sixty-five kilometers south of Seoul, Pyeongtaek is home to Osan Air Base and Camp

Humphreys, a former helicopter base that, after an $11 billion expansion, is now the largest overseas US military installation in the world and reputedly the US Department of Defense's largest construction project on record.[7] The Park compound in *Parasite* thus symbolizes a pivotal node in America's settler garrison. It is a heterotopic space; what it means and symbolizes depends on one's positionality within the contours of US militarist settler imperialism. For Geun-se, it is at once a refuge but also a kind of prison, given his indebted fugitivity. It is the site of the US frontier narrative, but also one that goes awry, for the "good Indian" does not get to save the "cake princess" after all and the fatalities pile up in unexpected and complex ways that depart from the prescripted "Indian cosplay." The departure, or improvisation, as it were, is precipitated by the appearance of Geun-se, a return of the repressed ghostly figure. *Parasite*'s inter- and intraclass warfare produces macabre collateral damage, yet as I have been demonstrating, the ultimately thwarted "Indian cosplay" through which that warfare plays out bespeaks US militarist settler imperialism's imbrications and complicities with global racial capitalism. As such, *Parasite* as an allegory of class is simultaneously an allegory of US militarist settler imperialism.

If *Parasite*'s revelation of the existence of the bunker that Geun-se occupies is a return of the repressed of the unended Korean War, his emergence from that bunker as the indebted fugitive makes gruesomely visible the exceptional temporality of debt regimes that structure and haunt US militarist settler imperialism. The film grapples with this third interlocking concern of *Settler Garrison* by making plain that for those without resources and privilege, it is difficult if not impossible to evade the punitive consequences of defaulting on debt. Short of disappearing from society, Geun-se is compelled to repay his debts with full usurious interest. Yet this disciplinary regime is differentially applied depending on the debtor's positionality within already existing asymmetries of power. To put it simply and mildly, there is a double standard in determining who must conform to the homogeneous time of repayment, whether the debtor is an individual or a whole nation. Moreover, by seeking shelter in the Park house bunker, Geun-se's indebted subjectivity is in a way redoubled, for he feels total indebtedness to the Park patriarch, who is at once his unwitting captor, commander, and host. In attempting to evade the homogeneous time of repayment of economic debt, Geun-se takes on an affective debt. Such a figurative debt, as I shall demonstrate throughout this book, is one that can never be fully repaid. Yet it must be performatively repaid over and over again, as we see with Geun-se's faithful and precise synchronization in turning on each of the stairway lights every time the Park patriarch comes home and ascends from the garage level. Unable to detect this synchronization, the Parks see it as an electrical malfunction.

It is precisely their vulnerability and proximity to debt that compels the fateful decisions of Geun-se and Moon-gwang and their doppelgängers the Kims. Household or individual debt of their kind, in both its figurative and economic registers, is connected to and also mirrored at the scale of the nation itself. In terms of the figurative debt, the South Korean nation's structure of feeling vis-à-vis the United States is one of gratitude or indebtedness for two successive putative liberations, first from Japanese colonial rule at the end of World War II and then from the specter of "totalitarian" Communist domination as World War II bled into what would be an escalating Cold War. As I examine in Chapter 2, South Korea "pays back" this figurative debt and demonstrates its gratitude to the United States in significant part by "hosting" a large number of US military bases. In terms of the financial debt, the "miracle" of South Korea's ultrarapid modernization and economic growth has generated a host of contradictions, notably a precariat class. The 1997 Asian Financial Crisis compelled the fateful decision of affected nations such as South Korea to borrow heavily from the International Monetary Fund (IMF) in accepting "bailout" money that comes with a host of conditions. These conditions included further deregulation, privatization, and austerity—namely, the privatizing of previously public sectors; the lifting of trade restrictions; the opening of the nation's capital markets to more foreign investment; and, of course, the cutting of public expenditures and an already-fragile social safety net. This led to massive unemployment, particularly for women. South Koreans were thus correct in their assessment that the purported solution to the crisis was worse than the original crisis itself. Hence, the crisis is called the "IMF Crisis" in South Korea, giving rise to jokes that IMF stands for "I'm fired." It has also given witness to the coining of phrases such as "IMF suicide" to mark the alarming rise in suicides in the wake of the crisis, and "IMF *chonyo*" (IMF maiden) to refer to the predicament of single women who delayed marriage because married women were the first to be subjected to layoffs.

This South Korean naming of the IMF as an exacerbation of the crisis rather than the solution to it points to a broader problem of representation and politics of knowledge. As Laura Hyun Hi Kang trenchantly analyzes, the moniker "Asian Financial Crisis" is not a neutral geographic designation but rather a racialization that obfuscates what forces and players outside of South Korea, Thailand, and Indonesia significantly contributed to the crisis. American schadenfreude when the crisis hit, and the identification of "crony capitalism" as the culprit, whose previous iterations include "Oriental despotism" and "Asiatic absolutism," belied the important role played by a US government increasingly beholden to Wall Street. Along with increased deregulation in the early 1990s, which led to the innovation of new financial instruments such as risky derivatives, the Clinton administration took an active role in compelling the "Asia-Pacific" region to open itself up to what is euphemistically called global market forces or free trade. Yet in effect, the region has been compelled to make itself available to the speculative, risky, and short-term interests of American banks and corporations. As for the IMF, former US Trade Representative Mickey Kanter called it a "battering ram" for American interests because of the outsize power and influence that the United States has in dictating IMF policies and "bailout" terms.[8] The IMF is thus accountable and transparent only to the owners of capital rather than to the nations and citizens it purports to save, and the conditions attached to its loans usher in a repetition and exacerbation of the vicious cycle of the very processes that caused the crisis in the first instance. Simply put, openness to global markets, such as South Korea opening itself up to short-term loans and risky new derivatives dreamed up by American financial corporations, precipitated the crisis. Yet the cause of the crisis is narrated and racialized, which is to say Asianized, as "crony capitalism" putatively peculiar to autocratic-leaning Asian nations and distinct from "Western" liberal capitalism. The conditions of the IMF "bailout" called for South Korea to continue to make itself available to foreign capital investment, eliding how such speculative investments had precipitated the crisis in the first place.

This is not to suggest that South Korean actors bear no responsibility. Rather, it is to suggest that such moments of "crisis" erupt as the result of specific policies, US imperial interests, and capitalist global interconnections that render parts of the globe differentially vulnerable when creditors and investors collectively panic and take flight. In this way, since their creation as part of the Bretton Woods Agreement in the World War II era, international financial institutions such as the World Bank and especially the IMF have increasingly engaged in a US-dictated "mission creep" beyond their original charge of providing social support and alleviating poverty. The US government, in turn, has increasingly become beholden to Wall Street interests. Ultimately, this hypercapitalist convergence of interests and influence has congealed as a "Wall Street-Treasury-IMF Complex."[9] The power of this complex is crystallized in this example: J.P. Morgan was at the forefront of the effort to convert the short-term debt of South Korean banks into sovereign debt. Why? Because J.P. Morgan held $2 billion in derivatives contracts with South Korean banks. Moreover, as Kang argues, the spatial and racial bracketing as an "Asian Financial Crisis" also has a temporal bracketing, insofar as calling something a crisis obscures the long "prehistory" leading to the crisis (the underlying as opposed to immediate causes) as well as its stubbornly distended aftermath persisting into and after "recovery."[10]

I have unpacked this "IMF Crisis" story, which is also a story about the interests of US militarist settler imperialism, with some detail here precisely because what at first appears to be a matter of strict political economic concern turns out to be a *story* as well. In other words, each word in the very naming of the political economic problem, *Asian, Financial,* and *Crisis,* is shorthand for a larger narrative that obfuscates more than it reveals. It is precisely this narrative and broader cultural valence of the debtor/creditor relation, in particular its sleight of hand tendency, that I will be elaborating throughout this book. US militarist settler imperialism operates significantly through the imposition of debt's manifold relations and forms beyond the strictly economic at multiple scales. How does the US imposition of debt operate as a sleight of hand and production of subjectivity in disciplining some players (whether individuals or whole nations) to conform to the homogeneous time of repayment, even as the United States reserves for itself an exception, or the right to be exempt from the very disciplinary protocols it imposes on others?

In another layer to this story, films such as *Parasite* and the work of Bong's cohort of fellow South Korean auteurs owe their material conditions of possibility in large measure to the South Korean government's efforts to recover from the IMF Crisis.[11] Part of this effort was to strategically invest in and promote the South Korean culture industry not only for domestic consumption but also for international export. This has produced what has been called the "Korean Wave," or *Hallyu* in Korean. The increasing international visibility and commercial success of Korean popular culture—especially films, television dramas, and K-pop boy bands such as BTS—have thus been significantly overdetermined by the South Korean nation's need to manage a debt crisis.[12] Yet for the working class, the IMF Crisis continues to be experienced as a never-ending crisis, producing precariat conditions of prolonged unemployment, underemployment, semi-employment, and thus ultimately household debt reaching epidemic levels.[13] The characters Ki-taek, Chung-sook, Moon-gwang, and Geun-se in *Parasite* would all have been in their early thirties when the crisis hit.[14] Living within this more recent distended shadow layered over the distended shadow of the division of the peninsula, these two couples' employment prospects at what would have been their prime working years were irreparably disrupted. This would explain why Ki-taek does not see the point of making plans and why he has had a string of unsuccessful stints, whether as driver, valet, chicken house owner, or Taiwanese castella cake shop franchisee. This would also explain Geun-se's indebted fugitivity and why he also, like Ki-taek, lost a great sum of money on the Taiwanese castella cake shop franchise. In South Korea, this cake shop franchise has become a symbol of economic failure because it became a common yet ultimately unsuccessful small business venture for employees laid off from large companies. It bears noting that in *Parasite*, Moon-gwang is the only gainfully employed one among the four at the beginning of the film. Even though the massive layoffs effected by IMF-mandated austerity restructurings differentially impacted women more than men, domestic work as particularly feminized labor is one circumscribed terrain "available" to women.[15] Thus, inasmuch as *Parasite* tells a universal tale of class hierarchy, these modalities of what we might call the "miracle's crises" are specific to the neocolony of South Korea and its place within US militarist settler imperialism's orbit.

In addition to displaying the contradictions of the "miracle's crises," *Parasite* also displays a refusal to submit to the homogeneous time of repayment on the part of vulnerable debtors such as Geun-se. This brings us to *Settler Garrison*'s fourth interlocking concern—how the transpacific imaginaries of cultural works such as *Parasite* display an aesthetics of settler imperial failure that gestures to world-makings and relations beyond the violence of US militarist settler imperialism. What I have called Geun-se's indebted fugitivity, his flight from whatever violent disciplinary punishment would be meted out by his creditors and their agents the debt collectors, and his unwillingness to use any significant portion of Moon-gwang's earnings to pay back his debts, constitutes a refusal to conform to the homogeneous time of repayment. Although Geun-se's flight is circumscribed by a kind of carcerality in the bunker and inaugurates a figurative indebtedness to his unwitting "host" Mr. Park, in the end it is still a refusal to submit to payback time and to the violence of his creditor. Through amplifying such refusals and rendering yet ultimately horrifically twisting the US frontier narrative, *Parasite* displays an aesthetics of settler imperial failure. US militarist settler imperialism continually needs to assert and renovate itself precisely because its ends and continued existence are never fully guaranteed. Indeed, the violence and fatalities it has produced and continues to produce are a mark or index of that very failure or incompleteness.

Parasite's aesthetics of settler imperial failure also emerges through seemingly insignificant details, such as the name of Dong-ik aka "Nathan" Park's tech company, Another Brick. In the audio commentary for The Criterion Collection's edition of *Parasite*, Bong reveals that Another Brick is indeed a nod to Pink Floyd; he was a "huge fan" of the band when he was in high school. "Another Brick in the Wall" (1979) has been interpreted by some as an enduring antiestablishment anthem, so it is a curious choice of name for a highly successful tech company. Yet on one level, it is fitting, given Silicon Valley's own enduring perception of itself as antiestablishment, though of course it has long become *the* establishment given the dominance and ubiquity of tech, big and otherwise. Indeed, as Geun-se observes in the film, the "send" button on a smartphone is like a "missile launcher," a "North Korean rocket, a North Korean missile button" when the content is sufficiently damaging to one's opponent. Moreover, it would seem that Another Brick, a South Korean company, is outcompeting US companies and technologies in producing a "Hybrid Module Map" of New York City, a virtual and augmented reality platform that allows users from anywhere in the world to experience and get to know the city. Finally, Pink Floyd's song has also been interpreted as a motif of isolation or a barrier, referring in particular to the band's isolation from fans and one another. It is ambiguous within *Parasite*'s diegesis if "Another Brick" means another brick or barrier (physical and otherwise) of the dominance of US tech companies destroyed through technological innovation and specifically South Korean hypercompetitiveness, or if it means another brick laid in the edifice of global racial capitalism. And to extend the metaphor of the Park house/compound as at once the desired isolated bastion of the wealthy and of the US settler garrison in Asia and the Pacific, has another brick of this fortification been blasted away or has a new one been laid? These ambiguities and possible interpretations constitute an aesthetics of settler imperial failure.

Parasite's aesthetics of settler imperial failure is also suggested by the ultimate ambiguity in the film's title, an ambiguity that turns on its head the initial presumption of who the parasite might be. This is related to the sleight of hand tendency of the cultural or narrative valence of debt that I examine throughout this book. Who owes what to whom? Are those who have been compelled to be debtors really, in fact, the creditors? For example, the "Heavily Indebted Poor Countries" or the HIPCs of sub-Saharan Africa have been compelled to be debtors and are stereotyped as "Third World debtors." Yet are they in fact creditors, when we consider that Europe owes them for colonial plunder? Yet this European debt to its African creditors is one that is not even acknowledged as such, along with the reality that the very reason why HIPCs need to borrow so heavily in the first place is because of colonial plunder and its distended shadow as manifested in the neocolonial practices of institutions such as the IMF. In a similar vein, *Parasite* asks who is actually the parasite (debtor), and who is the host (creditor)? In dramatizing exactly how easy it was for the Kims to infiltrate the Park house/garrison in order to leech off the Parks' wealth as paid members of the household staff, it would seem that the Kims are the parasite of the film's title. Yet by ingeniously invading the Park house(hold) through exploiting and exposing the weaknesses, insecurities, and failures of the Parks—and by extension US militarist settler imperial domination—the presumably parasitical Kims represent the ungovernability and unpredictability of that domination. We are thus compelled to ask: Who is leeching off whom; who is the parasite and who is the host? Are the Kims leeching off the Parks, or is it that the Parks are leeching off the invisible labor that the Kims provide? This labor, though absolutely essential to the smooth running of the Park household, is at once invisible and disposable or interchangeable, for as we saw in the film, the laborers themselves can be quite easily replaced. One might argue that the parasite and the host can in certain instances be interchangeable. Yet on a macro level, the creation of value and accumulation of wealth are made possible in the first instance by exploitation and by the violent processes of what Karl Marx calls "primitive accumulation," such as colonial plunder and racial chattel slavery, which I discuss in the next chapter.

Parasite's concluding moments poignantly punctuate an aesthetics of settler imperial failure. The film ends with Ki-woo's class aspirations of one day owning the Park house himself getting articulated as a filial desire to liberate his father, who has replaced Geun-se as the fugitive in the bunker evading arrest and prosecution for the killing of Dong-ik Park. This earnestly filial epistolary moment, captured like a dream sequence, is preceded in the film with absurdist moments of Ki-woo laughing uncontrollably, and often at inappropriate moments, after he emerges from brain surgery. This medical aftereffect displays its most absurd moment when we see Ki-woo laughing at a photo of his sister when he and his mother visit the columbarium, where the funerary urns containing cremated remains are stored. As Bong relates in his audio commentary, it is "quite sad" that even after death, impoverished people such as the Kims are confined to the "basement," a "condensed space," whereas "rich people have a huge space for their grave." Bong laments that "it's cruel." Indeed, burial plots are sold as pieces of real estate priced in accordance with the market of the city in which they are located. Unsurprisingly, plots or "cemetery property" in global cities such as Seoul or Los Angeles are quite expensive.

In this light, what are we to make of the prefiguration of Ki-woo's filial earnestness in his letter to his father with the absurdity of his laughter in his visit to his sister's cremated remains? On the one hand, we could say that Ki-woo's class aspirations of one day buying the Park house are absurdly delusional, as suggested by the dreamlike quality of that sequence. Yet on the other hand, the ultimate absurdity of Ki-woo's laughter points less to an individual delusion and more to the collective or structural dynamic in which capitalist cruelty follows one even into death. This is the ultimate absurdity, and *Parasite*'s aesthetics of settler imperial failure suggests that perhaps one of the best ways to expose and mock that very absurdity is to laugh at it. In this sense, what at first appears to be the absurdity of wildly inappropriate laughter turns out to be wildly *appropriate* laughter in the face of the absurdity of a capitalist cruelty whose postmortem temporality outlives or follows the dead to their graves. Yet in this instance, that idiom has lost its literal resonance because the cruelty is that the grave itself as expensive real estate or "cemetery property" is increasingly prohibitively out of reach while (premature) death is all too easily within reach for the Kims of the world.

Militarist Settler Imperialism and the Relational Analysis of the Distinct Yet Linked

I begin this introductory chapter with the film *Parasite* because it provides quite a productive point of entry into *Settler Garrison*'s analysis of how transpacific cultural productions articulate decolonial and antimilitarist imaginaries that at once diagnose and envision alternatives to what I conceptualize as militarist settler imperialism and the attendant making of America's settler garrison in Asia and the Pacific. I analyze cultural forms such as *Parasite* precisely because they do the important work of mediating and making critically visible the contours of US militarist settler imperialism and of America's settler garrison, yet also gesturing to world-making imaginaries beyond such contours through an aesthetics of settler imperial failure. In conceptualizing US militarist settler imperialism within and across Okinawa, the Philippines, South Korea, and Guam (Guåhan), *Settler Garrison* offers a *relational* analysis that departs from the geographic and cartographic privileging of continental landmasses and emphasizes as well the terraqueous and the oceanic alongside island, archipelagic, and peninsular spatialities.[16] With attentiveness to both Asia *and* the Pacific, my book bears in mind Teresia Teaiwa's analysis of the conjoined pitfalls of either marginalizing the Pacific altogether or of engaging in a "rhetoric of Pacific exceptionalism."[17] Moreover, in offering an interrogation of distinct yet linked forms of colonial domination, the conjunction of US settler colonialism and military empire in particular, *Settler Garrison* departs from a focus on one form that tends to elide completely or deemphasize the other. As Lisa Lowe observes, these "operations that pronounce colonial divisions of humanity . . . are imbricated processes, not sequential events; they are ongoing and continuous in our contemporary moment, not temporally distinct nor as yet concluded."[18]

The aesthetics of settler imperial failure contained in the transpacific cultural works I analyze allows us to think through the relationship between settler colonialism and military empire in this way: settler colonialism is at once military empire's proving ground, obscured condition of possibility, and imbricated partner in violence. The United States as the literal testing ground for biopolitical tactics and technologies that are geopolitically and militarily projected abroad has produced and continues to produce Native American displacement and dispossession, and that geopolitical and military projection abroad in Asia and the Pacific in turn produces Asian migration and Indigenous Pacific Islander displacement and dispossession. Indeed, as Jodi A. Byrd asks, "Given all these difficulties, how might we place the arrivals of peoples through choice and by force into historical relationship with Indigenous peoples and theorize those arrivals in ways that are legible but still attuned to the conditions of settler colonialism?"[19] As I elaborate later in this Introduction and throughout *Settler Garrison*, to think through distinct yet linked formations and experiences across and within Asia and the Pacific, and to analyze Asian, Asian diasporic, and Indigenous Asian cultural forms alongside Indigenous cultural forms from different parts of the Pacific is to think broadly and relationally about obscured connections without losing sight of local specificities, hierarchies, and incommensurabilities. What I call the "relational analysis of the distinct yet linked" is a method for apprehending circuits of US power specifically concentrated in Asia and the Pacific, the power of US militarist settler imperialism and its making of the settler garrison.

Focusing on the post–World War II era, I conceptualize militarist settler imperialism as the conjunction of US settler colonialism and military empire and argue that it is an ensemble of relations significantly structured and continually reproduced through a conjoined set of temporal and spatial exceptions. As I have analyzed, in the film *Parasite*, temporal and spatial exceptions come into play first through the representation of economic and affective indebtedness at multiple scales whose disciplinary regime of the homogeneous time of repayment the United States imposes but exempts itself from, and secondly, through the transpacific garrison, a juridically ambiguous zone of US military power. In thus focusing on temporal and spatial exceptions, the goal of *Settler Garrison* is not to magnify the dichotomies of the exceptional and normal, the extraordinary and the quotidian. Indeed, the exceptional and the unexceptional are coimplicated and coconstituted. Rather, at stake is an analysis of how the very creation and perpetuation of temporal and spatial exceptions enable the projection of US militarist settler imperial power and metapolitical authority. Metapolitical authority, as distinct from mere political authority, is the ability to define and prescribe the very content and scope of "law" and "politics" as such.[20]

In analyzing temporal and spatial exceptions, I conceive of the exception as the modality through which the United States attempts to impose a kind of metapolitical authority that in turn fortifies its militarist settler imperial power.

US metapolitical authority is such that the United States has the power to render itself exempt from, or as an exception to, the very rules that it imposes and enforces on others, whether it is abiding by the homogeneous time of debt repayment or fully respecting the sovereignty of nations and territories. Crucially, metapolitical authority is the power not simply to create these temporal and spatial exceptions but to discursively obfuscate and render these exceptions as precisely their opposite, as unexceptional. Metapolitical authority is thus a kind of sleight of hand: its very exercise or imposition is accompanied by a vanishing act that causes it to disappear. As such, temporal and spatial exceptions as I conceive them are distinct from Giorgio Agamben's highly influential work on the camp and the "state of exception" (which I discuss in Chapter 3) insofar as temporal and spatial exceptions are related not only to biopolitical space but also to the geopolitics of statehood and geopolitical territoriality.

Temporal and spatial exceptions as the technology of US metapolitical authority also give a new meaning to American exceptionalism. Against the dominant "shining city on a hill" thesis, American exceptionalism(s) can also signify the ways in which the United States has a tendency to render itself exempt from, or exceptional to, the very order of things that it imposes on others.[21] As I discuss in my analysis of the Fourteenth Amendment in Chapter 1, US exceptionalisms in this sense are no mere hypocrisy; indeed, they are the animating constitutive contradictions integral to the very founding of the United States as a settler state and continuing on through the post–World War II metastasizing growth of its military imperium in Asia and the Pacific. In this sense, metapolitical authority is a kind of exceptional power not simply exercised through the normalization of an exception but more substantively exercised without the need to declare a state of exception at all in the first instance.

A related alternative frame through which we can think about exceptionalism as it relates to settler state power and sovereignty is offered by Marie Lo in her brilliant analysis of plenary power. Lo argues that plenary power is "a particular technique of the racial regime of settler imperialism founded on a constant state of emergency." It is not simply that plenary power relies on a rhetorical construction of exceptionalism in order to rationalize "extraconstitutional" measures to counter threats. More crucially, "such exceptionalism is a structural and constitutive feature of the powers inherent in U.S. sovereignty."[22] Prior to the metastasizing growth of US military empire in the post–World War II conjuncture, the US exercise of settler imperial sovereignty was consolidated and codified as plenary power in a set of legal cases in the late nineteenth and early twentieth centuries. These cases pertained to Chinese immigration exclusion, the abrogation of treaties with Native Americans to enable further theft of land, and congressional power over the unincorporated territories ceded to the United States after the defeat of the Spanish in 1898. In granting congressional power over these domains, the cases codified plenary or absolute power as specifically an extraconstitutional or exceptional power whose exercise is justified in regulating the borders of the nation and defending it against "external" threats. As I elaborate in my discussion of Guam in Chapter 4, whereas extraconstitutional plenary power as the alibi for ruling over acquired territories presumed that such territories would soon be incorporated as US states, Guam still remains an unincorporated territory. Thus, we might say that the permanence of plenary power over the spatial exception of the unincorporated territory is metapolitical authority.[23]

As I will elaborate further in the next chapter and throughout the book, the temporal exception is debt imperialism. That is, debt is a form of imperialism, or more specifically a temporal exception that the United States grants to itself of rolling over its significant national debt indefinitely even as it imposes the homogeneous time of repayment and an indebted subjectivity on others at multiple scales. Speaking of debt, or a condition of great indebtedness, as a form of imperial power might at first sound counterintuitive. The ability to leverage great indebtedness into a form of imperial power demonstrates how debt can function in such counterintuitive ways because it is not simply a financial economy. Indeed, debt is undergirded by historically persisting asymmetries of power and thus also manifests in crucial ways as a figurative economy or narrative structure. Far more than indexing the sum of money owed, debt thus constitutes manifold regimes, relations, and forms. It is a broader social relation, production of subjectivity, sleight of hand, and creation of a temporal exception through which US militarist settler imperialism functions and continually attempts to re-create itself.

As *Settler Garrison* demonstrates, it is then no wonder that in this varied relation, debt can oddly appear in two forms that seem to be antonymous: as a form of imperialism, on the one hand, *and* as a form of freedom, emancipation, or liberation, on the other. How, in other words, can debt be the foreclosure of freedom *as well as* its effect? That is, debt as imperialism is a twin operation. First, vulnerable populations and nations are compelled to go into debt and must pay it back at often-usurious interest rates under threat of discipline and punishment and the imperial protocols of international financial institutions such as the IMF or the gendered racial predatory lending practices of banks and payday lenders. This is debt as the foreclosure of freedom. Simultaneously, debt imperialism is also the temporal exception through which the United States does not have to conform to this homogeneous time of repayment that it imposes on everyone else. Though this form of debt as imperialism is tethered to a straight economic valence, the form of debt as (the effect of) freedom or liberation refers to the production of an indebted subjectivity or gratitude for a figurative debt, the "liberation" from a range of unfreedoms, whether racial chattel slavery, military occupation, or colonial domination. Yet the production of this indebted subjectivity, and the attendant injunction to pay the figurative or affective debt back properly, is a sleight of hand. For the enslaved would not have required emancipation had they not been enslaved in the first place, and what is narrated as "liberation" from military occupation or colonialism elides how the liberator often becomes the new colonizer. As I analyze in Chapter 4, the United States' colonial domination of Guam has been narrated as Guam's "liberation" from centuries of Spanish colonialism and from Japanese military occupation during World War II.

This is to speak about promises, and the transpacific cultural forms I analyze in this book—literature, film, and performance—critically grapple with the promise made in bad faith, the promise that can be rolled over indefinitely, the promise that does not have to be made at all, the necropolitical promise that cannot be settled even with death. The *promise*, in other words, is another word for debt, and while debt imperialism certainly has an economic valence, it is also crucially a broader cultural operation and logic. As such, the cultural forms I analyze are a privileged site that renders visible and grapples complexly with the counterintuitive and manifold forms of the debtor/creditor relation and of the temporal exception that is debt imperialism.

The temporal exception of debt imperialism operates in tandem with the spatial exception. I analyze the ways in which the transpacific cultural texts in my study make visible how three types of spatial exceptions in Asia and the Pacific—the military base and attendant camptown, the POW camp, and the unincorporated territory of Guam—are remade into America's settler garrison. The spatial exceptions I focus on are the material sites on which the temporal exception of debt imperialism, the cultural operation, gets imposed in especially protracted ways. I conceive of these three types as spatial exceptions and have chosen to focus on them in particular, because they are juridically ambiguous spaces on which the operative logics of US aspirations to seize metapolitical authority get negotiated and revealed. Such spaces are laboratories, as it were, where we see the convergence of hypermilitarization, legal liminality, and negotiation of metapolitical authority. Neither domestic nor strictly foreign, these spatial exceptions are a part of the US settler garrison but not the United States of America insofar as they are not within the fifty states. To the extent that US dominion over spatial exceptions has not been "naturalized" via formal incorporation as US states, sovereignties at once pro-liferate, compete, and cancel one another out as the United States attempts to supersede local sovereignty. Thus, although Hawai'i is also certainly a heavily militarized and colonized site in the Pacific, I do not include it in this book precisely because it has been incorporated as a US state and is therefore not a legally liminal spatial exception as I conceive it.

Though *naturalization* commonly refers to the incorporation of people, the legal process through which those who are not "natural-born" US citizens can become so-called naturalized citizens, we can also think of it in the context of the settler colonial and imperial incorporation of territories. Formal incorpora-tion or admission of colonized Indigenous territories as US states "naturalizes" colonization, which is to say that the very granting of statehood renders natural or invisible the colonial conquest that makes territories available for statehood in the first place. In this sense, we might say that the granting of statehood is US metapolitical authority's ultimate disappearing act, for it converts *metapolitical* authority into *political* authority by incorporating territory into the "proper" federal jurisdiction of the US nation-state. Yet the granting of statehood as metapolitical authority's formal fait accompli is simultaneously its incomplete-ness or failure. For as I have observed, US militarist settler imperial power con-tinuously needs to assert and renovate itself in the face of challenges to it.[24]

The cultural productions in this book defamiliarize and estrange this nat-uralization by linking the land seizures of US settler colonialism to those of military empire. How do transpacific cultural forms articulate a theory of dis-tinct yet connected varieties of land seizure? They name and link the process through which Indigenous land has been successively incorporated into the white settler nation as the fifty states constituting the United States of Amer-ica *and* the process through which a proliferating expanse of Asian and Pacific sites (the legally liminal spatial exceptions I have named) has been converted into the bases, camps, and territories constituting the US military imperium and settler garrison. In other words, to speak about the very making of the US nation-state is to speak about the growing contours of its militarist settler imperial power or its continued aspirations to exercise metapolitical authority as the kind of disappearing act that I have described.

Even as the United States attempts to impose metapolitical authority in this way, its ends are never fully guaranteed. Indeed, the ongoing violence generated by settler colonialism and military empire is a mark or index of their very incom-pletion or failure, as are the solidarities, oppositions, and continued survivals of communities and peoples against whom (and often ostensibly *on behalf* of whom) such violence is waged. While Patrick Wolfe's important conceptualization of settler colonialism is that it is a "logic of elimination" whose dominant feature is the acquisition of land via the elimination of the Indigenous population and its replacement with the settler population, Maile Arvin theorizes settler colonialism as a logic of "possession through whiteness" precisely because possession rather than elimination more fully highlights the incomplete or continually deferred status of Indigenous elimination and replacement.[25] And although for Wolfe settler colonialism is a structure and not an event, insofar as settler colonialism is not an absolute fait accompli but rather a process that requires continual renewal and renovation, I comprehend it as *both* a structure *and* a processual series of ongoing events.[26] I link it, moreover, to military empire, observing how the United States is at once a settler state and imperial power whose militarist logics condense in a particularly heightened form specifically in Asia and the Pacific in the post–World War II era. Yet still, as Iyko Day and others have importantly argued, we need to go beyond a binary theory of settler colonialism structured around a settler-Indigenous dialectic. Day maps out "the triangulation of Native, alien, and settler positions" in North America with an attentiveness to how divergent conditions of both forced and voluntary migration are significant features of US settler colonialism.[27]

Alongside such important work, my concern is to apprehend the nexus of settler colonialism *and* the orders and outposts of military empire—a militarist settler imperialism—in Asia and the Pacific. The Obama administration's decision to "pivot" from the Middle East to the "Asia-Pacific," revealed in the then secretary of state Hillary Clinton's October 2011 policy plan, called "America's Pacific Century," gives renewed vigor to an already-protracted history of violence. Indeed, the transformation of the Pacific into an "American Lake" has been over a century in the making. In Clinton's recent articulation of this ongoing history, the "Asia-Pacific" is identified as the most crucial sphere of US influence in the twenty-first century and the region where US military resources will be concentrated. An "emerging" China is named as a new global reality to which the United States will need to pivot.[28] Yet crucially, a group of scholars from around the world practices a "decolonial political geography" in offering island perspectives on what it calls "China threat discourse." This discourse increasingly describes China's overseas activities as "neocolonialism," "imperialism," "creditor imperialism," "debt trap diplomacy," and "sharp power." The charge of neocolonialism and imperialism, however, becomes the alibi for retrenchment of the West's own neocolonial and imperial interests.[29] Indeed, the continuation and escalation of military buildup in the Pacific are rationalized by the concern that the "American Lake" is in threat of becoming a "Chinese Lake." In the case of island territories such as Okinawa and Guam, which I analyze in Chapters 2 and 4, respectively, this has witnessed an escalation of already-hypermilitarized geographies. If the sheer pervasiveness of US militarism and military violence in Asia and the Pacific constitutes what Sasha Davis calls a "banal colonialism," then we need to make obvious the brutality of that banality.[30] The transpacific cultural texts in this book make obvious the brutality of that banality and imagine alternatives to it through an aesthetics of settler imperial failure.

In what follows, I offer a further elaboration of the book's central concepts and terms of settler garrison, regimes of militarism, and transpacific imaginaries, while I devote the next chapter to a sustained discussion and contextualization of debt imperialism. Each chapter thereafter is organized around a specific spatial exception: the military base and camptown, the POW camp, and the unincorporated territory of Guam.

The Settler Garrison and "Astounding Political Creativity"

The territoriality of US settler imperial projections of power include not only the fifty states (or incorporated territories) but also a variety of unincorporated and discontiguous territories.[31] It is crucial to note that the Marshall Islands, Micronesia, and Palau in the Pacific were effectively annexed, falling under US trusteeship at the end of World War II and governed by the US Navy until 1951, then by the Department of the Interior until 1978, as the UN Trust Territory of the Pacific Islands.[32] This granted the United States the right to establish military bases on the islands, and US military control did not end even after they were granted formal independence by signing "compacts of free association" with the United States because the compacts gave defense responsibilities to the United States. This, combined with the 1946 "Truman Proclamation," which extended the littoral state to two hundred miles out to sea, instantiated what Elizabeth DeLoughrey calls a new "ocean territorialism" that tripled the size of the United States and saw its emergence as a dominant Pacific power. President Truman's violation of the freedom-of-the-seas doctrine in turn triggered a "scramble for the oceans" and led to the protracted and contested United Nations Convention on the Law of the Sea (UNCLOS).[33] More recently, with the development of new mining technologies, the Pacific Ocean is being called a new "El Dorado" in the scramble for submarine mining rights.[34]

Indeed, the Pacific is an intense locus not only of "ocean territorialism" but more critically of an ever-expansive US "transoceanic militarism." In a significant recent development, the US military renamed its largest command, the Pacific Command (located in Hawai'i), to the "US Indo-Pacific Command"

(USINDOPACOM), expanding its maritime regime to 100 million square miles, or an incredible 52 percent of the earth's surface.[35] The presumption of *terra nullius* (nobody's land) that abets settler colonization of land becomes conjoined with the presumption of *aqua nullius* (nobody's water) that abets the military imperium's colonization of the seas, or land seizure coupled with oceanic seizure. Indeed, oceanography has been from its very inception a military-funded science, growing in step with US naval power and empire since the nineteenth century. We might speak, then, of *terra nullius* and *aqua nullius* as the legal grammar of US militarist settler imperialism's seizures of land and sea. America's settler garrison in Asia and the Pacific is thus constituted not only via the seizure of land but oceanic seizure as well, or the colonization of the Pacific Ocean itself.

This transformation of the Pacific into the "American Lake," though certainly heightened in the post–World War II era, has a long-standing history and prehistory. Indeed, US imperial practices long predated the acquisition of overseas territories such as the Philippines and Guam at the conclusion of the Spanish-American War in 1898. Before that war, the United States had already claimed numerous guano islands located throughout the Caribbean, Pacific, Atlantic, and even Indian Oceans.[36] Yet still, US imperial practices also predated the acquisition of guano islands. US imperialism, while often presumed to be in reference to "overseas" territories, needs to be reframed. In theorizing "continental imperialism," Manu Karuka writes, "To conceive of the United States in national terms is to naturalize colonialism. There is no 'national' territory of the United States. These are only colonized territories." Karuka goes on to elaborate that what we call the United States is composed of hundreds of colonized Indigenous nations, so invoking the United States as a "nation" in this context functions to provide an alibi for imperialism.[37] This process, as I have observed, is US metapolitical authority's ultimate assertion as well as its disappearance. The alibi obscures not only continental and extracontinental imperialism (or the process through which successive territories extending from the Atlantic and into the Pacific were incorporated as US states) but also the ongoing US domination of the territories that it has *not* incorporated as states, namely Guam, American Sāmoa, the Commonwealth of the Northern Mariana Islands, the US Virgin Islands, and Puerto Rico. Yet still, the alibi also obscures the existence of a US military empire, the tentacular reach of US power on military bases throughout the globe numbering about eight hundred, close to 40 percent of which are disproportionately concentrated in Asia and the Pacific.[38] Continental imperialism has been linked to the extracontinental seizure of land and sea in Asia and the Pacific for explicit and what is turning out to be enduring military (ab)uses. This makes possible the very making, persistence, and exponential growth of America's settler garrison and at once manifests and enables militarist settler imperial projections of power.

This is to speak about the United States as what Walden Bello calls a "transnational garrison state."[39] This is also to speak about the spatialities and geographies of militarism, as distinct from military geography. Whereas military geography (as a subfield of the discipline of geography) is closely aligned with the state and is "aimed at the application of geographical tools and techniques to the solution of military problems," geographies of militarism, as I conceive them, constitute the transformation and malformation of space and social relations for militarist purposes.[40] As such, geographies of militarism index militarism itself as the problem. If geographies of militarism are thus a variety of what Katherine McKittrick calls geographies of domination and enclosure, they also give rise to antimilitarist and decolonial geographies and imaginaries.[41] We witness this interplay on the settler garrison, the spatial manifestation of militarist settler imperialism.

As a geography of militarism, America's settler garrison is constituted by the spatial exceptions of the military base/camptown, the POW camp, and the unincorporated territory, where multiple sovereignties at once compete and cancel one another out as the United States aspires to metapolitical authority. Observing the declension of European imperial power and the ascension of that of the United States in the interwar years, Carl Schmitt recognized what he considered to be America's "superiority and astounding political creativity." He observed that a historically meaningful imperialism is constituted not only by military and economic superiority but also crucially by the ability to define and determine the very content of political and legal concepts as such. A nation is thus conquered in the first instance when it surrenders to a foreign "vocabulary" or concept of law, particularly international law.[42] What we might euphemistically call sites of US "political creativity" are subjected, then, to its metapolitical authority. These sites or spatial exceptions are multiscalar "strategic hamlets" set off not only physically and legally but also conceptually and morally.[43]

The settler garrison, as both a term and concept, is meant to highlight precisely how these connected geographies and spatialities of militarism are produced. The settler garrison links US settler colonialism and military empire by amplifying how the latter also involves the theft of Indigenous land, especially when such land is transformed into US military bases and attendant camptowns, the first type of spatial exception in my study. Transpacific cultural productions generate and respond to a crucial set of linked questions: On whose land are US military bases in Asia and the Pacific built, and through what means was that land acquired? Within the context of the land constituting the United States itself, Winona LaDuke reminds us that much of what is today US military land was seized from Native peoples through a variety of violent means—gunpoint, massacres, forced marches, starvation, broken treaties, acts of Congress or state legislatures, or presidential authority.[44] This terrain is the proving ground or laboratory for practices and tactics that get projected overseas, and these projections then also rebound in revised form back to the "domestic" United States in a recursive manner that bootstraps militarist settler imperialism. This is amplified, for example, in the US military's very naming practices, such as referring to enemy territory as "Indian Country" in the Vietnam War, or "Geronimo EKIA" (Enemy Killed in Action), the moniker given to Osama bin Laden, the leader of al Qaeda and the United States' initial principal enemy in its so-called war on terror. The military also abounds with weapons and machinery called, for example, Kiowa, Apache Longbow, and Black Hawk helicopters or Tomahawk missiles.[45] And though the common presumption is that military bases are temporary "wartime" structures, they are durable and enduring. In short, they are proving to be permanent insofar as it is much easier to change functions at existing bases than to move or shut down the bases altogether.[46] Or as Chalmers Johnson asks, "Have these bases become ends in themselves?"[47]

As the cultural works I analyze reveal, while US military bases at once manifest and enable the projection of US militarist settler imperial power, they themselves also constitute settler projects or settlements. And as I elaborate further later in this Introduction, insofar as militarism's logic is the preservation of military institutions whether they are needed for war or not, these settlements of the settler garrison have become permanent outposts whose raison d'être and justification are no longer connected to questions of military preparedness or necessity, nor are they contingent on strong congressional oversight. Rather, they have taken on a life of their own, a tautology in which the raison d'être is d'être. In other words, the permanence of the base itself is a kind of temporal exception. Thus, although the US military, its personnel, and its contractors are not settlers in the classic sense, the enduring spatial logic and architecture of military bases and facilities—indeed the sheer amount of actual space they take up—constitute a settlement that violently displaces and dispossesses the Indigenous or local population.

Though the second type of spatial exception in my study, the POW camp, is a temporary wartime structure by definition, this temporariness is characteristic of specific POW camps. As a general form, however, the POW camp is a permanent feature of war, and the United States is a permanent warfare state. As my analysis reveals, the POW camp within the contours of America's settler garrison becomes a preeminent site or laboratory for the making of US metapolitical authority. Whether a question of abiding by new international human rights protocols governing the treatment of prisoners of war or applying new forms of psychological warfare in which human subjectivity itself is treated as a new figurative settler frontier to be conquered, the effects of such post–World War II negotiations of US metapolitical authority are enduring.

Finally, the third type of spatial exception in my study, the unincorporated territory, specifically Guam, has been remade into an effective military colony, a site of intense hypermilitarization. Neither a sovereign nation nor incorporated as a US state, Guam's political status remains ambiguous. The indefinite deferral of the possibility of incorporation or statehood for Guam, now for over a hundred years and counting, constitutes another kind of temporal exception. Taken together, the spatial exceptions of the military base and attendant camptown, the POW camp, and the unincorporated territory of Guam function as America's settler garrison for the creation, perpetuation, and projection of a militarist setter imperial power.

On America's settler garrison, the unincorporated territory already lacks sovereignty, yet even formally sovereign nations can only assert merely nominal sovereignty in the face of US metapolitical authority. However, as the transpacific cultural texts in my study powerfully reveal, there are alternative decolonial and antimilitarist imaginaries, relationalities, and futures, another kind of "political creativity," if you will, that at once reveal the violence of US settler imperial metapolitical authority and transcend it through an aesthetics of settler imperial failure. These cultural texts ask and imagine what it would mean, as Mishuana Goeman suggests, to "unsettle settler space."[48]

"The Cunning of Capitalist Militarism" and Regimes of Militarism

To speak of the militarization that produced and continues to reproduce the United States as a white settler state and military empire is to speak of a way of life. President Eisenhower warned the nation in his 1961 farewell address about the dangers of a "military-industrial complex" acquiring unwarranted power.[49] This sober warning, from a man who had himself reached the highest ranks of the US military as a five-star general and supreme commander of the Allied Forces in Europe during World War II, turns out to have been prescient and necessary, but ultimately unheeded. Indeed, even as far back as over one hundred years ago, in the era of the First World War, significant critiques of militarism were being articulated. Notably, in the last chapter of *The Accumulation of Capital* (originally published in 1913), Rosa Luxemburg observed that "militarism has yet another important function. From the purely economic point of view, it is a pre-eminent means for the realization of surplus value; it is *in itself* a province of accumulation."[50] Put simply, militarism is big business, from "the purely economic point of view." Karl Liebknecht, writing in 1917, punctuated this symbiosis between militarism and capitalism in dissecting a "capitalist militarism." Yet militarism is not purely economic, nor purely (geo)political, nor is it even purely military. As Liebknecht aptly put it, "The cunning of capitalist militarism is characterized by the diversity of its activity." This cunning allows a militarist logic and militarist institutions to pervade all of society, both our public and private lives.[51]

The pervasiveness of militarism as a broad ethos and the "diversity of its activity" have not abated since Luxemburg's and Liebknecht's critiques over a hundred years ago. My analysis and conceptualization of militarism build upon older works by figures such as Luxemburg, Liebknecht, and Alfred Vagts, as well as more recent critiques by feminist scholars.[52] Such work, while in some cases emerging from different political-intellectual traditions and historical as well as geographic contexts, ranging from European Marxism of the late-nineteenth and early twentieth centuries to Indigenous, decolonial, and women of color feminisms of the late-twentieth and early twenty-first centuries, can collectively cohere as an archive of antimilitarist critique. My juxtapositions of such thinkers and activists generate an analysis of the stubborn endurance of militarism and its imbrication with settler imperial state power, colonialism, and racial capitalism. This stubborn endurance and imbrication, while obvious or predictable on some levels, is also counterintuitive on other levels.

Just as debt has a counterintuitive valence, so too does militarism. Rather than presuming that the meaning of militarism is obvious, I defamiliarize it instead. Though we can use the terms *militarization* and *militarism* interchangeably, we might also think of militarization as the process that both contributes to and is the effect of militarism. Next, militarism, in turn, indexes something much more pervasive than the collusion between the military and the arms industry named by Eisenhower's "military-industrial complex." We might conceptualize instead "regimes of militarism" as the colonial and neocolonial nexus of state and capital that generates a proliferation of military logics beyond formal military institutions and sites, and beyond the war-making, peacekeeping, and security functions of the military itself. Put simply, militarism's logic is the preservation of military institutions whether or not they are needed for war, transcending, as Vagts observed in his classic study, "true military purposes."[53] Thus, regimes of militarism constitute US military empire but are not reducible to it, nor are they reducible to the collusion between the military and the arms industry. Regimes of militarism pervade the ideological and institutional, the material and discursive, the global and local, and act as a structuring force and logic not only in international geopolitical relations but also in the daily and intimate lives of (neo)colonized and gendered racial subjects.

As the process that both contributes to and is the effect of militarism, militarization exceeds the temporal parameters of war, the spatial demarcations of military bases, the functional ends of military institutions, and the enlistment of military personnel. Militarization, in other words, is all of these things, yet more. Today, a constellation of phenomena, historical processes, and subjectivities can be properly characterized, and need to be urgently critiqued, as militarized. These include militarized humanitarianism, militarized diaspora, militarized adoption, militarized sex work, militarized kinship, militarized capitalism, militarized tourism (what Teaiwa calls "militourism"), militarized entertainment, militarized settler colonialism, militarized logistics for the transportation of the world's oil supply, and militarized carbon emissions.[54] Crucially, there is also militarized nuclearization, or a "radioactive" militarism producing an "irradiated transpacific."[55] What does it mean that the term *militarized* serves as a proper adjective, appearing in a host of modifier-noun couplings that at first seem oxymoronic or unlikely but upon closer critical examination are compatible, co-constitutive, and verging on the tautological? Alongside a "military-industrial complex" there is what Teaiwa calls a broader "military cultural complex" generated by militarism as a phenomenon that "bleeds" across formal boundaries or military institutions and seeps into the significantly more fundamental aspects of social and cultural life. Teaiwa thus draws a distinction between military studies and studies of militarism.[56] In a similar vein, Catherine Lutz observes that the "massive entangled system can go by the knotted moniker of the military-industrial-Congressional-media-entertainment-university complex." This draws attention to the broad array of institutions and groups benefiting and profiting significantly from a large military budget.[57] Within the context of the Pacific in particular, Victor Bascara, Keith L. Camacho, and Elizabeth DeLoughrey conceive of a "critical militarisation studies" that analyzes state regimes of violence in the Pacific in relation to issues of ethnicity, Indigeneity, gender, and sexuality. They ask, moreover, how such regimes produce "new cultural practices and modes of expression in literature, the arts, activism and politics."[58]

The proliferating contours of US military empire constitute a crucial manifestation of regimes of militarism. This empire, what has been called an "empire of bases," proliferated globally, especially in Asia and the Pacific, during and after World War II, the Cold War, the more recent war on terror, and now the new twenty-first-century "Asia-Pacific pivot."[59] Yet if we consider, again, the very "founding" of the United States, we would recall that the young nation's ever-westward expansion during the nineteenth century depended on the stationing of soldiers in more than 250 military forts. The establishment of an overseas empire beginning significantly with the 1898 Spanish-American War also depended on the expansion of overseas bases. Then, during World War II, "island hopping" across the Pacific (through Guam, Saipan, Tinian, and Okinawa) for the bombing of Japan witnessed an expansion of US bases, as did the inheritance of the British basing structure. By 1945, more than 44 percent of all US military facilities overseas were located in the Pacific, with the extensive global network stretching from the Arctic Circle to Antarctica.[60] And although the more than 2,000 overseas installations during World War II had dwindled to 582 by 1949, as the Cold War escalated (especially in Korea), the number had risen to 815 by 1957 and yet higher to 1,104 by the peak of the Vietnam War. Two-thirds of these bases were in South Korea, Japan and Okinawa, and West Germany, and the majority continue to be located there as of the release of the 2018 *Base Structure Report* of the US Department of Defense (DoD).[61] Notably, before the closure of US bases there in 1992, the former US colony of the Philippines hosted one of the most significant and vast US military complexes in the world, employing seventy thousand Filipinos and thirteen thousand US military personnel. Clark Field became the second-largest US airbase on the planet, and Subic Bay became the largest American naval facility outside the United States.[62] Yet even after the historic base closures, US military presence has persisted not only in terms of ecological harm and environmental damage but also via a direct remilitarization in which the United States compels the Philippines to make itself available as a logistics hub. A series of military agreements, formally bilateral yet effectively an extension of US neocolonialism, facilitates the renewed and growing presence of US military forces on small bases or "lily pads" throughout the Philippines. In short, the DoD manages what it calls "a worldwide real property portfolio" that is extensive. The United States, in other words, is not only the biggest military power in the world but it is also the world's biggest landlord and leaseholder.[63] It is not surprising, then, that the United States accounts for nearly 40 percent of the *world's total* military expenditures each year.[64]

Transpacific Imaginaries, Decolonial Genealogies, and the Oceanic

In focusing on Asia and the Pacific as a crucial site of militarist settler imperialism in the post–World War II conjuncture, when the US settler state also becomes a military empire heavily concentrated in Asia and the Pacific, it is not my intent to reduce the complexities, heterogeneities, entanglements, and hierarchies within the region to a homogenized whole.[65] Different encounters with colonial formations and subjectivities of race, ethnicity, Indigeneity, and power more broadly work against facile conflations and generalizations. For example, there are incommensurable differences between neocolonialism experienced by an Asian site, on the one hand, and Indigenous Pacific Islander dispossession, on the other. Yet still, within the domestic space of the United States, Asian American concerns such as immigration exclusion and civil rights can ultimately reinforce the power of the settler state and of what Byrd calls "liberal multicultural settler colonialism" because they presume or leave uninterrogated Indigenous deracination and dispossession.[66] This difference and incommensurability are heightened even further in the specific context of Hawai'i, where we see the formation of Asian settler colonialism.[67] Further still, both among and within Native American, Pacific Islander, and certain Asian communities (such as Okinawa), Indigeneity has local specificities and differences, so we might speak of Indigeneities in the plural.[68] But to the extent that Asia and the Pacific have been and continue to be strategic sites and staging grounds of US militarist settler imperialism, or the locus of a militarized interconnectedness, we can speak of linked futures, productive solidarities and relationalities, and oppositional imaginaries.[69] For while militarist settler imperialism deploys specific modalities across smaller scales of time and space, there is also a significant consistency in its continual engulfment of larger scales of time and space in attempting to renovate itself for the perpetuation of US hegemony and metapolitical authority. Alongside the local specificities and hierarchies within Asia, within the Pacific, and across Asia and the Pacific, the vast contours of US militarist settler imperialism in the region have produced and continue to produce militarized intersections. This necessitates intellectual, political, and cultural projects that can take those crossings and that interconnectedness into critical account while also being attentive to incommensurable local specificities, histories, and hierarchies.

Bearing this in mind, my intent, goal, and hope are to interrogate *the very production* of the "Asia-Pacific" as a site of US strategic and geopolitical interest as opposed to a geographic given. As such, unless I am referring specifically to and querying this dominant ascription of "Asia-Pacific," I use *Asia and the Pacific* as the preferred naming practice to reference the region in more straightforwardly descriptive rather than ascriptive terms. While the hyphen in *Asia-Pacific* can tend to homogenize the region, the *and* in *Asia and the Pacific* links the two without necessarily conflating them. Further, as I elaborate in what follows, my use of *transpacific* in conceptualizing "transpacific imaginaries" is less about a singular geographic designation and more about what I have called an aesthetics of settler imperial failure articulated in cultural productions. As such, I do not use the terms *Asia-Pacific*, *Asia and the Pacific*, and *transpacific* interchangeably. Even as it would seem that all three name the same region, each comes freighted with its own particular context of deployment and purpose. To the extent that the "Asia-Pacific" is not only a geopolitical production but also a geo*historical* and geo*colonial* production, it calls for what I have called the "relational analysis of the distinct yet linked."

Yet further, *Settler Garrison* takes its inspiration from *alternative* theorizing of what scholars have more recently called the "transpacific."[70] I focus on what Lisa Yoneyama calls a "dissonant reading" and "decolonial genealogy" of the transpacific precisely because the term itself also has potential limitations and pitfalls.[71] Indeed, mindful that the term *transpacific* has increasingly been adopted as a shorthand for transnational Asian American or Asian diasporic critique, Erin Suzuki cautions that there is a risk of repeating "colonial evacuations" of the Indigenous Pacific performed by earlier "Pacific Rim" discourses unless scholars of the transpacific rigorously investigate "material and cultural entanglements within the Pacific itself . . ." That is, "scholarship that frames itself as '*transpacific*' *must* engage with Indigenous Pacific histories, frameworks, and methodologies, or else the term loses its unique critical purchase."[72] Given this, *Settler Garrison*'s engagement with *alternative* theorizing of the transpacific is not to create or reify a new object or method. Rather, my conceptualization of "transpacific imaginaries" gestures to the transpacific as a placeholder of sorts for naming at once a differentiated and vexed geocolonial site, method of decolonial critique, and multivalent keyword. This holds critical possibility for interrogating the dominant ascriptions of "Asia-Pacific" or "Pacific Rim" and substantively engaging with Indigenous analytical frames and subjectivities that have hitherto been ignored or insufficiently considered. As a geocolonial site, while the transpacific is tied together by ongoing histories of the conjunction I have named as US militarist settler imperialism, it is not reducible to it. As I have observed, hierarchies and local specificities within the transpacific, as well as decolonial epistemologies and movements, work against reductive ascriptions. We can thus think of the transpacific as constituted by "distinct yet densely interconnected political geographies," to cite what at times is the overlooked part of Ruth Wilson Gilmore's important formulation of racism.[73]

As such, the *trans* in *transpacific* is certainly not meant to invoke a "pan" Pacific harmony or homology. Moreover, the prefix *trans* calls to mind Chadwick Allen's conceptualization of "trans-Indigenous" in his call for a global Native literary studies. For Allen, given ongoing colonial histories, *trans* seems the best choice to convey the analytic and ethos of the "together (yet) *distinct*," for it "may be able to bear the complex, contingent asymmetry and the potential risks of unequal encounters borne by the preposition *across*. It may be able to indicate the specific agency and situated momentum carried by the preposition *through*. It may be able to harbor the potential of *change* as both transitive and intransitive verb, as both noun and adjective."[74] Allen's methodology of focused and purposeful juxtapositions, with mindfulness of the etymological difference between *compare* (which unites *together* with *equal*) and *juxtapose* (which unites *close together* with *to place*), is productive in thinking through and juxtaposing the "complex, contingent asymmetry" and at times incommensurability of the Indigenous and non-Indigenous transpacific.[75] My book *places* these parts of the settler garrison alongside one another as together yet distinctly constituting America's settler garrison in a manner that is attentive to the particularities of Indigenous place-based relations. The methodology of focused and purposeful juxtapositions is connected to a *relational* analytic rather than a comparative one that tends to presume or effect equivalence or homology.

Moreover, my engagement with *transpacific* departs from the sole privileging of continental landmasses by emphasizing as well the geographies and spatialities of the island, the archipelago, and the peninsula, alongside the terraqueous and the oceanic. As I elaborate in Chapter 2 and especially Chapter 4 as well as the Epilogue, the emphasis on the terraqueous and the oceanic is particularly important for island sites such as the Philippines, Okinawa, and Guam, as well as low-lying Pacific islands facing existential threat due to climate change. In a linked yet different way, it is also pertinent to peninsular South Korea and its subjugation of Jeju Island. Epeli Hau'ofa theorizes this powerful shift to the oceanic in his influential essay "Our Sea of Islands." Hau'ofa argues that switching the frame of reference from the terrestrial or continental to the oceanic opens up the world of Oceania and allows us to see the worldliness of islands. He writes, "There is a world of difference between viewing the Pacific as 'islands in a far sea' and as a 'sea of islands.' The first emphasizes dry surfaces in a vast ocean far from the centers of power. Focusing in this way stresses the smallness and remoteness of the islands. The second is a more holistic perspective in which things are seen in the totality of their relationships."[76] In short, the concern is to be attentive to the Pacific Basin, not just the Pacific Rim.[77]

This is to speak about nissology, "the study of islands on their own terms," or a perspectival shift away from both continental and Pacific exceptionalisms.[78] *Settler Garrison* thus also takes inspiration from interdisciplinary island studies approaches, in particular island and decolonial feminisms, in adopting a critically oceanic lens that takes into account the interrelation between the oceanic and the terrestrial, or "aquapelagic assemblages."[79] The militarized and colonial dynamics of islands are such that they undergo a simultaneous process that seems disjunctive but is violently conjunctive: "de-islanding," or the alienation of the island's inhabitants from its geography and ecosystem, and "islanding," or the imperial offshoring of militarism, tourism, and extraction along with their attendant infrastructures.[80] Yet we can also think of islanding, or *island* as a verb form, in a quite different or antipodal way. As Teaiwa argues, to make *island* a verb is to embrace and practice a way of living that centers an ethics, epistemology, and ontology of care for multispecies life-forms and ecologies. In this sense, to island and to be islanded is to awaken "from the stupor of continental fantasies" and to crowd out such fantasies with a care-centered way of life. Teaiwa declares, "Let us 'island' the word!"[81] This alternative conceptualization of islanding as care is thus the challenge to and antithesis of islanding as militarist settler imperial processes of offshoring. Within the context of my analysis, to speak about this twinned process of de-islanding and islanding is to speak about the violent transformation of the spatialities, topographies, and ecosystems—of Okinawa, Guam, the Philippines, and increasingly to a certain extent the South Korean island of Jeju—into the "offshore" sites or pivotal "aquapelagic assemblages" of America's settler garrison. Moreover, to speak of Teaiwa's alternative sense of islanding in opposition to imperial processes of islanding or offshoring is to speak about the aesthetics of settler imperial failure in the transpacific cultural forms I analyze.

Yet still, the "imaginaries" in my formulation of "transpacific imaginaries" foregrounds cultural texts—literature, film, and performance—as a potent figurative site for at once rendering visible and disarticulating the geocoloniality of the transpacific. Cultural works such as *Parasite* contain a powerful aesthetics of settler imperial failure, opening up to antimilitarist and decolonial world-makings that aspire to shatter "another brick" in the wall of America's settler garrison. Grouping such texts together into a transpacific collective or archive also departs from the limitations of adhering to nation- or region-bound designations of literatures and cultural forms. By being attentive to and highlighting the decolonial and antimilitarist contours of transpacific cultural productions, my book takes seriously Albert Wendt's declaration in his 1976 foundational essay, "Towards a New Oceania," that works of art contribute significantly to a "genuine decolonisation" and the creation of a "new Oceania."[82]

Settler Garrison proceeds with a focus on debt imperialism in the next chapter, and each chapter thereafter is organized around a particular spatial exception: the military base and attendant camptown, the POW camp, and the unincorporated territory of Guam. Chapter 1, "Perverse Temporalities: Primitive Accumulation and the Settler Colonial Foundations of Debt Imperialism," provides an elaboration of debt imperialism as the temporal exception. In situating debt imperialism within the multiple linked genealogies of the US nation-state's manipulation of debt since its very founding, of the longue durée of racial capitalism and primitive accumulation, and of the debt form and relation more broadly as a manifold regime of gendered racial and colonial asymmetries of power at multiple scales, the chapter conceptualizes debt anew. What is at stake in this conceptualization is twofold. First, it is an interrogation of the elision of the conditioning and ongoing violence of US militarist settler imperialism. Second, it is an analysis of the US attempt to possess metapolitical authority specifically through a split between militarist settler imperialism's imposition of the homogeneous time of repayment on others and its own inhabitation of an exceptional temporality.

Chapter 2, "The Military Base and Camptown: Seizing Land 'by Bulldozer and Bayonet' and the Transpacific Masculinist Compact," begins with a discussion of the linked yet differentiated ways in which sites across Asia and the Pacific are targeted to house US military bases and camptowns. Island spatialities such as Okinawa (Japan) and Jeju (South Korea) are especially targeted because they are doubly subjugated, by both the United States and the respective East Asian nations of which they are a part. These nations also enjoy a relatively privileged subimperial status within Asia vis-à-vis poorer and less powerful nations such as those of Southeast Asia. The chapter then examines how a range of transpacific cultural productions critically magnifies the land grabs that make possible the formation of the spatial exception of the perduring military base and camptown. How is this variety of land grab connected to the settler colonial seizures of land that make possible the very constitution of the United States of America? The base and camptown are the result of the wholesale spatial transformation of seized Indigenous or local land into a virtual "America Town" where US metapolitical authority reigns. How, moreover, do transpacific cultural works grapple with the ethics and politics of how to represent the necropolitical contours of the camptown, insofar as camptown sex workers perform a necropolitical labor that functions as a form of debt bondage and are also vulnerable to gendered racial and sexual violence that can be fatal? Focusing on the Philippines, Okinawa, and South Korea, I begin with an analysis of Rachel Rivera's documentary *Sin City Diary* (1992). I then turn to Okinawan literature: Kishaba Jun's short story "Dark Flowers" (1955), Higashi Mineo's novella *Child of Okinawa* (1971), and Medoruma Shun's short story "Hope" (1999). Next, I turn to South Korean and Asian diasporic literature and film, beginning with an analysis of *Bloodless* (2017), Gina Kim's

VR (virtual reality) documentary based on the 1992 murder of a South Korean camptown sex worker by an American soldier. My analysis meditates on how this transpacific cinematic form deploys the relatively new technology of VR to grapple in sophisticated ways with the politics and ethics of representing the gendered racial and sexual violence of US militarist settler imperialism perpetrated on the settler garrison. I then turn to Ahn Junghyo's *Silver Stallion: A Novel of Korea* (1990) and the documentaries *The Women Outside: Korean Women and the U.S. Military* (1995) and *Camp Arirang* (1995). Throughout, I ask how this constellation of transpacific cultural productions, collectively cohering as a critical archive of US militarist settler imperialism, articulates decolonial and antimilitarist imaginaries even as it leaves unresolved complex questions about the politics and ethics of representation.

Chapter 3, "The POW Camp: Waging Psychological Warfare and a New Settler Frontier," focuses on how Ha Jin's transpacific novel *War Trash* (2004) renders the POW camp of the Korean War (1950–53) as a particular kind of spatial exception. The POW camp as a laboratory and later general form for the aspirational goals of US metapolitical authority emerges out of the Korean War's introduction of the "voluntary repatriation" program, whose goal was to increase the number of anti-Communist defections, or POWs choosing not to repatriate back to China and North Korea. *War Trash* demonstrates how the "voluntary repatriation" program was a form of psychological warfare flouting both international law as well as the national sovereignties of China, North Korea, and South Korea. Coconstituted by biopolitical space and geopolitical territoriality, the POW camp as the site for the practice of psychological warfare and attendant fears of Chinese Communist "brainwashing" of American POWs reanimate the US settler imperial state's foundational tropes. Human subjectivity and loyalty become the new figurative "frontier" for American expansion that would in turn enable the widening of the literal frontier of US Cold War spheres of influence. The brainwashing scare breathes new life into the fear of captivity, drawing on a long-standing American trope dating back to the colonial era about the ever-present Indian threat faced by white settlers. The permanence of the US POW camp as a general form and the United States as a militarist settler imperial and permanent warfare state link as conjoined temporal exceptions operating in tandem with the temporal exception of debt imperialism. Moreover, the production of nonrepatriates or refugees would in turn generate an indebted subjectivity vis-à-vis the anti-Communist host nations, a figurative debt that can never fully be repaid even as refugee status was the result of psychological warfare.

Chapter 4, "The Unincorporated Territory: Constituting Indefinite Deferral and 'No Page Is Ever Terra Nullius,'" focuses on the unincorporated territory of Guam and offers an analysis of the poetics and what we might call a nondidactic archive and pedagogy of antimilitarist decolonization in Craig Santos Perez's multibook poetic project: *from unincorporated territory [hacha]* (2008), *from unincorporated territory [saina]* (2010), *from unincorporated territory [guma']* (2014), and *from unincorporated territory [lukao]* (2017). Perez's antimilitarist and decolonial poetics critically illuminates Guam's status as an unincorporated territory, a spatial exception made and remade into America's settler garrison or effective military colony. I argue that *from unincorporated territory* also provides a complex rendering of US militarist settler imperialism's temporal exception of debt imperialism. How does the temporal exception at once condition and obscure the imposition of the disciplinary temporality of an indebted subjectivity onto the Chamorro for their putative "liberation" by the United States from Spanish colonialism and Japanese occupation? For the unincorporated territory, there is another valence to the temporal exception that is connected to the spatial exception. The legally ambiguous status of the unincorporated territory, determined over a hundred years ago in the *Insular Cases* (1901–22), is characterized by the indefinite deferral of the possibility of statehood. This as-yet-perpetually deferred decision, the denial of even the promise of any definitive or final status, is also a kind of temporal exception. Against the logics of these spatial and temporal exceptions, *from unincorporated territory*'s aesthetics of settler imperial failure gestures to the urgency of how we might refuse and thwart US militarist settler imperialism's fatalities.

In the Epilogue, "Climate Change, Climate Debt, Climate Imperialism," I analyze *Moana: The Rising of the Sea* (2013/2015), a multimedia stage production that dramatizes climate change and sea-level rise in Oceania and significantly features the poetry of Kathy Jetñil-Kijiner, the Marshallese poet, performance artist, and educator. The forced migrations and displacements of the people of Oceania and other disproportionately impacted parts of the world are only one among the many devastating effects of climate change. Zoonotic diseases, and most certainly the COVID-19 pandemic, are also linked to climate change and industrial agriculture. I analyze how climate change brings to the fore another form of the manifold debt relation—that of the climate debt that nations with the largest carbon footprints, such as the United States, owe to the nations with significantly smaller footprints. As with the debt owed to Indigenous nations and groups, this, too, is a debt that is predominantly unacknowledged. It is also a debt that is generated by US militarist settler imperialism, specifically by the disproportionate carbon emission rates of the US military in securing the flow of oil. *Moana* grapples complexly with the climate debt and the vexed politics of what it means to be labeled a "climate refugee" insofar as it functions as a trope of victimhood and object of imperial humanitarian rescue. I thus close *Settler Garrison* with yet another urgent and necropolitical debt produced by militarist settler imperialism, the climate debt implicated in the Anthropocene, or, more accurately and critically, the Racial Capitalocene. *Moana*'s aesthetics of settler imperial failure refuses the trope of victimhood in embracing and demanding a complex ethics of survival and critical reckoning.

1. PERVERSE TEMPORALITIES: *Primitive Accumulation and the Settler Colonial Foundations of Debt Imperialism*

In 2005, the United States announced that as part of an agreement with Japan, it planned to transfer eight thousand marines and nine thousand marine dependents from Okinawa to the US unincorporated territory of Guam. Issued as the "United States-Japan Roadmap for Realignment Implementation" in 2006, this agreement proposed a further massive military buildup of an already heavily militarized island that functions as a US military colony.[1] The Indigenous Chamorro people of Guam effectively opposed the proposed buildup through a variety of actions, including protests, teach-ins, a "swim-in" at Guam's port Apra Harbor, lawsuits, international solidarity efforts, and a comment drive organized by the group We Are Guåhan. This comment drive resulted in over ten thousand comments submitted in response to the US government's 2009 Draft Environmental Impact Statement (DEIS) detailing the structural changes and environmental effects of what would be the biggest military base relocation in the twenty-first century.

The mobilization also included a series of Heritage Hikes to Pågat, the proposed site for the construction of a US Marine Corps live firing range complex.

An ancient Chamorro village and burial site of cultural significance to Chamorros, Pågat has been designated as a site of historical significance by the US National Park Service and is one of the few remaining and best preserved precolonial sites owned by the Government of Guam. Registered since 1974 as an archeological site in the Guam National Register of Historic Places, the village contains the remains of lattes (prehistoric structural stone foundations), stone mortars, freshwater caves, medicinal plants, pottery, and tools.[2] As part of the campaign to save Pågat, when a representative of the Department of Defense visited on July 23, 2010, to inspect it as the proposed site of the firing range, he was met by hundreds of protesters. Calling for the preservation of the village and protection of the environment in particular and for the decolonization of Guam more broadly, the protesters spanned multiple generations and included the dance group Taotao Tåno'. Their decolonial demands were inscribed on signs such as "Leave Pågat Alone," "Federal Dictatorship," and "Pågat Should Be Filled with Butterflies NOT Bullets" (referring to the endangered Mariana Eight-Spot Butterfly).[3]

Crucially, the multiple and ongoing mobilizations against the proposed military buildup constituted the "linking of diverse performative appearances of people at and across different stages into a powerful public space."[4] The mobilizations centered Chamorro cultural memory, performance, and values. This was articulated in the slogan *prutehi yan difendi* ("protect and defend") in the campaign to save Pågat, and was exemplified more broadly via the foundational Chamorro cultural framework of *inafa' maolek*. Literally translated, inafa' maolek means "to make things good for each other" by restoring harmony and order. It presumes mutual respect, collectivity, reciprocity, and interdependence rather than individualism and compelled dependence.[5] As such, we can think of inafa' maolek as an alternative concept of debt, a lateral form of reciprocity, mutuality, and obligation, or the very thing that makes sociality possible.

I begin with a discussion of these diverse performative appearances of people affirming Indigenous Chamorro cultural frameworks against the hyperescalation of US militarism and settler colonialism on the military colony of Guam because they articulate an alternative concept of debt that has not been, as David Graeber suggests, "corrupted by both math and violence."[6] Yet the corrupted form of debt has become the common, dominant understanding of what a debt means, crowding out earlier and ongoing concepts and inhabitations of debt, such as inafa' maolek, as mutual obligation and reciprocity. How has debt come to be not only understood but leveraged in such manifold ways?

In this chapter, I focus on what Graeber calls a "perversion of a promise" by math and violence, or the story of how the United States has been able to leverage massive indebtedness into a form of imperial power operating as a kind of temporal exception.[7] I offer an elaboration of the temporal exception of debt imperialism by situating debt imperialism within multiple linked genealogies: of the US nation-state's manipulation of debt since its very founding, of the longue durée of racial capitalism, and of the debt form and relation more broadly as a manifold regime of gendered racial and colonial asymmetries of power at multiple scales. My analysis lays bare debt's counterintuitive, paradoxical, and manifold manifestations: as at once a financial and figurative imperial economy; as both the foreclosure *and* effect of freedom; as a cunning sleight of hand in which the actual debtors transmogrify into creditors (and vice versa); and as a production of an indebted subjectivity that radically circumscribes multiple possible futures and ways of being in the world. At stake is a demonstration of how debt imperialism functions as the conditioning and ongoing violence of US militarist settler imperialism. I reveal, moreover, how that violence has been elided via the attempt to possess metapolitical authority through a split between US militarist settler imperialism's imposition of the homogeneous time of repayment on the spatial exceptions that constitute the settler garrison and its own inhabitation of an exceptional temporality that exempts it from having to conform to the very rules of the game that it creates and imposes.

Primitive Accumulation, the Public Debt, and Dispossession

I begin by observing that transpacific entanglements and hierarchies within Asia, the Pacific, and the United States, and the making of multiple Asian diasporas as well as Indigenous Pacific Islander displacements and dispossession, are animated by what might be called a colonial and gendered racial transpacific debt relation and militarism. So, too, are subimperial dynamics and desires among Asian and Pacific regions and nations as well as decolonial aspirations among the peoples of colonized territories. I ask, moreover, how debt functions as a necropolitical regime for those impoverished, gendered racial, and colonized nations and subjects whose promissory notes must be fully repaid with interest. How has the militarist settler imperialism of the United States been constituted by this usurious necropolitics of the promise, even as it continually confers upon itself the temporal exception of debt imperialism, or the right not to keep its promises? In some instances, the United States can also evade the very need to promise. My analysis reveals that what is at stake is not only the elision of settler colonial conquest and genocide as the conditions of possibility for military empire, economic power, and the avowed defense of liberal democracy but also for the attempt to possess metapolitical authority.

By way of a brief contextualization, I begin the story of debt imperialism, or the temporal exception, with a few flashpoints in the history of the United States' relationship to debt and militarism, and I connect this to the history of capitalism as analyzed by Marx in his discussion of "so-called primitive accumulation." First, the constellation of the strategic leveraging of debt, public debt, and militarism emerges in the British colonial era of the Thirteen Colonies and continues through the very founding of the United States of America, especially in terms of the concerns about the tremendous debt incurred by the "War of Independence."[8] To speak about this "founding," or the transformation of the thirteen British colonies in the "New World" into the nation-state of the USA through a revolutionary war, is to speak about the "breakaway" of thirteen white settler colonies from the metropole through a "settler revolt."[9] These colonies would then constitute themselves into a settler state, then later also a military empire and new metropole, of their own. Thus, while the United States might be formally "postcolonial" vis-à-vis Britain, the singular focus on this postcoloniality obscures ongoing US settler colonialism vis-à-vis Native and Indigenous groups. It also obscures, as I observed in the Introduction, the relationship between settler colonialism on the territory that incrementally became "incorporated" as the fifty United States of America and the discontiguous territories, unincorporated territories, military bases/camptowns, and neocolonies in Asia and the Pacific that constitute the proliferating orders and outposts of US military empire.

Indeed, even before the formation of the United States, in what K-Sue Park calls the "contact economy" of the pre-independence colonial era, the emergence of the American real estate market was made possible by the English expropriation of Indigenous lands. This seizure of land was in turn made possible by colonial lending practices that were essentially predatory, creating Indigenous debt. "Land therefore became a money equivalent not through positive sale, but through debt and loss; foreclosure was a tool of indigenous dispossession."[10] This long predates the subprime housing crisis of the first decade of the twenty-first century, and bespeaks a genealogy of Indigenous and later racial dispossession—via the mechanism of debt and land foreclosure—that also predates the very founding of the United States itself.[11] Moreover, it is worth recalling that the British used their colonies in North America, and later to a larger extent Australia, partly as a penal colony governed by a system of indentured servitude. This points to a long history of how the land-labor nexus is tethered to debt as a mechanism of dispossession and domination.

The constellation of debt, public debt, and the waging of war continues on through the US Civil War. A notable instance is the ratification of the

Fourteenth Amendment of the US Constitution in 1868, one of the Reconstruction amendments passed in the immediate aftermath of the Civil War. This amendment holds juridical significance because it extended citizenship to all persons born or naturalized in the United States regardless of race, and it guaranteed due process of law as well as equal protection of the laws. Citizenship, due process, and equal protection have come to be the hallmarks of US liberal democracy and political modernity. This constitution of the rights-bearing subject is spelled out in Section 1 of the amendment. Yet the rote familiarity of the key terms of this section has come to overshadow what is named in the other sections of the amendment. I draw our attention to Sections 2 and 4, and query how these lesser-known sections of the reified Fourteenth Amendment reveal the very contradictions that make possible citizenship, due process, and equal protection. Section 2 states, "Representatives shall be apportioned among the several States according to their respective numbers, counting the whole number of persons in each State, excluding Indians not taxed . . ." Here, we are told that "Indians not taxed" are excluded from the head count of proportional representation because of the nation-to-nation relationship between the US government and Native American tribes. Itself an amendment to Article I, Section 2 of the Constitution, this section retains the original Indian exclusion but does away with the three-fifths compromise.

Section 4 states, "The validity of the public debt of the United States, authorized by law, including debts incurred for payment of pensions and bounties for services in suppressing insurrection or rebellion, shall not be questioned. But neither the United States nor any State shall assume or pay any debt or obligation incurred in aid of insurrection or rebellion against the United States, or any claim for the loss or emancipation of any slave; but all such debts, obligations and claims shall be held illegal and void." In this section, we are told that the US government is obliged to pay its debts unless such debt is incurred "in aid of rebellion or insurrection against the United States" or because of "any claim for the loss or emancipation of any slave." Following the Civil War, this section served the double function of relieving the US government of having to pay back Confederate war debt and of having to pay Confederate states for the value of their emancipated slaves.

Taken together, these sections of the Fourteenth Amendment display at once the apotheosis of liberal democracy as well as its contradictory and violent conditions of possibility. The "exclusion of Indians not taxed" named in Section 2 cannot but reveal the US Constitution as the document of a white settler state whose frontiers would continue to expand far beyond its mid-nineteenth-century borders. Section 4 names the racial chattel slavery that, conjoined with settler colonialism, provided the labor and land in the consolidation of an ever-expanding United States of America. Both sections reveal the contradictory and violent conditions of possibility of liberal democracy via the language of exemption/exception. In Section 2, the "whole number of persons" in each state will be counted for apportioning representatives, *except for* "Indians not taxed." In Section 4, the validity of the public debt of the United States "shall not be questioned," *except for* "any debt or obligation incurred in aid of insurrection or rebellion against the United States, or any claim for the loss or emancipation of any slave." I point out these exceptions, legally enshrined in the Constitution, to demonstrate how such exceptions are pivotal to US nation-state formation as a settler imperial power. As I elaborated in the Introduction, we can thus reframe the discourse of US exceptionalism. The dominant "shining city on a hill" variant of US exceptionalism is at once made possible and contradicted by the obscured settler imperial and racial capitalist variant of US exceptionalism(s) dating back to the very founding of the United States.

Moreover, these sections of the Fourteenth Amendment also bear the residues of an early moment of US attempts to seize metapolitical authority via the imposition of exceptions. The power to render exceptional "Indians not taxed" is a metapolitical authority over Native nations; and the power to render exceptional or illegal certain public debts is a metapolitical authority over the Confederacy. This metapolitical authority is then converted into political authority through acts of what we might call domesticating incorporation—the affirmation of congressional plenary power over Native American nations and the dissolving of the Confederacy back into the Union. In the more recent post–World War II era, as I have argued, US militarist settler imperialism congeals and renovates itself through a conjoined set of temporal and spatial exceptions as the United States aspires to metapolitical authority by superseding local sovereignty in legally ambiguous militarized geographies. In terms of the temporal exception of debt imperialism, I have noted the appearance of the figure of debt, particularly US government debt, in Section 4. I offer this discussion of the Fourteenth Amendment as an early instantiation of how the United States would continue to deploy and manipulate debt, as at once a literal and figurative economy, an arithmetic and grammar, in brokering its power as both a settler colonial and imperial state.

If in the Fourteenth Amendment public debt functions as a narrative of transition in the political and economic maturation of the United States, we find a parallel narrative of transition in Marx. He writes that primitive accumulation forms the prehistory of capital, and in his classic case of England, this took the form of enclosure, or the expropriation of the agricultural producer or peasant from the land. Yet elsewhere in the world, "The discovery of gold and silver in America, the extirpation, enslavement and entombment in mines of the indigenous population of that continent, the beginnings of the conquest and plunder of India, and the conversion of Africa into a preserve for the commercial hunting of blackskins, are all things which characterize the dawn of the era of capitalist production. These idyllic proceedings are the chief moments of primitive accumulation."[12] In other words, it would seem that for Marx, settler colonialism, franchise colonialism, and the Atlantic slave trade constitute the prehistory of capitalism rather than what Cedric Robinson would describe as the history of racial capitalism.[13]

What is particularly interesting, however, in Marx's discussion of primitive accumulation is the appearance of public debt and the US Civil War. He writes, "The public debt becomes one of the most powerful levers of primitive accumulation. As with the stroke of an enchanter's wand, it endows unproductive money with the power of creation and thus turns it into capital . . . the national debt has given rise to joint-stock companies, to dealings in negotiable effects of all kinds, and to speculation: in a word, it has given rise to stock-exchange gambling and the modern bankocracy."[14] In terms of the US Civil War, he observes that it "has brought in its train a colossal national debt and, with it, a heavy tax-burden, the creation of a finance aristocracy of the vilest type, and the granting of immense tracks of public land to speculative companies for the exploitation of railways, mines, etc."[15] So even as Marx crafts a schematic narrative of transition from the prehistory of capital to its proper history, by focusing specifically on public debt, he complicates the political and economic teleology that the Fourteenth Amendment juridically formalizes. Political enfranchisement granted in Section 1 of the amendment is attenuated and contradicted by the growth of finance capitalism resulting from Section 4's recognition of the validity of public debt. That is, political emancipation within a capitalist mode of production has limitations and should not be conflated with what Marx calls "universal human emancipation" in "On the Jewish Question."[16] His reference, moreover, to the "granting of immense tracks of public land" for capitalist speculation lays bare how Section 2's naming of "Indians not taxed" inadvertently serves as an archive of the settler colonial abrogation of Native American sovereignty and treaty rights in the theft of Native land and the transformation of that land into property.

Even as Marx is clearly invested in charting a teleological history of capital, his invocation of public debt generates an interrogation of that presumably linear trajectory. Indeed, we have witnessed how primitive accumulation in the form of national debt has given rise to speculative enterprises of all kinds.

Primitive accumulation has multiple, overlapping, and still enduring temporalities. It is thus neither simply the prehistory of capital nor an anachronistic or belated practice appearing in the history of capital, which is to say that overt state and extra-state violence is an enduring and constitutive structure or feature of the capital relation.

Marx's analysis in *Capital* has met with debate and critique across a range of critical traditions, significantly because his analysis implies that primitive accumulation is a discrete historical stage rather than an ongoing structure, a prehistory dripping in blood, that will be succeeded by the general law of capital accumulation in which extra-economic force and violence will be replaced by the "silent compulsion of economic relations."[17] Rosa Luxemburg, in an important reformulation, viewed primitive accumulation not as an already completed historical stage but as a lens through which to apprehend imperialism and imperial violence as continuing and constitutive features in capitalist expansion.[18] Along with Luxemburg, we might think of primitive accumulation as the concept that helps to make visible the violent process (as opposed to historical stage) of not only imperial capitalism but also settler colonialism, franchise colonialism, racial chattel slavery, and gendered racial labor exploitation, or the very ground that continues to make capital accumulation possible. If anything, as postcolonial Marxists and others have noted, rather than a historical transition from extra-economic violence to "silent compulsion," there has been a continual *spatial* displacement of such violence to the imperial periphery.[19] David Harvey calls one important aspect of primitive accumulation, privatization, "accumulation by dispossession," arguing that it is peculiar to call such an ongoing and persistent process "primitive" or "original."[20]

More recently, in a generative rereading, William Clare Roberts argues that the crux of Marx's account of primitive accumulation in Part Eight of *Capital* has been missed by critiques that focus on the temporal and spatial contours of primitive accumulation. For Roberts, the crux of Marx's analysis is an account of the relation between capital and the state, specifically capital's capture of the state. Capital needs but cannot itself carry out primitive accumulation, and primitive accumulation in turn is an "ongoing necessity internal to *capitalism*, but always anterior to the specific operations of *capital*." In other words, since capital cannot itself carry out the so-called dirty work of primitive accumulation, other agents are necessary in the ongoing life of capitalism. This other agent, the primary agent, of primitive accumulation is the state. The state in turn is also specifically a "dependent agent" of capital, a "servile and corrupt henchman," because the state's own existence has become dependent on continued capital accumulation.[21]

Yet still, feminist and Indigenous studies scholars, such as Silvia Federici and Glen Coulthard, respectively, have also provided important critiques, demonstrating how shifting the central subject of analysis from the waged male proletariat to women or the colonial relation makes visible how primitive accumulation is a necessary and ongoing condition of capitalism rather than its precondition.[22] Building on such insights, Siddhant Issar theorizes "racial/colonial primitive accumulation" to elucidate how the capital relation is intertwined with the colonial relation *and* the anti-Black relation. This departs from important revisions of Marx's original formulation (such as Harvey's) that proceed in a "functionalist" manner to emphasize primitive accumulation's role in solving the crises generated by capitalism, rather than seeing it as a constitutive feature of capitalism. Issar's theorization also departs from accounts that do not take into consideration a key structuring logic of ongoing primitive accumulation, "namely the productive power of white supremacist racial and colonial domination."[23]

For the purposes of my analysis of US militarist settler imperialism and debt imperialism, Marx's work on primitive accumulation is helpful not only because of the appearance of public debt and the US Civil War but also because of what it might reveal about dispossession, land, and temporality in the context of the settler colonial and imperialist United States. In a useful analysis disaggregating the four elements of primitive accumulation—dispossession, proletarianization, market formation, and the separation of agriculture and industry—Robert Nichols focuses on Marx's influential phrasing "theft of land" in explaining dispossession. Nichols notes that to speak of dispossession is to "indicate something of the ways in which capitalism disrupts or disturbs our orientation in space, our place-based relations."[24] Although Marx analyzed dispossession in *Capital* as a way of explaining proletarianization, Nichols contends that it can be recast as a distinct category of violent transformation not conjoined to processes of proletarianization and market formation. This ultimately yields the conclusion that dispossession is a distinct logic of capitalist development that appropriates, monopolizes, and converts the planet into a homogenized means of production in a manner that is connected to dislocation, class stratification, and exploitation. Moreover, this logic is both constitutive and contemporary.[25] Along these lines, Iyko Day usefully encapsulates that in the chapter of *Capital* entitled "The Modern Theory of Colonization," Marx's recounting of the work of political theorist E. G. Wakefield recognizes crucial differences between the British metropole and its colonies. So in addition to the invocation of public debt that I discussed previously, Marx himself goes against the developmentalist and teleological assumptions that primitive accumulation as a "prehistory" tends to generate. Day observes that we can thus approach primitive accumulation as "both structure *and* stage of capital accumulation" in her analysis of how nuclear wastelanding on Indigenous lands is a uniquely recursive form of primitive accumulation.[26]

I would like to build on these insights by noting that dispossession names not only a "distinct logic of capitalist development" ordering class stratification but also the colonial, imperial, and gendered racial dynamics that are conjoined with capitalism and through which capitalism often dispossesses and exploits. Moreover, the relationship to land that capitalism disrupts is a specifically European one and does not account for other relationalities, in particular Indigenous ones. As such, Indigenous critiques of dispossession highlight an ambiguity in the term itself, because it is through its very theft that land gets transformed into property. In offering an alternative framework through which to view dispossession, Nichols compellingly demonstrates how dispossession transforms nonproprietary relations into proprietary ones while at the same time systematically transferring title and control of this newly formed property. That is, dispossession in the context of Anglo settler states merges the process of "propertization" and theft into one moment, or fuses the making and taking of property. So what gets created in the "making" of new property is not so much a material object but rather a juridical and abstract object at once manifesting as and undergirding settler relations of right and power, particularly the right to exclude. This is to speak about a peculiar recursive logic in which theft simultaneously precedes and produces property.[27] We might say that this strange recursive logic is a kind of temporal exception as well insofar as a stolen object only becomes that object after or by virtue of the event, after the event of it having been stolen.

As Nichols notes, it may thus appear that Indigenous critiques of dispossession are contradictory because they are demanding the return of something that wasn't property at all (or as yet) when it was stolen. However, when we consider that Indigenous peoples come into sight as the "original owners" of the land "but only retrospectively, that is, refracted backward through the process itself," it becomes clear that Indigenous critiques of dispossession are not contradictory but rather *belated*.[28] If dispossession is constituted by the conjoining or fusing of two things—both the taking and making of property—then undoing dispossession is less about taking property back (repossession) and more about unmaking property itself. It is to undo the very process of "propertization" that has effected alienation, deracination, and desecration, or the severing of a particular relation to land in which relation is not one of ownership and land is not alienable property.[29]

Thinking through the undoing of dispossession as the unmaking of property itself returns us to what I opened this chapter with—the Indigenous Chamorro concept of inafa' maolek. As an alternative form of debt, relationality, and obligation, inafa' maolek is also framed by a nonpossessive, anticapitalist relationship to land. In Hawai'i, there is a related Indigenous Kānaka Maoli concept called *aloha 'āina*. Literally translated as "love for the land," aloha 'āina is closely related to *'āina momona*, abundant or fertile land.[30] This conceptualization of land as relationality and responsibility rather than possession and property, and centering of abundance rather than capitalism's fabrication of scarcity and austerity, is an alternative form of debt and relationality. As Brandy Nālani McDougall pithily puts it in thinking through island sustainability and island-human relationality, "The island provides, the human marvels." This is a model of abundance based on lateral kinship and intricate interconnection among humans and all other parts of the island.[31] Recognizing what the island provides, what the island gives, is a relationality that is quite different from the racial capitalist and settler imperial mandate of what the human takes, extracts, accumulates, has dominion over, alienates from others, and ultimately depletes. This conceptualization of abundance is also quite different from racial capitalism's and nuclear modernity's presumption that Indigenous lands are wastelands, degraded and therefore available as sacrifice zones. Kānaka Maoli epistemologies and ways of life thus radically disrupt the two key features of Western liberal philosophy and political organization, the Rousseauian social contract and the Lockean liberal subject. We might think of the Rousseauian social contract, or human-human relationality, as another word for debt. And we might think of the Lockean liberal subject, or human-land relationality, as another word for possession. Aiko Yamashiro and Noelani Goodyear-Ka'ōpua write of a different kind of contract, a "*compact* of mutual obligation" that "contrasts sharply with the *contracts* that have allowed the (over)development of urban, suburban, and resort construction in ways that do not typically balance social, environmental, cultural, and spiritual impacts against the financial bottom line."[32] In other words, a "*compact* of mutual obligation" is an alternative form of debt or sociality that offers a sharp contrast to the contractual obligations that undergird the liberal settler state's conceptualization of both personhood and possession.

The Fatal Double Standard: Militarist Settler Imperial Time and the Homogeneous Time of Repayment

The spatial component of primitive accumulation, the conversion of the planet into a homogenized means of production, also has an attendant temporal component. Just as heterogeneous spaces are violently incorporated into the logic of capital, heterogeneous conceptualizations and inhabitations of time are homogenized into what we might call militarist settler imperial time. Writing within the context of Indigenous studies, Mark Rifkin warns against efforts at temporal recognition—or the attempt to overcome temporal distancing or denial of coevalness by insisting on a shared modernity or presentness—precisely because such recognition would be a homogenization into settler time. This would hardly be a neutral designation, for settler institutions, interests, and imperatives would define and authorize it. It would be a denial of what Rifkin calls Indigenous temporal sovereignty insofar as *one* particular concept or experience of time, the settler one, would be reified as the *only* one, or "the baseline for the unfolding of time itself."[33] Rather than approaching time as a singular or homogeneous unfolding, as a universal movement along a single axis, Rifkin suggests that we can think of it as multiple, plural, or varied. Thus, as opposed to a singular normative temporality, what Elizabeth Freeman in the context of queer studies calls chrononormativity, we have temporalities in the plural with their own rhythms.[34] We cannot speak, then, of a global coevality, insofar as simultaneity depends upon a shared frame of reference that fails or refuses to take into account the coexistence of multiple and qualitatively different frames of reference.[35] As I will elaborate, the homogeneous time of repayment is the imposition of a militarist settler imperial time, a denial of temporal sovereignty, that forecloses multiple futures and ways of being in the world. This, as we shall see, is coeval with the United States' metapolitical authority to confer upon itself the temporal exception of not having to conform to the very homogeneous time of repayment that it imposes on others. That is, US national debt is not so much a burden or obligation to be fulfilled but a weapon to be leveraged in the imposition of a militarist settler imperial time.

Since the mid-nineteenth century, national debt has played a vital role in the predatory practice of the nexus of capital and the settler state in which the state often plays the role of dependent agent of capital. The "enchanter's wand" through which the national debt begets speculative capital has more recently been endowed with an even greater magic. The Fourteenth Amendment recognizes and validates the public debt, and debates about the "debt ceiling" have attempted to make urgent the question of the US government's ability to pay back its loans. Still, the United States is the greatest debtor nation in the world, and thus far, its debt has been rolled over indefinitely.[36] This is the story of how the United States rigged the game of world finance in 1971. It is the story of debt as imperialism, or what economist Michael Hudson calls super imperialism.[37] The United States exercises debt imperialism by virtue of, and not despite, its status as the greatest debtor in the world. How has the United States been able to convert indebtedness, a position of weakness, into a position of relative strength and indeed into the very basis of the world's monetary and financial system?[38] Significant elements in the cruel magic of this alchemy are gold and paper. In 1971, Nixon floated the dollar, de-pegging it from the gold standard. The gold standard had been set up after World War II in Bretton Woods. This new monetary system replaced the old gold standard with a new gold *exchange* standard. Whereas currencies had previously been pegged to a fixed price of gold, they would now be pegged to the dollar, and the dollar itself was pegged to the value of gold. In other words, Bretton Woods created a gold standard system in which the US dollar provided the central link in the global monetary chain. In 1971, Nixon ended this Bretton Woods framework by de-pegging the dollar from gold in order to alleviate pressures on the dollar. There was justifiable concern that the United States did not have enough gold holdings to cover the dollars in circulation at the fixed exchange rate. This was due in significant part to growing trade deficits largely caused by the Vietnam War and other nations engaging in "competitive devaluation" via weakening their currency in order to improve their competitiveness in trade.

It could thus be said that Nixon's de-pegging of the dollar from gold is a kind of default, and while his 1971 announcement was that it would be a temporary suspension of the Bretton Woods framework, he made the suspension permanent in 1973 because Bretton Woods constrained the policy options, particularly domestic ones, available to him.[39] As I elaborate, the Bretton Woods creation of the gold exchange standard that anointed the US dollar as a central link in the global monetary chain, then Nixon's abandonment of the gold exchange standard altogether, ushered in a fatal *double* standard. Nixon's de-pegging of the dollar from gold made it into a nonconvertible or fiat currency. This in turn made it possible for the United States to exercise full monetary sovereignty: the power to issue not only its own currency but also specifically a fiat currency not tethered or pegged to gold or another currency.[40]

Since Nixon's suspension of the dollar's convertibility into gold, the United States has become the world's greatest debtor and has reached a level of indebtedness without world-historical precedent. The United States replaced the gold standard with a transformed US Treasury Bill, a government-issued debt, as an international monetary standard. Essentially, what this has meant since the early 1970s is that foreign banks with a surplus of dollars can no longer exchange them for gold. Rather, the banks must purchase US Treasury bonds, meaning US Treasury debt, thereby extending a continuous loan to the United States. This, counterintuitively, is an important source of US imperial power, an effective debt imperialism and strong exercise of monetary sovereignty through which the United States keeps itself afloat by inflating its capital markets and generating growing levels of budget deficits via foreign capital investment. It is a debt apparently *without* ceiling, precisely because the loan that the world continues to extend to the United States has become an integral, structural feature of the world economy. That is, US hegemony is significantly leveraged via a debt that is rolled over indefinitely and does not have to be repaid.

This loan that the world is continually compelled to extend to the United States is in many ways a form of "tribute" or, more accurately in recent decades, a protection racket.[41] US debt has been significantly incurred via military spending, and it is no coincidence that the United States has a strong military presence in nations whose institutional investors hold US Treasury bonds, like Germany, Japan, and South Korea.[42] The public debt of settler colonialism has been linked with a more specific debt driven by military spending in the post–World War II conjuncture. Debt imperialism is at once the literal cost and effect of military empire; regimes of militarism drive US debt imperialism. The US military budget typically accounts for over 50 percent of all federal discretionary spending, and as I related in the Introduction, this budget represents over 40 percent of the *world's total* military spending each year.[43] As Melinda Cooper so aptly puts it, "The irony here is that the exorbitant military expenditure of the United States has been financed through the very debt imperialism it is designed to enforce!"[44] It is no wonder, then, that US debt imperialism has been described as the "greatest rip-off ever achieved."[45] Thus far, even the entrance of China and China's status as the United States' greatest creditor have not witnessed a radical destabilization of US debt imperialism, even as this has disrupted the United States' long-standing fantasy since the latter half of the nineteenth century about gaining unfettered access to China's fabled market. The question remains, then, of what would radically threaten the US dollar's unique position as the global reserve currency. Moreover, even as these regimes of militarism incur a debt that the United States does not need to repay, as I elaborate throughout this book, they install a figurative economy of what we might call militarized indebtedness onto the colonized. That is, the colonized and occupied are made to feel indebted to the United States for its military intervention, often rescripted as "liberation."

How can a global superpower also be a global superdebtor? As Giovanni Arrighi and others have asked, how, in other words, can the United States have hegemony without hege*money*?[46] How can what Wolfgang Streeck calls a "debt state" be a global hegemon?[47] Given the central role of US global finance in the world economy, a US default on its massive debt would radically destabilize the architecture of racial capitalism. The specter of such a destabilization and

attendant fears of apocalyptic risk are in effect exploited as a form of US imperial domination. As such, one significant feature of US militarist settler imperialism is debt imperialism, or the creation of a temporal exception through
which the United States is able to roll over its debt indefinitely. The United
States does not need to conform to the homogeneous time of repayment even
as it imposes that standard temporality on other populations and nations.
Moreover, those who have been subjected to US military and imperial intervention are structurally positioned within a financial and especially affective
economy of an indebtedness for being "liberated." The affective indebtedness
is perpetual, for it can never be fully repaid. As for financial indebtedness, the
threat or actual use of institutional violence (via, for example, effective unilateral veto power in formally multilateral institutions such as the IMF and the
World Bank) and the threat of military retaliation compel the world to submit
to the rigged rules of the game.[48] This, as I have suggested, is a kind of metapolitical authority, or the authority not only to apply or enforce laws as well as
discipline and punish when necessary but also to define the very contours of
what constitutes law and political authority as such.

What I have called the homogeneous time of repayment is one particular
aspect and imposition of militarist settler imperial time, and this homogeneous
time is coconstituted by the temporal exception of debt imperialism that does
not have to conform to it. Whereas Fordism and Taylorism in the early twentieth century were concerned with homogenizing time as related to workflow
and labor efficiency within the capitalist mode of production, the homogeneous time of repayment is related to but not reducible to this. That is, the
debtor/creditor relation is not reducible to the labor/capital relation. So even
as US militarist settler imperialism imposes a homogeneous time on everyone
else at multiple scales, it reserves for itself the singular and unique privilege of
enjoying a different temporality, a different frame of reference. Counterintuitively, this double movement—the US settler imperial imposition of the homogeneous time of repayment, yet its own refusal to conform to it without the
risk of suffering disciplinary or punitive consequences—instantiates multiple
temporalities. There is a split, in other words, between the settler imperialist's
imposition of time on others and its own *inhabitation* of time. This split is one
instance of the exercise of US metapolitical authority.

US militarist settler imperialism is thus a debt relation linking statecraft
and capital. If militarist settler imperialism is an incomplete project, an ensemble of relations requiring continual recreation and renovation, it mirrors
the capitalist "delirium" of debt imperialism and of the debt form. As Cooper
argues, "In the sense that the debt can never be redeemed once and for all and

must be perpetually renewed, it reduces the inhabitable present to a bare minimum, a point of bifurcation, strung out between a future that is about to be a past that will have been. It thus confronts the present as the ultimate limit, to be deflected at all costs."[49] Cooper goes on to observe that the American state, insofar as its continued self-reproduction coincides with the temporality of perpetual debt, is a nation that in economic terms has become purely promissory or fiduciary. This suggests a double movement in which the United States is able to refound itself perpetually precisely because of the very loss of foundation, and this refounding occurs in the most violent and material ways. In this sense, debt imperialism is at once deterritorializing and reterritorializing, at once speculative and materialist; the endless refounding or revolution (rolling over of debt) is inseparable from the restoration of nationhood.[50]

This dialectic of revolution/restoration, to elaborate on the contextual remarks I provided earlier on the very founding of the US nation, is the very logic of settler colonialism as both a structure and a processual series of ongoing events and practices. Moreover, settler colonialism, the foundational and literally territorial condition of possibility of the United States, cannot be acknowledged as such, as the debt that is owed to Native Americans. This proving ground, this stolen land and water, or fatally irradiated territory in the case of the Marshall Islands, is the promise that does not have to be made at all. Settler colonialism, the promise never made (or unacknowledged debt) that makes possible and is conjoined with debt imperialism, the promise never kept (or the perpetually unpaid debt), attempts to deterritorialize and revolutionize, yet the US nation must also reterritorialize and restore or refound itself through the establishment of a military empire. The attendant temporal logic of this spatial dynamic, as Cooper writes, is a paradoxical time warp where the future and the past morph into one another without ever finding grounding in the present.[51] If the unmade promise resides in an unacknowledged past, and the unkept promise can only be said to be that when the future itself becomes a past that will have been, then the present is the time of holding to final account.

In this way, the US nation has become purely promissory or fiduciary, not only in economic terms but also in cultural and ideological terms. The indefinitely deferred promise of substantive freedom (which the formal and juridical form of liberal civil rights has failed to deliver or guarantee) is what Heidi Hoechst calls "speculative nationalism." Crucially, as Hoechst explains, speculative nationalism's challenge to democracy is not to be found in the gap between the US nation-state's promises and actual practices that fail to live up to its avowed ideals and potential. Rather, the true challenge to democracy is that such national promises themselves exacerbate and create the very problems of inequality and injustice that they claim to resolve. If, as I discussed previously, the problem of dispossession has a recursive or belated temporal dynamic, speculative nationalism's cultural promises have a temporality of indefinite deferral and capitalist speculative futures in which a "not yet" freedom predatorily converts "racialized risks into speculative advantages."[52] Put differently, the promises of an in(de)finitely deferred "not yet" freedom are the debts that the United States, a white settler imperialist state, owes to those it subjected to genocidal conquest, land theft, racial chattel slavery, and gendered racial labor exploitation. Not only are these debts rolled over indefinitely, but that very process of continual rolling over is itself a form of speculative racial capitalism that exploits anew—and produces as raw material for further extraction of value—the very colonized and racialized subjects to whom the freedom has been promised.

The deflection of the present makes possible the continual reproduction and renovation of militarist settler imperialism through a variety of literal and figurative debt relations. It is a debt regime that functions in multiple ways. On the one hand, it is the debt *to* Indigenous communities that is unacknowledged.[53] On the other hand, it provides the collateral for various debtor/creditor schemes. It is also, as I have elaborated, debt imperialism, or the debt that does not have to be repaid. Yet still, it continues to produce debt *for* various populations who are vulnerable to crushing indebtedness, or what Harvey calls "debt incumbency."[54] These seemingly antonymous forms of debt, or the deft ability of debt to operate as a sleight of hand, make crushingly clear how debt is not a strict economic relation.

Debt as the Foreclosure *and* Effect of Freedom

The colonial and capitalist nexus of race, gender, and sexuality distributes debt and vulnerability to debt unevenly. This uneven distribution, or debt as governmentality, is what I call the necropolitics of the promise. The etymology of promise, from the Old French *promesse*, is a pledge, vow, guarantee, or assurance. From Latin, *promissum* is the noun use of the neuter past participle of *promittere*, which is to send forth, let go, foretell, or assure beforehand. Keeping in mind this temporal dimension of what a promise means and what it means to promise, I contend that the United States' abandonment of the gold standard has ushered in a fatal *double* standard. Even as the United States rolls over its debts indefinitely, it imposes structural adjustment policies, austerity measures, and foreclosures on other debtor countries and populations. Variously labeled Third World debtors, subprime borrowers, and "Heavily Indebted Poor

Countries" or the HIPCs of sub-Saharan Africa, these debtors are compelled to keep their promises, for failure to do so results in punishment and discipline. Some promises demand repayment more than others, and some must conform to the homogeneous time of repayment more than others.

As I have been arguing, the debtor/creditor relationship is governed not simply through the borrowing and lending of money but is animated and enforced by an already existing asymmetry in power relations. As such, debt indexes not only the state and sum of money owed but a broader social relation structured by violent disciplinary protocols compelling the indebted to conduct themselves in a manner that will maximize the likelihood of repayment. In this sense, to be indebted is not simply to owe money. It is to inhabit a subjectivity that robs one of the possibility of having multiple futures, multiple ways of conducting oneself and being in the world. This, then, is the relationship between debt and time; debt neutralizes time so that it conforms to the homogeneous time of repayment.[55] Writing on the ascendance of neoliberalism and the debt economy since the 1970s, and following Friedrich Nietzsche as well as Gilles Deleuze and Félix Guattari on Christian theology's notion of indebtedness and guilt derived from original sin, Maurizio Lazzarato observes that unlike labor, which deploys our physical and intellectual abilities, the credit relation mobilizes the debtor's morality, mode of existence, and ethos. What the debt economy thus exploits and appropriates is not simply chronological labor time but also crucially nonchronological time, meaning time as action, choice, decision, or a wager on the events and forces that make action and choice possible in the first place.[56] Indeed, as Curtis Marez writes, debt colonizes the future, "tying present activities to plans for servicing its imperatives . . ."[57] Precisely because debt forecloses multiple possible futures in this way, it is not, as I observed earlier, reducible to regimes of labor. This is the case whether one is economically or affectively indebted, for both forms of debt demand continual repayment.

Indeed, whole nations and populations of the world have been saddled with permanent debt and cannot liberate themselves from the debt bind.[58] They are subjected to what Gayatri Chakravorty Spivak calls "credit-baiting," and what Miranda Joseph more recently has called a "pedagogy of 'entrepreneurial' subjectivity."[59] On a broader level, in a critique of development discourse and the presumption that it is only driven by an economic rationality, Sylvia Wynter writes of "the phenomenon of the debt burden, whose *oracular mechanism* transfers wealth steadily from the South to the North, from the inner cities to the suburbs, and intensifies a systematic misallocation of resources."[60] Wynter uses the term *oracular* and italicizes it to emphasize the systemic rather than purely economic nature of this transfer of wealth. The debt burden, in other words, is not simply economic. More fundamentally, the indebted, that is to say the "underdeveloped," are also marked with a metaphysical lack through the epistemological or what Wynter calls the "culture-systemic" logic of the North/West. So the debtor/creditor relation is determined not by economics but rather *pre*determined by the broader culture-systemic valence that constitutes "the a priori premises of the discourse of economics itself." As such, the solution to this problem in which economic underdevelopment is presumed to be merely an epiphenomenon of a deeper metaphysical lack cannot be an economic one that follows the path to greater "development." Rather, Wynter proposes that the only viable strategy is an epistemological revolution.[61]

This epistemological revolution would lay bare how the culture-systemic order of the Global North effects a sleight of hand. Indeed, we witness a role reversal in which the actual debtors have transmogrified into creditors, and vice versa. As Frantz Fanon writes, "Europe is the literal creation of the Third World."[62] That is, insofar as what was violently extracted from the Global South (via colonialism, racial chattel slavery, and labor exploitation) made possible the riches that developed the Global North, we must ask: Who owes what to whom? The Global North owes a huge debt to the world that created it. Yet the afterlife of colonial plunder persists through the neocolonial policies, for example, of institutions like the IMF and World Bank, whose officials are "the conquistadors of today."[63] For persons and places marked by a debt that "cannot be settled even with death," what is a debt?[64] As I see it, debt in this instance is itself both a relation and instrument of violence converted by the strange math of militarist settler imperialism and racial capitalism into a promissory note that binds for some but not for others. To promise, and to be promised, can mean radically different things depending on where the debtor, whether a nation or an individual, is located within asymmetries of power that are at once shifting and enduring.

This asymmetrical relation is now triangulated by China. Unlike the United States, however, China is manipulating debt as a newly emergent creditor. It is deploying what has been called "debtbook diplomacy," or more pointedly "debt-trap diplomacy," a strategic leveraging of debts made to economically vulnerable nations across Asia and the Pacific for political influence and economic advantages.[65] Yet as I related in the Introduction, critiques of China's imperial interests that cohere as "China threat discourse" can be deployed as an alibi to retrench the West's own imperial and neocolonial interests. The notion that the Chinese threat must be contained, and that vulnerable nations must be protected from that threat, is the covering rationale for what could be seen as a new interimperial competitive "Scramble for Africa" that is at once literal and figurative insofar as the terrain certainly includes but is not limited to Africa.

The creation of crushing indebtedness through the necropolitics of the promise, or debt as the *foreclosure* of freedom, futurity, and at times life itself, is captured pithily in this lyric by Jamaican artist Mutabaruka: "Life an' debt freedom not yet." Featured on the soundtrack of a 2001 Canadian documentary of the same title, *Life and Debt* (which compellingly reveals Jamaica's debt-bind and the devastating effects of the IMF, the World Bank, and "free trade" on the nation), Mutabaruka's song amplifies freedom's antinomies by questioning freedom's content and temporality. To live a life excruciatingly tethered to debt is to live a conjunctional "life an' debt."[66] In Mutabaruka's formulation, life and debt are one and the same; debt owns your life, and in doing so, it owns your freedom. By taking residence as the content of formal freedom, debt works in this instance to vacate or evict the substantive meaning of freedom and to forestall the event and temporality of freedom as a "not yet." In this sense, we can speak of debt as a "shifting grammar of life" that perpetually recedes before our horizon into a future tense, a vanishing point through which a "not yet" freedom is perhaps glimpsed but always foreclosed.[67] Haunting this vanishing point is the term that Mutabaruka self-consciously substitutes debt for: *death*. A life of debt forecloses an intimacy with freedom, which is to say that it forces an intimacy with forms of social and physical death. Debt, in other words, can be a death sentence, and while some might be able to have their sentences commuted and still live a social death, others experience a literal physical death flashing blindingly forward, a fatal present tense. If, to cite Graeber again, a debt is "just the perversion of a promise," a promise "corrupted by both math and violence," then who can have their debt/death sentences commuted, who can have their debts forgiven altogether, and who must fully repay their debts with interest?[68] Within this economy, who must keep their promises? Mutabaruka, and his Jamaican nation, must do so; they must pay their promissory notes. The reason lies in the "math and violence" to which they have been subjected, a history of colonialism and racial chattel slavery succeeded by more recent forms of neocolonial domination and an international uneven division and proliferation not only of gendered racial labor but also of debt. This is to speak about the uneven distribution of risk and vulnerability to risk. In the ultimate instance, it is to speak about the uneven distribution of life itself and death itself.

Debt as the foreclosure of freedom enjoins us to ask how debt as both a literal and figurative economy also emerges as the *effect* of freedom, emancipation, or liberation. The continued corruption of the promise by math and violence perpetually keeps Mutabaruka's longing for freedom, the promise of freedom, in the future tense. His future tense grammar, as at once a specific temporality of freedom as well as a broader system of signification, calls to mind other similar grammars, such as that of Hortense Spillers. Tracing the total objectification of the captive body as flesh within the US context of chattel slavery, Spillers calls and theorizes the symbolic order instantiated by the African slave trade an "American grammar." One of the distinctive features of this grammar is that it "remains grounded in the originating metaphors of captivity and mutilation so that it is as if neither time nor history, nor historiography and its topics, show movement, as the human subject is 'murdered' over and over again . . ."[69] This, as Saidiya Hartman writes, is the afterlife of slavery, an afterlife not only symbolic but crushingly material.[70] That is, formal emancipation for the enslaved in the United States did not represent a radical rupture but rather a "nonevent." The whip of chattel slavery was replaced with the "burdened individuality of freedom," constituted by the tethers of liberalism: a guilty conscience; notions of responsibility modeled on contractual obligation; calculated reciprocity; and most importantly, indebtedness, since "debt played a central role in the creation of the servile, blameworthy, and guilty individual and in the reproduction and transformation of involuntary servitude."[71] That is, emancipation for the enslaved in the United States instituted indebtedness via a calculus of blame and responsibility through which the newly freed were obliged to repay their emancipators' "investment of faith" or "gift of freedom" and demonstrate their worthiness. This figurative economy of indebtedness compelling submission and servitude was conjoined to a literal one in which Black laborers were rendered vulnerable to peonage and debt servitude. In this way, the transition from slavery to freedom, argues Hartman, constructed "an already accrued debt, abstinent present, and a mortgaged future. In short, to be free was to be a debtor—that is, obliged and duty-bound to others."[72]

The longue durée of the "nonevent" of emancipation from a range of distinct yet related forms of unfreedom throughout the globe—whether racial chattel slavery, colonial subjugation, racial genocide, debt peonage, contract labor, apartheid, or incarceration—has produced and continues to produce increased levels of privation and debt. Though this immiseration and dispossession are certainly not distributed evenly or uniformly, whole portions of the globe experience greater vulnerability to being rendered surplus populations of essentially disposable lives. This is what we might call a precarious grammar of life. It is debt as at once a form of extraction, as the effect of freedom or liberation, and crucially as a sleight of hand. Haiti is a particularly egregious example of this. When Haiti liberated itself from French colonial domination and plantation slavery through a revolutionary war of independence, it was forced to pay an "independence debt" to France for over one hundred years and was subject to a fifty-eight-year embargo. Effectively, Haiti was crushingly punished for its audacity and for becoming a beacon of Black freedom; the debt regime that it was subjected to became a template for "financial colonialism."[73] France imposed an indemnity of 150 million francs in 1825, which the international community compelled Haiti to repay to slaveholding plantation owners. In other words, France imposed the indemnity as reparation to slaveholders for the loss of income incurred by the emancipation of the enslaved in the Haitian Revolution. In exchange, the newly independent nation of Haiti would receive national recognition. Although the total amount of the debt was eventually lowered, payments that are estimated to have ultimately amounted to $22 to $40 billion were extracted for decades via heavy taxation of the peasant economy. The first payment in 1825 was of a high interest loan from French banks, while later payments involved loans from American banks. So rather than paying Haiti reparations *for slavery*, the debtor/creditor relation was reversed via France's imposition of reparations *to slaveholders*. This is what I have been calling debt as a sleight of hand.

In 1893, the indemnity was finally paid off; meanwhile, in 1862, Texas industrialists formed the American West India Company "to promote mining, land speculation, and the annexation of both Haiti and the Dominican Republic."[74] Moreover, by the 1890s the Haitian treasury was placed under the direct supervision of the French Société Générale and was later "literally moved to vaults on Wall Street via the National City Bank (today's Citibank)." The US invasion and military occupation of Haiti in 1915, which lasted until 1934, were the direct result of the attempt to ensure the collection of $500,000 from Haiti's national bank. It was not until 1947 that Haitian debts to American banks would be paid off. Yet this, over a century after the first 1825 payment, did not end the debt trap for Haiti. More recently, the neoliberal practices and loan mechanisms of the World Bank and the IMF have prolonged and exacerbated the entrapment of Haiti in what is an endlessly vicious cycle of borrowing and debt repayment.[75] Though capitalist extraction generally refers to the extraction of natural resources and labor, this debt regime also functions as an economy and logic of extraction.

Yet what of debt when whole nations are also "liberated" not through self-liberation or revolutionary war but via a bestowal by an imperial power? In this instance, gratitude is enfigured as indebtedness through the scripting of military intervention and imperial violence as a bestowal or gift of national liberation. If the literal financial economy of debt can be rewritten as a form of US imperial power, debt can also function as a figurative economy or narrative structure animating that power. The United States is able to leverage, convert, and narrate indebtedness into imperial might. Yet the structure of feeling imposed on those who are "liberated" from imperial or colonial domination is one of gratitude or indebtedness, even as such "liberation" would not have been necessary in the first place had the United States not intervened. Writing in the context of US imperialism in Asia, Lisa Yoneyama argues that the "imperialist myth of liberation and rehabilitation" confers belatedness and indebtedness.[76] The newly liberated nation, a pre- or protodemocracy, experiences a belatedness vis-à-vis political modernity. Yet it must demonstrate again and again an indebtedness to its imperial liberator for making the presumed eventual arrival at political modernity possible in the first place. But in the end, this moment of arrival never quite arrives, so the debt cannot ever be fully repaid.[77] This is a perverse temporal economy: belatedness transmogrifies into the future tense grammar of "freedom not yet."

In this way, the figurative debt that cannot ever be fully repaid is preconditioned by failure or impossibility. Yet this built-in failure, which drives repeated demonstrations of gratitude on the part of the indebted for their putative liberation, is also the mark of US militarist settler imperial failure. The perpetual performance of gratitude is demanded precisely because the ends of militarist settler imperialism are never fully guaranteed. The transpacific cultural forms and imaginaries that I analyze in the chapters that follow critically magnify the conjoined imposition of the settler imperial homogeneous time of repayment and of an indebted subjectivity for a putative liberation, while also demonstrating through an aesthetics of settler imperial failure how the ends of this conjoined imposition are never fully guaranteed. Insofar as debt imperialism as the temporal exception is imposed on (neo)colonized spatial exceptions, literal geographic colonization is coupled with the figurative colonization of both chronological and nonchronological time. The transpacific imaginaries in my study ask what it would mean to refuse this foreclosure of multiple possible futurities.

2. THE MILITARY BASE AND CAMPTOWN: *Seizing Land "by Bulldozer and Bayonet" and the Transpacific Masculinist Compact*

In "Backbone" (2005), Okinawan poet Tōma Hiroko writes:

> Across the sea from my island I cry out
> Age of Yamato, land battle, Age of America, wire fence, fighter jets
> The man closes his ears and grins
> Blue skies, white beaches, burnt orange roof tiles, tropical
> lemon-limes, red hibiscus . . .
>
> The streets bright with neon are the man's playground
> My playground is a would-be place where the wire fence is
> swept away
> I just want to stand up tall and stride through my backyard[1]

Traversing over one thousand years of history in invoking the "Age of Yamato" and the "Age of America," the poem highlights how the traditional land battles of the former have long made way for the omnipresent militarist geographies and weapons of the latter. The natural landscape of Okinawa, replete with "white beaches" and "red hibiscus," is ironically juxtaposed with its militarized landscape, overrun with "wire fence[s]," "fighter jets," and "neon lights." Okinawa, in other words, has become the "playground" of the US military, crowding out the narrator's own playground and backyard. The narrator's playground no longer exists because of the ubiquity of US military presence, as metonymically figured by the wire fence. For as long as the wire fence remains, this playground is only a "would-be place." Okinawa, an island chain doubly colonized by Japan and the United States, shoulders the disproportionate burden of US military bases in Japan. It is an island sacrifice zone. Yet in expressing the possibility of the wire fence being "swept away," and the desire to "stand up tall and stride through my backyard," Tōma's poem leaves open the possibility of an Okinawa imagined otherwise, that "would-be" otherwise. Having this kind of "backbone," as reflected in the poem's title, displays an aesthetics of settler imperial failure.

In *Reiterations of Dissent* (2011/2016), an eight-screen installation of different looped video fragments playing simultaneously, Korean diasporic artist Jane Jin Kaisen evokes the violent and spectral history of South Korea's Jeju Island.[2] Given the hegemony of national frames of reference and units of analysis, Okinawa and Jeju are viewed as Japanese and Korean, respectively. They are, however, linked as islands within the Kuroshio Current, the world's second-largest ocean current after the Gulf Stream in the Atlantic. Islands along the current share a distinctive and interconnected oceanic culture and thus in some ways have more in common with one another than with the respective nations of which they are a part.[3] In addition to this interconnectedness via the Kuroshio Current, Jeju is distinct from yet linked to Okinawa insofar as it is also an island subjected to militarist geographies and spatial development policies whose relationship to the mainland is one of subjugation and ongoing contestation. It, too, is an island sacrifice zone. Through what Crystal Mun-hye Baik theorizes as "durational memory" in her illuminating analysis of Kaisen's work, *Reiterations of Dissent* grapples with the buried history of US military atrocities in Jeju and the island's more recent remilitarization. Durational memory constitutes multiple and nonlinear temporalities that are intentionally at odds with official South Korean national history and the chrononormativity of Cold War historiography.[4] *Reiterations of Dissent* displays durational memory through a defamiliarizing array of video images (including US military films), contemporary footage from multinational media outlets, and original documentation shot by Kaisen in Jeju that are constellated across eight looped video fragments or film shorts. In one of these shorts, "History of Endless Rebellion," black-and-white archival footage of armed military vehicles in Jeju's narrow streets, the burning of houses, and the panicked fleeing of villagers is bookended with contemporary footage of a Daewoo bulldozer tearing into a shoreline and of international and local activists clashing with South Korean police as they protest the construction project. These images are paired with this voice-over: "Standing at a distance, the United States subjugated without getting blood on their hands at all, that was 4.3. The naval base is a continuation of this."

What was "4.3," what is the naval base whose construction is being protested, how are these things connected, and why is the United States culpable? The number "4.3" names and refers to the date of the "red hunt" or mass killings and torture of Jeju residents that took place between 1948 and 1954 following an uprising by leftists on April 3, 1948. This anti-Communist massacre began during the post–World War II US military occupation, when the southern part of the Korean Peninsula was under the rule of the US Army Military Government in Korea. The atrocities continued with the South Korean Interim Government, effectively a US puppet. With estimates varying, this devastating counterinsurgency resulted in thirty thousand to sixty thousand deaths, or 20–30 percent of Jeju's civilian population.[5] The island thus came to be known as "Red Island" and "Island of Rebellion" before its more recent designation in 2005 by the then president Roh Moo-hyun as an "Island of Peace" in remembrance of 4.3. Yet this attempt at reckoning with the atrocity of 4.3, which had actively been suppressed by the US and South Korean governments until they were pressured to launch a formal investigation in the late 1990s, was performative and short-lived. For Roh's government also advocated the construction of a naval base on Jeju. *Reiterations of Dissent* displays fragments from ongoing protests against the construction of the base as one of the ways in which Jeju's strong history of dissent against and difference from mainland South Korea reverberate into the contemporary context. In doing so, and in channeling a "History of Endless Rebellion," Kaisen's critical "durational memory" work is also an aesthetics of settler imperial failure.

Jeju's island spatiality and liminal political status tether the island to the external shocks produced by the central government's priorities and policies of capitalist development and militarized neocolonial relationship with the United States. The island is an autonomous subnational island jurisdiction (SNIJ) and self-governing province of South Korea.[6] Dubbed as the nation's "Hawai'i" and located at the southernmost maritime border of South Korea (about ninety kilometers south of the peninsula), Jeju has been developed as a tourist destination by South Korea's central government. More recently, it has been remilitarized from its days as a Japanese military base during World War

II, then the site of a brutal anti-Communist purge dictated by the US military, and on through the contested construction of a naval base at the fishing village of Gangjeong. In response to ongoing local and international opposition to the construction of the base, the South Korean government proposed that the base would also have civilian or commercial uses as a port for cruise ships and insisted that its military uses would be strictly South Korean.[7] In other words, the "Jeju Civilian-Military Complex Port" would *not* be a de facto US military base. Yet although the base is officially under the aegis of the South Korean government, this is merely a technicality. For the base is a site designated as a US cooperative security location. Under the current forms of the Mutual Defense Treaty and Status of Forces Agreement between the United States and South Korea, "the U.S. state is able to mobilize South Korean military facilities at its own discretion."[8] Accordingly and unsurprisingly, since the completion of the base in February 2016, US naval vessels, including a nuclear-powered attack submarine, have docked there.

Such dockings have witnessed renewed protest and confirmation of the position articulated all along by critics and activists that the true impetus for the base's construction was the US desire to contain China. In October 2018, the Association of Gangjeong Villagers Against the Jeju Naval Base protested the arrival of an armada of warships from thirteen countries, particularly the USS *Ronald Reagan* aircraft carrier. Linking the atrocities of 4.3 to the naval base, activists declared, "The US military killed Jeju residents back then, this is why we don't want a naval base. . . . Everyone knows this naval base is made for the US, even though the government insists it isn't. . . . We want to hear an apology from the US for the murder of innocents."[9] By laying bare these dynamics, and by demanding an apology from the United States, these Jeju activists upend the sleight of hand of the dominant debtor/creditor relation imposed on South Korea by the United States. They refuse to be interpellated by the injunction to feel gratitude for being "liberated" from Japanese colonialism and Sino-Soviet Communist domination. Instead, the activists radically reveal that the United States is actually the debtor, and they demand repayment in the form of an apology. Yet even as ongoing asymmetries of power determine who can script the sleight-of-hand narrative, and who can evade repayment of the debt even when the sleight of hand is revealed for what it is, the revelation itself and attendant demand for repayment are significant. For these activist refusals enact a performative aesthetics of settler imperial failure through the force and power of the very demand for repayment.

I begin this chapter with a discussion of "Backbone" and *Reiterations of Dissent* because these transpacific cultural works showcase the three related concerns of this chapter. The first concern is the linked yet differential targeting of particular sites in Asia and the Pacific as sacrifice zones or homes to US military bases and camptowns. Islands such as Okinawa and Jeju, though respectively part of East Asian nations that enjoy a relatively privileged subimperial status within Asia vis-à-vis their less powerful neighbors, are especially targeted not only because of their geostrategic locations but also because they are doubly subjugated. Focusing on the Philippines, Okinawa, and South Korea, sites of heavy US military presence, as pivotal locations of the settler garrison, in this chapter I trace the ways in which transpacific cultural productions connect the land grabs that constitute the US settler state and military empire. That is, the transpacific cultural works in my analysis generate a theory of the different yet linked varieties of land seizure through which what became the fifty states constituting the United States of America were successively incorporated into the white settler nation *and* through which proliferating Asian and Pacific sites were transformed into the bases and outposts constituting the US military imperium. I theorize how this latter variety of land seizure, for explicit and what has turned out to be perduring military uses, produces America's settler garrison. The cultural works I analyze reveal that while military bases at once manifest and enable the projection of US militarist settler imperial power, they themselves also constitute settler projects or settlements.

The second related concern of this chapter is the complex ethics and politics of how to represent the necropolitical contours of the spatial exception that is the military base and its camptown. *Reiterations of Dissent* foregrounds through its formal techniques the complexity of grappling with the buried and silenced history of a murderous US campaign of counterinsurgency or "red purge" that began during the formal US military occupation of what became South Korea. What is at stake is not a simple "recovery" of an invisibilized history into visibility but an interrogation of the ongoing dynamics of US militarist settler imperialism whose sleight of hand is what Baik incisively calls a "beautifying practice," one that alchemically transfigures violence into beneficent nonviolence and, I contend, death into the necessary precondition for life.[10] Alongside this, the transpacific cultural productions I analyze in this chapter also reveal a conjoined representational and epistemological conundrum: the ethics and politics of how to grapple with that which is not invisible but rather problematically hypervisible, objectified, and spectacularized. As the end of formal US military occupation transmogrified into a de facto one via the proliferation of US military bases on South Korean soil, an attendant camptown system of militarized sex work promoted and regulated through what I call a transpacific masculinist compact between the United

States and South Korean governments proliferated as well. This was also the case in the Philippines until the base closures in 1992 and remains the case in Okinawa. The network of militarized sex work or "camptown prostitution" in turn generates the question of how we can reckon with camptown sexual violence without spectacularizing it. And how can we work against what Laura Hyun Yi Kang calls the "enforced visibility" of camptown sex workers?[11] In *Traffic in Asian Women,* Kang queries more broadly what it would mean to think through "Asian women" as "bodies of knowledge and ways of knowing rather than resort to benevolent, nominal inclusion or empathetic identification with *those* bodies in pain." She poses "Asian women as method?" as an open-ended question toward deimperializing US interdisciplinary knowledge formations.[12]

The transpacific masculinist compact that at once generates and obscures camptown sexual violence has endured thus far for several decades. The third related concern of this chapter is that this compact, a "military-sexual complex," creates ever-renewed cycles of what is effectively a form of debt bondage for camptown sex workers, many of whom are now trafficked from the Philippines and Southeast Asia, preceded by trafficking from Russia and the former Soviet republics.[13] These trafficked women are a kind of migrant "guest worker," yet the racialized women who labor as sex workers on America's settler garrison are *all* a kind of guest worker, even when they are laboring in their very hometowns or nations. For the camptown, made in the image of "America Town," is not *their* town but rather a nonsovereign space made manifest as a militarized factory floor of compelled economic dependence, biopolitical surveillance, and gendered racial and sexual violence. It is within this context of US metapolitical authority that the debt bondage regime is forged. Yet through an aesthetics of settler imperial failure, the transpacific cultural forms I analyze in this chapter encourage us to ask: What debt do we owe camptown sex workers, those who are still living and those murdered by US servicemembers? How are we indebted to them?

In what follows, I provide a brief overview of US bases and basing networks before turning to the Philippines with an analysis of Rachel Rivera's documentary, *Sin City Diary* (1992). Next, I analyze Okinawan literature: Kishaba Jun's short story "Dark Flowers" (1955), Higashi Mineo's novella *Child of Okinawa* (1971), and Medoruma Shun's short story "Hope" (1999).[14] I then turn to South Korean and Asian diasporic literature and film: Gina Kim's virtual reality (VR) film *Bloodless* (2017), Ahn Junghyo's *Silver Stallion: A Novel of Korea* (1990), and the documentaries *The Women Outside: Korean Women and the U.S. Military* (1995) and *Camp Arirang* (1995).[15] This constellation of transpacific cultural texts collectively coheres as a critical archive that contains a significant theory of America's settler garrison and gestures to a future beyond it through an aesthetics of settler imperial failure.

What Is a Base?

The logic of militarism, as I have observed, is not reducible to strictly military functions; indeed, its ultimate logic and goal are the preservation of military institutions, hierarchies, and values whether or not they are needed for war. As such, bases are no longer temporary wartime structures but have become permanent outposts, or settlements of the settler garrison, whose raison d'être and justification are no longer reducible to questions of military prepared- ness or necessity. Nor are they contingent on the active existence or waging of actual war(s); instead, the inverted presumption is that "if we build them, wars will come."[16] Nor, moreover, are bases contingent on strong congressio- nal oversight. Rather, they have taken on a life of their own. In other words, the permanence of the base itself is a kind of temporal exception; it bespeaks what is effectively a US military occupation. The guest/host metaphor used to describe the United States and the sites on which its bases are located, respec- tively, obscures and inverts occupation and its attendant power dynamics. The "host" in this instance, far from possessing the power of resources and benefi- cence connoted by the word, is subjected to a "structural humiliation" vis-à-vis its "guest," the US military.[17]

We witness on these bases not only military hardware but architectures, infrastructures, personnel, and families of personnel effecting a wholesale spa- tial transformation of seized Indigenous or local land into virtual "America Towns" or replicas of American suburbs projected overseas. Indeed, on Okinawa, this sprawling complex contains not only headquarter buildings, ammunition depots, hospitals, family housing units, commissaries, and schools but also the facilities and amenities of leisure, entertainment, and recreation that we asso- ciate with a comfortable middle-class suburban American life. These include tennis courts, golf courses, swimming pools, baseball and football fields, and bowling alleys. On Okinawa, what soon became "permbase" grew exponen- tially into the most enormous complex of American military facilities out- side the United States, only to be perhaps outdone by the recent expansion of the Camp Humphreys garrison in South Korea that I described in the In- troduction.[18] Chalmers Johnson observes that such base amenities include the military equivalents of Disneyland and Club Med, already significant yet ever expanding.[19] In addition to such America Towns and amenities, US military personnel have also in recent years had access to even more exclusive entertainment and getaway spots, such as a ski and vacation center in the Bavarian Alps, a resort hotel in downtown Tokyo, and over two hundred golf courses worldwide, as well as jets to fly them there, including luxury jets in the case of admirals and generals.[20] Crucially, these bases and amenities not only involve the seizure of land but also a US military maritime regime whose control of the oceanic, as I observed in the Introduction, extends to 52 percent of the earth's surface.

These developments generate a perhaps counterintuitive but productive question: What exactly is a base? Indeed, David Vine begins *Base Nation: How U.S. Military Bases Abroad Harm America and the World* by posing this very question. While it might initially seem obvious what a base is, definitions and terminology vary widely, with each branch of the military deploying its own preferred terms, such as *post, station, camp,* and *fort.* The Pentagon's definition of its generic term, *base site,* is that it is a "physical (geographic) location"— meaning land, a facility or facilities, or land and facilities—"owned by, leased to, or otherwise possessed" by a component of the US Department of Defense (DoD). For his part, Vine explains that in order to avoid linguistic debates and to adhere to the simplest and most widely recognized term, he generally uses "'base' to mean any place, facility, or installation used regularly for military purposes of any kind."[21] I would like to draw our attention to a few key facets of the Pentagon definition of a base. First, there is the explicit inclusion of "land" and not just facilities, which is pertinent to this chapter's analysis of America's settler garrison in Asia and the Pacific. Second, such land and/or facilities are "owned by, leased to, or otherwise possessed by" the DoD. As I demonstrate in this chapter, an interrogation of how the DoD came to own, lease, or otherwise possess such land in Asia and the Pacific makes visible how military bases are constructed via land seizures and constitute a particular kind of settlement. Moreover, the term *lease* is misleading in many situations, particularly in places such as Okinawa, where landowners effectively had no choice but to rent their land to the US military at rates they had no power to negotiate. Third, the Pentagon definition is not explicit about the function of a base site; instead, we are to infer its military function because it belongs to and is occupied by some component of the DoD. Vine explicitly names the function as "military purposes of any kind." Yet as capacious as this is, it is even more capacious when we consider, as I elaborated in the Introduction, that US militarism is not reducible to the functions of the military. Rather, militarism exceeds the parameters of war temporally, spatially, and functionally, to the extent that the very existence of America's settler garrison has become the sine qua non of US militarist settler imperial power rather than the fighting of specific wars for national defense. Indeed, as early as 1970, the Senate Foreign Relations Committee conceded that, "Once an American overseas base is established it takes on a life of its own. Original missions may become outdated but new missions are developed, not only with the intention of keeping the facility going, but often to actually enlarge it."[22]

Guantanamo Bay in Cuba (seized by the United States during the Spanish-American War in 1898 and leased to the United States in 1903) is generally identified by scholars as the first US military base "abroad." Vine observes that, strangely, scholars tend to overlook the bases created immediately following the Revolutionary War. This is to speak about the hundreds of frontier posts that were instrumental in the westward expansion of the United States, posts that were built on land that was "very much abroad at the time." The first among these was Fort Harmar in the Northwest Territory, built in 1785, followed by Forts Deposit, Defiance, Hamilton, Wayne, Washington, and Knox in present-day Ohio and Indiana. Though these forts were not semipermanent settlements (of the kind we have witnessed in Asia and the Pacific in the post–World War II conjuncture), they made possible the westward migration of Euro-American settlers via the displacement of Native Americans and the seizure of their lands. By 1830, within the context of President Jackson's "Indian removal policy" of forcing Native Americans to give up their lands east of the Mississippi River, Fort Leavenworth in Kansas was understood to mark the "permanent Indian frontier" and thus the "very western edge of civilization." Yet it was not to be, as this "very western edge" edged ever farther westward. By the middle of the nineteenth century, Native Americans who had been forcibly relocated west of the Mississippi by Jackson's removal policy and those already there were met with sixty major forts as well as 138 army posts in the western territories.[23] This describes, in other words, the process of "continental imperialism" that I discussed in the Introduction.[24]

In this way, the US army played a pivotal role in making possible the US settler colonial project across the continent. The "very western edge of civilization" thus encountered the Pacific Ocean. Yet rather than presenting an impasse, this vast oceanic space was opened up for traversal via naval and later air power, with the fabled China market on the mind. Vine notes that the Obama administration's "pivot" to Asia and the Pacific has an original, pre–Civil War antecedent. As early as 1842, President John Tyler possessed a desire to establish Pacific naval bases. Within two years, the United States had opened up five Chinese ports to US trade and military forces through a system of "unequal treaties" imposed on China by the United States as well as European powers. Crucially, as base experts explain, while these treaties did not formally create bases, "they guaranteed forward access to US naval vessels, and enabled the Navy to purchase and establish warehouse facilities in any" of the ports.[25] As such, the treaties effectively marked the beginning of what would become a proliferating, metastasizing presence of the US military in Asia and the Pacific. This, in addition to the "opening" of Japan and Okinawa (with Commodore Perry establishing the first US military base in Okinawa); the annexation of Jarvis, Baker, Howland, and Midway Islands; the purchase of Alaska from Russia; and the annexations or seizures of Hawai'i, American Sāmoa, Guam, Wake Island, and the Philippines all by the end of the nineteenth century, established the United States as a global military power with a particular interest in Asia and the Pacific.[26] Although this nineteenth-century militarized globality of the United States pales in comparison to what would emerge out of and after World War II, it demonstrates the longue durée of US militarism in general and a prehistory of the post–World War II contours of America's settler garrison in Asia and the Pacific.

World War II witnessed a significant expansion of the basing network, with the goal of "island hopping" (to use a term coined by the US military) across the Pacific via Guam, Saipan, Tinian, and Okinawa in order to bomb Japan. With Japan's defeat, the United States occupied Japan and Korea, establishing bases in both nations while also acquiring former Japanese bases throughout the region. Thus, by 1945, almost half (more than 44 percent) of the total number of US overseas military bases was in the Pacific. Indeed, at the Potsdam Conference in 1945, President Harry Truman gave his full endorsement of the idea of a forward-deployed base network, stating, "Though the United States wants no profit or selfish advantage out of this war, we are going to maintain the military bases necessary for the complete protection of our interests and of world peace. Bases, which our military experts deem to be essential for our protection, we will acquire."[27]

Although US basing presence did recede significantly immediately after World War II, the Korean War (1950–53), within the context of a rapidly congealing Cold War, provided the impetus for a significant expansion of the basing network. Indeed, Kent E. Calder observes that, "Of all the fateful critical junctures of the past century, the 1943–45 and 1950–53 periods probably shaped global basing profiles most profoundly, with consequences that persist to this day."[28] And the signing of bilateral security treaties with Japan, the Philippines, Australia, New Zealand, South Korea, and Taiwan in the 1950s, though security oriented, served to buttress a broader framework of trans-Pacific political-economic integration. In this framework, the bases were a "linchpin."[29] Yet further, while during the Cold War the bases fulfilled the dual functions of serving as operational staging areas and as tools of strategic deterrence, since the 1970s this military concern has been increasingly coupled with strengthening the security of resource flows such as oil, especially from the Middle East. In effect, this network of bases is designed to be a *permanent* infrastructure, enabling the post-Fordist shifting of military power from some parts of the world to others with "just in time" efficiency and as dictated by crises that are perceived to pose a threat to US hegemony.[30] More recently, in the post-9/11 period, bases have become important also for "antiterrorist" campaigns and operations. In this so-called war on terror, the military significance of sea and air control has decreased in favor of a capacity for rapid intervention requiring "lighter" yet a greater number of bases distributed across remote regions of the world.[31] Indeed, the US "empire of bases" is so vast that the US military itself does not know the exact total because of poor reporting practices and shifting definitions of what constitutes a base. Grappling with this as well as the Pentagon's secrecy and lack of full transparency, Vine estimates that there are, as I related in the Introduction, approximately eight hundred US bases and "lily pads" (small bases) abroad. Of these, almost three hundred (close to 40 percent) are disproportionately located in Asia and the Pacific.[32]

Crucially, the reigning trope figuring such long-standing US imperial interests and desires in Asia and the Pacific has been the gendered metaphor of sexual conquest or consummation. As far back as 1868, for example, US Navy Commodore Robert W. Shufeldt described the Pacific as "the ocean bride of America" and used the metaphor of heterosexual marriage and sexual consummation: "It is on this ocean that the East & the West have thus come together, reaching the point where search for Empire ceases & human power attains its climax." In 1882, after orchestrating the treaty that would "open" Korea to US and Western trade, Shufeldt again made recourse to this metaphor, calling the relationship an "amicable intercourse."[33] Yet as I will demonstrate in the analysis that follows, this reigning metaphor of sexual consummation, as problematic as it is, is only the tip of the iceberg in what would become literalized as the provision of militarized sex work to US soldiers across camptowns in Asia and the Pacific, euphemistically called "Rest and Recreation" or "R&R" facilities and zones. This provision, at once promoted, institutionalized, and regulated via what I call the transpacific masculinist compact between the US government and that of the "host" nation or territory, would see sexual relations transmogrify into sexual violence, assault, and sometimes murder perpetrated by GIs against sex workers. Indeed, we witness an epidemic of rape, such that during the Korean War era of the 1950s, the GI slang for R&R leave could also mean "Rape & Restitution" or "Rape and Ruin."[34]

The transpacific cultural productions on bases and camptowns in the Philippines, Okinawa, and South Korea that I analyze in this chapter allow us to see how such crimes go unpunished via the projection or export of US sovereignty, whose metapolitical authority affords the protection of extraterritoriality (or effective impunity) to US military personnel who commit crimes. The spatial transformation effected via land seizure, making possible the creation of the spatial exception that is the US military base and its attendant camptown, are not only the outposts of an attempted (yet ultimately failed) world security but also the settlements of a presumably temporary (yet stubbornly enduring) kind of world-making in the image of "America Town." Indeed, it is also the projection and export of the American way of life as such. In the cultural works I analyze, these spatial and temporal registers of America's settler exceptions are at once made visible and thwarted through an aesthetics of settler imperial failure, or the crafting and imagining of decolonial and antimilitarist spaces and times that blast open the spatiotemporal continuum of the settler garrison.

An "Inexorable Liaison": The Philippines and the United States

In Rachel Rivera's documentary *Sin City Diary* (1992), Richard Gordon, the mayor of Olongapo City in the Philippines, makes a sobering observation about the city that lies next to Subic Bay, the largest US naval base in Asia until its closure in 1992. He states, "Does the city recognize prostitution? No, but we recognize that there will be that inexorable liaison ... the liaison that will have to come about because there is a US facility here, there are navy ships coming here and government but take into consideration that when you have these things going on that you'll be able to regulate it." Mayor Gordon reveals how the military camptown constitutes a spatial exception by highlighting the paradoxical conditions under which sex work is at once unrecognized or illegal yet regulated. The "inexorable liaison" of which he speaks is a euphemistic reference to the assumption that wherever the US military is based, so too will there be a local provision of "rest and recreation," itself another euphemism for militarized sex work.[35] Yet in such spaces, where the sovereignties of the United States and the host nation would presumably compete, or where the sovereignty of the host nation on whose land the base and its camptown are actually situated should logically reign, the "inexorable liaison" indexes economies of neocolonial dependence, gendered racial violence, and extraterritorial impunity for US military personnel who commit crimes. As I will elaborate in this chapter, the hybrid space that is the military base and its attendant camptown may be an ambiguous contact zone that blurs national boundaries and sovereignties, yet insofar as it is a part of America's settler garrison, US military authority and its own juridical apparatus often trump all else. As such, US military authority, negotiated through formally bilateral yet effectively neocolonial Status of Forces Agreements, functions as a type of metapolitical authority.

Ceded to the United States at the conclusion of the Spanish-American War in 1898, the Philippines was subjected to a genocidal war of conquest, with the United States declaring victory and colonial possession in 1902 and lasting until 1946. A central feature of US colonialism and ongoing neocolonialism in the Philippines is military presence.[36] Until the withdrawal of the US military in 1992, due in no small part to the end of martial rule in the Philippines and to the activist work of organizations such as General Assembly Binding Women for Reform, Integrity, Equality, Leadership, and Action (GABRIELA) and Co- alition Against Trafficking of Women-Asia Pacific (CATW-AP), the bases in the Philippines constituted one of the United States' largest and most significant military complexes in the world.[37] Subic Bay Naval Base and Clark Air Base were deployed as crucial staging grounds for the Vietnam War and more re- cently the Gulf War. It is crucial to note that after the 1992 withdrawal, the Philippines was remilitarized by the United States and once again made avail- able as a logistics hub through a series of agreements, specifically the Visit- ing Forces Agreement in 1999, the Mutual Logistics and Support Agreement of 2002, and the Enhanced Defense Cooperation Agreement of 2014.[38] Such agreements have facilitated the growing presence of US military forces on sev- eral "lily pads" in the Philippines, particularly for efforts in combating local insurgents and containing the perceived Chinese threat.[39] Militarized vio- lence such as the 2014 brutal murder in Olongapo of Jennifer Laude, a trans- gender Filipina woman, by a US marine on leave after participating in joint US-Philippines military exercises, makes crushingly visible how the 1992 base closures failed to extricate the Philippines fully from America's settler garri- son. This ongoing history of US military presence in Asia and the Pacific is not unique simply to former colonies like the Philippines, and in addition to remilitarization, the afterlife of base closures includes the ongoing effects of the environmental and ecological devastation wrought by the bases. Given the tendency of the United States to ignore the "polluter pays" principle, cleanup efforts have been difficult.[40]

Just as Olongapo City's mayor Richard Gordon's comments reveal the spa- tial exception, women who labor as sex workers in military camptowns am- plify the temporal exception. In *Let the Good Times Roll: Prostitution and the U.S.*

Military in Asia, a transgeneric text of interviews, critical essays, photo essays, and testimonials by sex workers at US military bases and camptowns in Asia, we hear from eighteen-year-old Lita, who worked at Olongapo: "I thought about our debt in the province. I said, 'Okay, I'll go with him.' I went with him. We went to a hotel."[41] Lita conceives of debt not as an individual one, but a collective "our debt in the province." Debt, as I have been elaborating, is the imposition of a militarist settler imperial temporality that demands and extracts repayment from people like Lita and her family. This compels economic dependence on the US military and the continuing presence of its bases and camptowns. Filmmaker Rachel Rivera's voice-over in *Sin City Diary* further reveals this protracted economy of not only compelled dependence but also gratitude, or the figurative debt that can never be fully repaid: "It was nearly fifty years ago that America gave up its rule here but the US military has since become the country's second largest employer. It's the payoff that's kept us grateful to the foreigner we've learned to love." A sex worker articulates this conundrum in the film: "If the base is gone, I don't know what happens. I think Olongapo is going down. No business here. Nothing. Business in Olongapo is restaurant and bar, if the business is gone, I don't know. I don't know what happen to people here." When the US military did withdraw its forces and shut down the base in 1992, business specifically in Olongapo did disappear, but camptown business as such did not. Just as Filipina women from the provinces had been compelled to follow where the business was to Olongapo, they then found themselves again compelled to follow where the business was, this time away from Olongapo and to bases elsewhere in Asia, especially in South Korea and Okinawa.

The migration of Filipina sex workers out of the Philippines to US military bases and camptowns elsewhere in Asia is but one stream of a much broader system of labor export and remittances. Robyn Magalit Rodriguez argues that the Philippines is a "labor brokerage state," engaging in what some have called legal human trafficking by offering and facilitating the export of Filipina/os to be used as a reserve army of labor throughout the globe. The Philippine state's "transnational migration apparatus," complete with a highly developed and efficient bureaucracy, functions much like an export processing zone. Except, in this instance, the export commodity is the human qua worker, one that is highly profitable.[42] This neocolonial labor export system builds upon the US colonial system that preceded it and functions as a "fix" for the unemployment, underemployment, and rural displacement produced in the Philippines as a result of neoliberal restructuring within US-led global capitalism.[43] Here, national debt plays a role, for unlike the United States, the neocolonized Philippine state occupies a subjugated position within ongoing asymmetries of power and is thus beholden to its creditors. Moreover, a significant number of households in the Philippines depends upon the remittances sent back home by family members who work overseas. In 2019, the amount in US dollars totaled over $35 billion, representing about 9.3 percent of GDP.[44] Just as Lita in *Let the Good Times Roll* is financially burdened by the obligation to help her family repay its debt, millions of overseas Filipina/o workers are burdened by the obligation to contribute to the household income of their families.

Neferti Tadiar argues that this debt-propelled and export-oriented strategy has led to the worldwide commodification of women of the Global South through the export and exploitation of their feminized and "cheap" labor power, especially in the sex trade. This sex trade takes both legitimate form (as tourism, hospitality, or mail-order bride businesses) and illicit form (as prostitution). Indeed, the Philippine nation itself has been hyperfeminized, symptomizing the condensation of patriarchy, modern heterosexism, colonialism, and imperialism. In particular, the production of the figure of the prostitute as a feminine ideal "has long been a cultural corollary to commodity fetishism in the age of capitalism."[45] Tadiar observes that for women coerced into what is euphemistically called the "entertainment industry," or in the context of military camptowns called "rest and recreation" zones, the difference between raw material and labor dissolves. For "the prostitute applies her labour power to her own body in the production of herself as a commodity." This process, in which the sex worker is at once raw material, labor, and machine, is a manifestation of the ever-increasing efficiency of global capitalism in hyperexploiting.[46] With militarized sex work in particular, what Katharine H. S. Moon calls "sex among allies," we see the symbiosis between capitalism and militarism that I discussed in the Introduction.[47] We also see that sex workers must contend with the spatial exception of the camptown as a site of competing sovereignties in which US metapolitical authority almost always supersedes local authority. This enables not only effective impunity or immunity for US military personnel perpetrating gendered racial and sexual violence but also an added layer of biopolitical surveillance and control imposed on the sex workers. Here, the process through which the sex worker is at once raw material and labor is particularly fraught.

In *Sin City Diary*, we see the racialized, gendered, and imperial optics through which men who serve in the US military view Filipina sex workers. One white, one Asian American, and two African American servicemen each comment on camera when asked by Rachel Rivera what they think about Olongapo. The white serviceman comments, "Don't come here mom, it's bad."

This is followed by an Asian American who claims, "This is like a guy's dream fantasy. I mean you think about it. You come here and a guy is treated like a king." Finally, the second African American serviceman is even more frank when he builds upon the first's remark that it's "fun . . . like an amusement park" by revealing, "I like your motherfucking women. Their shit is fresh. The women here—you would never find them like this here in America. It's easy, you know what I'm saying." The Asian- and African American men, though racialized as men of color within the United States and thus targeted by white supremacist violence in linked yet distinct ways, also carry the power of their US imperial citizenship and heteropatriarchy with them when they travel overseas, especially to neocolonies like the Philippines. As such, their remarks about Filipina sex workers are clearly not simply heteropatriarchal but are spoken as the agents of US militarist settler imperialism. Filipinas who labor as camptown sex workers are subjected to these logics and attendant practices. Vexed neocolonial relations, however, instantiate a dialectic of dependency, desire, and betrayal in which US servicemen continue to be viewed as avenues of escape and rescue from poverty.

Yet when US servicemen travel overseas, they not only carry their imperial citizenship but are also vectors of sexually transmitted diseases. The US military thus regulates and subjects the sex workers to biopolitical surveillance. In *Sin City Diary*, we learn about a "social hygiene clinic" run by the city and the US Navy. Women are required to go there every two weeks to get tested for sexually transmitted diseases, and a tracing system subjects the women to further surveillance by providing a way for US sailors to report the names of women whom they suspect of having given them a disease. The US Navy also begins funding HIV tests, but with no plans for actually treating women with AIDS. A woman who reveals on-screen that she had tested positive for HIV says, "I wanted to commit suicide." There couldn't be a starker contrast from the casual comments of the US servicemen and the serious testimonies of Filipina women. What is a hedonic "amusement park" for the former is a necropolitical minefield for the latter. Here, the blurring of raw material and labor in the Filipina's production of herself as a commodity is such that the raw material, her body, is vulnerable to exhaustion in both its senses.

What I have called this transpacific masculinist compact—of securing sexual access for the US military while surveilling and in some cases detaining women to protect the military from venereal disease—has been heightened in the post–World War II era. But it dates back to the Philippine-American War, the US conquest and colonization of the Philippines at the turn of the century.[48] Thus, while US bases in the Philippines were shut down in 1992, this longer genealogy preceding those closures by almost a century, and the escalating export of Filipina migrant labor following those closures as well as the more recent remilitarization of the Philippines, bespeak an enduring transpacific military-sexual complex whose "raw material" is composed not only of seized land but also the very bodies of the women who have been displaced and dispossessed by that seizure.

From this discussion of the Philippines, I turn next to Okinawa, another site on America's settler garrison with an enduring transpacific military-sexual complex. Like the archipelagic Philippines, Okinawa is also an island. Okinawa's dual domination by the United States and Japan has transformed and malformed the island itself into a base. To the extent that Okinawa is still colonized by Japan and is thus disproportionately targeted by US militarist settler imperialism compared to other parts of Japan, it is one among many islands in the Pacific with an Indigenous presence seeking a decolonial and antimilitarist future. From the Philippines to Okinawa and beyond, the vast contours of US "transoceanic militarism" necessitate a decontinentalizing oceanic analytic that can critically apprehend those contours. Craig Santos Perez writes that "no island is an island because islands exist in dynamic relationality to a larger archipelago and ocean." Moreover, "no island is an island because any island is itself an archipelago, or an 'auto-archipelago'" of complex and multilayered dynamics.[49] This vital inter-island and intra-island relationality, though significantly constituted in part by the dizzying proliferation of US bases, is not reducible to that proliferation. An oceanic analytic can also apprehend the transpacific imaginaries that at once critically diagnose and gesture beyond US militarist settler imperialism through an aesthetics of settler imperial failure.

Okinawa: "The Island Itself Is the Base"

"The military doesn't have bases in Okinawa. The island itself is the base." A navy officer made this observation to Morton Halperin, a high-ranking Pentagon official.[50] Similarly, Saundra Sturdevant argues that, "In many ways, it is a case not of the U.S. having a military presence in Okinawa, but of Okinawans living within a U.S. military preserve."[51] Annexed by Japan in 1879, occupied and controlled by the US military from 1945 until 1972, then "returned" or "reverted" to Japan in 1972, Okinawa's ongoing militarized dispossession is reflective of what Ayano Ginoza calls the "intimacies of US and Japanese empires" and what Lisa Yoneyama calls the "transpacific complicity" between the United States and Japan.[52] It is what I have been calling the transpacific masculinist compact. Although Okinawa constitutes only 0.6 percent (under 1 percent) of the total land area of Japan, almost 75 percent of US military bases, facilities, and troops in Japan are stationed there. Approximately 20 percent of Okinawa, the main island in the Ryūkyū Archipelago, is occupied by US military bases. Although many had hoped the "Reversion to the Mainland" in 1972 would also reverse this heavy military presence, it was not to be, leading to the question of whether Okinawa serves as the "garbage dump" where mainland Japan and the United States can dispose of their concerns about security.[53] Moreover, in critical recognition of how US militarism produces gendered spaces of violence, such as a militarized sex industry and sexual violence, Suzuyo Takazato argues that Okinawa is the "prostituted daughter of Japan. Japan used her daughter as a breakwater to keep battlefields from spreading over the mainland until the end of World War II. And after the war, she enjoyed economic prosperity by selling the daughter to the United States."[54] Indeed, Japan itself had also been feminized as "America's geisha ally" in its transformation from a racialized and demonized World War II enemy to submissive Cold War junior partner in Asia.[55]

The Cold War alliance between the United States and Japan, indeed an asymmetrical "transpacific complicity" structured by Japan's client state status vis-à-vis the United States, has made possible and desirable the continued expropriation of Okinawa. The 1952 San Francisco Peace Treaty ended the US military occupation of Japan, except Okinawa. Moreover, the US-Japan Security Treaty (initially signed in 1960 and automatically renewed since its second signing in 1970) and the Status of Forces Agreement (SOFA) of this treaty allow the United States to use and control the Okinawan land it seized during the initial phase of the occupation.[56] However, the treaty's Article 6, which allows the United States to station troops in Japan, specifies that it is to be "for the purpose of contributing to the security of Japan and the maintenance of international peace and security *in the Far East*." Yet since 1990, the marines have been deployed from there repeatedly for wars in the Gulf, Afghanistan, and Iraq. It is important to note that the marines are not a defensive, Far Eastern force but rather an expeditionary attack force.[57]

Although it was nominally incorporated into Japan, a constitutionally pacifist state, Okinawa is effectively an American military colony, "a militarized, dual-colonial dependency of Japan and the United States."[58] Here, it is important to note that Indigenous Okinawans are not Japanese in terms of culture and language but are a colonized and minoritized group.[59] Indeed, Okinawans are racialized by mainland Japanese, who see them as *gai-chi*, or those outside the orbit of central power. Media caricatures of Okinawans persist into the contemporary context, with descriptors such as *"naïve, slow, lazy, uncultured, unmannered, provincial, less civilized,* and so forth."[60] Although in 2019 the Japanese government passed a bill to formally recognize the Ainu of Hokkaidō, Japan's northernmost prefecture, as an Indigenous group and to promote and protect Ainu culture (after the Diet passed a nonbinding resolution in 2008), Indigenous Okinawans (Uchinānchu) have yet to receive formal recognition as either an Indigenous or minority group. Yet, as I will elaborate, there is a growing movement among Okinawans to articulate their Indigeneity within the context of global Indigenous peoples' movements as well as the local context of antibase activism in Okinawa. Ayano Ginoza, Megumi Chibana, and others offer powerful analyses of how feminist and Indigenous frameworks, articulated at the intensely local scale even as they might be connected to broader global movements, have animated the demilitarization movement.[61]

On Okinawa's ongoing doubly colonized condition, Yoneyama observes that Okinawa is a space of at least three overlapping liminalities—epistemically, legally, and materially. These liminalities are captured by Okinawa's ambiguous status as a "liberated yet occupied" space under US occupation in the post–World War II conjuncture.[62] Its legal liminality has effectively functioned to defer its decolonization perpetually, another kind of temporal exception. The post–World War II "transfer" of Okinawa from a defeated Japanese empire to the United States was conditioned by two provisions: the United States' recognition of Japan's "residual sovereignty" over Okinawa and uninterrupted US control over Okinawa continuing through what was initially imagined to be its eventual approval as a United Nations trusteeship. The legal mechanisms of "residual sovereignty" and "pending trusteeship" thus ensured that sovereignty as it pertained to Okinawa would reside outside of Okinawa itself. Yet the very liminality, out of which a "no longer formally colonized but not yet sovereign" Okinawa was created, at once enabled the continuation and disavowal of colonial expropriation and violence.[63] It is this twinned logic of the continuation and disavowal of the violence through which Okinawa has been transformed into America's settler garrison that is revealed in the Okinawan literature I analyze.

Let us begin with a common Okinawan refrain, that the violent expropriation of their land by the US military was undertaken by "bulldozer and bayonet."[64] Kishaba Jun's short story "Dark Flowers," set during the Korean War (1950–53), links this land seizure in Okinawa to settler colonialism within what became the United States.[65] The story is told from the third-person perspective of Nobuko, a sex worker who labors in a place called "K Town" in the story. When the story was published, readers logically assumed that "K Town" was Koza, a city on Okinawa Island that caters to US military personnel.[66] Describing Nobuko's trip home to the countryside to see and give money to her family, as well as her ambivalent feelings about her transactional relationship with an American GI, the story contains very little action. Instead, it is a powerful meditation on the spatial transformation of Okinawa from a predominantly agricultural land to a dense network of military bases and towns at a pivotal earlier moment in the US occupation and the Cold War, when the Korean War called for an expansion of an already heavily militarized presence. "Dark Flowers" generates a crucial analytic for apprehending the connected yet distinct land seizures that have come to constitute US settler state power and its specific formation as a settler garrison state in the post–World War II era. Moreover, Kishaba's short story imagines a future beyond such settler seizures by gesturing to the possibilities of a transpacific, transwar, and transcolonial Indigenous solidarity between Okinawans and Native Americans.

As Nobuko takes an uneventful walk to her friend's place, we see Okinawa's "weird landscape":

> To get to Michiko's room, Nobuko had to walk along the asphalt military highway, turn at the corner gas station, go down a gravel road lined on both sides with tire repair shops, car washes, and other stores, then walk in the direction of the seacoast along narrow footpaths between rice paddies. Here and there among the paddies were rows of brand-new houses, built on gravel landfills, with gleaming red-tile roofs. It made for a weird landscape. . . . They were, without a doubt, fine houses. But by this time none of the farmers, who'd been relocated here in this forced migration, were living inside. Instead, they lived in tin-roof shacks that had been built onto the kitchens or put up in the backyards. The interiors of these "fine houses" had been partitioned into eight-by-eight foot private rooms where yellowed bras and dresses in many colors now hung outside the windows, fluttering in the wind. At night these "fine houses" became bars and cabarets. (101–2)

This "weird" checkerboard of rice paddies, houses with red-tile roofs, and tin-roof shacks is a blueprint of US military land seizures, and the multiple displacements and forced migrations of farmers bespeak the transformation of Okinawa from a self-sustaining agricultural economy to one increasingly dependent on the US military.[67] The Battle of Okinawa during World War II obliterated much of the island and killed almost one-third of its population. Forced into internment camps and resettled after the war, then forced to migrate from one part of Okinawa to another multiple times, forced again out of their houses with red-tile roofs and into makeshift tin-roof shacks, more and more Okinawans are compelled to make their living within the terms of a distorted military economy and war "boom." The repurposed house with a red-tile roof, now a bar, a cabaret, and a brothel, was itself the site *to* which Okinawan farming families were displaced, yet it soon also becomes the site *from* which those families are again displaced so that they can survive.

The "weird landscape" described in "Dark Flowers" is a geography of militarism, or the landscape of America's settler garrison. By defamiliarizing this landscape within the context of what has become an unrelentingly quotidian militarized presence and infrastructure in Okinawa, the story provides a critical mapping of the *land* that must be expropriated in order for military settlement to occur. As I have suggested, the US military (not just its personnel but extending to dependent family members and contractors) are not settlers in the classic sense. There is, however, a permanence to the enduring spatial logic and architecture of military bases, camptowns, and facilities. This, coupled with the sheer amount of actual space they take up, constitutes a type of settlement that violently displaces and dispossesses the Indigenous population. Land, livelihood, and way of life had been intricately connected for Indigenous Okinawans. The making of America's settler garrison severs this connection and tethers Okinawans to the distorted auspices of the US Department of Defense.

This making of America's settler garrison by "bulldozer and bayonet" began during World War II's Battle of Okinawa in 1945, when the military violently seized large tracts of land and bulldozed or otherwise demolished many houses, family graves, and sacred sites.[68] Within a year, it had taken possession of forty thousand acres and 20 percent of the island's arable land. By 1950, this had risen to 40 percent, displacing approximately 250,000 Okinawans, or almost half the island's population.[69] In this process of dispossession and displacement, the United States determined both the land-use rules and land values.[70] Such a seizure of land, at once unilateral, uncompensated, and orchestrated on a massive scale, was in violation of the 1907 Hague Convention's Article 46 prohibiting the confiscation of private property.[71] In 1953, to legitimize the confiscations of land, the US military issued Ordinance No. 109 (Land Acquisition Procedure), which outlined the terms for acquiring new leases, "including the ability to take private land with armed force in the case of noncompliance."[72] After "reversion" to Japan in 1972, the Japanese Diet passed a land-use law called the "Special Measures for Law and Land Required by the U.S. Military Bases." Under this law, landowners are mandated to lease their land to the government of Japan, which in turn subleases it to the US military for no charge.[73]

The seizure of Indigenous Okinawan land by "bulldozer and bayonet," the production of the "weird landscape" limned in "Dark Flowers," was met with a dramatic series of protests in the mid-1950s by local resident farmers. Crucially, one forgotten yet significant series in this earlier moment of ongoing antibase activism that continues to this day is the Isahama land struggle. In Isahama, a region in the center of Okinawa Island, farming women articulated a radical set of demands based on their Indigenous place-based relations to the land and social relations to one another. In her stunning analysis of this struggle, Wendy Matsumura notes that the women did not fight explicitly for the removal of the bases. Yet the radicality of their demands can be apprehended by focusing on what they did explicitly fight for, which was the preservation of Isahama as a place and the social relations they had created to build it together. Through a Marxist feminist lens, Matsumura argues that the "Women's Appeal," in demanding continued access to farmlands, rejected altogether the very terms of compensation that dominated official negotiations among the landowner representatives (who were male), the local government of the Ryūkyū Islands, and the US military. This privileging of access to farmlands, rather than monetary compensation, radically articulated an Indigenous worldview that was not only anticapitalist but also revealed a prescience about the precarity of wage labor within a US-dictated military economy. By centering relationship to land rather than money as the condition that would secure their livelihood and more broadly the social reproduction and well-being of their larger community, the women forcefully articulated an Indigenous resistance to dispossession and capitalist enclosure. Plots of paddy land, even tiny ones, made it possible for them to harvest rice for sale, and it also crucially gave them access to "what they described as inexhaustible supplies of water for laundry, cooking, farming, drinking, and so on. In their appeal, the women called themselves some of the 'happiest people in all of Okinawa' for living in a place where water did not have to be purchased."[74]

In thus shifting the very terrain and terms of struggle by rejecting the imposition of US militarist settler imperialism's property regime on ever-growing parts of Okinawa, the "Women's Appeal" was not simply pointing to land and water as physical resources. Indeed, as Matsumura argues, the women's insistence on the incalculability or impossibility of converting what they would lose into a monetary sum (which goes beyond simply contesting the undervaluation of the land by the United States) points to how such losses would not only be tangible but also crucially intangible.[75] As I see it, the women were insisting on the incalculable value of a specifically Indigenous place-based epistemology, ontology, and mutuality of being situated on land that they had collectively rebuilt after the previous wartime displacements of World War II and the devastating Battle of Okinawa. Moreover, as "Dark Flowers" reveals, women in particular were being subsumed into wage labor within US military bases and camptowns, particularly into service work and militarized sexual labor, at the very same moment of the "Women's Appeal." The emergence of the "fallen woman" trope as a social problem, increased biopolitical surveillance, and vulnerability to sexual violence—these were some of the processes that the Isahama women farmers were attempting to preempt. In so doing, what they were striving to protect was not just livelihood but also autonomy and the very ground that makes possible mutuality. Such mutuality or lateral sociality, as I have been suggesting, is an alternative form of debt.

This earlier moment in Indigenous Okinawan resistance to the imposition of what Brenna Bhandar calls the "colonial lives of property" at once challenges and amplifies what would become the fast-growing contours of America's settler garrison on Okinawa and beyond.[76] Indeed, as Mark L. Gillem observes, this is a "mortgaged empire." However, "at least one thing comes cheaply— the land America's outposts occupy."[77] This militarist thirst for land, which has grown unquenchably in the post–World War II era, is expressed aptly by Patrick Lloyd Hatcher, a retired US Army colonel and historian, who writes, "Foreign real estate has the same attraction for American defense planners that Nimitz-class aircraft carriers do for admirals and B-2 stealth bombers and heavy Abrams tanks do for generals. They can never have enough."[78] It is no wonder, then, that the DoD refers to its vast network of bases, structures, and facilities as a "worldwide real property portfolio."[79] And in this way, the island of Okinawa was remade from self-sufficient agricultural villages to military-dependent Cold War suburbs with new forms of spillover—"clamor, calamity, contamination, and crime."[80]

Okinawa's "weird landscape" is the landscape of what I have been calling the spatial exception, in this case the strategic centerpiece or "keystone of the Pacific" of a vast network of bases constituting America's settler garrison. The land grab in Okinawa, the flagrant violation of the 1907 Hague Convention I noted above, and the continued occupation of that land after the 1972 reversion give witness to the US settler state's metapolitical authority. As I will elaborate later, this authority not only pertains to the violent means through which land was acquired but also the acts of violence perpetrated by US military personnel on that land against local populations. When US military personnel are stationed overseas, extraterritoriality, or adjudication by US military courts as opposed to local national courts, goes with them. What also travels with them is "America Town," or the spatial model of a suburb.[81] Unsurprisingly, this spatial model of the suburb, with a focus on conformity and consumption, requires great amounts of land.

Franchised shopping, that sine qua non of the American suburb, has also become the sine qua non of the American outpost, what Johnson calls a "consumerist Sparta."[82] Army and Air Force Exchange Service (AAFES), the biggest franchise, was established in 1985 to meet what was then the purchasing needs of over 11.5 million "authorized" consumers spread across US military installations throughout the globe. Dictating development plans on every base, AAFES builds shopping malls, called base or post exchanges (BX on an air force base or PX on an army post) that are the "military equivalent of Wal-Mart."[83] AAFES's demand for bigger stores and even bigger parking lots in service of industrial-scale retail consumption and its prioritization of profit over all other planning concerns for the "host" base give new meaning, as Gillem argues, to the phrase "military-industrial complex."[84] This phrase can no longer refer just to the weapons industry; it must also include the military equivalent of Walmart. "America Town" is where US military personnel and their families live while stationed overseas, and this town is accompanied by an "R&R" entertainment area catering to the US military, often a camptown.

In "Dark Flowers," we see the early design of an entertainment district or camptown that is at once the site not only of US militarism but also of cultural imperialism. Yet the story thwarts conventional assumptions about what kind of consumers and spectators the locals, in this case the Okinawans, might be. Nobuko spends time with her boyfriend, a GI named Joe, in the entertainment district: "K was the main business district in the middle part of Okinawa Island. It had the shabby postwar look of a town born and grown up along the military highway that ran through it from north to south. Its streets were lined up with a jumble of souvenir shops, movie theaters, foreign import-export companies, bars, game centers, vendors' stalls, and brothels—all fronted with signs written in English. Hidden behind its neat, modern buildings were countless one-story shacks" (103). "Dark Flowers" dwells at relative length on the American film that Nobuko and Joe watch and contains a detailed plot summary of a group of white settlers heading west, led by Gregory Peck, in a convoy of covered wagons. Their great challenge as they cross the prairie is a tribe of "Indians," whom the Peck character almost single-handedly annihilates. This unnamed film in the story could be a combination of the many epic Westerns that Gregory Peck appeared in starting in the 1940s. Interestingly, it could be a version of the "The Plains" sequence starring Peck in the grand epic How the West Was Won (1962), released several years after the publication of "Dark Flowers" in 1955. Author Kishaba marks here what became a familiar trope in the genre of the Western—the manifest destiny of white settlers heading west, led by a heroic man who defends the group against many dangers, including and especially "savage Indians." This trope attempts to cover over the very question of "how the west was won"—through the settler colonial genocidal conquest of Native Americans and the theft of their land.

Yet as "Dark Flowers" illuminates through the ekphrastic description of this film, the genre of the Western and the trope of the heroic and pioneering white settler cannot fully predict or contain oppositional spectatorial practices, interpretations, and identifications. After the summary of the film's diegesis, "Dark Flowers" reveals how it has been interpreted by Nobuko. Rather than identifying with the white settlers, in particular the Peck character's female romantic interest, Nobuko identifies with the massacred Indians: "Why did the Indians have to be massacred, Nobuko asked herself. It had filled her with anger to see them desperately defending their homeland as old Indian women died in terror, young Indian men tumbled to their deaths from cliffs, and camera close-ups showed the faces of men trampled to death after falling from their horses. Why would Indians ever agree to perform in such a film, she wondered. The whole thing made her sick" (105). In naming the massacre *as* a massacre, the annihilation *as* an annihilation, the story names US settler colonial violence as that of genocidal conquest of Indigenous populations. Moreover, multiple references to the encounters between settlers and Indians as that of Indians "defending their homeland" draw the reader's attention to the settler theft of Native land. In doing so, the story exposes one of the foundations of international law, the doctrine of *terra nullius* ("land belonging to no one") as a legal fiction abetting the white settler "discovery" of "empty" land.

Nobuko's anger and ultimate disgust, her questioning of why "the Indians [had] to be massacred," indeed her recognition of their humanity as "old Indian women" and "young Indian men" who die in "terror" on-screen, expose the failure of the ideological labor of US cultural imperialism on the settler garrison. Not only is Nobuko angry but the "whole thing made her sick," and she wonders why "Indians [would] ever agree to perform in such a film." On this point, Michelle H. Raheja develops a theory of "redfacing" in *Reservation Reelism: Redfacing, Visual Sovereignty, and Representations of Native Americans in Film*. Emphasizing the complex performances of Hollywood Indians negotiating a circumscribed context of uneven power relationships with European American filmmakers and producers, Raheja argues that "redfacing signals the ways in which the work of Indigenous performers, like that of the trickster, is always in motion and therefore creates acts that operate ambiguously, acts that open themselves up for further reading and interpretation."[85] The dying Indians that Nobuko sees on-screen, though compelled to play the role of the "vanishing Indian," a reigning trope in the settler colonial imaginary, indeed open up further reading and interpretation on Nobuko's part. She questions why they would take such roles, yet that very querying, the very disagreement she has with their decision, registers the alternative and critical interpretations that redfacing can generate.

"Dark Flowers" does not end with Nobuko's sympathetic feelings about the massacred Indians. Indeed, the story establishes a compelling point of identification between the Indians and the Okinawans. After viewing the film, Nobuko cannot forget the faces of the Indian men:

> Then, walking alone, she again recalled the faces of the Indian men in the movie. They brought back a horrible memory. It had been a sweltering dawn in mid-July when she witnessed this brutal scene. Just before sunrise, across the military highway from her room, she'd seen the faces of men and women huddled together, trembling with rage. They had just been dragged outside the barbed-wire fence that now surrounded their land, and the young men among them were being arrested. She had seen it with her own eyes. And she could still hear the endless clanging of an alarm bell at dawn as everything these people owned was being taken from them. "Gregory Peck, 'Mr. Handsome.' Hah! What a fraud," Nobuko grumbled to herself. (106)

In having the film trigger Nobuko's memory of this horrible scene, "Dark Flowers" establishes a connection between the genocidal conquest of Native Americans and the dispossession and criminalization of Indigenous Okinawans. The story thus links the violence of settler colonialism to the militarized violence of the settler garrison and also links the theft of Indigenous lands on what became the "domestic" United States to that of its military empire in Asia and the Pacific. The "barbed-wire fence that now surrounded their [Okinawan] land" marks the militarized enclosures that would increasingly dispossess and displace Indigenous Okinawans. Indeed, "fence-line landscapes," "detour mentalities," and "checkpoint cultures" are now all too common features of militarist spatialities and geographies.[86] This renders all the more prescient the "Women's Appeal" of the Isahama women farmers in recognizing what the loss of access to their farmlands would ultimately mean.

"Dark Flowers" gestures to the possibilities of a global Indigenous solidarity and linked decolonized future by making these Indigenous place-based transpacific connections and affective identifications through an aesthetics of settler imperial failure. Moreover, it interrogates the temporality of settler colonialism. The slaughter of Native Americans in the story's film depicts a historical period about a century or several decades before the roundup of Okinawans that Nobuko recalls. Yet if *we* are to recall settler colonialism's ongoing "present tenseness," if you will, it conjoins with the post–World War II formation of military empire and of the settler garrison in Asia and the Pacific. As such, decolonization for both Native Americans and Okinawans resides in the future. Despite different histories (including, for example, that Okinawa has a triangulated history with its colonizer Japan and with that nation's client state status vis-à-vis the United States), what I hope to have demonstrated are the recursive workings of settler violence. These recursive workings are the projections of settler state power overseas as also increasingly a militarist and imperialist transnational garrison state power. In turn, those projections also at times rebound in renovated forms to the "domestic" sites of the settler state.

These recursive workings of power are also those of resistance to that power. We have seen this with Nobuko's oppositional interpretation of the film. Her ultimate pronouncement is that Gregory Peck qua "Mr. Handsome" is a "fraud." This lays bare the fraud that is US militarist settler imperialism, or the sleights of hand through which metapolitical authority functions. Moreover, at the end of "Dark Flowers," we see that such critical disidentifications are not unique to Nobuko. Through an aesthetics of settler imperial failure, we are here reminded that Okinawan resistance has been there all along, in step with and in opposition to the metastasizing contours of America's settler garrison, as with the "Women's Appeal" of the Isahama women farmers. Nobuko's brother, it turns out, is part of a reading circle that discusses not only books but also "organizing" and "unions" (109).

Having focused my foregoing discussion of "Dark Flowers" on the spatial exception that is the settler garrison, I turn now to an analysis of Higashi Mineo's novella *Child of Okinawa* and its critical imagining of the temporal as well as spatial exceptions. Told through the eyes of Tsuneyoshi, an adolescent boy, and set in 1950s Okinawa, the novella depicts the island's increasing dependence on the military service economy. Displaced to a town next to a large air force base, Tsuneyoshi's family undergoes a series of failed business ventures, including a noodle shop and grocery store, before deciding to go into the bar (and effectively a brothel) business. Here, in the business that also doubles as a home, young Tsuneyoshi witnesses and must sometimes give up his bed for the bar's sex workers and their GI clients. *Child of Okinawa* demonstrates how in the linked economy of figurative and financial debt, the US military incorrectly assumed that Okinawans would feel indebted to the occupying power for providing the protection of a military service economy. Tsuneyoshi's displacement from his own bed, the claustrophobia-inducing ways in which the military service economy encroaches upon ever-greater spaces and lives, reveals that what is assumed to be protection and beneficence is actually compelled dependence via the wholesale destruction of a previously self-sufficient agricultural economy and way of life. One significant feature of this compelled dependence, as we shall see, is a transpacific masculinist compact in which Okinawan men control sex workers through the mechanism of perpetual debt, or an effective debt bondage system of sexual labor. As pithily observed by Kyle Kajihiro, in "the military economy, some 'get paid,' while others 'pay the price.'"[87]

This transpacific masculinist compact is forged through the US military's demand for sexual labor and Okinawa's provision of it.[88] Yet it is an asymmetrical compact because it is taking place within a US settler garrison, itself already colonized by Japan. Tsuneyoshi's father, complicit in this compact, is compelled to participate because, in his words, as lousy a business as it might be, "There's no use complaining. It's how we eat, you know" (81). The debt scheme through which he plans to extract profit from the sex workers is not his own unique brainchild; rather, it is the general economic form and logic of America's settler garrison. After his father learns his new trade from a man already in the business of managing bars, Tsuneyoshi recounts the afternoon when he came from school to find that the "girls had arrived" (85). He overhears his father telling his mother how he intends to maximize profit: "'See, you make loans to the girls who bring in lots of money. That way they have to keep working for you to pay off their debts. Of course, nobody lends money to the girls who can't sell, so they just drift around from bar to bar.' He talked so matter-of-factly about women who are lured into debt and then held like slaves. How could he sit there and gossip about their misery while chewing his food with such pleasure?" (86). As I will elaborate further in my discussion of South Korean camptowns, this debt bondage system, an effective form of indentured sexual slavery, is such that it is virtually impossible to pay off the loans completely.[89] Even an adolescent Tsuneyoshi can see the cruelty of this system, observing that "women . . . are lured into debt and then held like slaves." He sympathizes with the women's misery and cannot fathom how his father can derive pleasure from it.

Child of Okinawa reveals how even in the earlier years of the construction of America's settler garrison on Okinawa, a debt bondage system was already developing. Women are disproportionately rendered vulnerable to this system. Already vulnerable to gendered racial and sexual violence at the hands of their American GI clients as well as their Okinawan bar/brothel owners, through the debt bondage system the women are subjected to another linked economic violence. In the face of physical violence or the threat of it, they are compelled to pay off their debts. However, as I discussed in Chapter 1, the United States can practice an effective debt imperialism by rolling over its massive national debt indefinitely, thereby granting to itself a temporal exception, or an exemption from the homogeneous time of repayment that it imposes on everyone else at multiple scales, whether individuals or whole nations.

This temporal exception is linked to the spatial exception. If even Tsuneyoshi's own bed is not exempt from the reach of the military service economy, neither is the neighborhood he explores. Littered everywhere are both the growing edifices of US bases, facilities, and surrounding enclaves as well as the all-too-real remnants and traces of the brutality of the Battle of Okinawa. The lacerated ecology and topography of the island, its "weird landscape" or geography of militarism, is littered with various forms of military hardware. Tsuneyoshi chances upon a wooden box hidden in the weeds among some gravestones that he thought was filled with canned goods. Yet it contained ten rifles instead. His grandfather had to live in a tent after the war because his house had been demolished in order to build a runway, yet the runway that was built in only a week was never used for an attack on the Japanese mainland because it surrendered after the atomic bombings of Hiroshima and Nagasaki. So instead, the runway becomes a space on which gathered weapons and ammunition are piled, then later dumped into the ocean. Tsuneyoshi's grandfather obtains a temporary job from the US military gathering up ammunition from the area, yet he is paid not in dollars but canned goods and cigarettes. When he then tries to resume farming in the tiny plot that remains of his field, only "shriveled bulbs covered with fuzz" will grow (109).

The spatial exception that is the settler garrison operates not only through this scarred landscape but also through a nonexistent or skewed juridical process. *Child of Okinawa* reveals the quotidian and unpunished acts of violence perpetrated against Okinawans by US soldiers. Tsuneyoshi witnesses and hears about these acts. His father's second cousin, a taxi driver, crashes into a telephone pole when his three US soldier passengers harass him while he is driving, one of them stamping on his accelerator foot and all three yelling, "Hurry hurry, hubba hubba!" (96). This vehicular incident calls to mind a much harsher actual 1963 incident in which a US marine driving a truck ran over and killed a twelve-year-old Okinawan boy. The US military court found this marine not guilty. Tsuneyoshi also overhears a conversation between his mom and Michikō, who works in his dad's bar, about what has happened to Michikō's friend Chiiko, who also works in a bar. A US soldier had a crush on Chiiko, but she would not go out with him. For that, he tosses a grenade into her bar, disfiguring her face with burns all over. These are the everyday acts of violence with impunity that Okinawans are subjected to at the hands of US soldiers. Women like Chiiko and Michikō are vulnerable to gendered racial and sexual violence. The pervasiveness of such violence makes it quotidian, yet this very ordinariness hides its extraordinary horror and terror. During the US occupation, the US military possessed ultimate civil and criminal jurisdiction over everyone on the island, both soldiers and civilians. Cases with American defendants were rarely prosecuted, and even when they were, sentences were relatively light despite guilty pleas to serious offenses.[90] Even after reversion to Japan in 1972, US military authority was not radically overturned because of Japan's client-state relationship with the United States and concessions such as the SOFA.

Gendered racial and sexual violence in the form of rape, a particular concern in the immediate postwar years, has been an ongoing issue in Okinawa. Nonexistent or radically curtailed justice for those who are subjected to it amplify the logics of what I have been calling metapolitical authority within the spatial exception. Nobuko Karimata, the former managing director of the Okinawa Women's Foundation and the former director of the Okinawa Women's Comprehensive Center, recalls of the immediate postwar years:

> "The Americans are coming! The Americans are coming! Hide!" That's what we used to scream when we heard the clang of the village bell. . . . In the immediate postwar years, there was a huge bell in each village. If it rang once, that meant there was a meeting in town. If it rang continuously, that signaled a problem, namely that an American soldier was in the neighborhood. Sometimes the soldiers entered residential areas to rape women. In fact, there were so many cases of rape in those early postwar years that whenever we spotted an American on our streets, we thought for sure he was a rapist.[91]

If Nobuko Karimata's recollection provides stark testimony of an earlier period in this long-standing gendered racial and sexual violence perpetrated by the US military, the 1995 case of the abduction and gang rape of a twelve-year-old Okinawan schoolgirl by three US military servicemen has generated renewed protest. The perpetrators, Navy Seaman Marcus Gill, Marine Private Rodrico Harp, and Marine Private Kendric Ledet, were initially taken into US military custody because of extraterritoriality, which gives legal jurisdictional authority to US military courts (and not Japanese courts) even though the crimes were committed on Japanese soil. As I have related, extraterritoriality, a common provision in US SOFAs with its host nations, extends US sovereignty beyond the territory of the United States and effectively negates local sovereignty wherever the US military stations itself. As such, it is a significant feature of US militarist settler imperialism, and in particular the power projected onto the settler garrison. Yet because of massive public outrage over the 1995 rape, the men were eventually turned over to the local authorities. Their trial and conviction in Japanese courts in Okinawa were unprecedented since the beginning of the US occupation a half century earlier. Gill and Harp were each given seven-year sentences on convictions of abduction and rape, while Ledet received a six-and-a-half-year sentence on a slightly lesser charge.

Yet this particular court conviction, precisely because it was such a departure from the norm and even then was only produced via mass protest, is in many ways the placeholder for a justice yet to come rather than a justice fulfilled.[92] Writing on the judicialization of the political and the fissure between the legibility and illegibility of violence, Yoneyama highlights the limits of redress and the need to rethink the idea of "justice" beyond the juridical. Even as the post-1990s "transborder redress culture" traversing Japan and the United States has belatedly rendered legible previously illegible forms of violence, this legibility can be read more as a trace of ongoing forms of US-Japanese interimperial violence and less as the achievement of a capaciously reconceived justice.[93]

In his short story "Hope," critically acclaimed Okinawan writer Medoruma Shun grapples with this impasse.[94] The 1995 rape serves as a backdrop for "Hope," published on June 26, 1999, in the *Asahi Shimbun*, a major Japanese newspaper. In this notably *short* short story, the unnamed protagonist, an Okinawan young man, commits an unthinkable act of violence by abducting and strangling to death the young son of a US serviceman. He then kills himself via self-immolation. Between these two killings, we are provided a glimpse into what motivated the protagonist. The story is on one hand disturbingly and profoundly devoid of hope despite its title. Yet on the other hand, if we are willing to interrogate why nonviolent resistance has been understood to be the only morally and ethically defensible form of political resistance, then Medoruma's story offers some hope for challenging our understanding of what separates violence from nonviolence and of the presumption that we are inhabiting a space and time of "post-violence."

The protagonist of "Hope" radically mocks and challenges the inefficacy of peaceful protest in Okinawa. He mails anonymously this declaration to the office of his local newspaper: "*What Okinawa needs now is not demonstrated by thousands of people or rallies by tens of thousands but the death of one American child*" (21, emphasis in original). The comparison here of thousands of Okinawan lives to one American life would suggest an asymmetry in terms of numerical calculation. Yet what the protagonist's declaration amplifies is a more profound asymmetry—not in terms of the counting of lives but in the valuation of lives. The actions, decolonial aspirations, and curtailed lives of a thousand or indeed even an infinite number of Okinawans cannot ever be worth more than the value of the life of *one* American child. This is the calculus of US militarist settler imperialism. It is both the arithmetic and grammar driving violence on America's settler garrison. Moreover, as I elaborate in what follows, "peaceful" protest within a structure thoroughly saturated by violence also implies a profound asymmetry that can function to abet the colonizer's instrumental distinction between "violence" and "nonviolence." This monopoly, not only over violence itself but also over the very epistemological registers of what gets recognized as (legitimate or illegitimate) violence in the first place, is itself a kind of meta-violence.

Why kill the American *child*, as opposed to his parent(s)? If we examine the child as a figure or trope, there are two reigning qualities ascribed in particular to the white child: innocence and futurity. Racialized or colonized children, especially Black and Brown children, are not allowed to be "children" in this sense. In the face of hypercriminalization and genocidal practices, they are not allowed to enjoy the privileges of the presumption of innocence or be the precious bearers of futurity. These privileges, and not just qualities or characteristics in this context, can only condense on the figure of the white child. Medoruma's protagonist, in killing the white American child, radically challenges any claims of American nonculpability (innocence) and articulates a decolonial and antimilitarist aspiration of extinguishing continued US military presence (futurity) in Okinawa.

A photograph of the protagonist's anonymous declaration is printed on the front page of the newspaper, and the murder is the lead story on the six o'clock news. As to be expected, both Japanese and US officials express outrage and revulsion, which leads the protagonist to think to himself:

> That Okinawans—so docile, so meek—could use such tactics was something the bastards had never even imagined. Okinawans, were, after all, a people who followed their leaders and, at most, held "anti-war" or "antibase" rallies with polite protest marches. Even the ultraleft and radical factions staged, at most, "guerilla warfare" that caused no real harm and never out terrorism or kidnapping against people in power or mounted armed attacks. Okinawans were like maggots who clustered around the shit of land rents and subsidy monies splattered by the bases. And Okinawa was called a "peace-loving, healing island." It made me want to puke. (22)

Here, the protagonist interrogates the racialization of Okinawans, by both the United States and Japan, as precisely a peace-loving, nonmilitant, and docile "island" people.[95] He also calls to task landowners who lease land to the US military and thus directly profit from its continued presence in Okinawa. Base workers who receive subsidies are also implicated. The use of the organic metaphors of *maggots* and *shit* to describe economic dependence on the US military, what I have called the distorted auspices of the Department of Defense, amplifies the literal disfigurement of Okinawa effected by its contortion into America's settler garrison. The scarred landscape I analyzed earlier, the ecological harm done to the land, air, and waters of Okinawa, the militarized harm done to Okinawan multispecies life—these have compelled Okinawans to be "maggots" feeding off of a topography littered with "shit."

Despite the victory of the 1995 rape case, and a continuing history of vocal protest on multiple scales, the presence of the US military in Okinawa has remained stubbornly persistent.[96] Mass demonstrations against land seizures, rallies in the 1960s on a variety of issues, the 1987 human chain of approximately 25,000 people around Kadena Air Base, massive demonstrations following the 1995 rape incident—these all give witness to collective Okinawan aspirations for a demilitarized if not decolonized future. A notable movement was the so-called one-*tsubo* antimilitary landlords' campaign initiated in 1982. The campaign's goal is captured by its slogan, "Change the military bases into places for life and productivity!" Tsubo is a traditional Japanese measure equal to the size of two tatami mats (about 3.3 square meters or 35.52 square feet), and the campaign supported antibase landlords by buying and sharing one tsubo or less of their land.[97] This strategy increased the number of antibase landowners through the purchase of land just big enough on which to lie down. The campaign can thus be seen as a creative act of land redistribution, repossession, or collectivization. Moreover, in solidarity with other linked movements in areas similarly subjected to hypermilitarization, feminist movements in particular have called for demilitarization rather than realignment or relocation. Much of this collective movement work has been done through the formation of organizations and networks such as Okinawa Women Act against Military Violence (OWAAMV), the Okinawa Peace Network, and the East-Asia-US-Puerto Rico Women's Network against Militarism.[98] Building upon Black feminist Patricia Hill Collins's theorization of "interlocking oppressions," Kozue Akibayashi writes that the work of OWAAMV constitutes an *"island feminism,* which suggests a challenge to the interlocking of military violence and colonial violence in its fundamental critique and a challenge to patriarchy."[99]

In "Hope," the protagonist's utter disgust and total impatience with these and other means of peaceful protest lead to a conjoined homicide and suicide. He mutters to himself that *"Only the worst methods get results"* (22) and kills himself at the site of the rally where eighty thousand people gathered to protest the

1995 rape of the twelve-year-old girl. Calling the rally "farcical," and feeling no remorse or "even any deep emotion," he explains that, "Just as fluids in the bodies of small organisms that are forced to live in constant fear suddenly turn into poison, I had done what was natural and necessary for this island" (23). Such a logic of what is natural and necessary, along with another organic metaphor of how being forced to live in constant fear turns small organisms into poison, suggests that in order for Okinawa and Okinawans to live and thrive, the US military must die/leave. This formulation echoes Glen Coulthard's "Five Theses on Indigenous Resurgence and Decolonization" in the conclusion of his book *Red Skin, White Masks: Rejecting the Colonial Politics of Recognition*. In his second thesis, "Capitalism, No More!," Coulthard concludes that "for Indigenous nations to live, capitalism must die."[100] Medoruma's "Hope" suggests a similar relation of mutual exclusivity between Okinawa(ns) and the US military. As the agent of processes of violent dispossession, environmental contamination, and compelled dependence on militarized maldevelopment, the US military is literally and figuratively poisoning Okinawa and Okinawans. In order to reverse this antisymbiotic, poisonous, and warped ecosystem—in which the US military thrives by parasitically extracting labor, land, and resources from Okinawa—the US military must go away. In the face of a persistent refusal of a US military withdrawal, "Hope" hopes to instigate one through the protagonist's act of killing. His dramatic self-immolation, moreover, accelerates the already-poisoned condition of Okinawans.

"Hope" thus generates complex questions about violence, in particular the relationship between colonial violence and anticolonial counterviolence.[101] The US military possesses the global monopoly on "legitimate" violence, formally through the waging of war and less visibly through questionable impositions of metapolitical authority. Yet this violence obscures the violence of the prior and ongoing means through which the US military has come to monopolize the use of "legitimate" violence in the first place. This is to speak about the making, remaking, and astounding growth of the US military and its capability. It is to speak, in other words, about how the bases of empire, or settler garrisons like Okinawa, are made, viz, violent processes of land seizure, dispossession, displacement, and compelled dependency. It is to inquire into the conditions of possibility of US military capability and settler imperial projections of power. Within this context, the temporal demarcation between violence (a time of declared war) and postviolence (a time of negotiated peace) becomes blurred. For the US military's very existence, whether or not it is engaged in a campaign, operation, or war, is made possible by the violent processes I have just named. In this sense, just as, to invoke Patrick Wolfe again, we can think of settler colonialism as a structure and not merely an event, militarist settler imperial violence is a structure and not just an event.[102] And the "natural and necessary" outcome of this violence, "Hope" suggests, is counterviolence. As such, "Hope's" aesthetics of settler imperial failure not only amplifies the violence that is US militarist settler imperialism but also reveals that this violence in turn begets more violence. Yet these multiple violences should not be conflated.

Counterviolence brings to mind the biblical notion of "an eye for an eye," the principle of vengeance, revenge, or retaliation. In *Payback: Debt and the Shadow Side of Wealth*, Margaret Atwood reminds us that the word *revenge*, according to the Oxford English Dictionary, is derived from the Latin *revindicare*. And *revindicare* is derived from *vindicare*, which means to justify, rescue, liberate, or emancipate, as in liberating an enslaved person. Thus, "to revenge yourself upon someone is to reliberate yourself, because before doing the revenge, you aren't free. . . . The score that needs to be settled is a psychic score, and the kind of debt that can't be paid with money is a psychic debt. It's a wound to the soul."[103] Seen in this light, we might say that "Hope's" engagement with the ethics of counterviolence is an ethics of liberation. In turn, revenge is connected to figurative debt when we consider society's rationale for incarceration: that criminals need to "pay for their crimes," that is pay their "debt to society," via a prison sentence or execution. If society is the creditor in this scheme and criminals are the debtors, how exactly is society receiving a repayment of the debt from criminals by locking them up or executing them? Atwood argues that society receives a psychic payment that basically amounts to vengeance.[104] In this dominant debtor/creditor scheme, the protagonist in "Hope" would be the debtor or criminal for killing the child. Yet the protagonist prevents the creditor, in this instance the US military, from obtaining its payment or vengeance by killing himself.

"Hope" thus upends even as it reveals how a debtor/creditor scheme undergirds carcerality and the differential criminalization of various forms of violence. If we go back to the etymology of revenge, we see that even as dominant power structures write themselves into the story as the creditors who settle the score or exact vengeance by locking up or executing criminals, we can imagine otherwise. That is, who owes what to whom in this story? Who is the creditor? "Hope" imagines a world in which the criminal might actually be the creditor, the figure who is owed revenge or reliberation. This is a radical rewriting of the dominant debtor/creditor narrative and related carceral regimes through an aesthetics of settler imperial failure. Indeed, as I elaborated in Chapter 1, in a sleight of hand or role reversal, the colonizer becomes the creditor and the colonized becomes the debtor. "Hope" reverses this role reversal; it settles the score or corrects the sleight of hand by reminding us, to cite Fanon again, that "Europe is the literal creation of the Third World."[105]

Yet on the settler garrison of Okinawa, even when the structure of violence seems to have responded to mass protest, we witness again the stubborn intractability of that structure. In 1996, as a result of the vocal and massive protest following the rape of the twelve-year-old girl, the Special Action Committee on Okinawa Agreement was signed. It called for the relocation of Futenma, a US Marine Corps Air Station, to the Henoko district of Naga City. This entails a move from a congested area of central Okinawa to a pristine area in the north that is rich with coral reefs and the dugong, an endangered species protected under Japan's Cultural Preservation Act and an important Okinawan symbol of abundance. Ongoing protests delayed the construction of the Henoko base, and in 2012 the United States agreed to deploy elsewhere nine thousand of its eighteen thousand marines in Okinawa. In 2014, an international petition to cancel the planned base gained attention, and that same year 80 percent of Okinawans expressed their opposition to the construction, forming the All Okinawan Council (AOC).[106]

Yet preliminary base construction began in August 2014, with the then Japanese prime minister Abe announcing a year later in August 2015 the suspension of construction for one month because of rising tensions. In July 2017, Okinawa prefecture filed a lawsuit against the central government of Japan in another attempt to halt the base relocation, citing as the basis of the suit a permit that expired on March 31 allowing the breaking of the coral reef in Oura Bay at Henoko. Okinawa also filed an injunction to suspend the ongoing construction while litigation was pending. Suits have also been filed to protect the dugong, with the Ninth Circuit US Court of Appeals affirming in August 2017 the right of Okinawan citizens as well as US and Japanese conservation groups to sue the US military for failing to consider adequately the effects of the base construction on the dugong.[107] Though this favorable legal ruling might have offered a glimmer of hope, it is tempered by what Jacques Derrida calls the "force of law"—the violence that law itself can enact by way of foreclosing justice rather than delivering it.[108] Indeed, in December 2018, landfill work began at Camp Schwab, the marine base at Henoko, that will facilitate the relocation and closure of Marine Corps Air Station Futenma.[109] Then, in February 2019, in a first-of-its-kind prefecture-wide referendum on the issue, 72 percent of voters in Okinawa voted against the planned relocation. However, the referendum is legally nonbinding, and the central government of Japan is ignoring the referendum vote and proceeding with construction of the offshore replacement facility at Henoko beside Camp Schwab.[110]

More recently, in early 2021, volunteer excavators searching for the remains of the victims of the Battle of Okinawa still scattered within the soil of the site of the battle (the southern part of the island) demanded that Japan's defense ministry halt the clearing of that land. Soil from this land will be used for a reclamation project to build an offshore runway at the Henoko base. The volunteer excavators' demand came on the heels of a previous attempt to prevent the clearing of the land, a petition submitted to Prime Minister Suga in late 2020. This petition, signed by about five hundred family members who lost relatives in the Battle of Okinawa, requested that the soil from the battle's site not be used to build the base at Henoko. According to a 2016 law, the Japanese government is responsible for collecting the remains of soldiers and civilians who died in World War II.[111] Yet the use of the soil containing the bones of war victims is not only a violation of this law but an affront to the human dignity of the dead and of their survivors. As in the film *Parasite*, it is another instance of the postmortem temporality of a capitalist and militarist cruelty that follows some even into their deaths. It is a variety of what Laurel Turbin Mei-Singh calls "geographies of desecration."[112]

The recent Henoko protests constitute a local articulation of Okinawan Indigeneity within and inspired by two linked contexts: the local context of the Japanese government's formal recognition of the Ainu of Hokkaidō in northern Japan as an Indigenous group and the global context of what has emerged as a broader Indigenous rights movement, an important achievement of which was the passage of the United Nations Declaration on the Rights of Indigenous Peoples in 2007. Megumi Chibana observes that the ecological focus of the Henoko protests is an appeal not only for environmental protection but also for the cultural and spiritual connection that Okinawans have with Henoko. In other words, the appeal is an expression of a place-based Indigeneity resisting the disruption of "Okinawans' ontological relationship with nature and their guardians."[113] Recognizing that discussions of Indigeneity in Asia can be quite complex, and that there are disagreements over whether Indigeneity is an appropriate political tool for Okinawan self-determination, Chibana departs from an "identity politics" focus that privileges the question of who is Indigenous. Rather, the focus is on questions of local agency to investigate when, how, and to what extent Okinawans have taken up various aspects of Indigeneity to practice self-determination.[114] Thus, although what we name as *Indigenous* is a relatively new political subjectivity for Okinawans, this genealogy of Indigenous Okinawan place-based activism against colonial property regimes and US militarist settler imperialism stretches back to the immediate post–World War II era of the Isahama "Women's Appeal." Yet it was not until

1996 that Okinawan or Uchinānchu assertions of Indigeneity at the supranational level began taking place, largely with delegations to the UN Working Group on Indigenous Populations (WGIP). The Association of the Indigenous Peoples in the Ryūkyūs (AIPR) has been at the forefront in working to achieve the international recognition of Okinawans as Indigenous.[115]

From this discussion of how transpacific Okinawan literature grapples with America's settler garrison and its temporal and spatial exceptions, I turn now to transpacific South Korean literature and film and focus specifically on the military camptown. Japan colonized both Okinawa and Korea, yet unlike Okinawa, Korea was not "incorporated" into the Japanese nation-state as a prefecture, and the US military occupation of South Korea only lasted from 1945 until 1948. But soon thereafter, in 1950, the Korean War erupted, and US troops have been stationed permanently in South Korea since 1955. Crucially, as of this writing, wartime operational control of the South Korean military still remains under the command of the US military. Although it was agreed that the United States would return wartime operational command to the South Korean military in 2012, it has been postponed and is now scheduled to occur in 2022. That is, South Korea continues to exist in the distended shadow of US neocolonialism and is also home to a heavy US military presence.

South Korea: Militarized Sex Work and Debt Bondage

Bloodless (2017), a multiple award-winning VR experimental documentary film written and directed by diasporic Korean filmmaker Gina Kim, grapples with the complex aesthetics and ethics of how to represent egregious acts of sexual violence on the military camptown (*gijichon* in Korean). *Bloodless* deploys the technique of virtual reality to re-create the last living moments of Yun Keum Yi, a twenty-six-year-old US military camptown sex worker in South Korea who was brutally murdered by a US soldier in 1992.[116] A US-South Korea coproduction with a transnational crew, *Bloodless* was shot on location in Dongducheon in Gyeonggi Province, home to a US military base forty kilometers north of Seoul where the murder took place.[117] Running twelve minutes in length, the immersive experience of virtual reality places the viewer into the camptown's alleys. The film opens with a day shot. We see a dog pick up a bone and drop it after hearing the off-camera sound of shattering glass. We wonder what has just happened when the camera cuts to a silent intertitle, small white text on a uniformly black background providing the film's framing of sorts: "Since the Korean War (1950–53), US military bases have spawned almost 100 'camp towns,' often squalid places inhabited by an estimated one million sex workers from Korea and other parts of Asia. The crimes perpetrated here by US servicemen and others impact those who live on the margins of Korean society."

We are then transported to the entrance of the Dongducheon camptown, euphemistically called a "Special Tourism Zone for Foreigners." We feel helpless, unable to control any of the action even as we are immersed in it. Yet unlike traditional two-dimensional films, we can control our own gaze by focusing on any part of the 360-degree environment. This feeling of total control and simultaneous lack of control is at once utterly immersive and disorienting. Day turns into night. We see the dimly lit alleys and businesses, mostly rundown bars and clubs of the camptown. But we cannot see her, Yun Keum Yi. We are still left wondering, with a sense of foreboding as if in a horror film, of what might transpire next and whether the sound of shattering glass we heard earlier is significant. We begin to hear her footsteps and try to turn in the direction of their sound even as the 360-degree experience of VR and the sonic form of echoing effects make it difficult to detect that direction. We finally catch a glimpse of her, in high heels and a black dress, only to have her disappear. She is frustratingly and spookily out of our grasp. She is a ghostly and haunting presence evading our full view, a "digital uncanny."[118] Yet suddenly, she appears right up close, so that we cannot but see her, and she goes through us. We turn around, and there she is, staring us down and sighing deeply. She disappears yet again, and we find ourselves in a cramped, claustrophobic motel room less than seventeen square feet (1.6 square meters), with barely any furniture. We see empty Coke and beer bottles scattered on the yellow floor and a full-length mirror. Slowly, we begin to see what appears to be blood seeping out from the burgundy floral-patterned blanket on the floor. At some point, reflected in the full-length mirror, we see that the spreading pool of blood on the floor is coming from a body. Yet we cannot see the whole body; we see only a part of a leg. The buzzing of the overhead fluorescent lights that we hear is interrupted by the sound of the woman's footsteps and then the return of the sound of shattering glass that we heard at the opening of the film.

Yun Keum Yi's murdered and mutilated body is an obscured and oblique appearance, visible only partially as a reflected image in the mirror. *Bloodless* only hints at the details of her gruesome murder. Yet our bearing witness to the violence of her death is at once inescapable and disorienting because we are immersed, trapped, as it were, in the claustrophobic confines of her tiny room through the medium of virtual reality filmmaking. At the same time, *Bloodless* also gestures to the impossibility of bearing witness in a full and fully ethical manner because the formal device of VR is such that it allows us as viewers a certain degree of control in where to focus our gaze. The reflected image in the mirror of Yun Keum Yi's murdered body might thus escape our gaze altogether. Why this obscured, oblique, and spectral appearance of Yun's body, which is at once a kind of disappearance that immersively places the viewer at the scene of the crime?

I begin this discussion of US bases and camptowns in South Korea with *Bloodless* because it foregrounds the vexed problematic of the "enforced visibility" of camptown sex workers through a vertiginous revisioning of the brutal violence of the camptown. Identified simply as "the woman" in the credits of *Bloodless*, Yun was certainly not the first camptown sex worker to be killed, yet her case was made to be hypervisible. It garnered support from a diverse range of organizations that formed the "Committee on the Murder of Yun Geum-i by American Military in Korea," which later led to the formation of the "National Campaign for Eradication of Crime by U.S. Troops in Korea."[119] This took place within the context of growing critiques among South Koreans throughout the 1980s and into the 1990s of both their own government and the United States. Anti-imperialist sentiment and desire condensed on the violated and murdered body of Yun. In an unprecedented move, the American GI who committed the murder was tried in South Korean courts as opposed to the standard practice of virtual impunity effected by the rights of extraterritoriality enjoyed by the US military via its SOFA with South Korea. As Grace M. Cho observes, this case marked a turning point. The camptown sex worker, pejoratively called *yanggongju* ("Western princess") and exiled to the shadows as a figure of national shame symbolizing South Korea's neocolonized status vis-à-vis the United States, was welcomed home as the nation's daughter. Yet the image of Yun's violated body, graphic and overcirculated, turned into a "transnational macrospectacle" even as her case became a rallying point for diasporic Korean feminists as well as anti-American activists in South Korea.[120] Mindful of this problematic, filmmaker Gina Kim refuses to circulate Yun's violated body yet again. With heightened attentiveness to this representational, ethical, and political conundrum, Kim revisits the 1992 murder through her haunting virtual reality film in order to draw attention to the enduring presence of the US military, and of military violence, in South Korea. Although the spectacular circulation of the image of the gendered racial violence inflicted upon Yun's body is unique, the very fact of that violence is not, for US military bases and attendant camptowns in South Korea still number close to one hundred.

While a first-year college student in South Korea, Kim took part in the mass protests demanding that the United States Forces in Korea (USFK) extradite the US soldier so that he could undergo a trial in the South Korean court system.

Eventually, he was convicted and sentenced to fifteen years in prison by a South Korean court. Kim's director's statement on *Bloodless* relates:

> We put posters on walls and marched while spreading flyers to civilians. The graphic and disturbing image of the crime scene was printed on each flyer. Every time I saw Yun Keum Yi's brutally mutilated body being endlessly reproduced in posters and flyers, I saw her dignity being once again destroyed. For 25 years, I have struggled to find a way to make a film about this tragic incident. But I kept coming up against the fact that I could not cinematically represent the story without exploiting the image and thereby reproducing the original violence itself. But with VR, the viewer is no longer a passive spectator, who can take voyeuristic pleasure from a spectacle in front of them (and at a distance). Upon realizing the potential of the VR, I came up with a way to tell the same violent story, without showing and exploiting the image of her.[121]

Kim's deployment of VR to amplify the gendered racial and sexual violence inflicted by the US military without spectacularizing that violence and the South Korean woman's murdered body is complex. For it turns out that the US military played a significant role in funding the development of VR technology because of the potential for its military applications. Indeed, the US military has been using VR both for training recruits and for treating PTSD.[122] Kim is thus attempting to "weaponize" a technological weapon developed by the US military against that very military.

Though the potential of VR technology has been more commonly discussed and deployed for its ability to produce immersive experiences of fantastical entertainment or consumption (such as games, shopping, and real estate) or travel to desired locations throughout the world, there is a parallel discussion of VR's potential as an "empathy machine" that exceeds conventional narrative forms.[123] Indeed, the tagline for *Bloodless* is "Experience what cannot be said," and for Kim VR means a "completely new way of creating empathy."[124] Her ethics of representation are such that for over twenty-five years, she grappled with the challenge of how to tell Yun's story in a nonexploitative way that upturns the voyeurism of the cinematic medium. As Kim relates in an interview, "We really wanted to be truthful to the actual event, but at the same time we aren't simply re-enacting the violence . . . as a matter of fact there is absolutely no violence in my film."[125] For her, VR technology makes possible this inescapably immersive yet highly oblique or inferred representation of an unimaginably gruesome violation of a woman's body and life. She observes that *Bloodless* is thus not a documentary but rather a poetic and indirect rendition of this violation.[126] This nongeneric form, this aesthetics of settler imperial failure, allows viewers to "experience," as opposed to view voyeuristically from a distance, the pain of others not through sentimental identification but as witnesses.[127] Yun's haunting and disorienting footsteps in that dimly lit alley—a carefully produced stereophonic soundscape of "de-spatialized sound"—sensorially enjoin us to reckon with the continuing presence of the US military in South Korea, a reckoning with the violence of that presence.[128] *Bloodless* thus works against the "enforced visibility" of camptown sex workers, even as it is compelled by a desire to bring attention to the pressing issue of militarized sexual violence and murder. The film also enjoins us to ask: What do we owe Yun Keum Yi and others like her? Kim gestures to a response in explaining what motivates her work: "The image on the flyer still haunts me, motivating me to return to these *non-sovereign spaces* and the many women exiled there whose voices have yet to be heard."[129]

If *Bloodless* thus provides a complex rendering of the violence that occurs within such nonsovereign spaces long after their proliferation and management via the transpacific masculinist compact, Ahn Junghyo's celebrated *Silver Stallion: A Novel of Korea* (1990) offers a critical genealogy of US military presence in South Korea by focusing on the early days of the establishment of what became an extensive and regulated camptown system.[130] The original 1986 Korean-language publication was translated by the author himself, and Soho Press in the United States published it in 1990. This transpacific text depicts what becomes of the residents of Kumsan, a rural farming village, as the Korean War (1950–53) encroaches ever deeper into their daily lives. The village is confronted with the arrival of sex workers who serve UN and US soldiers. In highlighting the agency of these women and their collisions with traditional patriarchal authority in the village, *Silver Stallion* reveals the early stages of US imperial violence and militarism in South Korea, or transformations that would produce what Seungsook Moon calls South Korea's "militarized modernity."[131] This would witness a proliferation of US bases and attendant camptowns, effectively colonized spaces. On this spatial exception of the settler garrison, US authority, a metapolitical authority, has the power to negate local South Korean sovereignty by defining the scope of law and politics.

Silver Stallion reveals the early makings of the infrastructure and personnel that would come to constitute the vast network of camptowns in South Korea. In this earlier era, camptown sex workers are not subjected to government regulation or surveillance, leaving room for a certain entrepreneurial agency and initiative. Early in the novel, Ollye, a young widow with two children, is raped by US soldiers. Subjected to vicious village gossip, she is treated as an outcast, a defiled woman whose experience of sexual violence is considered a source of shame. Old Hwang, the county chief, embodies this patriarchal stance. He could not "visit Ollye and offer her words of consolation. He could not free himself from the thought that, victim or not, she was a dirty woman. Loss of feminine virtue, under any circumstance, was the most profound shame for a woman . . ." (67–68).

In narrating how Ollye later becomes a sex worker and staging clashes between Old Hwang and the new women who arrive, *Silver Stallion* exposes how the intersection of sexual violence and sex work within a militarized context generates complex negotiations of circumscribed choice and agency. Soon after Ollye's rape, the village residents are confronted with the arrival of "strange" women, whom they learn are sex workers serving UN and US soldiers. Ahn writes:

> What the Yankee wives had said proved to be true. The Yankee wives were on the move constantly, traveling up and down the country with the *bengkos* [big noses]; whenever the soldiers moved to a new place, they would pack up and migrate with their "steady customers" or "temporary husbands." They were scouting for their new business sites near the base the Americans were about to build on Cucumber Island. That afternoon and the next morning, more "U.N. ladies" came across the river looking for a house to let, but not a single farmer would discuss the matter with them. The villagers respected Old Hwang's instructions. Besides, nobody wanted the indecent women, who associated with the rapist soldiers, to live next door. (107)

Sister Serpent, a sex worker who had already purchased a house in the village before the villagers had been warned, has a confrontation with Old Hwang: "'What the hell does this old cock think he is anyway?' said Sister Serpent, not a bit intimidated. 'An MP or something? What right did you have to tell us to stay away from this place? I bought this house with my own money, and nobody is going to drive me out of my own house. You think you can treat me like dirt because I'm a whore, but, you fucking bastard, you'll see that you have it all wrong'" (111). Refusing to represent these women as abject victims, the novel instead emphasizes their acts of survival, persistence, and defiance of patriarchal authority in a rapidly changing landscape. By amplifying the entrepreneurial energy and agency of women like Sister Serpent, Ahn exposes an early moment in what would later congeal as a highly regulated, surveilled, and institutionalized system of camptown sex work. It is one that is yet to be captured by the metapolitical authority of US militarist settler imperial power.

Yet within the novel, we begin to see the contours of what would soon become the exceptional space of the camptown:

> Omaha was not the only sign that was put up in the islet. Somebody erected a sign in the shape of a milepost that, like the Omaha sign, carried both in English and Korean the words "Texas Town," at the entrance to another village a few hundred yards distant from Camp Omaha's main gate. This second village was not constructed by the *bengko* [big nose] soldiers, but by dozens of Korean carpenters and workers brought in from the town. With broken planks from ammunition boxes, tin plates from beer cans and sturdy cardboard from C-ration cartons, a team of two or three carpenters worked a miracle, creating one shanty a day. Built wall-to-wall, the board shacks on the barren slope looked like one big beehive. As the shanties were completed one after another the Yankee wives, carrying big bulging suitcases, came to Texas Town. Soon the shanty town was fully occupied by the prostitutes. (109–10)

Here, we see in "Texas Town" an improvised prototype of what would rapidly become institutionalized by the early 1960s as the camptown, adjacent to the bases' "America Towns."[132] Though we might say that military supplies and rations are creatively "repurposed" as building materials for shanties, their overall function of ultimately serving the US military remains the same. The "miracle" of the ultrarapid construction of the shanties, their appearance one after another, bespeaks what would fast become the metastasizing proliferation of US bases and camptowns in South Korea. Indeed, as Katharine H. S. Moon writes, "sex among allies," or the buying and selling of sex between Americans and Koreans, has been a staple of US-South Korea international relations since the Korean War and the permanent US troop presence in South Korea since 1955.[133]

In what has become a sine qua non of US-South Korea relations, camptown sex work in South Korea is sponsored, negotiated, and regulated by the US and South Korean governments. Camptown sex workers have been viewed as occupying the role of "cultural ambassadors" in their interactions with American servicemembers.[134] Although sex work is prohibited and illegal in South Korea, the promotion of regulated camptown sex work has been the effective exception to that rule.[135] Korean nationals, except registered sex workers, are legally barred from camptown clubs and bars catering to US soldiers. Moreover, as I have related, camptowns and bases are governed under extraterritoriality, rendering them as virtual US territories where South Korean sovereignty ceases to exist.[136] Indeed, as Johnson writes, "America's foreign military enclaves, though structurally, legally, and conceptually different from colonies, are themselves something like micro-colonies in that they are completely beyond the jurisdiction of the occupied nation." Extraterritoriality, negotiated via SOFAs, is a modern legacy of the nineteenth-century imperialist practice vis-à-vis China, extracted at gunpoint because white men refused to submit to what they perceived to be the barbarity of Chinese law.[137]

In addition to being a significant feature of US-South Korea geopolitical relations, the influx of American dollars generated by camptown sex work has benefited South Korea's development, economy, and modernity. Even as this is symptomatic of US militarist settler imperial domination over South Korea, it has in turn contributed to South Korea's relatively privileged subimperial status within Asia, especially vis-à-vis Southeast Asia. Yet the singular and uncritical focus on the "miracle" of South Korea's ultrarapid economic development, called the "Miracle on the Han River," elides its contradictions and violently uneven contours and effects. Jin-kyung Lee writes that two dimensions have been overlooked in studies of South Korean development—sexuality and race, and in particular what she calls the "proletarianization" of sexuality and race. Race, gender, sexuality, class, and Korean ethnonationality articulate with one another in the context of a transnational racial hierarchy in ways that generate a class of workers specifically for productive and socially reproductive labors.[138] Camptown sex work is a particular type of this kind of marginal transnational proletarian labor, and Lee argues moreover that it is a necropolitical labor insofar as it is labor extracted from lives that are disposable or condemned to death. In this instance, any "fostering" of life that occurs is already conditioned by disposability and is limited to serving labor demands. The coercive economic, physical, and psychological conditions that camptown sex workers are subjected to exist on a continuum with more overt forms of sexual violence. The disturbing frequency with which camptown sex workers are murdered "can be viewed as a material extension of [the] figurative violence" of the symbolic erasure or murder of the sex worker's subjectivity at once required by and resulting from the commercialization of sex.[139] Indeed, as I observed about the murder of Yun Keum Yi, while the attention it drew might have been unique, the fact of the murder itself of a disposable gendered racial, sexualized, and proletarianized laboring body was unremarkable. For as Lee argues, necropolitical laborers are already condemned to death, so their actual death is simply the material extension of that prefigured and figurative death.

If America's settler garrison as a spatial exception is thus the site of a proletarianized labor at once gendered, racial, sexualized, and necropolitical that is made possible by the deprivation of local sovereignty and submission to the metapolitical authority of the United States, the attendant temporal exception of debt imperialism deprives women of their futures. I now turn to an analysis of the camptown's relationship to this temporal exception of debt imperialism by focusing on two Asian American documentary films, *Camp Arirang* (1995) and *The Women Outside: Korean Women and the U.S. Military* (1995). I begin with a consideration of the fraught power dynamics as well as the politics and ethics of representation in documentary films such as these. While Kim's challenge leading up to the making of *Bloodless*, as I discussed earlier, was how to represent the dead (how not to recirculate the image of Yun Keum Yi's gruesomely violated body in a voyeuristic way that would itself be a form of violence), the challenge in *Camp Arirang* and *The Women Outside* is how to represent the living. These films attempt to center the voices and perspectives of camptown sex workers themselves, interspersed with talking head commentary from academics, former members of the US military, and activists. As I demonstrate, the very problematics and challenges of representation generated by these films are themselves an index of the power of the transpacific masculinist compact between the US and South Korean governments in creating the exceptional space of the camptown where sex work is facilitated, regulated, and legal yet illicit and morally condemned everywhere else.

What does it mean to attempt to give voice to camptown sex workers, some of whom do not wish to disclose their identities or even to be captured by the filmmakers at all? Although militarized sex work is a staple feature of US-South Korea geopolitical relations, the women who are compelled to provide that labor are judged and cast aside by South Korean society. Indeed, as Eun-Shil Kim writes, even though camptown sex workers are Korean women, "their bodies are deterritorialized as Korean." Within Korea's patriarchal system, the woman's body is obtained through the male family member—the father, husband, or son. So according to this system, "the bodies of women who sell their bodies to American soldiers in exchange for money are no longer the territory of the Korean nation or race."[140] Thus cast outside of traditional patriarchal norms, they undergo a civil or social death; it is a deterritorialization from the Korean nation that results in the loss of civil protection and social recognition. Yet as laboring bodies within the spatial exception that is the camptown, they are subjected to its governmentality as brokered through the transpacific masculinist compact between the South Korean and US governments. This governmentality comes in the form of surveillance, mandatory checks for sexually transmitted diseases, and often a debt bondage labor system. In this way, deterritorialization from the Korean nation via the politics of heteropatriarchal and neo-Confucian respectability is conjoined with a reterritorialization to the camptown via the metapolitical authority of US militarist settler imperialism.

This double bind, as it were, of deterritorialization and reterritorialization is particularly onerous when we consider the diplomatic significance of camptown sex work in US-South Korea geopolitical relations and its multiscalar economic significance to the nation, to the laboring women's families, and to the women themselves. Moreover, the post-1965 Korean American population, though constituted in significant part by women who married US soldiers and sponsored the migration of multiple family members, would rather keep buried the conditions of its own making. This is also an unacknowledged debt, for it is, as Cho writes, the shame of the "diaspora of camptown."[141] Yet still, faced with the reduction of US troop presence in the 1970s, camptown establishments began sending their "madams" and sex workers to military sites within the domestic United States (heavily concentrated in the South) via brokered marriages with US servicemen. By the 1980s, this Korean American sex trade spread to other parts of the United States, with militarized sex work proliferating and taking form as illicit massage parlor businesses catering to local troops. In this way, just as there is a "diaspora of camptown," the camptown itself is what Yuri W. Doolan calls a "transpacific phenomenon."[142]

In her trenchant analysis of *Camp Arirang* and *The Women Outside*, Laura Hyun Yi Kang foregrounds these fraught issues of representation and representability. What are the problematics of Korean American women attempting to represent Korea and Korean women (in particular a group of impoverished and subaltern women) through the medium of expository documentary film?[143] Kang highlights the vexed contours of the documentary form as a seemingly unmediated yet heavily mediated form, compounded by the dynamics of uneven power/knowledge in the "presumed urgency" to represent exploited and silenced groups who putatively "cannot represent themselves." She argues that even as these films can be seen as anti-imperialist articulations of a transnational feminist solidarity, the productive force of such significant Korean American critiques of US imperialism, immigration policy, and racialized and sexualized labor regimes is attenuated by what is often a problematic representation of Korean sex workers. These women appear in the films as the most visible bodies on display and as the object of analysis and commentary by "expert" talking heads.[144] Ultimately, Kang contends that rather than a wholesale refusal to represent, the challenge is to not efface the material specificities and differences of positionality, power, and privilege between the documentarian and the documented. This would "temper the impulse toward any grandiose, homogenizing and disembodied claims about and on behalf of those Korean women sex workers."[145]

Mindful of Kang's important critique, what interests me about *Camp Arirang* and *The Women Outside* is precisely not any grandiose claims they might make about and on behalf of camptown sex workers, but specifically what the films amplify about regimes of debt in the spatial exception of the camptown created by the transpacific masculinist compact between the US and South Korean governments. This compact, moreover, though formally bilateral, is driven by the power of US militarist settler imperialism. Indeed, the significance of the imposition of regimes of debt in relation to complex questions about volition and agency were highlighted in a recent South Korean court case in which dozens of former camptown sex workers filed a lawsuit against the South Korean government, demanding that the government acknowledge its significant role in creating, managing, and regulating a vast network of camptown sex work. In 2017, the Central District Court in Seoul issued a landmark ruling that, though falling short of the admission and apology that the women sought, did recognize that the South Korean government had acted illegally and in violation of human rights in detaining camptown sex workers and forcing them to undergo treatment for sexually transmitted diseases during the 1960s and 1970s. The government was ordered to pay each of the fifty-seven plaintiffs the equivalent of $4,240 as compensation for physical and psychological damage. After the ruling, one of the plaintiffs, sixty-two-year-old Park Young-ja, highlighted how the women had effectively been conscripted as "comfort women" for the US military and held in a state of debt bondage: "They say we walked into *gijichon* [the camptown] on our own, but we were cheated by job-placement agencies and were held in debt to pimps. I was only a teenager and I had to receive at least five G.I.s every day with no day off. When I ran away, they caught and beat me, raising my debt."[146] This case highlights the "transpacific complicity" of the South Korean government and represents a limited victory for the plaintiffs. Yet in doing so, it simultaneously amplifies the asymmetrical power relations undergirding the transpacific masculinist compact between South Korea and the United States. In this instance, the US government, or the agent of US militarist settler imperialism, was not and could not be named as a codefendant.

Camp Arirang prominently features Yun Ja Kim, who was a camptown sex worker and "madam" for twenty-five years. In 1987, a friend paid off her procurer ("pimp"), allowing her to pursue a new life as a missionary. As the film relates, unlike others who prefer anonymity, Kim was willing to discuss life as a camptown sex worker. She and the filmmakers go to America Town at Kunsan Air Base, where she used to live and work. Here, Kim recollects the stress caused by the system of debt bondage: "I had to work at the club till I paid off my debts. Whenever American GIs came in, I urged them to buy drinks. Every sale counts towards the debts. It's very stressful. So whether giving them massages or nuzzling up close, we have to persuade American GIs to buy alcohol. We only get

20 percent of any business we make." In *The Women Outside*, it is explained that while many women are kidnapped and held against their will, many more are held by debt.[147] And as revealed by Katharine H. S. Moon in *Camp Arirang*, the lives of camptown sex workers are circumscribed by a system of debt bondage. In some cases, even before their arrival at the clubs, they have been set up with a room, furniture, and clothing by the club owners. This inaugurates not only debt but a system of debt bondage insofar as the debts for these living expenses accrue at such a rate, thousands of dollars, that they cannot ever be fully repaid in most instances. It is a vicious cycle in which the women are then compelled to keep working at the clubs indefinitely. They are compelled to repay their debt through the threat or actual use of violence. "Slicky boys" or gangster figures are hired by "madams" to rough up the women if they do not pay back their debt.

Although the United States can reserve for itself the exceptional temporality of debt imperialism, of not having to pay back its enormous and escalating debt, the homogeneous time of repayment is imposed on camptown sex workers. This disciplinary temporality of debt bondage strengthens the indispensability of camptown sex work to US militarism in South Korea, yet camptown women themselves are dispensable. They are treated as disposable bodies, the raw material that can easily be replaced. They are, in other words, performing necropolitical labor. South Korea's uneven development has produced a population of women who are compelled into camptown sex work by financial exigencies like debt and the need to support their families. Contending with both the spatial exception that is the camptown and the temporal exception of debt imperialism, these women are disparaged as *yanggalbo* ("Western whore") and yanggongju ("Western princess"). Yet as I have observed, they have played a pivotal role in US-South Korea relations and have significantly made possible the post–World War II migration of Koreans to the United States through the sponsorship of multiple family members.[148]

Even as this Korean diasporic cinematic archive reveals the force of deprived sovereignties and futures, it also contains an aesthetics of settler imperial failure that gestures to alternative spaces and times that such deprivations cannot fully obliterate. In *Camp Arirang*, we see Yun Ja Kim's three-room house, which she shares with her mother. Kim has converted this house into a center for Amerasian children, the True Love Mission.[149] These children, the mixed-race offspring of US military personnel, largely abandoned by their fathers, are in many cases prevented from attending school because of discrimination.[150] At True Love Mission, they receive an alternative education, learning English from student volunteers. While some viewers might be critical of and find disturbing the Christian religiosity as well as the "claiming of America" taught in Yun Ja Kim's lessons, we can also view this pedagogy and site of alternative collective caretaking as constituting a time beyond compelled debt repayment and a space beyond compelled deference to US metapolitical authority. Indeed, in a reversal of the debtor/creditor relation, the children are taught that they are entitled to a repayment of the debt that America and their American fathers owe them. That is, they have been left behind by their fathers, and they are taught to desire a future in America, not South Korea. This is a pedagogy of another trajectory of debt repayment.

In giving visibility to the children who have been left behind and in holding their absent fathers accountable, *Camp Arirang* calls to mind the camptown as a space of what Lee calls an "imperial translocality." This imperial translocality is constituted by movements of people: the continuous influx and outflow of US soldiers, the migration of Korean military brides to the United States, the return of these brides to South Korea in cases of divorce, the Amerasian children left behind in South Korea by US servicemen, and the migration of these children to the United States as adoptees. The camptown as an imperial translocality is also constituted by the social relations and networks generated by these movements of people.[151] Indeed, as I have written elsewhere, Korean American novels such as Heinz Insu Fenkl's *Memories of My Ghost Brother* (1996) and Nora Okja Keller's *Fox Girl* (2002) give narrative form to this imperial translocality and to the "diaspora of camptown."[152]

Rather than unquestioningly accepting the negation of South Korean sovereignty, Yun Ja Kim expresses a desire to challenge the seat of US sovereign power itself, the US Congress. She states, "Someday, if God leads me to US Congress, I'll tell them about camptown women and children. This situation has continued for more than fifty years and it's still happening today." What might at first appear to be the expression of a naïve hope is instead an act of powerful testimony and bearing witness. It also reminds viewers that even the US Congress is not fully cognizant of the Pentagon's activities on America's settler garrison. Moreover, an act of resistance that began at the intimate scale of Yun Ja Kim's home through the transformation of that private sphere into the site of an alternative inhabitation of space and time generates a transpacific imaginary, a "scaling up" to the transnational and global scale of bearing witness before the US Congress. This multiscalar enactment and imagining gesture to a different kind of politics, akin to what Sasha Davis conceives of as a project whose aim is toward "expanding circles of affinity" and a departure from a politics based on hegemony and, I would add, identity.[153] Kim chooses to focus on providing an alternative education for children while their mothers are at work at the camptown, even though she herself is not a mother. By way of helping other women who are mothers, she also imagines a different future by caring for the generational bearers of that future. This expanded ethic of care, teaching, and collective parenting, as well as this transgenerational scope, creates a circle of affinity not based on circumscribed identity, consanguinity, or self-interest but on the protracted presence of the US military in South Korea. If the US network of bases proliferates globally, and if the projection of US militarist settler imperial power threatens to respect no bounds, then the Venn diagram of circles of affinity is overwhelmingly constituted by unions and intersections. These convergences point toward not only the global scale of US militarist settler imperialism and its concentration in Asia and the Pacific but also the relationalities, responsibilities, and resistances that it has in turn generated.

Thus, while we see Yun Ja Kim escaping debt bondage and thriving, I close this chapter by observing that many like her do not share the same fate. Indeed, the haunting presences and absences of camptown women make America's settler garrison a site of ungrieved and ungrievable loss, both of the women's actual lives in some cases and in others of lives that might have thrived beyond compelled dependence on militarized maldevelopment and subjection to debt bondage, biopolitical surveillance, and sexual violence. This is another sense in which the space and time of America's settler garrison is exceptional, where a loss cannot be grieved *as* a loss. In the next chapter, I turn to the POW camp, focusing on how Ha Jin's novel *War Trash* generates a theorization of the POW camp as another spatial exception through which US militarist settler imperial power constitutes and renovates itself.

3. THE POW CAMP: *Waging Psychological Warfare and a New Settler Frontier*

A November 1951 *New York Times* article entitled "Chinese Prisoners Shift Allegiance" bears this subtitle: "Many at Huge Compound off Korea Are Reported to Have Renounced Communism."[1] The "huge compound" referred to in this news report on the Korean War (1950–53) is a POW camp, located on Koje Island off the southern tip of the Korean Peninsula and under United Nations (UN) Command. The article goes on to report that many of the POWs, captives from the Communist armies of China and North Korea, have branded themselves with "Down with Communism" tattoos. Other marks of anti-Communist sentiment as revealed by the article include blood-signed pleas not to be repatriated back to Communist China and North Korea and the waving of the anti-Communist flag of the Nationalists led by Chiang Kai-shek in Taiwan along with that of the UN. Anti-Communist sentiment is also displayed through a pair of statues: a statue of an angry Chinese POW "hammering away at the head of a fallen figure of Mae Tse-tung, leader of Communist China," standing close to another statue of a Chinese soldier shaking hands with an American GI. The article raises a constellation of questions. A key question is this: What explains the seemingly high number of renouncements of Communism and a desire not to be repatriated back home among the Chinese and North Korean soldiers? In other words, what explains the high number of anti-Communist would-be defectors? Also, what explains the high levels of tattooing if it was an essentially taboo practice both in China and Korea due to the Confucian belief that body decorations are impious or unfilial? According to Confucian thought, marking the skin was defilement and a show of disrespect to the ancestors who provided it. Thus, tattoos in the early 1950s were relatively rare and strongly associated with criminals or the branding of vassals by their feudal lords.[2]

The article does not itself pose these questions, yet it hints at the answers, if only obliquely and unintentionally, and only through what it obscures. The depiction of the Koje Island POW camp, its activities, and its treatment of prisoners reads like a Cold War anti-Communist, pro-American propaganda piece. We learn that most of the POWs in the camp "live better than they did in the Communist army. They are warmly dressed, they are learning to read and many attend trade schools. Their rice diets have been adding one pound each month on the average prisoner." In addition to learning trades, they are learning history and the principles of democracy and citizenship from a group of Taiwanese and Korean civilian instructors under the guidance of chief instructor John Benben of Chicago, head of the Civil Information and Education section of the camp. Benben comments that the instruction received by the POWs was "sowing seeds of independent thinking." After what essentially amounts to a cataloging of such "positive" aspects of the camp, the article closes with a brief mention of a possible negative, only to contain it in the end. There is mention of open clashes between political factions and "some riots" in the camp compounds, but that generally "'the climate'" of the camp is "said to be well within bounds."

This article reports on the early moments in what would become a significant issue in the armistice negotiations of the Korean War in particular and the ideological front of the Cold War more broadly. Although the "cessation of hostilities" came in July 1951, the Korean War armistice agreement was not signed until July 1953 because of protracted negotiations precisely over the issue of exchanging POWs. In the absence of a military victory, the United States adopted the strategy of prolonging the negotiations so that it could gain greater credibility and capture "hearts and minds" toward a "substitute victory."[3] Indeed, in early 1951 the National Security Council (NSC) pledged to "encourage and induce" as many defections as possible.[4] By early 1952, as the military conflict stalemated, both sides increased their efforts in winning the ideological or propaganda front of the war by capturing greater shares of world opinion. As part of this effort, the armistice negotiators at Panmunjom, with President Truman's backing, formally proposed what they called a "voluntary repatriation" program. Though ostensibly made available in order to give would-be defectors the option of evading harsh treatment by their Communist governments should they choose repatriation, "voluntary repatriation" was a euphemistic moniker for what was essentially a program of compelled or coerced defection deploying methods of psychological warfare and violence that began before the formal announcement of the program in early 1952. Thus, the *New York Times* article's brief mention of open clashes between political factions and riots hints at but ultimately obscures both the level of extreme violence in the POW camp on Koje Island as well as the significant metapolitical role that the United States played in abrogating the rights of POWs to ensure as many defections as possible.

"Voluntary repatriation," it turns out, was hardly voluntary. This was a significant aspect of the Korean War and an important earlier moment in America's development and deployment of psychological warfare. Yet for the most part, Korean War historiography, with a few notable exceptions, has hitherto shed insufficient light on this significance.[5] Charles S. Young writes that "many accounts do not give any details of the POW issue, attributing the armistice delay to some murky Oriental/Red obstinance."[6] For the purposes of this chapter, the *New York Times* article is revealing precisely because of what it *fails* to reveal through a structuring absence. It is not difficult to read the article critically, against the grain, and conclude that the UN Command, effectively a US Command, was essentially indoctrinating the POWs with anti-Communist, pro-American propaganda via history and civics lessons. It is also not difficult to wonder if the article is downplaying the seriousness of the "open clashes" and "riots" between political factions. Yet in claiming that the "climate" of the camp is "said to be well within bounds," the article begs the question of precisely what those bounds are. What are such bounds or thresholds within the physical bounds of a particular space such as a POW camp?

In this chapter, I grapple with this question of bounds or thresholds through an analysis of how Ha Jin's transpacific novel *War Trash* (2004) critically magnifies two linked bounds: the figurative psychological bounds of human subjectivity in the production of the temporal exception of an indebted subjectivity, and the literal bounds of the POW camp as a spatial exception. Moreover, in dramatizing the violations that made possible the US practice of psychological warfare, and a POW revolt against such violations within the camp, *War Trash*'s aesthetics of settler imperial failure reveals the multiple fictions or "beautifying practice[s]" that US metapolitical authority requires.[7] In terms of the psychological bounds of human subjectivity and the temporality of debt, *War Trash* reveals that insofar as the goal of the "voluntary repatriation" program was to increase the number of anti-Communist defectors, that is to say refugees, it was a mechanism for the production of indebted subjectivities vis-à-vis the anti-Communist host nations that would welcome these refugees. As I have observed, this is a figurative or affective debt that cannot ever be fully repaid. For the trope of the "gift of freedom" is a "beautifying practice" that alchemically transfigures the violence of US militarist settler imperial intervention into a beneficent liberation from the putative evils of Communism. Psychological warfare and attendant fears of Chinese Communist "brainwashing" of American POWs breathe new life into the US settler imperial state's foundational tropes. Human subjectivity, interiority, and ideological affiliation are conceived as the new "frontier" for American expansion, much like the opening of successive new parts of territory for settler acquisition on what became the United States. The "turning" of human subjectivity and loyalty would in turn enable the Cold War expansion of a literal territorial sphere of US influence. This form of psychological warfare, euphemistically called the "voluntary repatriation" program, allowed the United States to claim its unalloyed commitment to rights, in this case the right of prisoners to refuse repatriation back to Communist China or North Korea. In other words, "voluntary repatriation" served as a euphemism for compelling defection via what was essentially anti-Communist psychological warfare.

Although the word *voluntary* suggested that the program presented the POWs with the option to choose whether to repatriate, this imposition of what turned out to be psychological warfare violated the Geneva Conventions and refused to recognize the national sovereignties of China and the divided Koreas, even though the United States itself had divided Korea at the 38th parallel in 1945.[8] Yet psychological warfare would also ironically and unintentionally generate as well the turning of American POWs opting out of repatriation back home to the United States, triggering an intense "brainwashing" scare. This scare draws on a long-standing American trope and narrative dating back to the colonial era—the white settler fear of captivity in the face of an ever-present "Indian" threat. Indeed, the production of spatial exceptions—in the form of the frontier, the colony, the camp, the reservation, the unincorporated territory— also dates back to the founding moments of an expanding United States.

In terms of spatial bounds, *War Trash* renders the POW camp of the Korean War as a particular kind of spatial exception, a coconstitution of biopolitical space and geopolitical territoriality. In doing so, the novel makes visible how the POW camp as a general form emerges out of the Korean War. This takes place, moreover, within the global post–World War II context of decolonization and the consolidation of a regime of international human rights. In *War Trash*, we see how the POW camp becomes a laboratory for the consolidation of a US metapolitical authority that attempts to supersede the force of international law as well as the sovereignties of China and the newly created North and South Koreas. The novel inspires a transpacific critique of how, under the sign of the Cold War, US militarist settler imperialism as an ensemble of relations requiring continual reassertion and reproduction witnessed a growing symbiosis between ongoing settler colonialism and a rapidly expanding military empire. *War Trash* also generates a conceptualization of the significance of the spatial exception in the reproduction of these relations. In this instance, it is the US POW camp, but as I have been arguing, spatial exceptions are constituted at multiple scales and in a variety of ways that make possible the imposition of US metapolitical authority. Though each particular POW camp erected during a time of war might be temporary, the POW camp as a general form is enduring, especially when we consider that the United States is a permanent warfare state. As such, *War Trash* amplifies broader questions about militarist settler imperial projections of power undergirded by the POW camp as a spatial exception. We might say that the US POW camp as a spatial exception has an attendant temporal exception given its permanence as a general form. This, along with the permanence of warfare, groups together as a conjoined pair of temporal exceptions operating in tandem with the temporal exception of debt imperialism. *War Trash* thus makes visible the significance of the POW camp and calls for an interrogation of and reckoning with not simply the continuation but also escalation of US militarist settler imperialism in Asia and the Pacific. This is to speak about the consolidation of the United States as a hypermilitarized national security and permanent warfare state from World War II and into the contemporary context of the twenty-first century.

Psychological Warfare on the POW Camp, or, Human Interiority as the New Frontier of Settler Expansion

Ha Jin, a post-Tiananmen exilic Chinese writer, fashions *War Trash*, winner of the Pen/Faulkner Award and a finalist for the Pulitzer Prize, as a realist historical novel told from the perspective of a soldier in the Chinese People's Volunteer Army aiding North Korea in the Korean War. The soldier survives the brutality of a POW camp under a US-led UN Command during the Korean War and travels to the United States decades later in the years immediately following 9/11. The novel is structured as a self-described "documentary style" memoir of narrator Yu Yuan's experiences surviving the POW camp on South Korea's Koje Island. Based on extensive research on actual camp practices at Koje Island during the war, especially the newly emergent US "voluntary repatriation" program, the bulk of the novel takes place at the POW camp and details the internecine violence among the prisoners. *War Trash* renders how the prisoners—composed of both Communist mainland Chinese and Nationalist Chinese, as well as Communist North Korean and anti-Communist South Korean soldiers—play out on a microscale the ideological divisions of the Cold War.[9] The novel reveals how the new voluntary repatriation program generates escalating levels of violence either ignored or instigated by the UN/US Command.

War Trash opens with a framing device of the first-person narrator, Yu Yuan, speaking in the present-day context of an extended trip to the United States in the years immediately following 9/11. The purpose of his trip is to write a memoir of his experience as a Chinese POW during the Korean War and to visit his son and grandchildren, who reside in Atlanta. He writes of the nervousness he felt upon arrival to the United States: "When I was clearing customs in Atlanta two weeks ago, my heart fluttered like a trapped pigeon, afraid that the husky, cheerful-voiced officer might suspect something—that he might lead me into a room and order me to undress. The tattoo could have caused me to be refused entry to the States" (3). The narrator's trepidatious encounter with the Transportation Security Administration (TSA), a US federal agency created as part of the new Department of Homeland Security within the context of the increased securitization and militarization measures taken in the wake of 9/11, draws attention to a post–Cold War context that mediates the interpretation of the account of the Korean War POW camp that will follow.

Framed by this more recent context, which is not only post–Cold War but also post-9/11, *War Trash*, as Joseph Darda compellingly argues, "interrogates the war on terror through the historical lens of the Korean War" and could thus be read as an exemplar of "literature of the long War on Terror."[10] In another compelling yet different analysis, Sunny Xiang contends that Yu performs a "neutral tone," in which neutral names a distinctly post–Cold War and post-racial affect of *Asian* that marks an ambiguity between global capitalism and Asian capitalism rather than presuming the triumphal universalizing of US capitalism.[11] Bearing these insights in mind, I focus in my analysis on how *War Trash*'s setting and the narrator's near-fetishistic avowal of neutrality index a logic of the spatial exception through which US militarist settler imperialism functions and continually reproduces itself. Moreover, the avowal of political neutrality, in particular the decision not to "voluntarily" repatriate but to go back home to mainland China for familial and not ideological reasons, is a refusal to be interpellated as an indebted refugee. This refusal of the "gift of freedom" within a bipolar and Manichean Cold War context is a kind of politics of nonalignment paradoxically articulated as apolitical or neutral.

Yu Yuan, our narrator, chooses repatriation back to mainland China, but not for any transparently ideological reasons that one might presume. *War Trash* takes as one of its central motifs the malleability of language despite the narrator's claim of telling his "story in a documentary manner so as to preserve historical accuracy" (5). Depicting the mandatory or forced tattooing, a kind of branding, of Chinese POWs by anti-Communist forces in US POW camps, the novel amplifies the ambivalent and strategic circuits of affiliation and alliance that Cold War Manichean binaries refuse to recognize. A soldier of the Chinese People's Volunteer Army aiding North Korea, Yu Yuan wishes to return home to Communist mainland China for personal, familial reasons rather than ideological ones. Yet those compatriots in the camp who have decided to align themselves with the anti-Communist Nationalist government-in-exile in Taiwan attempt to compel Yu Yuan to refuse repatriation by tattooing FUCK COMMUNISM on his stomach. *War Trash*'s amplification of Yu Yuan's forced tattooing responds to the question I posed at the beginning of this chapter, of why such a large number of POWs would choose to go against Confucian strictures on body purity. Just as voluntary repatriation was not quite voluntary, so too, was tattooing. Forced defection went hand in hand with forced tattooing, for the political branding via tattooing would make it difficult for the POWs to not go through with the defection. Despite this, Yu Yuan is able to return home to China after all and has a doctor alter his tattoo such that it reads FUCK US with the removal of most of the letters in COMMUNISM except the *U* and the *S*. This simple procedure transforms an explicit and expletory anti-Communist slogan into its opposite, and it explains his nervousness about clearing customs upon arrival in the United States. Yet if we were to read US as *us* rather than the US (United States), we are led to reckon with slippages and ambiguities of meaning—and more broadly of alliance and ideological affiliation—that Cold War bipolar logics elide. Slippages and ambiguities of meaning are also evident in a favorite tattoo at the actual Koje Island camp, "Kill the pig for its hair," which is a play on words of Chinese homonyms mocking Mao Zedong (hair) and his military commander Zhu De (pig).[12]

Indeed, we see on a microscale the Chinese civil war played out in the Chinese compound in the Koje prison camp, within the context of yet another civil and decolonial war erupting on the Korean Peninsula linked to the ongoing legacies of Japanese colonialism. This is also occurring within the even broader global context of the Western interimperialist war *between* the United

States and the Soviet Union or a civil war *within* the West that came to be called the Cold War.[13] These layered spatialities of the Cold War, and the US military empire that was forged under the sign of the counterinsurgent Cold War against global movements of decolonization and race wars, are revealed in *War Trash*.[14]

Yu Yuan's refusal to pick sides based on ideological affiliation, indeed his desire for a "third choice so that [he] could disentangle [himself] from the fracas between the Communists and Nationalists" (313) is, as has been observed, a symptom of how *War Trash* is mediated by post–Cold War developments. As I see it, this insistence on the neutral voice, repeated throughout the novel, is as much an amplification of the contemporary economic threat posed by China as it is a symptom of the Cold War's failure to resolve militarized, ideological, and geopolitical tensions between the United States and China. This is not to suggest that these two things are not related; the former can be seen as a manifestation of the latter. Nor is it to suggest that there have not been significant changes and ruptures brought about by the end of the Cold War. The rapid economic growth of China would itself suggest perhaps a world-historical shift from Europe and the United States to Asia.[15] Rather, I am interested in how a twenty-first-century novel like *War Trash*, both through its formal and thematic elements, diagnoses what we might consider the longue durée of US militarism in particular and settler imperialism more broadly in Asia and the Pacific. Indeed, the Cold War failure is also indexed when shifting the focus from Europe to Asia. Although the US Cold War might have ended in Europe with the fall of the Berlin Wall in 1989 or the failed Soviet coup in 1991, it is unclear when, if at all, it ended in Asia. Hence, we witness references to a "new Cold War" with China, and as much as the so-called war on terror in the Middle East has been observed to be the unfinished business of the Cold War, the "pivot" from the Middle East to Asia and the Pacific as articulated in Hillary Clinton's "America's Pacific Century" policy plan in 2011 also symptomizes the unfinished business of the Cold War in Asia.[16] This military pivot attempts to contain what we might see as Cold War remainders, or tensions with China and North Korea. The ongoing division of the Korean Peninsula, and the still formally unended Korean War, are also Cold War remainders.[17]

War Trash refracts the increasingly militarized Cold War relation between Communism (China and North Korea) and anti-Communism (the United States and South Korea) through the POW camp. The camp emerges not simply as a setting for the novel but more crucially as an organizing logic governed by a proliferation of violence enabled and instigated by its constitution as a spatial exception. Highlighting a longer history of spatial exceptions, A.

Naomi Paik powerfully writes that camps constitute one particular type of spatial exception among many. Indeed, the deployment of spatial exceptions dates back to the very origins of the United States, both to imperial spaces such as the frontier and the colony and to internal zones of exclusion. These spatial exceptions, where we witness the suspension of rights, have in fact counterintuitively enabled the United States to claim to defend rights. Building on Paul A. Kramer's insight that spatial exceptions are not exceptional at all despite US proclamations that they are, Paik contends, "Thus, although camps, particularly those located outside formal US territory, are understood as extreme and external to the United States, such ideological divides between the normal and the exceptional, or the foreign and the domestic, obscure their co-constitution and connection to each other."[18]

Before we turn our focus to *War Trash*'s rendering of the POW camp as a particular kind of spatial exception, it bears noting why it is significant that it is a *Korean War* POW camp located on an island off the southern coast of South Korea. Indeed, the entire island of Koje is the camp, which calls to mind the observation I discussed in the previous chapter that the entire island of Okinawa is a military base. It also brings to mind the particular proximities that island spatialities have to being transformed and malformed as militarist and carceral geographies. Koje's wholesale transformation into a POW camp, and the repurposing of Guam's military bases as refugee camps and detention centers that I discuss in Chapter 4, literalizes Michel Foucault's metaphor of the "carceral archipelago."[19] The relatively "short" length of the Korean War and its fuzziness in US popular memory belie its singular significance in inaugurating a national security and militarist state waging permanent warfare that outlasts the historical life of the Cold War itself. During the US military occupation of the Korean Peninsula south of the 38th parallel after World War II, the US military transformed itself organizationally and rhetorically. The National Security Amendments of 1949 have rhetorical significance in transforming the former Department of War into the Department of Defense (DoD). This discursive shift allowed the United States to refashion itself as the defender of a "normatively defined global humanity" no longer through wars but through "conflicts," "hostilities," or "operations." In this new discursive scheme, World War II was deemed to be the last "true" war.[20] Alongside the creation and violent manipulation of spatial exceptions, we see here how US militarist settler imperialism functions by exceptionalizing (and thus ultimately normalizing) war itself as precisely *not* that through rhetorical sleights of hand constituting a host of obfuscating euphemisms. In terms of the actual military budget, NSC-68 (regarded as the blueprint of Cold War containment policy) attempted to raise it significantly by hyperbolizing the Soviet threat. President Truman initially refused the budget request when he received the document in April 1950, but the Korean War that June effected a reversal, quadrupling the defense budget and opening a floodgate of military appropriations that has not closed since. The Korean War also crucially stimulated Japan's economy, the United States' important Cold War junior partner in Asia. Finally, Chinese participation in the war unprecedentedly militarized US-China relations through the proxy of Korea.

Moreover, in her stunning multiscalar analysis of the global significance of the UN/US POW camps of the Korean War, Monica Kim compellingly demonstrates how the camps and in particular the POW repatriation issue became an important crucible or testing ground, "a dense node of global politics," for a new world order inaugurated by the end of World War II. Central to this analysis is the interrogation room of the Korean War, through which we can apprehend a shift in the very objective of war itself in this period. Whereas previously official warfare had been waged over geopolitical territory, this changed in the mid-twentieth century to war being waged over "human interiority."[21] The script of war, or the discursive grounds for waging war, underwent a transformation. Although in previous eras nation-states could wage self-interested wars without having to rationalize them as "just wars," the end of World War II witnessed the rise of a moral universalism that, following Carl Schmitt, only allowed "wars over humanity."[22] This, as I relayed above, ushered in a host of euphemisms for war, and the one used in Korea was "police action." That is, "war could now only be conducted as a disavowal of war itself."[23]

This new imperative of moral authority went hand in hand with the growth of an international nation-state system as newly decolonized territories, or emergent nation-states, sought recognition within the system even as they attempted to challenge the very terms of that recognition. In other words, rather than simply entering into a Eurocentric Westphalian system that long preceded them and was founded upon their very exclusion and nonrecognition, newly independent nation-states attempted to revise the limits of sovereignty. For liminal states such as Korea—colonized by Japan, then divided at the 38th parallel and occupied by the United States and the Soviet Union—the war amplified the unfinished project of decolonization and attendant conundrums of recognition and authority. How, for example, could the United States wage formal war, and subsequently negotiate POW repatriation, with North Korea, the Democratic People's Republic of Korea (DPRK), if it did not recognize that entity as politically legitimate? Ultimately, as Kim argues, the Korean War became a test case of evolving notions of sovereignty not only in the making of nation-states but also the making of subjects or gaining "territory" by winning access to human interiority itself. A subsequent articulation of this goal of anti-Communist ideological "conversion," if you will, would be during the Vietnam War, when the strategy of winning "hearts and minds" came to have increasing significance in the face of a guerilla war that the United States was ill-equipped to manage.

The question of how POWs were to be treated, and whether they were to be repatriated, not only presented contradictions between national sovereignty and the new regime of international humanitarian law but also generated competition for who could lay legitimate claim to the correct interpretation and application of the 1949 Geneva Conventions on the Treatment of Prisoners of War.[24] This, as we shall see, became a crucial issue because Korean War POWs in US camps were composed of Koreans from both sides of the 38th parallel as well as Chinese. The players involved were thus an entity the United States did not recognize (the North Korean DPRK), what amounted essentially to a US puppet regime (the South Korean Republic of Korea, or ROK), and what came to be the United States' principal Cold War enemy (the Chinese mainland People's Republic of China, or PRC).

War Trash highlights such questions of sovereignty and law(lessness) in the POW camp. In doing so, it amplifies a variety of linked, as yet unresolved, concerns in the wake of questions arising out of World War II and amid the era of the decolonization of territories and subjects formerly constituting European and Japanese empires. Put simply, these questions concerned issues such as norms of warfare, sovereignty, and treatment of POWs. In *War Trash*, such questions condense around two related issues: voluntary repatriation and the 1949 Geneva Conventions governing the prompt release of POWs upon the cessation of military hostilities. The Korean War saw an attempt to apply the Geneva Conventions soon after their ratification.[25] Although China and North Korea had not signed the conventions, and the United States had not ratified them, all parties agreed to observe them.[26] As such, these issues magnify yet further the ongoing yet obscured significance of the Korean War. Indeed, while the contemporary war on terror has brought to public consciousness the problem of "indefinite detention," we find in the Korean War an earlier genealogy of US implication in this practice.

Caught between the Nationalists and Communists and shuffled instrumentally by the two sides because of his superior knowledge of English, our narrator Yu Yuan in *War Trash* bears witness not only to his own violent experience but also to that of his fellow POWs. Indeed, the novel renders Koje Island as an incubator or laboratory of violence, both physical and psychological, perpetrated by all sides. Psychological warfare (or compelled ideological indoctrination via "education" sessions); forced branding via tattooing; compelled repatriation or nonrepatriation; coerced anti-Communist vows made in public; petition drives for nonrepatriation; the creation of secret societies; reprisals against the UN (effectively the US) Command; crushing counterreprisals by the Command; uneven camp conditions, malnourishment, and medical care based on ideological affiliation; and brutal beatings, starvation, or fatally difficult labor—these all graphically demonstrate what *War Trash* reveals to be the banality of violence in the spatial exception of the POW camp. Mandatory or universal tattooing, though not necessarily particularly violent on the surface in this brutal chain of violence, turns out to have been otherwise. Many were initially resistant because it violated a Confucian stricture or because it made it difficult to go back home to family. This resistance was crushed with brute force. Survivors later testified to witnessing such acts as public beatings and the tearing out of a man's heart and displaying it in front of resisting POWs to scare them into submission. Among those already tattooed, some tried to "erase" the characters by scraping them off with razor blades, while a few others reportedly "attempted suicide by eating glass."[27] Young writes that what was required was an "extravagantly cruel spectacle of dominance. To brand the POWs, barracks bosses required ultimate control: ownership of the skin."[28]

Though formally run by the UN Command, the POW camp was effectively subjected to "local rule" in the compounds, often by agents trained by the US Civil Information and Education section of the Far Eastern Command in collaboration with the anti-Communist governments of Taiwan and South Korea. These agents posed as POWs.[29] Yu Yuan relates such an instance:

Liu had once been a sergeant in the Nationalist Army, but the Communists had captured him in a battle and put him into a logistic unit after a month's reindoctrination. Because he could drive, they gave him a truck. After his division crossed the Yalu River, at the first opportunity he drove three tons of salt fish to the American position and surrendered. Rumor had it that he was sent to Guam for two months' training and then returned to Korea. That was why he was appointed to a battalion commander as well as the vice chief of the regiment—to help Han Shu keep order in the compound, since Han was a man of mild disposition and seemed indecisive. Liu Tai-an hated the Communists so much that he often publicly flogged men who wanted to return to Red China. The Americans had adopted a let-alone policy and didn't care what happened in the compounds as long as the POWs remained behind the barbed wire, so Liu ruled this regiment like a police state. Even some GIs called him Little Caesar. (68–69)

Here, we see the ways in which the space of exception that is the POW camp coconstitutes the norm. On the one hand, the camp's exceptional status and internecine violence would seem to be a departure from the juridical and social formation of the sovereign space of the home front of the US nation-state. On the other hand, this passage's detailed description of the itinerary (including the unincorporated US territory of Guam) that led Liu to the camp reveals a projection or extension (rather than disruption or aberration) of US settler imperial power. Racialized and colonized subjects, both at home and abroad, are rendered vulnerable to the brutal biopolitics of settler imperialism. They are the disposable and unexceptional "war trash" of the novel's title, even Liu.

During the war, the US ambassador to South Korea, John Muccio, referred to barracks bosses as "Gestapos," while another State Department functionary observed that the Chinese compounds holding would-be defectors were "violently totalitarian" and run by "thugs."[30] The irony of such assessments, of course, is that such "totalitarian" conditions were at once instigated and condoned by the United States in its effort to win the ideological Cold War. Within this scheme, the repatriation interrogation room of the camp also becomes an exceptional space, one where the POW presumably exercises the free choice to repatriate or defect. Yet as Kim compellingly demonstrates, this assumption about the liberal bureaucratic interrogation room, coupled with contemporary debates about torture as a symptom of the horrors of war, is problematic. What gets elided in this assumption is that the liberal bureaucratic interrogation room is a site of intense violence insofar as the primary concern is not the production of information but the production of a new subject molded as the putative object of US liberal humanitarian rescue from Communist totalitarianism.[31]

Such violence, transforming the camp itself into a war zone, or a war within the Korean War, was largely due to the application of new concepts of psychological warfare deployed by the United States with the aim of maximizing the number of POWs choosing not to repatriate back to mainland China or North Korea. In other words, the goal was compelled mass defection via psychological warfare, but it was discursively obfuscated as "voluntary repatriation." Insofar as the Korean War was one "hot war" within the broader context of the Cold War, winning the ideological front via the production of indebted refugee or defector subjectivities was crucial. In the context of a military stalemate and the increasing significance of the ideological valence of the Cold War, the Korean War provided an ideal occasion to apply theories of human communication that had recently formalized as "psychological operations" or "psyops," basically interchangeable with the term *political warfare*. As early as 1949, the National Security Council had recommended expanding "foreign information programs and overt psychological operations." This led to the creation of "Project Troy," aptly named to reflect the ambition of destroying an enemy from within via psychological warfare.[32] Project Troy helped to inaugurate the Psychological Strategy Board (PSB) in April 1951, just a few months after the opening of Koje Island's POW camp.[33] Yet even before this, in September 1950, the Joint Chiefs of Staff had ordered a pilot program to investigate the possibility of exploiting POWs for "psychological warfare purposes," whether for propaganda or as spies and conspicuous defectors. By mid-1951, the pilot program was expanded to include all POWs.[34]

The production of indebted refugee subjects through psychological warfare or "psyops" was institutionalized through Truman's issuance of an executive directive for the PSB. This directive stated that the PSB was "for the formulation and promulgation, as guidance to the departments and agencies responsible for psychological operations, of over-all national psychological objectives, policies and programs, and for the coordination and evaluation of the national psychological effort." The second director of the PSB, Raymond Allen, stated that its goal was to "combine with the forces of military and economic strength in the free world a systematic U.S. psychological effort under a single strategy" that would enable the United States to "put to work something more powerful than dollars and weapons—the power of ideas."[35] Although this notion of winning "hearts and minds," as I have observed, would later gain visibility during the Vietnam War, it was the Korean War that became the first "testing ground" for the newly created PSB to show the significance and efficacy of psychological warfare. The term *psychological warfare* was a new name for a set of practices that the US military had in fact already been deploying for different ends in the previous few decades. During World War II, for example, psychological warfare was conceived as "information" that would influence individual opinion. What was new, then, was the creation of the PSB as the first fully institutionalized oversight structure for and coordination of psychological warfare, which continued the existing, earlier goals of educating a broad global public about the benefits of American liberalism. Also, as I will elaborate, there was a distinct shift in attitude about psychological warfare as constituting a new "frontier" of American expansionism.[36]

In the summer of 1951, the energies of the PSB condensed on the figure of the POW as a "potentially useful fulcrum on which to turn the 'political course' of the war."[37] Indeed, this tactic ultimately evolved into a centerpiece of the United States' war strategy. Brigadier General Robert A. McClure, the US Army's chief of psychological warfare, recognized that the United States could take advantage of the fact that many of the Chinese POWs had started in the Kuomintang's

(KMT's) anti-Communist Nationalist arm during the Chinese Civil War, but had been captured and indoctrinated in Maosim, then later sent to fight in Korea as part of the Communist Chinese army. Similarly, some of the North Korean POWs had actually been South Korean soldiers captured by the North, reuniformed, and sent to fight as part of the North's army.[38] In addition to the use of force when necessary, the propaganda arm of psychological warfare involved an array of educational and cultural materials. Materials from Japan, used during the US occupation there following World War II, were sent to Korea by the Civil Information and Education section of the Far Eastern Command, along with agents and teachers from Taiwan and South Korea. Hollywood films such as *High Noon* and *Young Mr. Lincoln*, Sears and Montgomery Ward catalogs, and radio station broadcasting over loudspeakers performed the ideological labor of "conversion," reinforced by the operatives from Taiwan and Seoul.[39]

As Kim observes, although the POW repatriation controversy is dismissed as mere propaganda and relegated to footnotes in histories of the Korean War, it was significant in policy debates as it was unfolding because what was at stake wasn't simply about propaganda. Indeed, at stake was the very meaning and justification for the war itself, on the one hand, and a concern over how the war would also become a template for future wars or conflicts, on the other.[40] This latter concern gained increasing significance because of the broader linked contexts of a rapidly congealing Cold War and demands for recognition and sovereignty among newly postcolonial nations in the era of decolonization. As such, the success of the PSB's voluntary repatriation program depended upon the continued refusal to recognize North Korea as a sovereign state. If North Korea was not a sovereign state, the logic presumed, then it had no claims over its POWs. It could not, in other words, demand that its POWs be repatriated. Rendered effectively stateless in this way, the POWs would then be under the auspices of international law, a law in this instance sanctioned by the UN but managed by the United States and regulated by the International Committee of the Red Cross.[41]

What is especially revealing about the increasing significance of psychological warfare in this era is the belief that it would aid in the acquisition of new territory. In other words, what I have called the new figurative "settler frontier" of gaining access to human subjectivity in the production of new loyal liberal subjects went hand in hand with the literal territorial frontier of US militarist settler imperial expansion. Indeed, Henry Loomis drew a connection between psychological warfare and settler acquisition of territory in explaining growing US government interest in using social science research for "political warfare" in the years after 1945. He wrote, "After the war, the atmosphere must have been similar to the opening of the Oklahoma territory to the settlers—each agency dashed in to stake out as large a claim as possible to the most fertile territory visible."[42] This figurative new fertile territory was human interiority itself, the control of which was becoming pivotal in a new kind of war to gain literal territory for an expanded dominion of US militarist settler imperialism and what would rapidly become a US-led global capitalism.

If the United States thus attempted to promote mass defection via another name, "voluntary repatriation," this program could also have unintended effects or a reverse trajectory: American POWs choosing not to come home, not to repatriate back to the United States but electing to go to "Red China." Much to the dismay and shock of Americans, this particular exercise of the right to refuse repatriation was indeed practiced by twenty-three American POWs. They explained their presumably inexplicable decision in a press statement, referring critically to the "murder of the Rosenbergs" and the "legal lynching [of] dozens of Negroes" in justifying their desire to work for peace in China. They saw China as a country where "there is no contradiction between what is preached and what is practiced."[43] This triggered a "brainwashing scare" in the United States, with most commentators presuming that the twenty-three non-repatriates had been indoctrinated. Some believed they were suffering an "artificially imposed mental illness" and spearheaded a letter-writing campaign among Sunday schools, civic groups, and homes for the elderly to encourage the group to come home. Those in the military, however, demonstrated less compassion, convinced that the group was full of collaborators.[44] Ultimately, of the original twenty-three, two changed their minds. The decision of the remaining twenty-one "turncoats" was deemed to be not only unfathomable but also unprecedented. Hyperbolic phrasings such as "never before in history" overlooked a long history of captives who had also refused to come back to their Euro-American communities. This intense focus on the twenty-one Americans who opted against repatriation virtually eclipsed the fact that 22,000 Korean and Chinese POWs turned their backs on Communism by refusing to be repatriated and choosing to go to Taiwan, even as this latter group was held out as validating the superiority of democracy.[45] However, this relatively high number of nonrepatriates could be explained by the fact that, as I stated, approximately two-thirds of Chinese POWs were actually former members of Chiang Kai-shek's anti-Communist Nationalist army who had been reeducated in Maoism, absorbed into the People's Liberation Army, and sent to fight in Korea.[46]

As with the issue of psychological warfare, the brainwashing scare or fear of captivity finds a long-standing genealogy connected to the settler colonial expansion of the United States. Dating back to the colonial era, captivity has held a privileged place in the settler colonial and imperial imaginary of the United States. In their passage across the Atlantic and arrival in the New World, the Puritans saw themselves as God's chosen people, as redeemed captives who had been liberated from bondage. The North American wilderness, however, seemed to be an inhospitable sanctuary with an ever-present threat of death, dismemberment, or captivity at the hands of what the settlers viewed as savage and marauding Indians. Susan L. Carruthers writes that this "national self-conception—a people under the perpetual shadow of a raised tomahawk—proved stubbornly persistent."[47] This stubbornly persistent national self-conception or preoccupation with the trope of an ever-threatening Indian is one reason why, as I have observed, militarist settler imperialism continuously needs to reassert itself. The precise content of the trope of the ever-threatening Indian (the savage enemy) might change over time, but what remains consistent is that US national self-conception and reconsolidation perpetually rely on such an (imagined) enemy, whether found on US shores or overseas. By the time of the Korean War in particular and the Cold War in Asia more broadly, the tomahawk was largely replaced with the hammer and sickle of "Red China." This was coupled with attendant fears of "menticide," coined by Columbia psychologist Joost Meerloo to refer to the "rape of the mind." To many at the time, the prospect of being subjected to menticide was more frightening than the possibility of atomic annihilation.[48] Brainwashing, moreover, was racialized as a specifically Orientalist technique, tethered to long-standing American tropes of Oriental inscrutability and cunning.[49]

The POW Camp as Biopolitical Space and Geopolitical Territoriality

The waging of psychological warfare on captured POWs amplifies the POW camp's coconstitution as biopolitical space and geopolitical territoriality. In an incident that amplifies competing interpretations of the Geneva Conventions and of how the suspension of law or the state/space of exception becomes the rule, *War Trash* dramatizes an account of the real-life kidnapping of General Dodd at the Koje Island camp in May 1952. The novel reveals how the POWs stage a kidnapping of a general in order to gain leverage and an audience for their grievance about camp conditions and the charge that the Geneva Conventions had been violated:

> To the Americans' credit, I should mention that they had posted the relevant clauses of the international law in every compound, in both

Chinese and Korean, and that they issued to every platoon a booklet containing the text. Before seeing the booklet, we had only heard of the Geneva Convention but hadn't known its contents. Having studied the document thoroughly, our leaders concluded that the Americans had contravened Article 118, which stated: "Prisoners of war shall be released and repatriated without delay after the cessation of hostilities." However, when the regulation had been drafted three years before, the world had been less complicated and none of the participating countries had been able to imagine our situation—in which more than two-thirds of the Chinese POWs wouldn't be going home. Still, whenever possible, we would confront our captors with their violation of Article 118, and most of the time we could get the upper hand. (157)

Here, we see the POWs taking up their captors' very language of humanitarianism and turning it against them. The accusation that the UN/US Command has violated its own laws governing the treatment of POWs is not so much an articulation of "pro-Communist" ideology as much as it is a demand for all prisoners' rights, above and beyond ideological divisions and loyalties.[50] Thus, what was at stake in the Dodd incident was the very definition of the prisoner of war as a particular kind of political subject with attendant rights.[51] In addition to the violation of Article 118 governing repatriation without delay, the Geneva Conventions' stipulation against the use of force or violence in extracting decisions as well as Article 7 specifying that prisoners could not renounce their right to return were also violated.

Inasmuch as *War Trash* self-referentially attempts to be an archive of the Koje Island camp by narrating the story of the POWs in a "documentary manner," the POWs involved in the actual Dodd incident were themselves also attempting to create their own archive. Collectively, they formed the "Korean Peoples Army and Chinese Volunteers Prisoners of War Representatives Association," and gave Dodd a document listing eleven items, a combination enumerating the functions of their association as well as the demands they were making. In addition to the demand that the US military cease the repatriation screening through which North Koreans were being forced not to repatriate via the imposed nonrecognition of their country as a sovereign state, the POW association also revealingly requested, "In order to secure the business of this institute . . . four tents, ten desks, twenty chairs, one hundred K. T. paper and two hundred dozens of pencils, three hundred bottles of ink and two hundred stencil paper and one mimeograph." Seeking political recognition beyond their wartime status as "prisoners of war," the members of the association were also demanding that the international community recognize the sovereignty of their state, the Democratic People's Republic of Korea. In this context, these two things—the category of "prisoner of war" and the issue of sovereign recognition in the post-1945 nation-state system—went hand in hand.[52] Ultimately, however, in the investigation of the Dodd incident by the US military, the political content of the POWs' demands, which the POWs were very careful to keep legitimate by not harming Dodd, was vacated by criminalizing the POWs and charging them with mutiny.[53]

The POW camp's violations, and the US ambassador to South Korea's observation that the Koje Island camp was run using Gestapo tactics, generate a consideration of Giorgio Agamben's important work on the camp and its relationship to modernity. Agamben calls for an inverse line of inquiry. Rather than arriving at a definition of a camp by studying the events that occurred there, he takes a step back and asks instead: "What is a camp, what is its juridical political structure, that such events could take place there?"[54] For Agamben, the most important issue is not the debate among historians about whether the first camps to emerge were the *campos de concentraciones* in the Spanish colony of Cuba in 1896 used to suppress popular insurrection or the "concentration camps" the English used for captured Boers toward the beginning of the 1900s. Rather, what is significant is that in both cases, "a state of emergency linked to a colonial war is extended to an entire civil population. The camps are thus born not out of ordinary law (even less, as one might have supposed, from a transformation and development of criminal law) but out of a state of exception and martial law."[55]

As *War Trash* reveals, the Koje Island camp, then, is on the one hand a spatial materialization of the state of exception and martial law in a time of imperial war. Though the Korean War was not a colonial war in the classic sense (since the Korean Peninsula was not a formal colony of the United States), it was an imperialist one in the Western interimperialist rivalry between the United States and the Soviet Union that came to be called the Cold War. Moreover, when the United States divided the peninsula at the 38th parallel and militarily occupied the southern part, this formal cessation of Japanese colonialism in Korea transmogrified into a US imperial succession that exploited and built upon Japanese colonial formations rather than radically disrupting or eradicating them. On the other hand, the Koje Island camp complicates Agamben's formulation, for the application of martial law by the UN/US Command also had to contend with the international law for the humanitarian treatment of POWs as ratified in the 1949 Geneva Conventions. Agamben's central concern, the Nazi concentration camp and how "its inhabitants were stripped of every political status and wholly reduced to bare life," thus predates and was one of the main impetuses for the 1949 Conventions and the post–World War II consolidation of an international juridical regime governing rules of warfare and crimes against humanity.[56]

As *War Trash* makes visible, the inhabitants of Koje Island presumably possessed internationally recognized political rights as POWs as well as the rights of national citizen-subjects, in this case split between Chinese and Korean and each respectively split even further into the PRC (Communist mainland China), the ROC (Nationalist Taiwan), the DPRK (Communist North Korea), and the ROK (anti-Communist South Korea). As such, the Koje Island camp is a space of multiple, proliferating legal structures rather than a total absence or suspension of them. Yet in *War Trash*, we see in graphic detail how the prisoners' rights were violated through a brutal political economy of violence instigated by the United States yet disavowable through "localization" or "delegation" to prisoners themselves. So while, for example, US officials did not start the practice of tattooing that quickly became mandatory, "they allowed in the tattooers and profited from the careening mess they set loose."[57] Indeed, according to an extensive Pentagon study, prisoners developed "private armies" organized, recruited, and trained by the compound chief, or *hancho*. That the POWs chose to defect or repatriate in blocks in line with their compound chief attests to how tightly controlled the barracks were. In this way, the "camps became a bloody war zone."[58] To be sure, POWs who identified as Communist also perpetrated violence, yet such violence, unlike that perpetrated by anti-Communists, was not under the auspices of the Command. This contradiction, or ability to act effectively in "extralegal" ways within a seemingly hyperlegal context, is an enabling and defining feature of modern power rather than an aberration. Agamben argues that asking how such atrocious crimes against humanity could be committed in the camps is incorrect and highly hypocritical. Rather, the correct, more honest, and above all more useful question to pose is this: What juridical procedures and deployments of power were operative such that "human beings could be so completely deprived of their rights and prerogatives that no act committed against them could appear any longer as a crime"?[59] In other words, the vital question is not so much how such atrocious crimes could be committed but rather how such acts were not even legible *as* crimes in the first place.

War Trash's rendering of the proliferation of violence within a seemingly hyperlegal context generates an important question about the relationship between the law and the camp, between cause and effect. Whether human beings can be put in camps as a consequence or effect of their loss of rights, or whether they are stripped of such rights as an effect of being put in a camp, or even whether they are presumably entitled to a new set of specific rights by virtue of being put in a camp (as in the case of POWs), violent atrocities against them can be committed in ways that are not rendered criminal. This is because the space of the camp itself constitutes what Agamben calls "a new and stable spatial arrangement" in which the state of exception, previously a temporary suspension of the juridico-political order, becomes permanent.[60] The camp is thus the "materialization of the state of exception," and "in this light, the birth of the camp in our time appears as an event that decisively signals the political space of modernity itself."[61] As the political paradigm of the West, the camp for Agamben constitutes the "nomos of the modern" rather than a breach or violent rupture.[62] Given this insight, it could be argued that the POW camp and the other spatial exceptions I have noted constitute the "nomos of US militarist settler imperialism" in Asia and the Pacific.

Yet Agamben's work must be extended in this context of US militarist settler imperialism in order to highlight how the camp not only is a biopolitical space but also is coconstituted by geopolitical territoriality. As Mark Rifkin compellingly demonstrates, Agamben's insights on the camp and sovereignty must necessarily be revised when analyzing the United States because focusing on the camp as the political paradigm of modern statehood can elide the geopolitics of statehood. At stake in an analysis of the geopolitics of statehood is an apprehension of the dynamics of settler-state imperialism.[63] The focus on the camp as a *biopolitical space*, in other words, effaces questions generated by *geopolitical territoriality*. By concentrating on the POW camp of an imperial war, and amplifying competing claims to legal authority, *War Trash* helps us grapple with how the biopolitical space and geopolitical territoriality coconstitute one another.

The convergence of biopolitical space and geopolitical territoriality also long predates the Korean War. An early and significant instance of the US creation of a spatial exception in Asia and the Pacific was the seizure of the Philippines as a colony so that it could be a "stepping-stone" to China. During the genocidal war of conquest leading to formal colonization, a policy of reconcentration was deployed from 1901 to 1902. A strategy to crush remaining resistance in hostile areas by waging war against the entire rural population, reconcentration sought to isolate and starve guerillas by deliberately obliterating the rural economy. Peasants in resistant areas were compelled to relocate to garrisoned towns with nothing but the most basic of provisions. These garrisoned towns were essentially policed "reconcentration camps." Outside of the perimeter of these fenced-in camps, troops would then practice a scorched-earth policy.[64] Although the use of such "reconcentration camps" by the Spanish in

Cuba during the final Cuban war of independence had generated US outrage (enough to be a putative factor in the US decision to intervene against Spain in 1898), by 1900 the United States found instructive their effective and supposedly humane use by the British in South Africa.

Yet what these seemingly opposite and contradictory reactions to the use of concentration camps—outrage in the case of the Spanish and emulation in the case of the British—have in common is a profound disavowal of how the United States itself had already been using concentration camps long before the debate at the turn of the century. The US federal Indian policy of removal in the decades leading up to the Spanish-American War effected the seizure of Native American land through the reservation system. Indeed, Native American reservations, many of which functioned initially like concentration camps, are the spatial exception within what became the fifty states (or incorporated territories) constituting the United States. They are thus the very ground that makes possible the formation of the United States as a settler state. A particularly infamous instance is the "reconcentration" of Navajos in the Bosque Redondo Camp. The 1848 acquisition of territory (what became the US Southwest) from Mexico in the US-Mexican War witnessed a US scorched-earth policy to crush Navajo resistance. Driven in 1864 to the New Mexico Bosque Redondo reservation, essentially a prison or concentration camp, the Navajo were subjected to a particularly harsh and ultimately failed experiment of reeducation to compel them to become Christian yeoman farmers under what amounted to four years of captivity. Over eleven thousand Navajo were incarcerated, and over 2,500 died as a result of the unrelentingly brutal conditions at the camp and 350-mile forceful march there.[65] This history demonstrates Scott Morgensen's important observation that the biopolitics of settler colonialism and the displacement of Native peoples and nations "form a transnational proving ground *within* settler societies to produce a white settler state for imperial projection abroad."[66] This brutal history of subjecting Native Americans to captivity is elided in America's fears of precisely the opposite—of facing captivity at the hands of Native Americans. This is, as I cited previously, the American national self-conception of living under the "perpetual shadow of a raised tomahawk." This kind of rewriting is not a simple forgetting. It is a kind of double operation in which one side of the chiasmus (the notion of Americans being held captive by Native Americans) covers over the other side (Native Americans being held captive by Americans). It is a particular variety of what Lisa Lowe calls "the economy of affirmation *and* forgetting."[67]

These instances of the United States' earlier settler colonial and imperial projections of power and aspirations for metapolitical authority through the creation of camps as spatial exceptions constitute the strategically forgotten political unconscious of the camp's "reemergence" in later wars and eras. This is not to argue, however, that all camps are the same. Rather, it is to observe that the camp as an exceptional spatial form is intimately linked to a logic of domination and/or extermination. The Korean War and Cold War POW camp is connected to this longer genealogy, yet its specificity lies precisely in how it is deployed by the US settler state as it increasingly makes and remakes itself as also a military empire in the post–World War II conjuncture. Its specificity also lies in how it became a laboratory for the early testing of a newly emerging international human rights regime that would clash with and ultimately be superseded by US metapolitical authority, even as the United States purported to be the strongest defender of such rights. Although the United States did not formally colonize South Korea, its imperial projection of power in the POW camp negated both local competing national sovereignties as well as the authority of a newly emergent international regime of human rights. The proliferation of law functioned ultimately to negate POW rights rather than to fortify or guarantee them. As such, what was at stake in the immediate post–World War II and rapidly intensifying Cold War context was less a matter of application of or control over particular laws and more a question of metapolitical authority. The Cold War, following Oswaldo de Rivero, was a struggle over who, the United States or the Soviet Union, would be the rightful inheritor of territories and bearer of Western political philosophical traditions within the context of the breakup of the classical European empires in the aftermath of World War II.[68] As such, it could be argued that the Cold War itself was a contestation over metapolitical authority. War Trash's rendering of the Korean War POW camp thus generates broader questions about US militarist settler imperialism's attempt to seize metapolitical authority through spatial exceptions that extend beyond what became the fifty states (incorporated territories) constituting the United States in an era when the settler state also becomes a military empire in Asia and the Pacific.

The longer genealogy of the Korean War POW camp stretches both back in time to the settler state's relations with Native American nations and forward in time to the camps of the more recent war on terror. This longer genealogy of the camp is suggested in War Trash through the post-9/11 framing device, which returns at the end of the novel. Before that very end, however, Yu Yuan critiques a Pulitzer Prize–winning journalist for having approached the Korean

War as a "publicity stunt, a game. She should have been given a rifle and made to fight like an infantryman so that she could undergo the physical suffering and take the bitterness of betrayal, loss, and madness. One article even concluded: 'Korea is her war.' Who can bear the weight of a war? To witness is to make the truth known, but we must remember that most victims have no voice of their own, and that in bearing witness to their stories we must not appropriate them" (299). This narrative and ethical injunction is precisely what author Ha Jin has putatively respected.[69] I would like to close this chapter by reflecting on the idea of "bearing witness." Precisely what is Jin attempting to bear witness to? Certainly, it would be the victims of war, ideological division, and what Yu Yuan as a self-described detached observer assesses to be political "fanaticism."

The very end of the novel, however, complicates the temporality of war. Here, Yu Yuan is inspired by an episode of the long-running animated television show *The Simpsons*, in which Bart gets a tattoo removed, to get his own FUCK US one removed as well. Yu makes an appointment with a doctor at Atlanta's Emory Hospital, and the procedure is set to take place "next Thursday" (349). This presents a kind of exceptional temporality of its own within the novel. Jin begins his narrative by having his narrator inform his readers that he will write a memoir and ends by noting that he has done exactly that. Yu's experience in Korea is told entirely in the past tense. Yet the tattoo removal procedure does not actually take place within the time frame of the novel; it is left to a future date of "next Thursday." Will Yu actually keep his appointment? We are led to presume so. But this future temporality leaves as yet untouched or unerased the trace of the brutal biopolitical and geopolitical violence of Koje Island. This trace, the tattoo, challenges us to regard *War Trash*'s "bearing witness" to the violence of the spatial exception, what I suggested is the "nomos of US militarist settler imperialism," not simply as a bygone history but, following Foucault, a "history of the present."[70] This makes *War Trash*'s aesthetics of settler imperial failure all the more urgent and timely.

In a short 2008 piece entitled "No to Biopolitical Tattooing," Agamben explains his refusal to submit to a new regulation requiring those entering the United States on a visa to have their fingerprints and photograph filed by the Department of Homeland Security. The imposition of this "biopolitical tattooing," he writes, "concerns the [increasingly] routine inscription and registration of the most private and most incommunicable element of subjectivity— the biopolitical life of the body," and therefore must be opposed.[71] Seen in this light, the six remaining letters on Yu's belly inscribe a "history of the present" of biopolitical tattooing as a technology of state surveillance and terror that is no longer exceptional but increasingly normal under the guise of national security. What has also been rendered normal and necessary, again under the guise of national security, is a steroidal militarism. In attempting to bear witness to the experiences of Chinese POWs under UN/US Command in the Korean War, *War Trash* diagnoses these conjoined histories of biopolitical violence and militarism that animate our present. How, in other words, have we arrived at a military pivot whose name goes by "America's Pacific Century?"

4. THE UNINCORPORATED TERRITORY: *Constituting Indefinite Deferral and "No Page Is Ever Terra Nullius"*

In her poem "AmneSIA," Teresia Teaiwa writes:

> . . . it's easy to forget
> that there's life and love and learning
> between
> asia and america
> between
> asia and america
> there's an ocean
> and in this ocean
> the stepping stones
> are
> getting real[1]

Just as the Midwest is thought to be constituted by "flyover states" within a dominant US continental cartographic imaginary that centers and privileges the coasts, the area between Asia and America is thought to be constituted by a vast yet mostly empty oceanic expanse within a Pacific Rim imaginary that privileges continental landmasses. When the Pacific Islands and the Indigenous people there are remembered or considered at all, as Teaiwa writes, they are done so as mere "stepping stones" for some other destination and in the service of some other project and population. Indeed, since the mid-nineteenth century, the United States' prolonged project of "China watching," overdetermined by its desire for the fabled Chinese market, has imagined islands in the Pacific such as the Philippines as strategically located "stepping stones" to China. More recently, America's nuclear modernity has been made possible by testing on sites such as the Marshall Islands whose human and animal inhabitants, land, water, and air are presumed to be expendable.[2] Yet still, in US imperial wars in Asia, islands such as Guam (Guåhan), a US unincorporated territory, have been used as military staging grounds and refugee camps. This was especially the case with the Vietnam War. Yet as Teaiwa reminds us, between Asia and America lies not just the detritus of what US power imperils and ruins, but "there's life and love and learning" that the optics of geostrategic use-value refuses to make visible, to make real. Against this ongoing violence, the "stepping stones" are nevertheless "getting real" on their own terms. In other words, Indigenous lives, relationalities, and epistemologies of the Pacific Islands offer powerful critiques of the cartographic imaginary and violence of US militarist settler imperialism. The optics of presumed use-value and disposability after use shift radically when we bring into central focus the Pacific Islands, the oceanic and the terraqueous along with the archipelagic, rather than adhering to a singular focus on the terrestrial and continental.[3]

Guam's "use-value" to the United States extends far beyond the island's deployment as staging grounds for war. Indeed, the Indigenous Chamorro (Chamoru) population of Guam has some of the highest enlistment and fatality rates per capita in the United States and its territories.[4] A significant reason for such high enlistment rates is the imposition of an indebted subjectivity onto Chamorros, the notion that they owe a debt to the United States for "liberating" their island first from centuries of Spanish colonialism in 1898 and then from brutal Japanese occupation during World War II. They are heavily targeted for enlistment in the US military as an important way of paying back this presumed debt. On many levels, the US unincorporated territory of Guam is effectively a military colony.

In her poetry collection *Inside Me an Island: Poems* (2018), Chamorro poet Lehua M. Taitano writes:

> Because two more of our sons and daughters have enlisted. Because their enlistment might return them home whole or in pieces or not at all.

Because diabetes has taken another pair of our eyes. Because we cannot tread on pieces of our own land without clearance. Because we keep words like *clearance* and *deployment* and *strategic* and *stationed* in the bowl with our keys by the front door. Because we can count to a thousand in Spanish. Because we can count to the apocalypse in English.

Because our crow song has vanished. Because our trees are blighted. Because our reefs are targets. Because we are always in the path of military maneuvers. Because I must write this to you in English.[5]

The anaphoric *because* that begins each sentence poignantly responds to a question that Taitano poses at the beginning of this section of her collection. The section, entitled "A Love Letter to the Chamoru People in the Twenty-first Century," begins by stating, "So you'll understand, I hope, if I pick up where we last left off, which is always at horizon. Who but a horizon feels how we are kept at each other's distance?"[6] Taitano then answers this question with a series of *becauses* that punctuates the hypermilitarization of Guam and successive colonizations by Spain and the United States. Taitano's line, "Because we can count to the apocalypse in English," signals not only the ongoing control that the United States exercises over Guam but more pointedly the apocalyptic threat that US domination poses to the health and vitality of the interlinked ecologies of the island: its land, water, air, and multispecies life. In the postliberation or post–World War II context, the relationship between what the US military desires and the desire for the military by Chamorros—a linked set of militarized desires—indexes an ongoing cycle of compelled dependence. The military has become the preeminent site through which such affects, desires, and needs are fulfilled. Indeed, a Chamorro major who teaches in the Reserve Officers Training Corps program at the University of Guam articulates his sense of militarized indebtedness: "My service is payment for a debt. I was taught since I was young about how we were liberated, and this is the least I can do."[7]

I begin this chapter with "AmneSIA" and *Inside Me an Island* because they amplify the violently liminal status of Guam as an unincorporated territory of the United States. "AmneSIA" interrogates the ways in which islands in the Pacific have been strategically deployed as "stepping stones," or in the case of Guam, as "the tip of the spear" pointed at China. And *Inside Me an Island* magnifies the militarist geography, what Tiara R. Na'puti calls the "colonial cartographic violence," that constructs and registers "places as existing exclusively for colonization and militarization."[8] As with the POW camp and military base and attendant camptown discussed in the foregoing chapters of this book, the unincorporated territory also functions as US militarist settler imperialism's spatial exception. In Asia and the Pacific, sites that experience a heavy US military presence, islands such as Guam in particular, are what Sasha Davis calls "sacrifice areas for an imperial national security."[9] Even as their lands, lives, and ways of life are thus sacrificed, they are interpellated into an economy of militarized indebtedness. The US seizure of Guam at the conclusion of the Spanish-American War in 1898 has been narrated as a "liberation" from centuries of Spanish colonization and the 1944 US victory over Japanese occupation during World War II as yet another "liberation." The US military controls 33 percent of the land in Guam thus far, leading some to call the island an "unsinkable aircraft carrier" and "USS *Guam*."[10] Indeed, as Catherine Lutz notes, "Guam, objectively, has the highest ratio of US military spending and military hardware and land takings from indigenous populations of any place on earth."[11] Militarized indebtedness, or the price to be paid for the promise of liberation, is on the one hand the violence of a promise made in bad faith. Yet as I elaborate, the promise of liberation is also not reducible to an easily refutable case of bad faith. Indeed, it is a structuring grammar and logic that indefinitely defer the possibility of decolonization for Guam.

In this chapter, I ask how these promises of US militarist settler imperialism— the promise made in bad faith, the promise that can be rolled over indefinitely, the promise that does not have to be made at all, the necropolitical promise that cannot be settled even with death—call on us to imagine an alternative politics of debt.[12] Indeed, how might we imagine and live a refusal of the debt relation altogether? I offer an analysis of how Chamorro poet Craig Santos Perez beautifully and at times comically captures both the seeming impossibility and urgent necessity of such refusals in a multibook poetic project: *from unincorporated territory [hacha]* (2008), *from unincorporated territory [saina]* (2010), *from unincorporated territory [guma']* (2014), and *from unincorporated territory [lukao]* (2017). *hacha* means "one" in the Chamorro language; *saina* means "parents, elders, spirits, or ancestors"; *guma'* means "house, home, shelter, refuge, or dwelling"; and *lukao* means "procession." Amplifying the militarist violence made possible by Guam's spatial exception as an unincorporated territory, the *from unincorporated territory* series also offers a layered meditation on how US militarist settler imperialism's temporal exception of debt imperialism conditions even as it obscures the imposition of the disciplinary temporality of an indebted subjectivity onto the Chamorro. Perez's aesthetics of settler imperial failure, his antimilitarist and decolonial poetics, thus gestures beyond the spatial and temporal exceptions by imagining a future in which refusals of the debt relation thwart US militarist settler imperialism's fatalities.

"A Disembodied Shade in an Intermediate State of Ambiguous Existence for an Indefinite Period"

To be an unincorporated US territory is to be a virtual colony. Before turning to Perez's *from unincorporated territory*, I offer here a contextualization and analysis of the historical and juridical making of an unincorporated territory as a specific kind of spatial exception. The US acquisition of Guam, Cuba, Puerto Rico, and the Philippines from Spain in 1898 set off a legal debate about imperialism. The animating question of this debate was whether the "Constitution follows the flag" into the territories acquired from Spain and the newly annexed territory of Hawai'i. Could the nation still remain a republic if it ruled over lands and peoples not subject to the US Constitution? In a series of legal cases known as the *Insular Cases* (1901–22), the question was answered ambiguously, and it remains so to this day. In *Downes v. Bidwell* (1901), the most well known of these cases, the US Supreme Court created the new category of the "unincorporated territory." Unlike other territories that the United States had annexed, this new type of territory would not be incorporated as a US state, and the Constitution and its attendant protections and rights such as due process would not apply. Specifically, the Court's decision deemed Puerto Rico to be "foreign to the United States in a domestic sense," a territory "belonging to" or "appurtenant to" but "not a part of the United States," its inhabitants neither aliens nor citizens.

Amy Kaplan writes that the *Insular Cases* allowed for a two-tiered, uneven application of the Constitution through the creation of the liminal space of the "unincorporated territory" that became the legal edifice for imperial rule. The designation of the unincorporated territory as neither foreign nor domestic was informed by a racist view that the inhabitants of that territory were absolutely unfit for self-government and US citizenship. This served the dual function of legitimating colonial domination while also protecting US citizens from acquiring a population seen as wholly uncivilized, as "absolutely unfit to receive" the full protections and responsibilities of the US Constitution.[13] Even as unincorporated subjects were thus denied the protections of the Constitution, such as due process and equal protection of the laws, they were treated as would-be citizens in terms of taxation, discipline, and punishment.

In his dissent, Chief Justice Melville Weston Fuller effectively captured what still remain the long-standing implications of the creation of a spatial exception called the "unincorporated territory": that the denial of sovereignty as a foreign autonomous nation left the territory and its inhabitants in limbo. Fuller argued that the "occult meaning" of the "unincorporated territory" granted Congress the power to keep any newly acquired territory "like a disembodied shade in an intermediate state of ambiguous existence for an indefinite period."[14] Indeed, the *Insular Cases* departed from the assumption that territorial status must eventually lead to statehood. This had been the pattern throughout the continuous westward expansion of the United States, a pattern outlined in the Northwest Ordinance of 1787. The ordinance enumerated three basic steps in the acquisition of a territory: 1. Federal plenary control for a period of one to eight years, in which Congress appoints a governor as well as a judiciary and other government officers and holds strong decision-making power; 2. The ability of territorial residents to elect their own legislature and form a constitution, with Congress still retaining the power to appoint a governor who can overturn the legislature's decisions; 3. Statehood and the attendant creation of an independent government within the federal system. The territories of the western United States were conceived as candidates for eventual membership into the Union.[15] The racialized insular territories of Puerto Rico, Guam, and the Philippines, however, were never conceived as such.

Denied both sovereignty as an autonomous nation and incorporation as a US state, the "unincorporated territory" continues to exist as a spatial exception. Its perduring liminal status is "like a disembodied shade in an intermediate state of ambiguous existence for an indefinite period." Yet for the unincorporated territory, conjoined with the spatial exception there is another set of valences to the temporal exception that I have been elaborating throughout this book. The deferred decision, the denial of even the promise of any final status, is also a kind of temporal exception. Whereas extraconstitutional plenary power over acquired western territories was merely temporary on the eventual road to incorporation or statehood, and whereas plenary power was also the alibi for ruling over the territories acquired from Spain, a crucial difference is that two of these latter territories, Guam and Puerto Rico, still remain unincorporated. We might then say that the permanence of plenary power over the unincorporated territory is metapolitical authority, insofar as that metapolitical authority has hitherto not been converted to political authority via the incorporation of the territory as a state. Moreover, this indefinite deferral of statehood is akin to indefinite rolling over of the debt; the refusal to make the promise is akin to the refusal to meet the promise. The constitutional crisis sparked by America's new possessions resulting from its victory in the Spanish-American War was thus managed through a deferral and to this day an unambiguous resolution still remains elusive.

In addition to the logic of indefinite deferral, yet another valence to the temporal exception inheres in the grammar of the very question of whether the "Constitution follows the flag." The question was posed, and answered in the affirmative, by the anti-imperialist candidate William Jennings Bryan in the 1900 presidential election as a challenge to the pro-imperialist policies of the McKinley administration. Yet as Brook Thomas argues, Bryan was unaware of the double meaning of the question. "Bryan clearly intended his question to imply that constitutional rule should coincide with the territory over which the flag of the United States flew. But the phrase can also imply that the Constitution is not coincident with but follows *behind* the flag."[16] This second meaning was implied in a quip made by Secretary of War Elihu Root during the debate: "As near as I can make out the Constitution follows the flag—but doesn't quite catch up with it."[17] This second meaning, of course, is the opposite of what the anti-imperialist Bryan intended in his belief that the Constitution should reign supreme in the nation and all its territorial possessions. Moreover, as Thomas analyzes, in invoking the flag as the symbolic stand-in for the nation, Bryan's phrase brought to mind an image of the nation leading the Constitution, as opposed to the Constitution leading the nation.

In the *Downes v. Bidwell* decision imposing tariffs on goods from Puerto Rico despite the constitutional guarantee that "all duties, imposts and excises shall be uniform throughout the United States," Justice White's use of the metaphor of incorporation "effectively let the flag lead the Constitution while maintaining the appearance that the two were coincident."[18] In arguing that the Constitution did apply to the US territories, but not fully until the territories were "incorporated" into the United States, Justice White left ambiguous precisely what he meant by "incorporated." Yet it is this very ambiguity, this "occult" meaning, of the metaphor of incorporation that gave it its productivity because it allowed the court to have its cake and eat it too—by permitting a differential, uneven application of select parts of the Constitution depending on the particular issue at hand. Crucially, the ambiguous metaphor of incorporation rendered moot the need for a constitutional amendment limiting the states of the Union to the continent only. Thomas argues that this, in turn, inaugurated a new relationship between the Constitution and the nation in which the United States moved from a model of the nation held together as a "compact of contracting entities to a corporate model of the nation-state."[19]

What was thus at stake in the *Insular Cases* was not just congressional power to impose tariffs. Indeed, the constitutional crisis was sparked not necessarily by the *general* fact that the United States had acquired new territories. After all, the very making of the "United States of America" had been and continued to be the acquisition of new territories by conquest and/or purchase. The *particular* fact was that these newly acquired territories of Guam, Puerto Rico, and the

Philippines were populated by a race deemed to be unfit for self-government and the full rights and protections of US citizenship. In his majority opinion in *Downes v. Bidwell*, Justice Brown claimed that territories were not a part of the United States but "appurtenant" to it, appended to it in a subordinate position. Congress *could*, he argued, extend full constitutional rights and protections to the territories, but *should* it? Congress could rule as it deemed proper, constrained only by "certain principles of natural justice inherent in the Anglo-Saxon character which need no expression in constitutions or statutes to give them effect."[20] This white supremacist conceptualization of "Anglo-Saxon character" informed and provided the racial context within which White came to the conclusion that the Constitution did not need to explicitly state, but merely imply, the nation's power to acquire and govern colonies just like the imperial powers of Europe. This power, he reasoned, is what it meant to be a modern nation. Noted lawyer and Harvard Law School professor James Bradley Thayer argued that it was necessary to read the Constitution in this way, and abandon "the childish literalness which has crept into our notions of the principles of government, as if all men, however savage and however unfit to govern themselves, were oppressed when other people governed them; as if self-government were not often a curse." The abandonment of "childish literalness" would make room for reading contextually, "in the atmosphere of the common law and of the law of nations."[21]

Downes v. Bidwell was preceded by a group of significant cases within the continental United States that also hinged on the question of whether racialized subjects were citizens or could be granted full constitutional protections. In 1896, just five years before *Downes v. Bidwell*, Justice Brown wrote the majority opinion in *Plessy v. Ferguson* upholding the constitutionality of racial segregation through what came to be known as the "separate but equal" doctrine. In *Cherokee Nation v. Georgia* (1831), the Court ruled that Cherokees were a "domestic dependent nation" or a ward to the United States lacking sovereignty. In *Dred Scott v. Sandford* (1857), Black people were uniformly denied citizenship, whether enslaved or free. Finally, *United States v. Wong Kim Ark* (1898) solidified jus soli or birthright citizenship regardless of race by ruling that a child of Chinese descent born in the United States to parents residing permanently in the United States is automatically a citizen upon birth. This would seem to be something of an anomaly compared to the other cases supporting racial segregation, abrogating Indigenous sovereignty, or denying citizenship. Yet if we recall that *United States v. Wong Kim Ark* was coeval with a constellation of laws restricting immigration, naturalization, and equality before the laws to Chinese, and also that the plenary power doctrine was established via *Chae*

Chan Ping v. United States (1889), also known as the *Chinese Exclusion Case*, what emerges out of the "disembodied shade" is the Court's creation of what Priscilla Wald calls "disembodied subjects."[22]

To this day, the doctrine of the *Insular Cases* still determines Guam's ambiguous legal status as an unincorporated territory. To speak of Guam's continuing existence as a spatial exception born of a "deferred decision," its liminal status as an unincorporated territory, is to speak of what Michael Lujan Bevacqua calls the "banal ambiguity of Guam's political existence." Bevacqua eloquently observes that Guam is "spectrally indistinct, meaning that whatever specters of colonization or injustice it conjures up, they remain the type that do not haunt."[23] In the continental United States, Guam is basically a forgotten colony. Yet in Guam itself, the motto is that it is "Where America's Day Begins" given its location in the Pacific.[24] But because Guam is not a US state, Guamanians are not full, or fully enfranchised, US citizens; they cannot vote in national elections nor can they have a voting representative in Congress.

What also remains "spectrally indistinct" is that although political tensions after the Japanese occupation during World War II and America's reoccupation in 1944 led to the passing of the 1950 Organic Act ending the military government in Guam by creating a civilian domestic legislature and conferring partial citizenship, the act granted only limited self-rule.[25] The governor would be appointed by the president, the government would be put under "'the general administrative supervision of the Secretary of Interior,'" and Guam would be under the Director of the Office of Territories within the Bureau of Land Management in the Interior Department. As such, observes Robert F. Rogers, "The Interior functioned in the twentieth century as the federal clean-up crew for the neocolonialist residue of American Manifest Destiny of the nineteenth century."[26] Although the Organic Act formally recognized Guam for the first time as an "unincorporated *organized* Territory," the federal government continued to treat Guam as an unorganized territory or possession.

The Organic Act, moreover, simultaneously effected a large-scale transfer of land into the hands of the US military.[27] Section 28 of the act mandated that all property, including utilities, used by the naval government for "civilian affairs" be transferred to the new civilian government within ninety days of August 1, 1950. However, Section 33 of the act "gave the U.S. president the extraordinary authority to designate any part of Guam a military reservation, even if privately owned. The president also retained the power to close Guam to vessels and aircraft of foreign nations."[28] In order to make the military's retention of Guam's land legal, on the day before the Organic Act went into effect, Carlton Skinner, Guam's first civilian governor, was instructed to sign a quitclaim deed transferring all condemned properties to the United States "for its own use." Truman then signed Executive Order 10178 on October 30, 1950, returning all property in the quitclaim deed to the navy so that it could apportion the land to the various branches of the military as necessary. This resulted in the navy and air force directly controlling about 49,600 acres, or over 36 percent of the island, all without consulting Guamanian officials or owners of leased properties.[29] To speak of Guam's continuing existence as a spatial exception born of a "deferred decision," then, is to speak of it as America's settler garrison, composed of "strategically positioned coaling stations, bases, testing grounds, and garbage dumps for US military power . . ."[30] It is to speak of one of the US Navy's many "lily pads" and refueling stations, and what some American pilots refer to as "the world's largest gas station."[31]

Although Truman signed the Organic Act of Guam into law on August 1, 1950, it was made retroactively effective as of July 21, the sixth anniversary of "Liberation Day" in 1944 when Guam was "liberated" by the United States from the Japanese occupation (1941–44) of World War II. As I will elaborate later in this chapter, such a tethering of Guam to the United States works to impose an indebted subjectivity onto Chamorros. This affective tethering through the retroactive alignment of the date of "liberation" parallels, moreover, Guam's legal tethering to the United States. The Senate report on the Organic Act bill before it was passed and signed by Truman made note of the fact that despite the change in government effected by the new law, Guam remained under the doctrine of the 1901 *Insular Cases*: "As an unincorporated territory, Guam like Puerto Rico and the Virgin Islands is appurtenant to the United States and belongs to the United States, but is not a part of the United States, as distinguished from Alaska and Hawai'i, which are incorporated territories. Unincorporated areas are not integral parts of the United States and no promise of statehood or a status approaching statehood is held out to them."[32]

The perdurance of US plenary power over Guam, what I conceive as metapolitical authority, was further reinforced in a more recent legal case, *Sakamoto v. Duty Free Shoppers, Ltd.* (1985). The Ninth Circuit Court of Appeals based its decision on this logic: "If the government of Guam is a federal agency, and if federal agencies are entitled to immunity from antitrust laws, then the Guamanian government's creation of an exclusive franchise must enjoy antitrust immunity."[33] As Gary Lawson writes, although Congress has granted Guam substantial powers of self-government, it is "purely a matter of legislative grace" insofar as the territory has "'no inherent right to govern itself'" and insofar as its government is thus an agency or instrumentality of the federal government.[34] Judge Schroder encapsulated the decision by stating that "the

Government of Guam is in essence an instrumentality of the Federal Government."[35] Self-governing as a matter of "legislative grace," thus still ultimately subject to the plenary power of the US Congress and economically dependent on the distorted auspices of the US Department of Defense, the unincorporated territory of Guam and its governance remain one of the most significant problems of American constitutional law. Yet, as the editors of *California Law Review* observe, "In modern times, however, issues of territorial governance have been reduced to the status of constitutional arcana."[36] Banal ambiguity, constitutional arcana, legislative grace, instrumentality of the federal government, spectrally indistinct, appurtenant to—these are the grammars generated by Guam's continuing status as an unincorporated territory, a territory militarized through its control by the US Navy when ceded to the United States by the Spanish over a hundred years ago and continually forged into America's settler garrison in the wake of being "liberated" again by the United States in 1944.

In the wake of the *Sakamoto v. Duty Free Shoppers, Ltd.* decision, Guam petitioned Congress for commonwealth status in 1986.[37] As part of that effort, Guam's poet laureate, Frederick B. Quinene, provided testimony before Congress and delivered some of his poetry. In his poem "Ignominy," from his 2018 collection *An Islander's Voice*, he laments the irony of partial citizenship: "What irony does befall us/That though Guam is of the USA/We are not yet full citizens/And still feel alienated to this day?"[38] He also articulates a trenchant critique of the temporal exception legally instantiated by *Downes v. Bidwell*, what I have been calling the indefinite deferral of statehood, or the promise made in bad faith. In his poem "Quest for a Commonwealth," he points out that despite the Organic Act and its rhetoric of self-determination and citizenship, Guam is still a US colony and a spoil of war. Quinene lays bare the temporal exception by reminding Congress of its unkept promise: "Years ago Congress declared/When Guam is ready she will nod,/And Guam will be self governed/Or was that only a façade?" He asks Uncle Sam if that intention was merely "promises ephemeral" or if such promises will "become true."[39] In calling out the Organic Act as "out-dated" and "antiquated" insofar as it unconstitutionally enables a master-slave dynamic, Quinene interrogates the present tenseness of colonialism. His appeal attempts to shame Congress into realizing the legal/constitutional and temporal contradictions of a present-tense colonialism. What does it mean for Chamorros to live this profound contradiction? In the introduction of his poetry collection, Quinene captures what it means in stark terms when he expresses, "Our problem is with the US and the way they treat us— they own us. I have never appreciated the fact that I am owned by someone."[40] For Chamorros, the temporal exception of indefinite deferral of statehood or "promises ephemeral" means they are owned by the United States. For Chamorros, the temporal exception of US debt imperialism, another kind of indefinite deferral, means they are owned by the US military.

More recently, the very condition of Chamorros as a colonized people with particular rights to assert decolonial aspirations was challenged. Although the 1950 Organic Act only conferred partial citizenship, it did give Chamorros the right to hold self-determination plebiscites. The plebiscite statute defines the eligible plebiscite electorate as "native inhabitants" of Guam (namely Indigenous Chamorros) who were granted citizenship via the 1950 Organic Act as well as their descendants. Crucial to note here is that this plebiscite electorate is thus defined by ancestry and residency, not race. In 1997, after many years of inaction by the federal government on the question of granting commonwealth status to Guam, the Self-Determination Commission was replaced with a newly formed Commission on Decolonization. This commission was charged with researching and conducting a plebiscite on the three processes of decolonization recognized by the United Nations: statehood, independence, and free association. Statehood would mean Guam would become the fifty-first state, with full political and economic rights. Independence would make Guam a sovereign nation, while free association would only extend Guam's ambiguous status. The Commission on Decolonization planned a plebiscite for 2002 after considering these options, but because convening a plebiscite formally requires the registration of at least 70 percent of qualified "native inhabitant" voters, difficulties in voter registration indefinitely delayed it.[41] Then, in 2016, Governor Eddie Calvo pushed an advisory plebiscite. But on March 8, 2017, a federal judge in Guam struck down Guam's plebiscite law as unconstitutional.

What led to this significant 2017 court decision, one that ultimately thwarted the Commission on Decolonization's efforts to conduct a plebiscite? In 2011, Arnold "Dave" Davis, a white, non-Chamorro retired US airman and longtime resident of Guam, filed a federal lawsuit against the Guam Election Commission for the right to participate in the plebiscite vote, arguing that Guam's plebiscite law violates the Fifteenth Amendment's prohibition on racial discrimination and the Fourteenth Amendment's equal protection clause. The case lasted over five years and involved an appeal before the 2017 decision. Judge Frances Tydingco-Gatewood, chief judge of the US District Court of Guam, ruled that a ballot restricted to Indigenous Chamorros violates the constitution's ban on racial discrimination.[42] She opined that "the U.S. Constitution does not permit for the government to exclude otherwise qualified voters ... because [they] do not have correct ancestry or bloodline" and that the plebiscite statute "impermissibly imposes race-based restrictions on the voting rights of non-native inhabitants." Her twenty-six-page opinion acknowledged that "the court recognizes the long history of colonization of this island and its people. However, the court must also recognize the rights of others who have made Guam their home." In April 2019, Tydingco-Gatewood also awarded Davis $947,717.39 as reimbursement for attorney's fees.[43] Her ruling was largely based on the 2000 Supreme Court case involving Hawai'i, *Rice v. Cayetano*, which ruled that non-Hawaiians could vote in Office of Hawaiian Affairs elections.[44] The state's law defines "Hawaiians" as "persons descended from people inhabiting the Hawaiian Islands in 1778."[45]

Guam appealed Judge Tydingco-Gatewood's decision. Guam Special Assistant Attorney General Julian Aguon argued to the US Ninth Circuit Court of Appeals that "it would be impossible for a colonized people under U.S. rule to exercise any measure of self-determination because the mere act of designating them, designating who constitutes as a colonized class would collapse automatically into a racial categorization. . . . The purpose of the law is to identify the group entitled to decolonization rights."[46] Aguon argued, moreover, that, "Neither the Fourteenth nor the Fifteenth Amendment was designed to prohibit this kind of political expression."[47] Constitutional law expert Erwin Chemerinsky, who joined Aguon's legal team appealing the ruling, argued that "*Rice* held only that ancestry may be a proxy for race, not that it always is. This case is an example of when it is not," because the "Guam Legislature intended to carve out a class of colonized people for the purpose of determining their views regarding their right to decolonization, as recognized by international law." Chemerinsky also added that the definition of "native inhabitants" was careful to identify a colonized people, and "whether one's ancestors experienced colonization."[48]

In July 2019, the Ninth Circuit Court of Appeals ruled against the Government of Guam (GovGuam), affirming US District Court Chief Judge Frances Tydingco-Gatewood's initial ruling. In the opinion, Judge Marsha S. Berzon ruled that Guam's self-determination plebiscite law violates the Fifteenth Amendment which states that the "right of citizens of the United States to vote shall not be denied or abridged by the United States or by any state on account of race, color, or previous condition of servitude." Sidestepping the question of whether Guam's interest in the self-determination of its Indigenous people is compelling, the court opined, "Rather, our obligation is to apply established Fifteenth Amendment principles, which single out voting restrictions based on race as impermissible whatever their justification. Just as a law excluding the Native Inhabitants of Guam from a plebiscite on the future of the Territory could not pass constitutional muster, so the 2000 Plebiscite Law fails for the same reason."[49]

Also in 2017, the federal government filed a suit against GovGuam and the Chamorro Land Trust Commission, alleging that the Chamorro Land Trust Act of 1975 is racially discriminatory and violates the federal Fair Housing Act. The Chamorro Land Trust holds public land, Chamorro homelands, for the benefit of Guam's native Chamorros, who under the act can apply for three types of leases: residential, agricultural, and commercial. Residential and agricultural leases are one dollar per year for a term of ninety-nine years, whereas commercial lease rates are based on property appraisals.[50] The Land Trust Act defines "native Chamorro" as those who became citizens as a result of the Organic Act as well as their descendants. In 1950, 96.8 percent of Guam's population was Chamorro, so since there were also some non-Chamorro people living on Guam in 1950, they are also eligible for leases under the Chamorro Land Trust Act. Interestingly, Chief Judge Frances Tydingco-Gatewood, who is Chamorro, recused herself, and she was replaced by District Court of Hawai'i Senior Judge Susan Mollway. For GovGuam, Assistant Attorney General Kenneth Orcutt argued that the Land Trust Act program is not racially discriminatory because eligibility for the program is not based on race but rather on a date when people living on Guam were granted citizenship. "Native Chamorro" is thus a political classification, and not one based on race or national origin. Moreover, Orcutt argued that GovGuam and the Land Trust Commission cannot be sued for violating the Fair Housing Act because they do not qualify as a "person" under federal law. In its motion for judgment, GovGuam requested that the court dismiss the claims against it and the Chamorro Land Trust Commission.[51]

Judge Mollway initially indicated that the *Davis v. Government of Guam* case could help guide hers and expressed a desire to wait for a decision in that case before moving forward. Then, about a month later, in December 2018, Mollway ruled that the federal government had failed to show *at that time* that the Chamorro Land Trust Act is racially discriminatory, thus denying the federal government's motion for partial judgment. However, the court also denied GovGuam's motion for judgment on the pleadings to dismiss the federal government's claims against it and the Chamorro Land Trust Commission.[52] Mollway opined, "This court agrees with Guam that, at this pleading stage, the court cannot conclude that the Chamorro Land Trust operates as a race-based entity. . . . The record must be further developed to address the question of whether the Chamorro Land Trust operates instead as a *compensatory entity* that seeks to implement the return to the people of Guam of land that the United States took from them."[53] Thus, crucial to note here is that unlike the Davis case, what is at stake in this case is the question of compensation—compensating "native

Chamorros" as defined by the Chamorro Land Trust Act for the theft of land by the US government. Yet ultimately, even this case could not preserve the designation of "native Chamorros" as specifically or exclusively entitled to the right of compensation. In December 2019, the Chamorro Land Trust Commission unanimously approved a settlement proposed by the US Department of Justice. A crucial concession made by the commission was the agreement to "expand the definition of eligible land trust beneficiaries to all those who owned, farmed, ranched, or occupied land taken by the federal government between 1898 and 1968, and their descendants." In short, the specifically Indigenous designation of "native Chamorros" was replaced with the broader and more vague category of "beneficiaries."[54] What connects these two cases is that the law disturbingly refused to recognize—through adjudicating the problematic charge of racial discrimination in a particular way—the designation of a colonized people as a political classification meriting measures of compensation or unique rights to express political desires for self-determination.

The *Davis v. Government of Guam* case in particular is yet another example, and an especially disturbing one, of the "return of the repressed" of the ambiguous and as yet ultimately unresolved legal status of the unincorporated territory. In this instance, the law's refusal to acknowledge the difference between colonized Indigenous Chamorros who have the right to express desires for self-determination and noncolonized residents of Guam who already exercise self-determination exemplifies the violence of the force of law. Going even further than this refusal to acknowledge such a substantive difference, the law effected a rewriting of that refusal as a constitutional upholding of racial equality on behalf of a white male plaintiff. Moreover, Tydingco-Gatewood's decision is symptomatic of the law's willingness to acknowledge what it perceived to be racial discrimination and its simultaneous unwillingness to acknowledge rights specific to a colonized Indigenous group. In this case, the avowed upholding of the Fourteenth and Fifteenth Amendments is a highly problematic validation that there can be such a thing as "reverse discrimination" against a white man who is a citizen of the nation colonizing the place where he has chosen to reside. This very ability to choose Guam as his place of residence is in large part by virtue of that colonization, and the fact that he is a military veteran amplifies Guam's status as a *military* colony.[55]

Thus, at a broad structural level, the perverse and profoundly contradictory logic of this legal ruling is such that it refuses to acknowledge that only Indigenous Chamorros, by virtue of being colonized, have the specific right to vote in a plebiscite regarding self-determination. It somehow extends that voting right to a white man even though he is not colonized and is actually in a broad sense an agent of the colonizing power, because to deny him that right would be racially discriminatory according to this contorted legal logic. In other words, by expanding the plebiscite electorate, the ruling acknowledges colonization in a particular way, yet it simultaneously vacates that acknowledgment of any meaning or force because it refuses to recognize that only the colonized, Indigenous Chamorros, have the right to vote in self-determination plebiscites. It refuses to acknowledge the crucial difference between Indigenous inhabitance and mere residence and treats colonization and a problematic notion of "racial discrimination" as if they are fungible. As I have argued, moreover, the particular case of putative "racial discrimination" here is especially problematic because the plaintiff is a white male.

Against such logics, Craig Santos Perez's *from unincorporated territory* series, to which I will now turn, offers an antimilitarist and decolonial poetics that grapples in complex ways with the spatial and temporal exceptions of US militarist settler imperialism. As part of a broader network of solidarity against militarism in Asia, the Pacific, and beyond, Perez's work can also be situated as an "affinity poetics," recalling Sasha Davis's conceptualization of an affinity politics that I discussed in the previous chapter.[56] Perez's affinity politics is articulated in his poetic series through an aesthetics of settler imperial failure.

"Liberation as Apocalypse," the Figurative Debt, and the Politics of (In)gratitude

Craig Santos Perez writes of his work, "My poetry draws from Pacific Islander, indigenous diasporic, and post/decolonial literary traditions. I envision my work as writing Guåhan and the Pacific—places that have often been erased from global historiographies—into existence."[57] Perez's multibook project, *from unincorporated territory*, confounds generic containment or categorization. Influenced by his study of the long poem, the series at once gathers together and scatters as poems, poem fragments, epigraphs, and long citations from an eclectic variety of sources: Asian American, African American, and postcolonial poetry (including Oswald de Andrade, Claude McKay, and Myung Mi Kim), canonical Western works, travel writing, government documents, maps, legal cases, the US Constitution, the aforementioned Section 28 of the Organic Act, governmental documents, the Bible, and autobiographical anecdotes.[58] Mostly in English but also containing Chamorro that is untranslated or translated later on a subsequent page, while also playing with orthographic conventions using strategic typography in the display of words, images, figures, diagrams, maps, and illustrations on a page, *from unincorporated territory* calls for multiple encounters or experiences with it. I engage the project as a poetics and what we might call a nondidactic archive and pedagogy of antimilitarist decolonization, or an aesthetics of settler imperial failure.[59] I focus in my analysis on the complex ways in which Perez grapples with the conundrum of the conjoined spatial and temporal exceptions governing the unincorporated territory of Guam. How might other articulations and inhabitations of space and time emerge out of and against these spatial and temporal exceptions which have reduced Guam to its use-value for US militarist settler imperialism?

Perez opens the first part of his multibook project, *from unincorporated territory [hacha]* (2008, hereafter *[hacha]*), with a preface that begins by citing Article IV, Section 3 of the US Constitution: "*Congress shall have Power to dispose of and make all needful Rules and Regulations respecting the Territory and other Property belonging to the United States*" (7, italics in original). This encapsulation of congressional power over US territories and properties is followed by a Bible verse, John 6:12–13: "*When they were filled, he said unto his disciples, Gather up the fragments that remain, that nothing be lost. Therefore they gathered them together, and filled twelve baskets with the fragments . . .*" (7, italics in original). What follows is precisely that—a gathering up of the fragments so that nothing will be lost. The fragments, in this instance, constitute a territory or property "belonging to the United States"—Guam. The gathering occurs through poetic stanzas explaining in the first person how small Guam appears in maps. At times it is so small that it doesn't even exist. Or it is simply an unnamed island on some maps, and at other times it is variously labeled "Guam, USA" or "Guam" on other maps. Depending on how Guam is (un)named on the map, the writer says, "I'm from here," "I'm from this unnamed place," "I'm from a territory of the United States," or "I am from 'Guam'" (7). This is followed by a short primer of sorts on what/where Guam is: its precise location in the Pacific; the underwater volcanic activity that formed Guam as well as the Mariana Trench (the deepest part of the earth's surface); what it means that Guam is an "unincorporated organized territory"; the etymology of the word *territory*; and how the *Insular Cases* in general and *Downes v. Bidwell* in particular ruled on the legality of imperialism after the United States' territorial acquisitions in the Spanish-American War.

[hacha] offers this nondidactic pedagogy of the where and what of Guam precisely because its literal nonexistence on maps indexes the US general public's complete lack (or at best hazy) knowledge of Guam's very existence as such or as a US territory. As Perez relates, though consciousness of Guam is largely submerged, it emerges in certain moments, such as in a poem by Robert Duncan. In "Uprising: Passages 25," appearing in the collection *Bending the*

Bow (1968), Guam surfaces in Duncan's critique of President Johnson and the Vietnam War. Perez provides this excerpt: "Now Johnson would go up to join the great simulacra of men,/Hitler and Stalin, to work his fame/with planes running out *from* Guam over Asia" (10, emphasis in original). Guam's colonial status as an unincorporated territory and strategic location in the Pacific allowed it to be used as a significant staging ground for America's war in Vietnam and for the processing of Vietnamese refugees displaced by the war. In a 1969 speech that came to be known as the Guam Doctrine, President Nixon, during a stopover in Guam, called for the shifting of the American military and its perimeter from putatively "contested bases" or sites to more secure areas throughout the Pacific.[60] Because Guam is a territory or possession of the United States and not a sovereign nation, the US military can be there and exercise metapolitical authority without the need to negotiate Status of Forces Agreements. Perez notes that "Uprising" is one of the few American poems that mentions Guam, yet in the poem Guam "only manages to signify a strategically positioned US military base (sometimes referred to as the USS *Guam*). This 'redúccion' of 'Guam' enacts the cultural, political, geographic, and linguistic 'redúccion' that has accrued from three centuries of colonialism" (11). *Redúccion*, Perez explains, is the term that the Spanish used in referring to their practice of subduing, converting, and encamping natives by establishing missions and fortifying them with stationed soldiers.

Guam has for centuries been captured and defined for its strategic position in the Pacific, first as a stopping area in the Spanish Galleon Trade Route, then as an important advancement for the Japanese army when it was occupied by Japan during World War II, and then for the US waging of World War II in the Pacific and attacks against Japan when the United States recaptured the island in 1944. More recently, Guam has been used as a staging ground for the Vietnam War and other subsequent wars. As Cathy J. Schlund-Vials observes, if Guam's current motto is "Where America's Day Begins" given its location in the Pacific, then its midcentury motto could be "Where the American War in Viet Nam commences."[61] In effect, the "redúccion" of Guam as a US military colony, as America's settler garrison, continues unabated. Since World War II, US military bases on Guam have been repurposed as facilities for migrant detention, "processing," or resettlement, becoming a central site in the United States' management and often restriction of asylum-based immigration. Not surprisingly, much of the asylum-based immigration has been the result of US wars. In addition to the 100,000 Vietnamese refugees held in temporary refugee camps after the Vietnam War, more recent groups include 6,600 Kurdish refugees displaced by the First Gulf War, almost 1,000 Burmese political refugees, and a significant yet "unreliably documented" number of Chinese asylum seekers. Guam's ambiguous political status and its island geography and spatiality make possible and desirable this militarization of space and the "repurposing" of that space for militarized migrations and detentions in ways that remain invisible to the wider US populace.[62]

Perez offers his poems against that imperial "redúccion," pivoting and generating an alternative strategic position from which "Guam" might emerge into "further uprisings of meaning" (11). Thus pivoted, to be *from* Guam, from unincorporated territory, signifies beyond the multiple meanings of the preposition and in particular beyond its reductively militarized appearance in Duncan's poem even as it appears in service of a critique of US militarism in Vietnam. Perez explains that his poems, *"from unincorporated territory,"* have been "incorporated from their origins (those 'far flung territories') to establish an 'excerpted space' via the transient, processional, and migratory allowance of the page. Each poem carries the 'from' and bears its weight and resultant incompleteness" (12). From the perspective of a diasporic Chamorro who migrated to California in 1995, his formal experimentation with language in creating a new visual vocabulary of what I have called a poetics of antimilitarist decolonization and aesthetics of settler imperial failure crucially include a "re-territorializing" of Chamorro language, culture, and history (12). In the second part/text of the series, *from unincorporated territory [saina]* (2010, hereafter *[saina]*), Perez elaborates this further by equating poetry and the page with land: "poetry, too, consists of textual land surfaces and the surrounding deep geographies of silence, space, and meaning— . . . no page is ever terra nullius— each page infused with myths legends talk story—" (65). *Terra nullius*, Latin for land belonging to no one, became the basis for international law justifying colonial and settler colonial conquest. Perez resignifies terra nullius from this settler colonial fantasy to a powerful poetic writing against it through the scattering of long poem fragments across the four texts of his project. This opens out to an expansive reconceptualization and reterritorializing of the unincorporated territory in ways that emphasize the oceanic and the worldliness of islands.

Perez's pivoting and alternative strategic positioning of those "far flung territories," those presumably tiny islands in the Pacific that sometimes do not even appear on maps, involves a dislodging of the dominant terrestrial, continental frame of reference and cartographic hierarchy. In *[saina]*, Perez engages with the notion of *préterrain*, a concept used in ethnography and anthropology. Literally meaning "fore-field," préterrain refers to the constellation of forces, both within and beyond the ethnographic frame of the "field," that constitutes the ethnographic experience. Such forces include, for example, modes of transportation, dwellings, relations of power, translations, and discursive practices. Perez observes that attentiveness to the préterrain "opens our eyes and our writing to the complexity, fragmentation, contradictions, and multiplicity of our historical and lived realities" (63). He draws our attention to how Epeli Hau'ofa articulates an "oceanic préterrain" in his essay "Our Sea of Islands" (1994). Hau'ofa argues that switching the frame of reference from the terrestrial or continental to the oceanic opens up the world of Oceania and allows us to see, as I elaborated in the Introduction, the worldliness of islands.

Following Hau'ofa, Perez allows us to see the worldliness of islands, an expansiveness, against the forces of "redúccion." Guam's "redúccion" to a spatial exception that negates its sovereignty and proliferates its militarized contours provides the occasion to think through and offer an enlargement of sorts through alternative "uprisings of meaning." A series of poems entitled "from TIDELANDS," scattered throughout the series, departs from the cartographic and geographic centering of land by emphasizing instead that our planet is terraqueous. Perez's poetic practice resonates with Kamau Brathwaite's theory of "tidalectics," an alternative to colonial historiographies and epistemologies of linear progress. A "tidal dialectic" departs from Hegel's dialectic by privileging a cyclical model that calls to mind the continuous movement and rhythm of the ocean. Elizabeth DeLoughrey interprets tidalectics as a geopoetic model of history that "destabilize[s] the myth of island isolation and . . . engage[s] the island as a world as well as the worldliness of islands."[63] In tidalectic fashion, the poems and poem fragments in *from unincorporated territory* do not unfold by beginning and ending without interruption in a linear mode. Because they are scattered across the pages of one text but also across all four texts, one must move continually and rhythmically, like the ocean, between the pages and across the texts when experiencing them.

Indeed, extending the recent archipelagic turn in American studies, Perez calls instead for a mapping of what he calls the "American imperial terripelago" in an essay entitled "Transterritorial Currents and the Imperial Terripelago":

> Even though the idea of the archipelago offers a "vision of bridged spaces rather than closed territorial boundaries"—emphasizing how the continent is produced in relation to islands—it remains essential to foreground the history and processes of territoriality that structure the origins and ongoing formations of American Empire. The word *territory* derives from the Latin *territorium* (from *terra*, land, and *-orium*, place). *Territorium* may derive from *terrere*, meaning "to frighten"; thus, another meaning for *territorium* is "a place from which people are warned off."

With this in mind, I propose a new term, *terripelago* (which combines *territorium* and *pélago*, signifying sea), to foreground territoriality as it conjoins land and sea, islands and continents.[64]

Perez's tracing of the etymology of territory and conceptualization of "terripelago" highlight not only the imperial dimensions of US power, but also the settler colonial. The meaning of *territorium* as "a place from which people are warned off" echoes settler colonialism's strategy of eliminating the native population and replacing it with the settler one.

Yet in an important extension of Patrick Wolfe's argument that "territoriality is settler colonialism's specific, irreducible element," Perez contends that territoriality is more than land.[65] For him, "Territoriality signals a behavioral, social, cultural, historical, political, and economic phenomenon. Territoriality demarcates migration and settlement, inclusion and exclusion, power and poverty, access and trespass, incarceration and liberation, memory and forgetting, self and other, mine and yours." In short, territorialities are not irreducible elements.[66] Perez's conceptualization of territoriality and of "terripelago" productively highlights how the United States is not just a continental power. Rather, what he calls the "discontiguous American Empire" draws attention to how the United States is quite literally "'the largest overseas territorial power in the world.'"[67] In a similar vein, Paul Lai's formulation of "Discontiguous States of America" emphasizes the imperial topography of the United States, "highlighting Native American reservation spaces within the boundaries of the contiguous states, offshore territories in the Caribbean and Pacific Oceans (including Guantánamo Bay, Cuba), and the two outlying states of Alaska and Hawai'i."[68] The question of territory is crucial to Guam's status as an unincorporated territory, for it is through the island's juridical construction as this spatial exception that it has been able to be shaped into a military colony or pivotal part of America's settler garrison. As I have explained, while military bases are not settlements in the classic sense, and military personnel (including their families and military contractors) are not settlers in the classic sense, such seizures of land, placement of people, and displacement of the native population endure and intensify in ways that belie the assumption that bases are temporary wartime structures.

In *[hacha]*, the colonization of Guam by the US military, both its imperial and settler contours, is rendered through an account of the introduction of the brown snake on the island during World War II and the effects of its subsequent proliferation. This account is spread across the bottom of several pages. First reaching the island as cargo ship "stowaways" during World War II, the brown snake's bite will not kill adults but can cause severe illness in young children and can be fatal for babies. By the mid-1960s, the snakes *"had colonized half the island. . . . [Their] population grew exponentially, reaching a density of 13,000 per square mile. At the same time, declining bird populations were noticed"* (91, italics in original). Immediately following this statement juxtaposing the proliferation of non-native life and the attendant declination of native life, is this: "[*8000 marines and their dependents will be transferred to Guam from Okinawa by 2014 through a joint effort of the United States and Japan.]" (91). Bracketed, and preceded by an asterisk as a reference mark, this statement explains or answers a somewhat vague question posed several pages earlier in the form of a number typographically enlarged and bolded on the page: "**8000?***" (83). Before encountering the explanation of the significance of the number 8000 several pages later, readers can only glean its meaning by heeding the "please visit" suggestion appearing below "**8000?***" on the same page. The suggestion is followed by the URLs of three websites petitioning and organizing against the planned transfer of eight thousand marines and nine thousand marine dependents from Okinawa to Guam as part of an agreement announced in 2005 and issued as the "United States-Japan Roadmap for Realignment Implementation" in 2006.[69] As I indicated at the beginning of Chapter 1, this agreement called for a further enormous military buildup of an already heavily militarized Guam.

[hacha] closes with a return to the story of the brown snake, at once a literal and allegorical story of the fatalities produced by invasion. *"About 100 times a year, a brown tree snake will scale a power line or transformer, electrocuting itself and causing a power outage that may span the entire island. At present, Guam has lost all its breeding population of seabirds, 10 of 13 endemic species of forest birds, 2 of 3 native mammals, and 6 of 10 native species of lizards. Also, there have been over a 100 infant deaths reported in the last 50 years"* (93, italics in original). Then, the story of the brown snake ends where it began: *"They say there were no snakes on Guam before World War II"* (95, italics in original). The story of the brown snake indexes the hypermilitarization of Guam in the post–World War II conjuncture. Already a militarized island under the governance of the US Naval Department, the US reoccupation of Guam after the Japanese occupation during World War II sets into motion an intensification of militarization and further land seizures. The Organic Act of 1950 might be seen to be a democratizing move, yet what does the conferral of partial citizenship and self-government mean within a space that has been remade into America's settler garrison? Indeed, as I have discussed, the Organic Act becomes the pretext for yet more transfers of land into the hands of the US military.

Joining the effort to stop the planned massive military buildup announced in 2005, Perez himself provided a testimony in October 2008 before the UN Special Political and Decolonization Committee.[70] The entire transcript of his testimony appears in *[saina]*, scattered throughout the poem fragments entitled "*from* tidelands." However, the testimony is typographically rendered in strikethrough font. Even as the strikethrough draws our attention to techniques and processes of erasure, it also forces or invites the reader to pay closer attention to the very text that has been stricken through. The line created by the strikethrough defamiliarizes the text, leading the reader to pay closer attention to that part of the page. This palimpsestically highlights the spectral quality of Guam itself and its colonized status in the imaginary of the general US public.

Indeed, as I cited earlier, Perez writes that "no page is ever terra nullius." Terra nullius, or the settler colonial fantasy of empty land that abets, as Sarita Echavez See captures succinctly, the genocidal emptying of that land, also leaves its traces.[71] That is, settler colonialism, and militarist settler imperialism more broadly, is not a fait accompli but rather an ensemble of relations that continually requires renovation. As Alyosha Goldstein, Juliana Hu Pegues, and Manu Karuka suggest, it would be productive to consider settler colonialism as a "structure of failure."[72] Perez's UN testimony, appearing as scattered footnotes all in lowercase and in strikethrough, attests at once to the United States' continued attempts at remaking ever-greater areas of Guam into a settler garrison and the very incompleteness of that project. This is to say that even as Guam is effectively a military colony of the United States, it is not reducible to that. It is not solely that. Perez testifies on behalf of the Guåhan Indigenous Collective, a grassroots organization "committed to keeping chamoru culture alive thru public education and artistic expression" (17). The very need for such an organization indexes the genocidal effects of the remaking of Guam as a settler garrison. The havoc wreaked by the brown snake makes a reappearance in the testimony. Perez also urges against "grave implications" for the Chamorro people of the continued "hyper-militarization" of Guam, explaining and detailing those implications as leading to premature death (45). Military dumping, nuclear testing, further land seizures, the mass unearthing of ancestral remains to build more hotels for wealthy Asian tourists—these are the violences of hypermilitarization that poison water, land, air, and life. Disproportionate rates of a host of ailments (including multiple sclerosis, Alzheimer's, cardiovascular disease, stillbirths, and infertility), incarceration, family violence, substance abuse, teenage suicides, school dropouts—these are the fatalities and "fatal impact statements" of the spatial exception of the unincorporated territory malformed into America's settler garrison. In short, "chamorus are being disappeared" (114).

The last part of Perez's testimony appears as footnote #10. It closes with one particular fatality: the disproportionate fatalities of Chamorro soldiers fighting in the US military. As a hypermilitarized US territory, Guam has been made to be economically dependent on the US military. This is to speak about a perverse economy—about what it means to be so heavily dependent on the very thing that is killing you. American occupation and reoccupation, narrated as liberation from the Spanish and then the Japanese, imposes militarized indebtedness onto the Chamorro. The production of this indebted subjectivity, linked to the ubiquitous presence of the US military on the island and aggressive recruitment tactics, is precisely why "military recruiters based in Guam almost always exceed their quotas. Headline: 'US Territories: A Recruiter's Paradise: Army Goes Where Fish Are Biting'—" (23). As I have related, this has led to Chamorros having some of the highest enlistment rates per capita in the US and its territories.[73]

Such disproportionately high enlistment rates, as payment for liberation and the price to be paid for restored masculinity and agency, is also, then, what has led to Chamorros having the highest fatality rates. Perez writes:

> joining the US military and dying in america's wars at alarming rates. in 2005, four of the US army's top twelve recruitment producers were based on guam. in 2007, guam ranked no. 1 for recruiting success in the army national guard's assessment of 54 states and territories. in the current war on terror, our killed in action rate is now five times the US national average. since the war on terror began in 2001, 29 sons of micronesia have died—17 of them from guam.
>
> in terms of population, chamorus constituted 45 percent of guam's population in 1980, in 1990, 43 percent, in 2000, 37 percent. in devastating contrast, the planned influx of non-chamorus will increase guam's overall population by about 30 percent, causing a 20-year population growth over the next five years. history repeats itself. more foreign snakes, fewer native birds. (127)

This, as I have suggested, is the violence not only of a promise made in bad faith but of an interpellating force and structure of affect governing America's settler garrison. Enlistment in the US military is the price to be paid for the unfulfilled promise of liberation. The temporal exception of debt imperialism that the United States enjoys, the perpetual rolling over of its debts, parallels the temporal exception of indefinitely withholding actual liberation (in the form of statehood or better yet, national sovereignty) for Guam. And yet Chamorros are made to repay the debt of (non)liberation again and again through their military labors, demonstrations of loyalty, and commemorations of "Liberation Day." For many, the ultimate payment is their very lives. Given this, in the third part/text of his poetic series, *from unincorporated territory [guma']* (2014, hereafter *[guma']*), Perez asks, "what are [our] bodies worth?" (75, brackets in original).[74] This is, of course, a rhetorical question, yet Perez provides an answer of sorts. According to the 1945 Guam Claims Acts, which granted settlements for property damage and loss of life during the Japanese occupation, the average death claim following a calculus based on age at death was approximately $1,900. This paltry sum of $1,900 demonstrates how subjects of America's settler garrison undergo at once an indispensability and disposability—indispensable soldiers and laborers in US military recruitment efforts and militarized service economies while also disposable lives in terms of disproportionate fatalities both in the fighting of America's wars and militarized environmental racism on the island.

Loyalty to the United States and to the US military is spectacularly displayed every year on July 21, "Liberation Day." A religious procession, marching bands, floats, games, a carnival, and young women selling fundraising tickets competing to become the next Liberation Day Queen congeal as the occasion for "Chamorros to express [our] loyalty and gratitude to the US. They say that [we] enlist in the military at such high rates to pay the debt of liberation" (*[guma']*, 34, brackets in original). Indeed, as Keith L. Camacho argues, the American discourse of loyalty has a long-standing history in Guam. In the first half of the twentieth century, efforts to garner the loyalties of Chamorros relied upon a broader history of white American perceptions of and dynamics with the colonized in the continental United States. The promotion of American loyalty in Guam was shaped by "strong racist undercurrents" that "reflected histories of indigenous dispossession and slavery in the United States."[75] During World War II and the period leading up to the passage of the Organic Act in 1950, the concept of loyalty was exploited by the American colonial government and Chamorro elites. The Organic Act itself had been passed in part to domesticate and neutralize Indigenous resistance to US naval rule. The conferral of partial citizenship and a certain measure of self-government were in some respects a counterinsurgent move renarrated as another instance of "liberation" in the form of US citizenship.

Camacho writes that leading up to World War II, "loyalty was, at best, an emergent, mutable concept of colonial control and indigenous adaptation."[76] Yet this changed with the outbreak of World War II and in particular with the return of American soldiers. Guam, already heavily militarized, underwent an intensification of militarization that required Chamorros to contemplate actively their loyalty to the United States. Indeed, during the brutal Japanese occupation, a popular song that Chamorros sang in resistance to the occupation contained these lyrics: Oh Mr. Sam, Sam, My Dear old Uncle Sam,/Won't you please come back to Guam![77] The ensuing American "liberation" of Guam from Japanese occupation "convinced Chamorros of the perceived humanitarian dimension of US military expansion into the Pacific. . . . Felix Torres Pangelinan wrote, for example, that Chamorros 'owe an everlasting debt to these gallant [American] men; a debt that we can never repay, but that we can show, in our humble gratitude, by being loyal, faithful, and patriotic to the United States of America.'"[78] Chamorros internalized the notions of loyalty and liberation more substantively and in far greater numbers than they had before, and from the 1950s onward, loyalty would be a key commemorative theme in Liberation Day celebrations. The celebration of Liberation Day has its roots in a 1945 Catholic religious procession held primarily to recognize the spiritual triumph of the Chamorro people in surviving the brutal horrors of the Japanese occupation, in addition to remembering the dead and expressing gratitude to the US liberators. But since the 1960s, this religious tone of the celebration has given way to the primacy of the displays of loyalty. Now a major commercial event resembling a carnival, Liberation Day involves a parade along Marine Corps Drive (the island's main thoroughfare named after the liberators), the "Liberation Queen" contest, and fundraising for charity.[79]

If the promise of liberation or freedom was made in bad faith, why such spectacular displays of loyalty and continued repayment of what Saidiya Hartman calls the "gift of freedom"?[80] As Vernadette Vicuña Gonzalez asks, "What alchemy transforms the terror of imperial violence and American . . . occupation to deeply felt understandings of American rescue, liberation, and benevolence?" These feelings, she compellingly argues, are not manifestations of false consciousness; they are "essential elements of a garrison state."[81] In a similar vein, building on Hartman's analysis of the contradictions of the "gift of freedom" for the formerly enslaved in the United States, Mimi Thi Nguyen argues that within the context of the Vietnam War, "the gift of freedom is not simply a ruse for liberal war but its core proposition and a particularly apt name for its operations of violence and power." More than a simple case of bad faith or falsehood, the gift of freedom is a force.[82] Whether as a formerly enslaved person, a Vietnam War refugee, or a subject of an unincorporated territory with only partial citizenship, the gift of freedom continues to exert an interpellating force that elides why the granting of such freedom was necessary in the first place. If the United States had not practiced racial chattel slavery, if it had not waged racist and imperialist war in Vietnam, if it had not captured Guam from the Spanish and indefinitely deferred the possibility of statehood—then the gift of freedom would not have been necessary in the first place. Moreover, the freedom that is granted is full of contradictions and contains within it forms of unfreedom, whether it's the "afterlife of slavery" and anti-Black racism, the refugee condition as a target of disciplinary knowledge and power through the medico-juridical diagnosis of abnormality and arrested development, or the transformation of a "liberated" territory into a military colony.[83] This elision of the *theft* of freedom through the sleight of hand amplification of the gift of freedom is precisely what gets instantiated again and again via Liberation Day. Yet still, what also gets elided is the United States' role in exempting Japan from all war reparations in 1951 as part of its Cold War alliance-building. This, too, is an instance of what I call the transpacific masculinist compact.

If Liberation Day is a performative conformity to the homogeneous time of repayment for the figurative debt imposed on Chamorros, it is paralleled with high enlistment rates in the US military as a more substantive and at times fatal form of repayment that reinforces and is in turn also reinforced by Liberation Day's spectacular gestures of loyalty as an annual event. In *[guma']*, Perez reveals an account of the targeting for military enlistment that he himself experienced, one that he and his parents were ultimately able to thwart. His family migrated to California in 1995, when he was a sophomore in high school. One reason for migrating was so that Perez could be better prepared to do well at a "mainland" university. Yet unsure of how his family would pay for his college education, Perez attended an army recruiter's presentation at his new high school. The recruiter, full of pride in his uniform, attempted to recruit Perez by informing him that the army would pay for college and reminding him that he had relatives in the military. Continuing with such aggressive recruitment tactics, about a month later the recruiter came to Perez's family house. In a phone conversation with Perez about that visit from the recruiter, his mother articulates a critique of the recruitment of children at such a young age and remembers wanting to find a different way to pay for Perez's college, ultimately expressing relief that he didn't join. His father, though a veteran, is similarly critical, expressing how he did not like the fact that the recruiter came to their house. He takes issue, moreover, with the recruiter's assumption that as a veteran he would automatically want his son to enlist as well, and with the assumption that parents would be naïve in the face of promises of free college, free travel around the world, free clothes, free food and housing. But, he asks, "what if you don't live? You went and you die and you don't get any college then . . . I could see a guy like that is just trying to make his quota as a recruiter" (22). Ultimately, Perez attends a university in California with scholarships, loans, work-study, and his parents' help. Within his own family history, we thus see on a microscale the vulnerability to engulfment by the military as well as a critique and evasion of it.

It was not until the 1990s that a Chamorro political activist group publicly criticized and protested the commemoration of Liberation Day as a colonial fabrication and imposition.[84] In a letter to the *Pacific Sunday News* on Liberation Day (July 21) 1991, Angel Santos, the then *maga'låhi* (male leader) or president of the United Chamorro Chelus for Independence Association, asserted that it was a misnomer to call July 21 "Liberation Day." Instead, he argued, it should be more appropriately called "Reoccupation Day." The US recapture of Guam from the Japanese was especially bloody and violent, what Rogers calls "liberation as apocalypse."[85] Santos voices a scathing indictment of US hypocrisy and of the genocidal effects of its ongoing colonial domination over Guam. It is worth citing at length:

> The only thing that the United States government cares for relative to our island is Guam's 210 square miles of land, Guam's strategic location in the Pacific, and the mining rights to anything within Guam's 200-mile Exclusive Economic Zone. . . . They only view Guam as a piece of real estate, the spoils of the Spanish-American War. . . . Could it be that by having all the Chamorros killed by the Japanese invasion or the US re-occupation, that the United States can claim sole possession of Guam? . . . Chamorros were relocated in a manner that would make them dependent on American handouts. . . . United States sovereignty and US Constitutional law which hinders the protection of Chamorro rights on Guam must be abolished. We must formally establish a "Chamorro Nation" in order to protect our rights to control our lives, land, resources and immigration. We must break down the walls of colonial slavery. . . . Consumerism, materialism, capitalism, alcoholism, and drugs are destroying the Chamorro family. We must stand together to save a dying nation of people . . ."[86]

Going beyond Guam's appeal to the US Congress in 1986 for commonwealth status, Santos calls for a formally independent, sovereign Guam, nothing short of a "Chamorro Nation." This, he urges, is necessary in standing up against the genocidal effects of "colonial slavery." Here, the horizon of political desire is set by the radical necessity and urgency of saving a "dying nation of people." Alongside and a part of the ecological harm wrought by US militarism in Asia and the Pacific is harm done to Chamorro life itself. This, Santos elucidates, is what is at stake. What we might call his politics of ingratitude or disloyalty challenges the very foundational grounds or sources of US authority in Guam—US sovereignty and constitutional law. Insofar as US sovereignty and constitutional law not only preempt "the protection of Chamorro rights on Guam" but are producing Chamorro death, they must be abolished. Indeed, as I discussed earlier, even though the unincorporated territory of Guam and its governance remain one of the most significant problems of American constitutional law, this problem has been relegated to the form of "constitutional arcana," or what I have been calling indefinite deferral.

"Fatal Impact Statements"

Such a genealogy of protest and urgent calls against the genocidal effects of US militarist settler imperialism on Guam find a more recent elaboration in [guma']. Perez powerfully engages with the protests against the massive planned transfer and military buildup outlined in the 2006 "US-Japan Roadmap for Realignment Implementation." Similar to how he scattered his UN testimony through a series of poem fragments bearing the same title in [saina], here, in a series of poem fragments entitled "fatal impact statements," Perez reproduces some of the comments submitted by Chamorros during the public hearing on the "Draft Environmental Impact Statement," one of a series of documents required by the National Environmental Policy Act (NEPA) enacted in 1969.[87] The 2009 "Draft Environmental Impact Statement (DEIS) for the Guam and Mariana Islands Military Relocation: Relocating Marines from Okinawa, Japan to Guam" is a document containing nine volumes, twenty-two chapters, and eleven thousand pages. It details the structural changes and environmental effects of what would be the biggest military base relocation in the twenty-first century—an additional eight thousand marines and nine thousand marine dependents on an island that is only 210 square miles, a relocation which would have resulted in the population of Guam becoming 42 percent US military.[88] Requiring more than five years to prepare, this is the longest DEIS in US history. Although Chamorros were given only ninety days (extended from an initial forty-five) to comment on an eleven-thousand-page document, over ten thousand comments were submitted, largely in response to a comment drive spearheaded by We Are Guåhan, an organization formed in opposition to what would be the biggest military buildup in the region since World War II. The final "Environmental Impact Statement" (EIS) did not contain any major changes but did include a tenth volume containing almost all the ten thousand comments submitted during the official ninety-day comment period. Perez's "fatal impact statements" is a poignant revision of "Draft Environmental Impact Statement."

Throughout [guma'], Perez includes and cites some of the comments. Though most of them are pointedly critical of the planned buildup, a few are supportive. Predictably, one supportive comment comes from the tourism industry—the Outrigger Guam Resort, OHANA Guam, and OHANA Oceanview Guam—testifying that the buildup will increase the number of tourists and customer "diversity" (27). Two other comments articulate the conundrum of Chamorro enlistment in and economic dependence on the US military. One comment reveals, "I don't think I'm allowed to say that I'm against the military buildup because both of my parents are for the buildup, and my dad is in the Air Force" (27). Similarly, another comment reads, "Hafa Adai [Hello]! My family has a long history of serving in and [being] in support of the US military" (44). Throughout, within the list of comments, Perez interjects his own comments in response to a particular one. He has a series of rejoinders to the comment cited immediately above. Through anaphoric repetition, he begins and ends each rejoinder as the commenter did, "Hafa Adai! My family has a long history of . . . in support of the US military." Yet what fills the ellipses is something different with each rejoinder—the variety of harms wrought by supporting the US military, whether diseases such as cancer and diabetes, dying in wars, land being taken, being relocated, or simply forgetting.

With the exception of the two comments cited above, the DEIS Public Comments or "fatal impact statements" included in [guma'] are articulations that pithily name and oppose the multiscalar violence of US militarist settler imperialism. Taken together, the comments focus on a variety of issues from multiple perspectives, but they are uniform in their opposition. They oppose sexual violence (recalling the rape of a twelve-year-old Okinawan girl in 1995); further theft of land; the displacement and outnumbering of the native Chamorro population; danger to wildlife; traffic, sewage, and solid waste; loss of recreational space and facilities (windsurfing and the racetrack); military usurpation of available bandwidth; and desecration of sacred, holy ground. A few comments question the process itself, asking for an extension of the comment period and wondering where the comments will be sent, who will see them, will the public see any of them? One comment pointedly critiques what a farcical and futile endeavor such opportunities for the public to comment can be: "Buenas. First off, thank you for the false sense of participation created by the comment period. The opportunity to vent, while completely meaningless, is at least very cathartic" (25). Scattered throughout Perez's poetics of antimilitarist decolonization and aesthetics of settler imperial failure, these "fatal impact statements" themselves constitute a poetics of antimilitarist decolonization. Though it may almost always very well be that an opportunity to weigh in provides a "false sense of participation," in this instance, it cannot be reducible to that. We can also read the tenth volume of the EIS, the volume containing almost all ten thousand of these comments, as a poetics of antimilitarist decolonization.

As I elaborated in Chapter 1, the outcry also came in the form of protests, teach-ins, hikes to threatened sites, a "swim-in" at Guam's port Apra Harbor, lawsuits, and international solidarity efforts. Yet more than the outcry, economic downturns in the United States and Japan led to the indefinite deferral of the buildup.[89] Moreover, in February 2010, the Environmental Protection Agency (EPA), after conducting a mandatory review of the DEIS, gave it the lowest possible rating, "Unsatisfactory: Inadequate information," and asserted that the buildup should not proceed as proposed because it would "significantly exacerbate substandard environmental conditions on Guam."[90] In particular, the EPA cited the lack of a specific water treatment plan as well as "unacceptable impacts to 72 acres of high quality coral reef ecosystem." Then, in response to a 2011 local lawsuit that charged the Department of Defense (DoD) with violating NEPA by selecting Pågat (the site of an ancient Chamorro village and burial site that is of cultural significance to Chamorros) for the construction of a live firing range complex, a revised EIS and supplemental EIS were to be submitted.[91] In 2014, when discussions resumed, proposed troop transfer numbers for Guam were lower and the focus shifted to other islands in the Mariana Islands north of Guam, Pågan and Tinian (a launching point for the *Enola Gay* during World War II).[92] Yet more recently, the Make America Secure Appropriations Act of 2018 provides the DoD with funding for defense-related projects on Guam, and even though the DoD acknowledges that climate change is a "threat," this does not prevent it from continuing to construct bases in locations differentially exposed to climate change at the cost of billions of dollars.[93]

Insidiously and perhaps counterintuitively, the United States practices what Perez calls "blue washing" or "blue capitalism" through the rhetoric of ocean conservation and the creation of national monuments and "Marine Protected Areas." This makes such areas exempt from environmental protections, making possible their availability for war training, weapon testing, the securing of shipping and military routes, maritime investments, and development projects.[94] Moreover, as I related in the Introduction, the United States practices a "maritime territorialism" through its control of the Exclusive Economic Zones (EEZs) extending two hundred nautical miles offshore of US states and territories. Recall that Angel Santos, in his letter to the *Pacific Sunday News* that I discussed earlier, notes that the United States controls not only the land constituting the island of Guam but also the mining rights of anything within Guam's two-hundred-mile EEZ. Constituting over thirteen thousand miles of coastline and 3.4 million square nautical miles of ocean, the US EEZ is larger than the combined landmass of all fifty states and is the biggest in the world.[95]

Although the particular indefinite deferral of the transfer of eight thousand marines (and nine thousand marine dependents) from Okinawa constitutes a victory for the moment that is not to be underestimated, it makes ever more urgent what antibase and antimilitarist activists recognize: that solidarities calling for overall demilitarization rather than realignment should be the expansive horizon of political possibility. Moreover, within the context of a still-colonized Guam whose possible statehood faces indefinite deferral (and in which statehood itself would be the placeholder for a decolonization yet to be realized), there still remains an urgent question posed by a commenter: "What if the people on Guam get outnumbered?" (64). This question and all of its implications build upon the history of Chamorro militarized death, dispossession, displacement, and diaspora. Indeed, along with the "fatal impact statements," scattered throughout *[guma']* is a roster of military fatalities, the names and details of Chamorro soldiers who have died while on active duty in the war on terror. Typographically, Perez does this: "[~~US Army Sgt.~~ Jesse Castro~~, 22, a Guam native, was killed when a roadside explosion destroyed their Humvee in Iraq~~]" (35). Rendering in strikethrough and in gray font everything except the name of the deceased soldier, Perez compels the reader to notice the individual names, even as the strikethrough and gray font indicating their age, place of origin, and details of their deaths suggest at once their now-ghostly presence and the inability of their ghostliness to haunt. That is, Chamorro deaths remain "spectrally indistinct" to the US populace, while Chamorro lives register only insofar as they can be targets of military recruitment or properly indebted subjects.

This aggressive targeting, and drafting during the Korean and Vietnam Wars, has not only produced fatalities but also a large-scale Chamorro diaspora in the continental United States, especially clustered in militarized cities such as San Diego, Long Beach, Vallejo, Alameda, and Fairfield. Perez accounts for the intensifying rate of migration out of Guam: "1980: 30,000 Chamorros live off-island *removed from*. 1990: 50,000 Chamorros live off-island. *removed from*. 2000: 60,000 Chamorros live off-island *removed from*. 2010: more of [us] live off-island than on-island. On YouTube, you can watch *red blood* Chamorros celebrating Liberation Day in *white bases* Hawai'i, California, Texas, South Carolina, Nebraska, Arizona, Nevada, Washington, Florida, and New York *blue passports*" (40, brackets and emphases in original). The italicized interjections—*removed from* (repeated three times), *red blood, white bases,* and *blue passports*—defamiliarize and challenge the presumption that migration to the continental United States is a desired teleology. The Chamorro diaspora is one of many militarized diasporas or displacements wrought by US militarist settler imperialism in Asia and the Pacific. Because Guam has been remade into America's settler garrison, there is a double movement: a heavy influx into Guam of US military personnel, dependents, and contract workers as well as a departure out of Guam of Chamorros in the US military for deployment in war (most recently the war on terror in Iraq and Afghanistan) or for stationing on the United States' vast chain of military bases. Moreover, the diaspora of Chamorros out of Guam has been long preceded by displacements within Guam itself in the wake of the US militarist settler imperial seizure of Indigenous land. Responding to the Land Acquisition Act of 1946, which allowed the US Navy to condemn private land and seize it, Guam's newly established Congress called the navy's land policy "a refugee-making policy" in a petition to the governor in 1947.[96]

Amid such testimony to loss, amid "fatal impact statements," Perez's poetics of antimilitarist decolonization and aesthetics of settler imperial failure also demonstrate the ability to find humor—even if a morbid humor—in the face of the ongoing violence of US militarist settler imperialism. Inserted within the DEIS Public Comment statements is a series of what we might call comic interludes. One such interlude captures the ambivalent love/hate relationship that we have come to have with Facebook: *"–The revolution will not be on Facebook/–If it isn't on Facebook, it probably wasn't very successful/–Or it was so successful that there is no more Facebook"* (64, italics in original). Perez's reference to Facebook—a recognition of the putative indispensability of Facebook that at once problematizes Facebook's reign—provides comic relief against the devastating effects that the planned massive military buildup would have on an already heavily militarized island. It also reveals a prescience about the scale of the dangers and recent critiques of the unethicality of Facebook's business practices. Even still, Perez comments that he posted some of the DEIS Public Comments to his Facebook account as status updates, suggesting that this particular revolution against further military buildup was successful enough to be on Facebook, but not so successful that Facebook no longer exists. In including the electronic space of online social media in activism against the military buildup, Perez creates a "public cybersphere" that enlarges the community of resisters.[97] In response to specific concerns, such as how much sewage and solid waste Guam can absorb, American mispronunciation of village names, and increased traffic, Perez responds with these comic quips: "—*Many comments address how full of ___ our colonizer is, but the real concern was never where our colonizer was going to put all that ___, especially with 80,000 [sic] more ___holes coming to Guam*" (25, italics in original); "—*Pronunciation before colonization!*" (27, italics in original); and "—*Traffic is the only issue that everyone is united against*" (47, italics in original). Here, Perez's politics of humor, far from making light of such concerns about the myriad effects of the planned buildup, amplifies the fatal absurdity of what the buildup would mean for such a tiny island already malformed by the distended contours of the US military.

Especially humorous and mordant are Perez's riffs on SPAM®. So much could be revealed about US militarism by following SPAM® as a trace. A "culinary legacy" of the US military in Asia and the Pacific during World War II, this unhealthy processed "meat" has high consumption rates precisely where US military presence is heavy—Guam, Hawai'i, the Philippines, Okinawa, and South Korea. Guam's consumption of SPAM® is the highest per capita in the world, with each Chamorro consuming on average sixteen cans per year. Guam is thus "considered the SPAM® capital of the world. . . . Welcome to Guam. Let [us] present you with the gourmet luxury of SPAM® at your birthday, wedding, and funeral. . . . In the devastating wake of Typhoon Omar, Hormel donated 40,000 cases of SPAM® to the Salvation Army's disaster relief effort. The end result of so much SPAM® can be found in [our] newspapers' obituary pages" (26, brackets in original). In other words, SPAM®'s ubiquity makes it the food staple of Guam. Yet it is a lethal staple that causes premature death.

Perez's continued riff on SPAM® is worth citing at length :

Rub the entire block of SPAM®, along with the accompanying gelatinous goo, onto your wood furniture. The oils from the SPAM® moisturize the wood and give it a nice luster. Plus, you'll have enough left over to use as your own personal lubricant (a true Pacific dinner date). Why didn't you tell me about the "In Honor of Guam's Liberation" SPAM®? I'm trying to collect them all! . . . SPAM® doesn't have to be unhealthy; I eat SPAM® every day and I'm not dead, yet—just switch to SPAM® Lite. . . . The name itself stands for *Specially Processed Army Meal, Salted Pork and More, Super Pink Artificial Meat, Snake Possum and Mongoose,* or *Some People Are Missing*. My uncle is the reigning Guam SPAM® king. He won the last SPAM® cook off with his Spicy SPAM® meatballs. I will never forget the two-pound SPAM® bust of George Washington he made for Liberation Day, toasted crispy on the outside with raw egg yolk in the hollow center—the kids loved it! (28, emphases in original)

SPAM®, a contraction of "spiced ham," may as well actually stand for "*Specially Processed Army Meal.*" For SPAM® is not only a metonym for US military presence but also of a militarized dependence upon, desire for, and literal ingestion of that which produces premature death. The connection that Perez makes between the consumption of SPAM® and demonstrations of loyalty on Liberation Day amplifies a kind of fatal coupling upon which the continued life and functioning of America's settler garrison depends. Elsewhere, Perez has called this "gastrocolonialism," a "structural force feeding." He writes, "My stomach is a colonial subject of the United States of SPAMerica. My Pacific body is an American SPAM dump . . . Indigestion is not an event; it is a structure."[98] This is to speak of militarized dependencies and desires that, in foreclosing resistance and alternatives, foreclose alternative futures or the possibility of having *any* future. That is, "*Some People Are Missing.*"

In the opening of *[guma']*, Perez also offers two pointedly humorous ways in which Guam itself can be an acronym for "Give Us American Military" and "Give Us Asian Money" (13). Commenting here on Guam's twinned economic dependence on the US military and tourism (especially from wealthy Japanese and pregnant South Korean women who travel to Guam's birthing centers so that their children can be US citizens), Perez likens Guam to an endangered species. Indeed, "Guam is no longer Guam" (13).[99] In a poem fragment toward the end of *[guma']*, he writes:

> invasion is
> a continuous chain of
> immeasurably destructive
> events in time—
>
> is the death of *[i sihek]*
> origins
> is a stillborn *[i sihek]*
> future—is the ending of
> all nests this
> choking thing [we] *[i sihek]* (71, brackets and italics in original)

The *sihek* is the Micronesian kingfisher bird native to Guam. Extinct in the wild because of the introduction of the predatory brown snake, it now only exists in small numbers in captivity. Immediately preceding the poem above is a paragraph explaining how two Guam Micronesian kingfishers were mated in a special breeding room of a zoo's bird house. One of the two fertile eggs that were laid was taken to an incubation machine in a lab where it is fed by keepers with tweezers and an oversized kingfisher hand puppet. In *from unincorporated territory [lukao]*, Perez calls this process "violent care" (23). This oxymoronic construction highlights the violence of militarist settler imperialism, the very violence that then necessitates a certain kind of care in the attempt to combat its environmentally devastating effects. Much like the gift of freedom, this "care" in the face of imminent extinction would not be necessary if the structure of militarist violence had not been imposed in the first place.

This story of the sihek also describes the fate of Chamorros in the wake of a never-ending invasion. Perez's conceptualization of invasion as "a continuous chain of/immeasurably destructive/events in time—" at once reinforces and complicates Wolfe's oft-cited argument that invasion is a structure and not an event.[100] As I have observed, invasion is at once a structure *and* an event. In the case of Guam, to think of invasion as "a continuous chain" of destruction is to think of it as a structure. Yet at the same time, as Perez writes, the immeasurable destruction is a set of "events in time—." The temporal element is crucial precisely because Guam's status as an unincorporated territory, as I have demonstrated, is underpinned by both a structural logic or militarist geography as a spatial exception and a temporal (il)logic of imbricated temporal exceptions. Inasmuch as US militarist settler imperialism is a structure of domination, it is also a "structure of failure." It is not a total fait accompli but rather an ensemble of relations that continually requires renovation and reassertion. It is precisely because of such incompleteness, inexhaustiveness, or failure that it requires continuous acts of invasion through "immeasurably destructive/events in time." Perez's aesthetics of settler imperial failure makes these conjoined structural and processual aspects of invasion visible.

By way of a conclusion, I draw our attention to Perez's reference to a "stillborn . . . future." To speak of the sihek's stillborn future is to speak also of the Chamorros' stillborn future. Yet there is yet another possible stillborn future—US militarist settler imperialism's stillborn future as a structure of failure. In Guam, the settler debt regime coexists with an alternative concept of debt. It is, as I explained in Chapter 1, inafa' maolek, which means "to make things good for each other." It presumes mutual respect rather than individualism, and a principle of interdependence rather than compelled dependence. If debt, as I have suggested, is this lateral form of reciprocity, mutuality, and obligation, the very thing that makes sociality possible, then inafa' maolek is a stubborn refusal that can generate a collective default, or another abolition, an abolition of the debt regimes of US militarist settler imperialism.

EPILOGUE: *Climate Change, Climate Debt, Climate Imperialism*

In a special folio of poems published in the journal *Shima* in 2019, Craig Santos Perez previews work to be included in the fifth book of his *from unincorporated territory* series.[1] The final poem in this folio, "Storm Tracking," focuses on the increasing convergence of disaster capitalism, colonialism, and the devastation caused by greater frequencies of climate change–induced hurricanes in the Pacific. Each line of the poem begins with the anaphoric "This is when" to convey a trio of linked forces that we witness in the wake of the storm: physical destruction, the privatizing and extractive practices of disaster capitalism, and acts of human survival against them. Perez writes of a particularly poignant and violently compelled act of survival: "This is when we migrate with or without dignity—."[2] Let us consider the poem's amplification of the multiple devastations wrought by climate change in general, and compelled migration in particular, with another Indigenous Pacific Islander cultural form that is the focus of this Epilogue. *Moana: The Rising of the Sea*, a multimedia dramatic stage production combining original music compositions, song, dance, theater, poetry, and video projection design, had its world premiere in December 2013 at the

University of the South Pacific (USP) in Suva, Fiji. The premiere was held in conjunction with the conference "Restoring the Human to Climate Change," organized by the European Consortium for Pacific Studies, a European Union (EU)–funded research project.[3] *Moana* dramatizes the fictional story of a Pacific Island community facing displacement because of climate-induced rising sea levels, storms, and floods.

Moana's staging of the differential impact of climate change, of differential vulnerabilities and fatalities, illuminates another valence in the manifold regimes of debt that I have been discussing throughout this book. Climate change instantiates what has been called climate debt. As with other forms of debt, climate debt is, following Nicholas Mirzoeff, a "structural violence." He explains that the so-called developed world of the Global North has accumulated wealth via its disproportionate use of fossil fuels per capita, producing ever-greater levels of carbon emissions. Given that there is general global agreement now that emissions have to be limited, the Global North "owes" emissions to the parts of the world it has subjected to compelled underdevelopment, the Global South.[4] What this climate debt means is that the Global North needs to cut emissions sufficiently enough so that it leaves room under the established overall global limit for countries in the Global South to expand their economies. This climate debt, or the means by which the Global North has become wealthy and has simultaneously underdeveloped the Global South, in turn generates monetary debt, what has been called "Third World debt," for the Global South. I have observed that the debt owed to Indigenous communities in the wake of land theft is the debt that is not even acknowledged as one at all. Climate debt is another variety of such unacknowledged debt, and the economy of unacknowledgment can operate because of what Mirzoeff calls "climate imperialism." The bitter irony is that the effects of climate change undergo an inversion such that the greatest carbon emitters are the least likely to be impacted. In other words, "because citizens in the developed world drive their gas-guzzlers, low-lying countries in the Pacific and Indian Oceans risk being permanently flooded."[5]

Performed by lead actor Allan Alo (the late great Sāmoan choreographer and artist), the Oceania Dance Theatre (founded by Alo), and the Pasifika Voices Ensemble, *Moana* features thirty-two performers representing Fiji, the Solomon Islands, Sāmoa, Kiribati, and the Marshall Islands. The 2013 world premiere at USP was followed by a tour in Europe in May and June 2015, specifically Scotland and Denmark, as well as performances at the EU Parliament in Brussels and the Bergen International Film Festival in Norway. This latter staging in Bergen was recorded for release online and as a DVD entitled *Moana Rua: The Rising of the Sea* (2015).[6] These performances were driven by the goal of sparking a collective international conversation about an urgent issue: the existential threat faced by low-lying Pacific Island nations and territories because of the escalating impacts of climate change, particularly sea-level rise and flooding, but also related threats to sustainability and security such as crop failures, limited water supplies, and extreme weather events.[7]

Moana is a powerful experimental poetic work, staged as "a dialogue between movement, projected image, and song."[8] Movement is composed of the performance of the Oceania Dance Theatre interwoven with aspects of ballet and modern as well as aerial dance. The musical composition similarly layers different elements, including prerecorded sounds of the Pasifika Voices Ensemble as well as live drumming and singing. Projected images are composed largely of documentary footage of the devastation and displacement wrought by climate change and of protests against it. Poetry is largely composed of the work of Kathy Jetñil-Kijiner, the Marshallese poet, performance artist, and educator who gained international acclaim following her powerful performance of "Dear Matafele Peinam," a poem written to and for her daughter, at the opening ceremony of the United Nations (UN) Climate Summit in New York in 2014.[9] In *Moana*, this piece, along with "Tell Them," is performed by the chief of the community, Chief Telematua, played by Alo. Throughout the staging, beautifully evocative movements of dance and song are sharply and suddenly interrupted by sonic effects, suggesting ominous danger. The performing bodies on stage collapse into chaotic movements and cries of flight and cover, coupled with video projections of actual documentary images of catastrophic floods. By the end of *Moana*, after a devastatingly fatal hurricane has killed many members of the community and drowned the islands, the surviving members are compelled to make the difficult decision to leave their homeland. Full-scale images of the sailing *vaka*, the voyaging canoe of Oceania used with sophisticated navigation techniques that rely on knowledge of the natural environment rather than instruments, are projected onscreen.[10]

Through this evocative poetics of performance, *Moana* grapples complexly with what can only be described as the immediate existential and ecological threat to Pacific Islander communities that climate change poses. In the official abstract of the filmed version of the stage production, director and producer Vilsoni Hereniko writes, "For most of us who live in the Pacific, our views of climate change are influenced by what we see happening in our own backyard: waves crashing against our homes, making obvious that we face a bleak and uncertain future." Hereniko's statement on the devastating effects of climate change on a local and concrete scale complicates recent discussions of the Anthropocene, a twenty-first-century term adopted by some scholars to call attention to how human activity is irreversibly changing the planet on the scale of a geological force.[11] Although we have witnessed in recent years something of a cottage industry of new publications and journals on the topic of the Anthropocene, Elizabeth DeLoughrey makes the important observation that Anthropocene discourse presumes the *"novelty* of crisis rather than being attentive to the historical *continuity* of dispossession and disaster caused by empire."[12] This is the case because of a lack of substantive engagement with postcolonial and Indigenous viewpoints, epistemologies, and experiences in favor of an almost-exclusive focus on the viewpoints of the Global North.[13] We see a similar absence in international climate regimes. Although Pacific Islanders are among those who are most likely to be impacted by climate change, their particular challenges are not taken into account in instruments such as the 1992 UN Framework Convention on Climate Change (UNFCCC) and the 1997 Kyoto Protocol. Only in the recent 2015 Paris Agreement did we finally see any acknowledgment at all that Indigenous knowledge could possibly be worthy of integration into relevant socioeconomic and environmental policies and actions addressing climate adaptation.[14] In centering the Pacific's devastating experience of climate change, Hereniko's abstract interrogates dominant Anthropocene discourse, as well as global climate change frameworks and protocols, and makes clear what kind of intervention *Moana* hopes to inspire. Critically reframed, the Anthropocene is more specifically the Racial Capitalocene and Plantationocene.[15] In the final instance, it is also the Necrocene.

Moana opens with Alo's performance of parts of "Tell Them" as Chief Telematua, cataloging the various effects of climate change experienced directly by his community and imploring his audience to "tell them that we never wanted to leave, and that we are nothing without our islands." His second poetic monologue comes about midway through *Moana*. This time, he addresses the UN directly. It begins in a manner similar to the opening performance, yet it takes an unexpected turn:

> Our islands are sinking, swallowed up by the rising seas, swallowed up by ways of life in which money and development and fossil fuels and greed have caused the rising seas to overcome us. Soon we will be forced to abandon these beautiful islands . . . what some of you call paradise. . . . You ask how can you help, what can you do. Here's how you can. Be our advocate. Wherever you are, spread the word about us, tell them we are drowning and that we may be forced to give up these islands that have given us life for thousands of years. Should we be forced to relocate, our desire is to be able to live with our dignity intact. *Do not call us climate change refugees*

because we do not deserve that label. Instead call us migrants to a new land, where we will rebuild our lives, piece by piece, slowly but surely.

Chief Telematua's complex invocation of the climate change refugee through the very refusal to ascribe that "label" to himself and to his people enjoins us to grapple with not only the urgent question of what is to be done about the state of emergency caused by climate change but also the fraught set of questions concerning representation, agency, ethical responsibility, and power.[16] The invocation of the climate change refugee as a problematic trope, one that indexes what I cited previously as Perez's poetic lament that "we migrate with or without dignity," makes visible the climate debt. Even as formal legal recognition or classification as a climate change refugee might come with certain protections and benefits, it is a vexed issue fraught with uneven power dynamics and (neo) colonial interests.

As I have been arguing throughout *Settler Garrison*, given the underlying asymmetries of power undergirding regimes of debt, the question of who owes what to whom must be continually posed anew. Who, really, is the creditor, and who, really, is the debtor? Compounding the unacknowledged climate debt is what has been called the "ecological debt" owed by the Global North to formerly colonized peoples and places because of the protracted environmental impacts of colonial plunder and resource extraction.[17] Ongoing asymmetries of power are such that the "ecological debt" is also unacknowledged. The Global North's refusal to acknowledge its conjoined climate-ecological debts is coupled with the imposition of monetary debt on the Global South and punitive mechanisms for compelled repayment. In this way, climate imperialism can be seen as a variety of debt imperialism insofar as it is also a debt that does not have to be repaid and can actually be leveraged as a form of imperial power in imposing strict policies and disciplinary protocols, such as austerity, on the Global South.

In turn, insofar as debt imperialism can be seen as the economic logic and form of US militarism, we must ask how the US military is implicated in climate change. The Pentagon, as it turns out, is the biggest consumer of energy on the planet and has the distinction of being the institution with the highest level of global carbon emissions. This might be surprising or shocking, given how emissions are often attributed to individual consumption, less often to corporate practices, and hardly at all to military expansion. Yet the US military, particularly the navy and its air force, emits some of the most polluting bunker and jet fuels because of the central role it plays in securing the smooth flow of the global oil supply, over 60 percent of which is shipped by sea. In turn, over 20 percent of the Pentagon's budget is dedicated to securing this supply. Indeed, the Pentagon both consumes energy and emits carbon in rates that are disproportionate to any nation. In short, "'militarism is the most oil exhaustive activity on the planet.'"[18] And yet, in another example of the extreme inversion I referred to earlier, the United States withdrew from the 2015 Paris Agreement on November 4, 2020, formally concluding the withdrawal process Trump announced in June 2017 and making the United States the sole nonparticipant in the world. Days later, President-Elect Biden announced that the United States would rejoin the Paris Agreement under his administration. Though this is a relatively positive development, what remains disturbing is that a commitment to combating climate change, and even the very belief that climate change is actually occurring, is not consistent but subject to the vicissitudes of the imperial presidential administrations of the United States.

Alongside plunder and extraction, imperial power can also be manifested and scripted as imperial largesse, generosity, or grace. This returns us to Chief Telematua's refusal of the "climate refugee" ascription in *Moana*. To be any kind of refugee, climate or otherwise, is to be the recipient of imperial "generosity" and hospitality. As I have observed, the bestowal of the "gift of freedom" elides the crucial question of why the recipients of freedom were unfree in the first place. In this sense, the economy of the gift of freedom is also a kind of unacknowledged debt; the freedom, which is to say the debt, that is owed to the enslaved, the colonized, or the refugee, is rescripted as a gift instead. This is a particularly insidious sleight of hand, for through it the debtor metamorphoses into the creditor, and the creditor metamorphoses into the debtor. Moreover, it is a denial of agency; the enslaved, the colonized, and the refugee become legible only as the bodies from whom freedom has been denied then later upon whom it has been bestowed by the powers that be. *Moana* is mindful of this scheme and is careful not to embrace the status of climate refugee, even as it dramatizes the compelled migration of Pacific Islanders because of climate-induced rising sea levels. The "host" nations of the Global North receiving displaced Pacific Islanders as climate refugees benefit from debt's form as a sleight of hand with a double operative logic: debt in the form of a figurative indebtedness or gratitude is imposed on the climate refugees, and the Global North can continue to leave unacknowledged the climate debt that it owes, or elide the fact that its own disproportionately high carbon emissions caused the existential threat to low-lying islands in the first place.[19]

Against such logics, *Moana* stages through Chief Telematua what the figure of the refugee—as a trope that conjures victimhood, helplessness, and the putative generosity and humanitarianism of the host country—all too often obscures: the agency and dignity of those who have been displaced. In this context, to refuse the refugee label is to highlight instead how Indigenous communities in the Pacific have used Indigenous forms of knowledge (what is called traditional ecological knowledge, or TEK) along with newer technologies in frameworks and practices of adaptation, mitigation, and climate activism and diplomacy.[20] Crucially, alliance building and initiatives among island nations both within Oceania and beyond are a significant part of this practice, whether working within the UNFCCC regime or beyond. Important developments include the Pacific Plan created by Pacific Island states at the 2005 Pacific Islands Forum in Papua New Guinea to strengthen regional cooperation and integration, which was later overhauled and replaced by the Framework for Pacific Regionalism.[21] Working within the UNFCCC regime, we have seen formations such as the Pacific Small Island Developing States (PSIDS) grouping and the Alliance of Small Island States (AOSIS).[22] Moreover, gatherings such as the Third International Conference on Small Island Developing States (SIDS) held in Sāmoa in 2014, following on meetings in Barbados and Mauritius, have been significant not only because they were held in the Pacific Islands but precisely because they highlighted the challenges faced by low-lying islands and coasts.[23] Finally, recent policy initiatives include the 2018 Vanuatu National Policy on Climate Change and Disaster-Induced Displacement, a policy that has helped to preserve Indigenous cultural heritage in the islands of Vanuatu.[24]

It is this crucial context that *Moana* amplifies. In the third and final closing poetry performance, Chief Telematua speaks the words of Jetñil-Kijiner's "Dear Matafele Peinam" to his baby:

no one's drowning, baby
no one's moving
no one's losing
their homeland
no one's gonna become
a climate change refugee

or should i say
no one else . . .

because baby we are going to fight
your mommy daddy
bubu jimma your country and president too
we will all fight

and even though there are those
hidden behind platinum titles

who like to pretend
that we don't exist
that the marshall islands
tuvalu
kiribati
maldives
and typhoon haiyan in the philippines
and floods of pakistan, algeria, colombia
and all the hurricanes, earthquakes, and tidalwaves
didn't exist

still
there are those
who see us . . .

The refusal to be called a climate change refugee is reiterated, but also augmented from its earlier iteration through a conjoined refusal to succumb to the
existential threat. Indeed, after Jetñil-Kijiner's powerful performance of her
poem at the 2014 UN Climate Summit in New York, the line "no one's gonna
become a climate change refugee" became a refrain for Pacific climate change
movements.[25] Jetñil-Kijiner's poetry and climate activism have been called a
"hydro-feminism" that centers Indigenous feminist epistemologies and posi-
tionalities to critique the continuities between colonial and neocolonial operations as well as the continuities between colonial and "environmental scopic
regimes" that limit climate change imaginaries.[26]

In *Moana*, Chief Telematua makes a pledge to his child that "we will fight,"
and as the performance unfolds, the "we will" gets articulated as a series of what
"we are": "fists raising up, banners unfurling, megaphones booming, canoes block-
ing coal ships, radios of solar villages, rich clean soil of the farmers, petitions
blooming from teenage fingertips, families biking, recycling, reusing, engineers
dreaming, designing, building, and artists painting, dancing, drawing." By asserting this Pacific-centered ontology and praxis in the face of differentiated
vulnerability to the impacts of climate change, *Moana* strategically grapples
with the dialectics of victimhood and agency. Rather than sending out an SOS
signal and hoping for "rescue," *Moana* instead offers an invitation to its European
audience to become a multilateral partner as opposed to a "savior" in combating
the climate crisis.[27] The focus on Indigenous agency and refusal to succumb to
the forces of climate change works against a "transnational politics of pity."[28]

Scholars in island studies and its broad productive intersections with critical political and human geography, settler colonial studies, Indigenous and

feist studies, critiques of militarism, and other related fields have grappled complexly with the notion of "island vulnerability." Mindful that vulnerability has become a problematically dominant trope in fetishizing islands as inherently, essentially, or naturally vulnerable rather than interrogating the multiple causes of vulnerability itself, Mimi Sheller reminds us that vulnerability is "not grounded in geography alone, but constructed within and through neocolonial conditions of deliberately weak states or non-sovereignty, neoliberal economic coercion, external military domination, and 'disaster capitalism.'"[29] In terms of climate change vulnerability in particular, Sheller argues that to the extent that it is the result of colonial pasts and neocolonial presents, it would be more apt to call it the "coloniality of climate."[30] So rather than fixating on notions of islands as singular and isolated laboratories for experimentation, the most extreme indicators of climate vulnerability, or compelled displacement, island studies scholars emphasize instead resilience against (neo)coloniality, mobilities, complex interconnectedness, relationality, multiplicity, cultural creativity, and ever-evolving social ecologies.[31]

Moana departs from a representational scheme in the Global North that either completely renders invisible climate change in the Pacific Islands or fetishizes the existential threat via two dominant tropes—newness and disappearance. The presumption is that climate change is something new, partly because it is only perceptible and representable as a disaster event, when its slow violence reaches an inflection point and erupts. This presumption also ignores the fact that Pacific Islanders have been adapting to changes in the environment for long periods of time far predating the twenty-first century. The refusal to apprehend Indigenous adaptation, resilience, and survival is in turn connected to the second trope, disappearance. It calls to mind the trope of the "vanishing Indian" within the context of the continental United States, and the related practice of salvage anthropology and ethnography, the late-nineteenth and early twentieth century preoccupation with capturing the "vanishing Indian" before it is too late. DeLoughrey observes that although this earlier generation of salvage anthropologists was focused on "dying culture," the contemporary genre of "salvage environmentalism" attempts to capture a "dying nature" in the era of the Anthropocene and Necrocene. Documentary films in particular, many produced in the years immediately following 9/11, do the ideological work of focusing on climate change in the Pacific Islands, but in a manner that denies coevality to Pacific Islanders with a primitivist stroke and obfuscates the Global North's causal role as the primary agent of climate change. DeLoughrey argues that while these films give a "human face" to the fraught political and juridical issue of "climate refugees," they "harness the characters' personal mourning for their inundated islands to figure as the western audience's anticipated loss of a universal 'nature.'"[32] This imperialist nostalgia is such that the mourning of the loss becomes a substitute for interrogating what or who caused the loss in the first place. Moreover, insofar as imperialist nostalgia is saturated by tropes of island primitivity and premodernity, it misapprehends the object of loss itself and the temporality of when the loss occurred. The Marshall Islands, for example, were violently engulfed into US nuclear modernity via irradiation and displacement several decades ago.[33]

Moana closes with an alternative vision for the future in the form of a pledge or promise. Chief Telematua promises his baby that the community will bring about change by saying, "You deserve to do more than just survive. You deserve to thrive." Like the Chamorro concept of inafa' maolek that I discussed in Chapters 1 and 4, this promise is an alternative form of debt, one based on mutual obligation and the responsibilities that humans have not only to one another but to the environment and to other species. How might these lateral forms of debt based on responsibility and mutual obligation, the very thing that makes sociality possible, crowd out the dominant debt relation that instantiates and perpetuates violent asymmetries of power? I am thus compelled to ask how we might abolish the debt relation altogether. To be clear, this call for debt abolition is different from debt forgiveness. The latter only clears particular debts, whereas the former eliminates debt as such.[34] Put differently, this is to ask about the difference between the abolishment of militarist settler imperialism and "forgiveness" industries and processes such as liberal philanthropy, truth and reconciliation commissions, reparations, and transitional justice. These processes, though significant in their own ways, are the symptoms of or the placeholders for an as-yet-unrealized horizon.

For the figurative debt, might it be possible to enact a politics that calls on us to view the debt not as an invitation to coevality or liberal political modernity that we cannot refuse but as an engulfment into the suffocating embrace of militarist settler imperial and gendered racial violence? For the literal debt, this politics calls on us to refuse the debt by harnessing the power of a collective default *against* the bullying threat of US debt imperialism and the homogeneous time of repayment. This is to embrace something along the lines of what Fred Moten and Stefano Harney call the place of bad debt, "the debt that cannot be repaid . . . the debt without creditor, the black debt, the queer debt, the criminal debt."[35] And the student debt. This debt without creditor gestures to an alternative social relation and economy and refuses quid pro quo calculations of reciprocity. Indeed, if debt in an alternative sense is, as I have observed, a lateral form of reciprocity and obligation, or the very thing that makes sociality possible, the debt regimes of US militarist settler impe-rialism have converted and perverted that sociality into necropolitical social hierarchy. In this sense, to inquire into this conversion is to perform a social autopsy, to encounter the mortuary of the already dead and the living dead, all the while apprehending that what remains and awaits our embrace are those stubborn refusals.

Throughout this book, I have written about debt in its manifold forms, both acknowledged and unacknowledged, and financial as well as affective. So it is fitting that in these acknowledgments, debt continues to linger. For there is a singular form of the affective debt that is at once acknowledged but never sufficiently repaid, not because it is an imposed or prescriptive debt whose continual repayment the creditor demands but precisely because the creditor in this instance does not expect or demand repayment at all. How to account for the debts that do not desire accounting, that indeed actively refuse it? I have written that this is an alternative form of debt, the counterintuitive antithesis of what we have come to know as the debtor/creditor relation. It is the very thing that makes sociality possible. And so what I offer now is intended less as an accounting and more as an acknowledgment and recognition of relations of mutuality and reciprocal obligation.

At UC Riverside, where I have taught since completing my graduate studies in 2004, I have learned so much from a wonderful collective of colleagues and friends. Many are still in Southern California and the Inland Empire; some have departed for other places; and one, sadly, has departed us for other worlds. I begin with the one who is no longer with us, the late Stephen Cullenberg, whom we affectionately called "Dean Steve." His visionary intellectual leadership as the dean of the College of Humanities, Arts, and Social Sciences, far surpassing perfunctory administrative or bureaucratic bounds, made it possible for us to build boldly, beyond the defeatist logic that can often limit resource-deprived institutions such as UC Riverside. I like to hope that the career-long conversation Steve had with Marx is now continuing, in another world. Then there are those who have departed for other places who, in their own ways, made lasting contributions to our collective formation. I miss and appreciate Fred Moten, Laura Harris, Nick Mitchell, Ashon Crawley, and especially Erica Edwards and Deb Vargas. Those who are familiar with the sprawl of

Southern California and also work at a commuter campus know that it can be a minor miracle when colleagues who are also your dear friends become your literal neighbors. Minor and short-lived miracle it was that I got to be Erica and Deb's (and Maceo's!) neighbor for a bit before the other coast beckoned them away. Our "undisciplined encounters" and happy hours sustained me, and I continue to learn from their important work. And speaking of SoCal traversals, I remember those important trips to LAX and how Deb took the Greyhound to Mariam's!

Then, of course, are those who remain my local coconspirators. I thank and am profoundly grateful to Amalia Cabezas, Mariam Lam, Sarita Echavez See, and Dylan Rodríguez for their steadfastness, wisdom, and wicked wit. I thank Amalia for all those fish tacos, for pushing me in exactly the right way when necessary, and for calling even when there is no immediate reason. I thank Mariam for giving shelter (literal and otherwise) at a moment's notice, for providing a model of work that is not ego driven, and for necessary doses of brutal honesty. I thank Sarita for encouraging me to write what we came to call "The Plot," for coming and making pork adobo, for patiently unspiraling what I have spiraled, and for being a model of ethicality. And I thank Dylan for all that chicken with the secret sauce, for seeing abundance and possibility where and when others don't, and for all that he did to build the Department of Ethnic Studies as chair for seven years. Thanks as well to David Lloyd, who never tires of fighting the good fight. I am also grateful to my colleagues in the Department of Media and Cultural Studies who welcomed me into the department and made a difficult transition much easier to navigate.

This project in particular, and my continuing development as a scholar in general, have also benefited immeasurably from the summer travel crew as well as friends and mentors elsewhere. I thank Grace Kyungwon Hong for her fierceness, committed generosity, and the stickers of Mia. Kara Keeling nudged me to get my chapter drafts done at exactly the right moment. My gratitude goes as well to Iyko Day for her abounding intellectual curiosity, true patience, and adeptness at brainstorming. Nadine Naber is an inspiration, a multitasking wizard, and an embodiment of courage. Thanks as well to David Hernández for his impeccable taste in music and ability to find the humor in things. I also thank Lisa Lowe and Lisa Yoneyama, not only for their support and mentorship over the years but for gifting us with their paradigm-shifting work. I remain grateful as well to the LOUD Collective for feedback on my project in its early stages. Our monthly meetings traversing multiple counties went strong for the better part of a decade and provided a formative model of peer mentorship, intellectual abundance, and generous engagement.

I have presented earlier versions of what became this book at a variety of gatherings over the course of many years. My gratitude goes to the many who generously extended invitations for me to share my work and to the many more in attendance whose active engagement helped me immensely in refining and strengthening my ideas. These occasions and sites include the "Between Life and Death: Necropolitics in the Era of Late Capitalism" Residential Research Group at the University of California Humanities Research Institute (UCHRI) that I coconvened with Grace Kyungwon Hong; the Asian Institute's Centre for the Study of Korea at the University of Toronto; the Five College Asian/ Pacific/American Distinguished Lecture Series; the "Global Asias" Symposium at Pennsylvania State University; the Distinguished Visitors Series at Haverford College; the Summer Institute in "Asian American Studies: Empire Reconsidered" at National Tsing Hua University in Hsinchu, Taiwan; the "Race in the Global Asias" Symposium at Brown University; the Militarism in Asia Working Group at UC Berkeley; the "Empires of Capital: Race across the Atlantic and the Pacific" Symposium at the University of Washington; the "Cold War in Asia" Conference at the University of Chicago; the "Poetics of Law, Poetics of Decolonization" Conference at UC Riverside; the "Africa-Asia: A New Axis of Knowledge 2" Conference in Dar es Salaam, Tanzania; the Inter-Asia Cultural Studies Conferences in Seoul, South Korea, and Singapore; the English Language and Literature Association of Korea (ELLAK) Conference in Busan, South Korea; the "Trans-Asia as Method: Exploring New Potentials of 'Trans-Asian' Approaches" Symposium at Monash University, Prato Centre, Italy; the "Except Asia: Agamben's Work in Transcultural Perspective" Conference at National Taiwan Normal University in Taipei, Taiwan; the "Histories of Violence" Symposium at Northwestern University; and the annual meetings of the American Studies Association and the Association for Asian American Studies.

At Duke University Press, I thank my editor Ken Wissoker, whose enthusiasm, encouragement, and support kept me on track and made it possible for me to cross the finish line. From the opening moments of our first conversation about my project and throughout the entire process, Ken demonstrated a model of thoughtful care, generous listening, and intellectual capaciousness. I am also grateful to the wonderful editorial staff and the whole team at Duke: Josh Tranen, Susan Albury, Emily Lawrence, and others. Thanks as well to the staff at Westchester Publishing Services. My deep gratitude also goes to the anonymous reviewers whose rigorous engagement with my manuscript and incisive comments were enormously helpful and generative.

An earlier version of a part of Chapter 1 was previously published as "Settler Modernity, Debt Imperialism, and the Necropolitics of the Promise," *Social*

Text 135 (June 2018). This is a special issue on "Economies of Dispossession: Indigeneity, Race, Capitalism," edited by Jodi A. Byrd, Alyosha Goldstein, Jodi Melamed, and Chandan Reddy. I thank all the editors, and Alyosha in particular, who worked with me on my essay. His generous and deep feedback made an immeasurable difference. An earlier version of a part of Chapter 3 appeared as "Settler Modernity's Spatial Exceptions: The US POW Camp, Metapolitical Authority, and Ha Jin's *War Trash*," *American Quarterly* 69, no. 3 (September 2017). This is a special issue on "The Chinese Factor: Reorienting Global Imaginaries in American Studies," edited by Chih-ming (Andy) Wang and Yu-Fang Cho. I thank Andy for extending a generous invitation to submit my essay to the special issue, and thanks as well to Yu-Fang, whose careful reading of my essay and insightful comments sharpened my analysis and lines of inquiry.

Finally, I am deeply grateful to my family. My father, who is no longer with us, lived to feed everyone around him even though he could not himself eat solid food for multiple decades because of the aftereffects of cancer treatment. I thank him for teaching me, by example, how to transform scarcity or lack into abundance and plenitude. Luna, who is also no longer with us and was taken way too soon, taught me how to be patient and that toy poodles really are the best. She converted me, someone who had strongly identified as not being an "animal person," and saw me finally make progress on my manuscript (after many fits and starts) before losing her valiant battle with liver failure. I am grateful to my sister, Kelly, for always being there for me and going beyond the call of sisterly duty. Thanks as well to my brother-in-law, Jason, for his support, and to my nephews Matthew, Andrew, and Colby for keeping things real. I must also thank Mia, all eleven maltipoo pounds of her, for keeping me on my toes and teaching me how to approach even the most familiar and mundane of things with animated curiosity.

INTRODUCTION

1 For an insightful analysis of how the claim that Asian *Americans* have nothing to gain by the success of *Parasite* actually misses the point, see Eng-Beng Lim, "Living in *Parasite* Country as Asian/American."

2 When *Parasite* won the 2020 Golden Globe Award for Best Foreign Language Picture, Bong notably began his acceptance speech, translated by Sharon Choi, in this way: "Once you overcome the one-inch tall barrier of subtitles, you will be introduced to so many more amazing films."

3 Dargis, "'Parasite' Review." In addition to reviews, academic essays that focus on the film's critique of capitalism include Gabilondo, "Bong Joon Ho's *Parasite* and Post-2008 Revolts"; and Noh, "Parasite as Parable."

4 "Bong Joon-ho Discusses PARASITE, Genre Filmmaking And The Greatness Of ZODIAC," YouTube Video, 5:08, posted by Birth.Movies.Death., October 16, 2019, https://www.youtube.com/watch?v=dXuXfgquwkM&fbclid=IwAR09ptKpv-MLikgHgCRRyWlvDZR2Ffj5-5LTcHYy_VogNxbg8b4PCOmPk9g.

5 As Alyosha Goldstein, Juliana Hu Pegues, and Manu Karuka suggest, it would be productive to analyze settler colonialism as a "structure of failure." See Goldstein, Pegues, and Vimalassery (now Karuka), "Introduction: On Colonial Unknowing." Similarly, in his critical history of Hawaiian statehood, Dean Saranillio argues that "U.S. imperialist ventures in Hawai'i were not the result of a strong nation swallowing a weak and feeble island nation, but rather a result of a weakening U.S. nation whose mode of production—capitalism—was increasingly unsustainable without enacting a more aggressive policy of imperialism." See Saranillio, *Unsustainable Empire*, 9.

6 Park, J-H., "Reading Colonialism in 'Parasite.'"

7 For an incisive and revealing analysis of how consent for the Pyeongtaek base expansion was strategically fabricated, see Martin, "From Camp Town to International City."

8 Kanter, quoted in Kang, "Uses of Asianization," 423.

9 Robert Wade and Frank Veneroso, quoted in Kang, "Uses of Asianization," 423.

10 Kang, "Uses of Asianization," 424, 412.

11 Joseph Jonghyun Jeon analyzes what he calls "Korea's IMF cinema" as a way to peri-
odize compelled political and economic restructuring following the 1997–98 crisis.
See *Vicious Circuits*.

12 The South Korean government's deep investment in its domestic film industry in
the wake of the 1997 Asian Financial Crisis was formalized by the Kim Young-sam
administration through the Basic Culture Industry Promotion Law in 1999. A national film culture has been transformed into an international culture export whose
market ranks now among the top ten film markets in the world. See Worthy et al.,
"Appeal of Korea." Although the South Korean government has a unilateral policy
of promoting the Korean Wave, it has increasingly relied on expanding private
sector resources. This is the case with *Parasite*, a private sector initiative, whose executive producer is Miky Lee, a Samsung heiress and early investor in DreamWorks
who established CJ E&M, an entertainment and media subsidiary within her family's
CJ Group's conglomerate.

13 In 2019, South Korea's Financial Services Commission (FSC) chairman, Choi Jong-
ku, warned of dangerous increases in the level of household debt, averaging $44,000
per family in 2018. According to the Bank of Korea, household debt hit a record of
$1.34 trillion at the end of September 2014, accounting for over 97.5 percent of South
Korea's GDP in 2017, markedly higher than the average of 67.3 percent of the OECD
member countries. See Lee Suh-yoo, "Average Seoul Household Debt over $44,000,"
Korea Times, July 8, 2019, https://www.koreatimes.co.kr/www/nation/2020/04/281
_271912.html; Jhoo Dong-chan, "FSC Chief Warns of Ballooning Household Debts,"
Korea Times, January 27, 2019, http://www.koreatimes.co.kr/www/biz/2019/12/367
_262749.html.

14 The *Parasite* screenplay indicates that all four of these characters are in their mid- to
late forties.

15 Kang, "Uses of Asianization," 430. See also Kim, H. M., "Work, Nation and
Hypermasculinity."

16 Guåhan is Guam in the Chamorro language; it means "we have." I have chosen to use
"Guam" and not "Guåhan" throughout my book because it is more apt for describing
and naming the island's status as an unincorporated territory and a specific type of spatial exception constituting America's settler garrison within the terms of my analysis.

17 Teaiwa, "On Analogies," 83.

18 Lowe, *Intimacies of Four Continents*, 7.

19 Byrd, *Transit of Empire*, xxvi. In theorizing the nexus of US settler colonialism
and military empire in Asia and the Pacific as militarist settler imperialism, I also
amplify Alyosha Goldstein's contention that focusing exclusively on imperialism
and empire can risk obscuring how territorial seizure, occupation, and expansion;
differential modes of governance; and their attendant justifications remain the
conditions of possibility for more indirect forms of rule, the vast network of military encampments, and global economies. See Goldstein, "Introduction: Toward a
Genealogy of the U.S. Colonial Present," 9.

20 My conceptualization of metapolitical authority has been informed by Mark
Rifkin's deployment of the term and analysis of it in the context of US sovereignty
over Native Americans. See Rifkin, "Indigenizing Agamben," 117.

21 American exceptionalism, the United States' mythical conception of itself that it alone has the right, either by "divine sanction or moral obligation, to bring civilization, or democracy, or liberty to the rest of the world, by violence if necessary—is not new. It started as early as 1630 in the Massachusetts Bay Colony when Governor John Winthrop uttered the words that centuries later would be quoted by Ronald Reagan. Winthrop called the Massachusetts Bay Colony a 'city upon a hill.' Reagan embellished a little, calling it a 'shining city on a hill.'" See Zinn, "Power and the Glory." Zinn provides a useful historical overview of how the myth has driven the conquest of Native Americans as well as military intervention abroad. Two additional related aspects of American exceptionalism are the notions that the United States is distinct from the "old world" of Europe in two ways: that it does not possess overseas colonies and that its lack of a landed aristocracy makes class mobility possible.

22 Lo, "Simultaneity and Solidarity in the Time of Permanent War," 43. See also Lo, "Plenary Power and the Exceptionality of Igorots." The plenary power cases Lo analyzes are *Chae Chan Ping v. United States* (1889, also known as the *Chinese Exclusion Case*) and *Lone Wolf v. Hitchcock* (1903).

23 Moreover, insofar as US metapolitical authority is asserted in reaction to and as an attempted negation of Indigenous and other national sovereignties, it is what Manu Karuka calls countersovereignty. Karuka writes that as a mode of political authority, countersovereignty is closely linked to counterintelligence, counterinsurgency, and counterrevolution. These are all modes of "reactive anxiety" betraying a profound anxiety about the future possibility of anti-imperialist and anticapitalist transformations of collective life. See Karuka, *Empire's Tracks*, xii, 183.

24 A stark example of this is the most recently admitted state, Hawai'i. Its incorporation into the United States in 1959 as the fiftieth state, occurring in the distended shadow of invasion, occupation, and annexation dating back to the late-nineteenth century, converted metapolitical authority into political authority. Although colonization was thus "naturalized," the living memories and vital decolonial movements of Native Hawaiians, Kānaka Maoli, continually denaturalize, or render visible, that colonization.

25 See Wolfe, "Settler Colonialism and the Elimination of the Native." In *Possessing Polynesians*, Arvin explains that possession highlights how settler colonialism is also a highly gendered project, for the "supposed consanguinity between the settler and the Native is necessarily produced through heteropatriarchy" (17). Arvin's conceptualization of settler colonialism is also useful: "Settler colonialism, as a structure of dominance, is particularly set on the domination and exploitation of land. Settler colonialism is not a structure limited to any discrete historical period, nation, or colonizer. Though never monolithic or unchanging, settler colonialism is a historical and a contemporary phenomenon. Its power usually operates simultaneously through economy (the turning of land and natural resources into profit), law (the imposition of the legal-political apparatus of a settler nation-state, rather than an indigenous form of governance), and ideology (culturally and morally defined ways of being and knowing resulting from European post-Enlightenment thought)" (15).

26 Wolfe, "Settler Colonialism and the Elimination of the Native," 388.

27 Day, *Alien Capital*, 19, 20. For a trenchant study along similar triangulated lines that goes beyond the Native-settler dialectic, see Le, *Unsettled Solidarities*. For an analysis of a "transpacific settler colonial condition" as "the interconnected nature of Indigenous struggles against settler colonialism across the Americas, Asia, and the Pacific Islands, given shared histories of American empire and military violence" (50), see Gandhi, "Historicizing the Transpacific Settler Colonial Condition."

28 Clinton's "America's Pacific Century" was published in the November 2011 issue of *Foreign Policy*. US imperial and militarist violence in Asia, previously rationalized under the sign of the Cold War, gets reanimated under the sign of "new global realities." The policy plan posits, "In the last decade, our foreign policy has transitioned from dealing with the post-Cold War peace dividend to demanding commitments in Iraq and Afghanistan. As those wars wind down, we will need to accelerate efforts to pivot to new global realities" (63). The "Asia-Pacific" is identified as the United States' "real 21st century opportunity" (63). The now-defunct economic arm of the Asia-Pacific pivot, the Trans-Pacific Partnership, has been called the NAFTA for the Pacific, or "NAFTA on steroids." See, for example, Lori Wallach, "NAFTA on Steroids," *Nation*, June 27, 2012, https://www.thenation.com/article/nafta-steroids/. The twelve participating nations were Australia, Brunei, Canada, Chile, Japan, Malaysia, Mexico, New Zealand, Peru, Singapore, and Vietnam. The United States withdrew from the agreement on January 23, 2017.

29 Grydehøg et al., "Practicing Decolonial Political Geography."

30 Davis, "Repeating Islands of Resistance," 1.

31 In the Pacific, these territories are the unincorporated organized territory of Guam, the unincorporated unorganized territory of American Sāmoa, the Commonwealth of the Northern Mariana Islands, and the three Compact of Free Association nations (or the "Freely Associated States") of the Republic of the Marshall Islands, the Federated States of Micronesia, and the Republic of Palau.

32 British constitutional law expert Stanley de Smith called it "de facto annexation." Quoted in Vine, *Base Nation*, 84. The Northern Mariana Islands were also part of the Trust Territory of the Pacific Islands. Yet unlike the Republic of the Marshall Islands, the Federated States of Micronesia, and the Republic of Palau (which signed Compacts of Free Association with the United States but are independent, sovereign states), the Commonwealth of the Northern Mariana Islands still remains an unincorporated territory and commonwealth of the United States.

33 DeLoughrey, "Heavy Waters," 705; DeLoughrey, *Routes and Roots*, 31. DeLoughrey explains that UNCLOS was formed out of complex dynamics between emergent postcolonial states and dominant Western powers because of contestations over ocean governance in the post–World War II context. The 1982 UNCLOS, "the most important remapping of the globe in recent history . . . expanded the sovereignty of coastal nations to 12 nautical miles, their contiguous zones to 24 nautical miles, and established an Exclusive Economic Zone (EEZ) of 200 nautical miles" (*Routes and Roots*, 33).

34 DeLoughrey, *Allegories of the Anthropocene*, 140.

35 DeLoughrey, "Toward a Critical Ocean Studies for the Anthropocene," 24. As defined by geographers, the Pacific Ocean is sixty-three million square miles and covers one-

third of the earth's surface area. However, to the US military, it extends all the way to India's western coast. India, along with twenty-four other predominantly Pacific Rim nations except China and Russia, has the largest naval force in South Asia and participates in RIMPAC (Rim of the Pacific) military exercises. In summer 2018, the twenty-sixth biennial RIMPAC exercise was held. The largest maritime exercise in history, it involved the participation in "war games" of 25,000 military personnel of twenty-five predominantly Pacific Rim nations. See DeLoughrey, "Toward a Critical Ocean Studies for the Anthropocene," 21, 24; DeLoughrey, "Island Studies and the US Militarism of the Pacific," 29. DeLoughrey also compellingly analyzes how "transoceanic militarism" is connected to the smooth flow of global energy sources, diasporic masculinity, and state power. See "Toward a Critical Ocean Studies for the Anthropocene," 23. Simeon Man trenchantly analyzes the making of US military empire in the Pacific by deploying the "decolonizing Pacific" as a methodology for illuminating the coevality of US imperial and race wars and anticolonial movements in the United States, Asia, and the Pacific after 1945. See Man, *Soldiering through Empire*, 8.

36 Burnett, "Edges of Empire and the Limits of Sovereignty," 781.

37 Karuka, *Empire's Tracks*, xii, 174.

38 As David Vine observes, the US military has so many bases that it itself does not know the exact total. It is impossible to compile a fully accurate and comprehensive list of all US bases throughout the world because of Pentagon secrecy, poor reporting practices, and shifting definitions of what actually counts as a "base" in light of the increasing pattern of constructing "lily pads" (small bases under ten acres in size or valued at under $10 million). Based on the Pentagon's count of "base sites" in its 2018 *Base Structure Report*, Vine estimates that there are about eight hundred US military bases abroad. Given the obvious errors and omissions in the *Base Structure Report*, Vine has created, updated, and made public a list. See Vine, "Lists of U.S. Military Bases Abroad, 1776–2019." See also Vine, *United States of War*, 350n1. According to Vine's continuously updated list, as of late 2019, of the approximately eight hundred overseas bases and lily pads, 285 are located in Asia and the Pacific. This does not include Hawai'i since it is a US state.

39 Bello, "From American Lake to a People's Pacific," 14.

40 Woodward, "From Military Geography to Militarism's Geographies," 720.

41 Katherine McKittrick has a generative conceptualization of geography: "Geography, then, materially and discursively extends to cover three dimensional spaces and places, the physical landscape and infrastructures, geographic imaginations, the practice of mapping, exploring, and seeing, and social relations in and across space." McKittrick deploys the term *traditional geography* to describe cartographic, positivist, and imperialist formulations upheld by a legacy of exploitation, exploration, and conquest, and argues that "if we imagine that traditional geographies are upheld by their three-dimensionality, as well as a corresponding language of insides and outsides, borders and belongings, and inclusions and exclusions, we can expose domination as a visible spatial project that organizes, names, and sees social differences (such as black femininity) and determines *where* social order happens." Although McKittrick is writing within the context of black women's negotiations

with the "traditional geography" of the legacy of transatlantic slavery, her work is useful in thinking through how America's settler garrison in Asia and the Pacific, a geography of militarism, is also a kind of "traditional geography" of domination. How, moreover, do the transpacific cultural works in my study contest this geography? See McKittrick, *Demonic Grounds*, xiii–xiv, emphasis in original.

42 Schmitt, quoted by G. L. Ulmen in Translator's Introduction, *Nomos of the Earth in the International Law of Jus Publicum Europaeum*, 19.

43 Constituted at multiple scales and in a variety of ways, spatial exceptions make possible, as Paul A. Kramer writes, "extraordinary power exercised at and through the interstices of sovereignty, often underwritten by essentialisms of race, gender, and civilization." See Kramer, "Power and Connection," 1357.

44 LaDuke with Cruz, *Militarization of Indian Country*, 80.

45 LaDuke with Cruz, *Militarization of Indian Country*, 18.

46 Calder, *Embattled Garrisons*, 35.

47 Johnson, *Sorrows of Empire*, 253.

48 Goeman, *Mark My Words*, 2.

49 In the original draft of the speech, President Dwight D. Eisenhower termed it the *military-industrial-congressional complex*. The full transcript of his farewell address to the nation, delivered on January 17, 1961, can be found in *Public Papers of the Presidents* (Washington, DC: US National Archives, 1961), 1035–40.

50 Luxemburg, *Accumulation of Capital*, 454, emphasis added. Giovanni Arrighi observes, "So-called 'military Keynesianism'—the practice through which military expenditures boost the incomes of the citizens of the state that has made the expenditures, thereby increasing tax revenues and capacity to finance new rounds of military expenditures—is no more a novelty of the twentieth century than finance capital and transnational business enterprise." See Arrighi, *Adam Smith in Beijing*, 266.

51 Liebknecht, *Militarism and Anti-Militarism*, 56, 39. More recently, Manu Karuka has theorized the "war-finance nexus." See Karuka, *Empire's Tracks*, 168. For an analysis of militarization as a "complex politics of diffusion" that pervades everyday power relations as well as resistance to such relations, see Henry and Natanel, "Militarisation as Diffusion."

52 These feminist scholars include Kozue Akibayashi, Megumi Chibana, Elizabeth De-Loughrey, Cynthia Enloe, Vernadette Vicuña Gonzalez, Catherine Lutz, Seungsook Moon, Tiara R. Na'puti, Margo Okazawa-Rey, Teresia Teaiwa, and others. There is an important body of scholarship analyzing militarism and the long and ongoing history of military intervention in Asia and the Pacific. In addition to the scholars I have already cited, notable recent work includes Juliet Nebolon's generative conceptualization of "settler militarism" as "the dynamics through which, in Hawai'i, settler colonialism and militarization have simultaneously perpetuated, legitimated, and concealed one another." Although Nebolon is writing specifically within the context of martial law in Hawai'i during World War II, her formulation of the symbiotic nexus between settler colonialism and militarization is helpful for analyzing other related contexts. See Nebolon, "'Life Given Straight from the Heart,'" 25. In the context of Asia and the Pacific more broadly, Setsu Shigematsu and Keith L. Camacho analyze militarization "as an *extension of colonialism* and its gendered and

racialized processes," interrogating how "colonial histories constitute the conditions of possibility for ongoing forms of militarization." See Shigematsu and Camacho, "Introduction: Militarized Currents, Decolonizing Futures," xv, emphasis in original. And Cynthia Enloe observes that Asia and the Pacific are strung together with a necklace of US military bases, violently producing a "militarized interconnectedness." See Enloe, *Bananas, Beaches and Bases*, 85.

53 Vagts, *History of Militarism*, 13.

54 On militourism, Teresia Teaiwa writes, "*Militourism* is a phenomenon by which military or paramilitary force ensures the smooth running of a tourist industry, and that same tourist industry masks the military force behind it. The roots of militourism in the Pacific go back as far as Ferdinand Magellan's first (and last) encounter with the natives of Guam in 1521." Teaiwa continues, "Militourism is complex. It goes beyond the simple presence of military bases and tourist resorts on the same islands or in the same archipelagoes. Often, the tourist industry capitalizes on the military histories of islands." See Teaiwa, "Reading Paul Gauguin's *Noa Noa* with Epeli Hauʻofa's *Kisses in the Nederends*," 251, 252. For an important work on militourism in Hawaiʻi and the Philippines, see Gonzalez, *Securing Paradise*.

55 For a useful overview of these manifold ways in which the transpacific is militarized, see Chen, "Transpacific Turns." On "radioactive militarism," see DeLoughrey, "Myth of Isolates," 172. On the "irradiated transpacific," see Bahng, *Migrant Futures*, 147.

56 Teaiwa, "Bleeding Boundaries," 2.

57 On the "military-industrial-Congressional-media-entertainment-university complex" as constituting the "military normal," see Lutz, "Military Normal," 29. Similarly, in *Maneuvers*, Enloe argues, "Militarization does not always take on the guise of war." It is a "pervasive process, and thus so hard to uproot, precisely because in its everyday forms it scarcely looks life threatening" (2–3).

58 Bascara, Camacho, and DeLoughrey, "Gender and Sexual Politics of Pacific Island Militarisation."

59 On "empire of bases," see Johnson, *Sorrows of Empire*, especially Chapter 6.

60 Calder, *Embattled Garrisons*, 14.

61 Höhn and Moon, S., "Politics of Gender, Sexuality, Race, and Class in the U.S. Military Empire," 7–8. According to the 2018 *Base Structure Report*, the Department of Defense (DoD) "manages a worldwide real property portfolio that spans all 50 states, 8 U.S. territories and outlying areas, and 45 foreign countries. The majority of the foreign sites are located in Germany (194 sites), Japan (121), and South Korea (83 sites)" (7). There are 4,150 sites in the United States, 111 sites in US territories, and 514 overseas, totaling 4,775 overall. The "DoD occupies a reported 279,240 buildings throughout the world, valued at approximately $749 billion and comprising approximately 2.3 billion square feet" (9). Recent *Base Structure Reports* of the DoD can be found here: https://www.acq.osd.mil/eie/BSI/BEI_Library.html (accessed June 10, 2019).

62 Calder, *Embattled Garrisons*, 12.

63 According to the 2018 *Base Structure Report*, the US military controls 26.9 million acres of territory, with approximately 538,000 acres of that located overseas and made available by host governments. In terms of cost, it would be close to $1.2 trillion to replace the Department of Defense's "existing inventory" of facility assets such

as buildings, structures, and linear structures using standards and codes updated
through the 2018 *Base Structure Report*. Although the report is not fully accurate or
comprehensive insofar as many bases are secret or officially "nonexistent" sites, it is
useful in providing a picture of the sheer scale of US military presence throughout
the globe. See 2018 *Base Structure Report*, 8, 9.

64 González, Gusterson, and Houtman, Introduction, 6, emphasis added.

65 To be clear, this is not a call for a more purportedly inclusive "Asian Pacific American" or "Asian Pacific Islander" designation by subsuming a Pacific or Indigenous
Pacific Islander within a presumably broader Asian American or Asian category. For
a useful overview of how a sustained engagement with Native and Indigenous theorizing challenges some of the prevailing concerns of Asian American studies (such as
immigration, diaspora, and civil rights), see Tiongson Jr., "Asian American Studies,
Comparative Racialization, and Settler Colonial Critique." For a critically trenchant
examination of the problematics and pitfalls of the "Asian Pacific Islander" designation, an attempt to make "Asian American" more inclusive by subsuming Pacific
Islander within it without taking into sufficient account substantive differences and
hierarchies, see Kauanui, "Asian American Studies and the 'Pacific Question.'" See
also Hall, "Which of These Things Is Not Like the Other." Alice Te Punga Somerville
makes a similar point as well, noting that Pacific studies and Indigenous studies
function as separate fields with distinct genealogies and methods, and any overlap is
partial. Moreover, each category—Pacific and Indigenous—in and of itself is complex,
which can lead to "rabbit holes of definitions and categorizations." See Somerville,
"Searching for the Trans-Indigenous," 100. Teresia Teaiwa also sees the Asia-Pacific
coupling as problematic, noting that the Pacific is relegated as a vague suffix of Asia,
when in fact the Pacific itself is an umbrella term containing diverse elements within
it. Similarly, Terence Wesley-Smith points to the sheer number of Pacific languages
and epistemologies, which means that "the architects of Pacific studies programs will
have to engage with a more diffuse and fragmented epistemological landscape than
they might like." See Teaiwa, "For or *Before* an Asia Pacific Studies Agenda?"; Wesley-
Smith, "Rethinking Pacific Studies Twenty Years On," 161. For a useful, concise
overview of these debates, see Suzuki, "And the View from the Ship."

66 Byrd, *Transit of Empire*, xvii.

67 Given the political, economic, and demographic power of Asian Americans, particularly East Asian Americans, in Hawai'i, they are "settlers of color" or "arrivants"
who are structurally complicit with settler colonialism. As Haunani-Kay Trask,
Noelani Goodyear-Ka'ōpua, Candace Fujikane, Dean Saranillio, and others have
written, this structural complicity does not and should not prevent Asian Americans from being "settler allies" in Hawaiian decolonization movements. Jodi A. Byrd
borrows the term *arrivants* from African Caribbean poet Kamau Brathwaite. See
Byrd, *Transit of Empire*, xix. See Trask, "Settlers of Color and 'Immigrant' Hegemony"; Goodyear-Ka'ōpua, *Seeds We Planted*; Fujikane, "Mapping Abundance on
Mauna a Wākea as a Practice of Ea"; and Saranillio, *Unsustainable Empire*.

68 For a useful discussion of Asian Indigeneities in sites such as Okinawa, Taiwan, and
the Philippines, see the 2015 special issue of *Amerasia Journal* on "Indigenous Asias,"
edited by Greg Dvorak and Miyume Tanji. For another special issue of a journal on

Asian Indigeneities, see the Fall 2018 issue of *Verge: Studies in Global Asias*, edited by Charlotte Eubanks and Pasang Yangjee Sherpa.

69 Indeed, Jinah Kim amplifies this militarized interconnectedness in calling the region the "Pacific Arena." See *Postcolonial Grief*, 17. Kim writes, "*Arena* references the tendency to refer to zones of combat as *theaters of war*. Unlike a theater, however, an arena more accurately describes the conditions of war and the ways that it is made into violent fantasy for consumption" (17–18, emphases in original).

70 For an important earlier articulation of the term *trans-Pacific* within critical Asian studies, see Sakai and Yoo, Introduction to *Trans-Pacific Imagination*. Writing specifically within the context of East Asia, they posit the "trans-Pacific imagination" as an analytic for grappling with the neo-imperial US-Japan alliance or complicity. For a "decolonial approach to fabulating transpacific futurity" that focuses on the transpacific as at once a geopolitical realm, material ecosystem, culturally produced imaginary called "the Pacific," and the temporal ascription called "the Asian Century," see Mok and Bahng, "Transpacific Overtures," 5, 4. For an analysis of transpacific critique that "knits together diverse memories of historical violence—settler colonialism, military expansion, and refugee displacement—into a layered story of US Empire in the Asia-Pacific region," see Espiritu, "Critical Refugee Studies and Native Pacific Studies," 483. For a study of "transpacific redress" in terms of the performance of "redressive acts" that challenge the erasure and denial of the history of Japanese military sexual slavery, see Son, *Embodied Reckonings*.

71 The term *transpacific* can be deployed, for example, in a purely descriptive, uncritical, or even celebratory sense to track the transnational movement of goods, people, ideas, and so on across the Pacific. It can re-center East Asia or the US mainland, whether unwittingly or wittingly. It can also be taken up in ways that elide Indigeneity and the Pacific Islands, even as the stated goal might be to do otherwise. Bearing this in mind, Lisa Yoneyama engages in what she calls a "conjunctive cultural critique of the transpacific" and "a dissonant reading of the transpacific as an alternative to the Cold War geography, which emerged out of transwar, interimperial, and transnational entanglements." See Yoneyama, *Cold War Ruins*, x. In a more recent article, Yoneyama elaborates further on her conceptualization of the transpacific and of transpacific critique. Calling attention to the problems of a transpacific critique that absents Indigenous and Pacific Islander epistemologies and interventions, she continues by noting the "potentials for developing alternative theorizing of the transpacific even further, through exposing the conjunctions among settler states, imperialisms, and the overseas military deployment whether in aggression, in peacekeeping, or as occupying forces." See Yoneyama, "Toward a Decolonial Genealogy of the Transpacific," 478–79. In a similar vein, for an analysis of "transpacific entanglements" as constituted by "historical and ongoing settler logics of invasion, removal, and seizure" as they intersect with racialized capitalism and overseas empire, see Espiritu, Lowe, and Yoneyama, "Transpacific Entanglements," 175.

72 Suzuki, *Ocean Passages*, 4, emphasis in original. In an earlier piece, Suzuki and Bahng pointedly query the potential pitfalls of deploying the term. They ask, "At the institutional level, does transpacific actually just rebrand more familiar methods of comparative analysis between nation-based settler units that pass over and

even obfuscate Indigenous place-based relations?" Bearing this in mind, they take inspiration from the Oceanic framework and suggest that it might be useful to refer to the transpacific not as a "singular geopolitical space or descriptor" but rather as a keyword or category. See "Transpacific Subject in Asian American Culture," 6. For important early work that critiques the celebratory capitalist articulations of Pacific Rim discourse, see Dirlik, *What Is in a Rim?*; Connery, "Pacific Rim Discourse."

73 This is the latter part of Ruth Wilson Gilmore's highly cited and influential definition of racism: "Racism is the state-sanctioned and/or extra-legal production and exploitation of group-differentiated vulnerabilities to premature death, in distinct yet densely interconnected political geographies." See "Race and Globalization," 261.

74 Allen, *Trans-Indigenous*, xiii, xiv–xv, emphases in original.

75 Allen, *Trans-Indigenous*, xvii–xviii, emphasis added.

76 Hauʻofa, "Our Sea of Islands," 152–53. This essay was originally published in *A New Oceania: Rediscovering Our Sea of Islands* (1993), edited by Eric Waddell, Vijay Naidu, and Epeli Hauʻofa. Indeed, the very terms that are used for the region, *Pacific Islands* and *Oceania*, reflect the difference between the two perspectives. Whereas the prevailing first term, *Pacific Islands*, denotes small areas of land, the second term, *Oceania*, denotes a large sea of islands full of people and places to explore. Drawing on Hauʻofa, David Hanlon writes that "the Pacific" evokes outlander visions, while "Oceania" highlights a vastness, diversity, fluidity, and complexity that require a more Indigenous conceptualization of history. See "Losing Oceania to the Pacific and the World," 286. Normative Eurocentric cartographic practices also minimize the Pacific, splitting it literally down the middle and relegating it to the left and right margins. As J. Kēhaulani Kauanui notes, this consignment to the literal margins has a distorting effect, reducing the vastness of Oceania as well as the islands in relation to each other. See Kauanui, "Imperial Ocean," 626. See also RDK Herman's *Pacific Worlds* (http://www.pacificworlds.com/), a web-based Indigenous geography project, and the related article "Pacific Worlds."

77 Kauanui, "Asian American Studies and the 'Pacific Question,'" 126.

78 McCall, "Nissology," 1.

79 For a discussion of island studies as a decolonial project, see Nadarajah and Grydehøj, "Island Studies as a Decolonial Project (Guest Editorial Introduction)." For a study of the institutionalization of island studies and where it might be headed in the future, see Randall, "Island Studies Inside (and Outside) of the Academy." For a discussion of island feminism, see Akibayashi, "Okinawa Women Act against Military Violence." As I discuss in Chapter 2, Akibayashi contends that the writings and activist work of Okinawa Women Act against Military Violence (OWAAMV) constitute an "*island feminism*, which suggests a challenge to the interlocking of military violence and colonial violence in its fundamental critique and a challenge to patriarchy" (39, emphasis in original). See also Karides, "Why Island Feminism?" Karides writes, "Island feminism is a theoretical orientation that understands 'islands on their own terms' and draws from feminisms of intersectionality, geography, and coloniality and queer theory" (31). On "aquapelagic assemblages," see Hayward, "Aquapelagos and Aquapelagic Assemblages." Hayward proposes *aquapelagic assemblages* as a term "to emphasize the manner in which the aquatic spaces between land around groups of

islands are utilized and navigated in a manner that is fundamentally interconnected with and essential to social groups' habitation of land" (1).

80 On "de-islanding," see Gómez-Barris and Joseph, "Introduction: Coloniality and Islands." On "islanding," see Sheller, "Caribbean Futures in the Offshore Anthropocene," 972; Sheller, *Island Futures*. Gómez-Barris and Joseph as well as Sheller are cited in an insightful essay by Gonzalez, "Target/Paradise/Home/Kin," 25.

81 Teaiwa, "Island Futures and Sustainability," 514.

82 Wendt, "Towards a New Oceania," 60.

CHAPTER 1. PERVERSE TEMPORALITIES

1 Frain, "'Make America Secure,'" 224.

2 Na'puti and Bevacqua, "Militarization and Resistance from Guåhan," 846–47.

3 In a video uploaded to YouTube, we can see the protesters singing and holding up signs. See "Save Pagat," YouTube Video, 10:00, posted by sixsixdegrees, July 25, 2010, https://www.youtube.com/watch?v=_j3k8_qidW8.

4 Heim, "How (not) to Globalize Oceania," 137.

5 Na'puti and Bevacqua, "Militarization and Resistance from Guåhan," 848.

6 Graeber, *Debt*, 391.

7 Graeber, *Debt*, 391.

8 See Hogeland, *Founding Finance*; Wright, *One Nation under Debt*; and Konings, *Development of American Finance*.

9 For an analysis of the American Revolutionary War as a "settler revolt" and the evolution of the United States as a "settler empire," see Rana, *Two Faces of American Freedom*.

10 Park, K-S., "Money, Mortgages, and the Conquest of America," 1009. Michael J. Shapiro also describes the process through which Indigenous cultural systems of meaning and exchange were negated in the imposition of Euro-American lending practices. See *Violent Cartographies*, 12.

11 For an incisive analysis of how property law, conjoined with white supremacist racial logic in the settler colonies of Canada, Australia, and Israel-Palestine, effected the colonial appropriation of Indigenous lands, see Bhandar, *Colonial Lives of Property*.

12 Marx, *Capital*, 915.

13 Robinson, *Black Marxism*. As Jodi Melamed writes, the capitalism that was Marx's purview "was always already racial capitalism" (80). See "Racial Capitalism."

14 Marx, *Capital*, 919.

15 Marx, *Capital*, 940.

16 Marx, "On the Jewish Question," 30.

17 Nichols, "Disaggregating Primitive Accumulation," 19.

18 Luxemburg, "Accumulation of Capital," 194.

19 Nichols, "Disaggregating Primitive Accumulation," 19.

20 Harvey, *New Imperialism*, 143–44. Harvey usefully elaborates the wide range of processes included in Marx's description of primitive accumulation:

> These include the commodification and privatization of land and the
> forceful expulsion of peasant populations; the conversion of various forms

of property rights (common, collective, state, etc.) into exclusive private property rights; the suppression of rights to the commons; the commodification of labour power and the suppression of alternative (indigenous) forms of production and consumption; colonial, neo-colonial, and imperial processes of appropriation of assets (including natural resources); the monetization of exchange and taxation, particularly of land; the slave trade; and usury, the national debt, and ultimately the credit system as radical means of primitive accumulation. The state, with its monopoly of violence and definitions of legality, plays a crucial role in both backing and promoting these processes . . . (145)

21 Roberts, "What Was Primitive Accumulation?," 15, 12, 5, emphases in original.
22 Federici, *Caliban and the Witch*; Coulthard, *Red Skin, White Masks*.
23 Issar, "Theorising 'Racial/Colonial Primitive Accumulation,'" 4.
24 Nichols, "Disaggregating Primitive Accumulation," 22.
25 Nichols, "Disaggregating Primitive Accumulation," 26.
26 Day, "Eco-Criticism."
27 Nichols, *Theft Is Property!*, 8, 31.
28 Nichols, *Theft Is Property!*, 114.
29 Nichols, *Theft Is Property!*, 29.
30 For analyses of aloha 'āina, see, for example, Goodyear-Kaʻōpua, Hussey, and Wright, eds., *Nation Rising*; Yamashiro and Goodyear-Kaʻōpua, eds., *Value of Hawaiʻi* 2; and Fujikane, *Mapping Abundance for a Planetary Future*.
31 McDougall, "What the Island Provides," 208.
32 Yamashiro and Goodyear-Kaʻōpua, "We Are Islanders," 1, emphases in original.
33 Rifkin, *Beyond Settler Time*, viii, 2.
34 Freeman, quoted in Rifkin, *Beyond Settler Time*, 37.
35 Rifkin, *Beyond Settler Time*, 21.
36 According to the US Congressional Budget Office, the total US national debt in 2021 was almost $28 trillion. See https://www.cbo.gov/publication/56970 (accessed March 15, 2021).
37 Hudson, *Super Imperialism*.
38 For an insightful explanation of debt imperialism and its connection to capitalist speculation in the life sciences within the context of neoliberalism, see Cooper, *Life as Surplus*.
39 For a useful discussion of this historical context, see Kelton, *Deficit Myth*.
40 Stephanie Kelton, an important proponent of Modern Monetary Theory (MMT), argues that we cannot think of US national debt in the same way that we think about household, corporate, or other kinds of institutional debts because the United States is a currency *issuer*, whereas the others are currency *users*. See *Deficit Myth*.
41 Graeber, *Debt*, 367.
42 Graeber notes that in most cases, such countries are effectively US military protectorates. See *Debt*, 6.
43 For fiscal year 2021, the US military budget was $705.4 billion, yet once you add components hidden in other budgets, it was $934 billion. For fiscal year 2022, it is expected to remain flat. See https://www.thebalance.com/u-s-military-budget

-components-challenges-growth-3306320?utm_source=emailshare&utm_medium
=social&utm_campaign=shareurlbuttons (accessed June 3, 2021); https://www
.defense.gov/Newsroom/Releases/Release/Article/2079489/dod-releases-fiscal-year
-2021-budget-proposal/ (accessed February 22, 2021); and https://www.defensenews
.com/pentagon/2021/03/10/research-procurement-could-get-squeezed-in-biden
-budget/ (accessed March 30, 2021).

44 Cooper, *Life as Surplus*, 164.

45 Hudson, *Super Imperialism*, xiii.

46 Arrighi, *Adam Smith in Beijing*, 193.

47 Streeck, *Buying Time*, 79–81. Building on Streeck's theorization of the European debt state, in *Public Debt, Inequality, and Power*, Sandy Brian Hager analyzes the US debt state, in particular the relationship between the public debt and inequality. Hager's empirical inquiry showed that, "since the 1980s, domestic ownership of the public debt had rapidly become concentrated in favor of the now-infamous top 1 percent of US households and the top 2,500 US corporations" (xi). The import of this is that "in essence, what the debt state means is that the US federal government has come to rely on *borrowing from elites instead of taxing them* . . . in choosing to furnish elites with risk free assets instead of levying taxes on their incomes, the debt state comes to reinforce the existing pattern of wealth and income inequality" (7, emphasis added).

48 Angela Mitropoulos writes, "Legal tender is a species of debt, and debt is organized on a contractual basis. Debts are guaranteed by violence, whether implied or deployed." See *Contract and Contagion*, 105.

49 Cooper, *Life as Surplus*, 31.

50 Cooper, *Life as Surplus*, 163–65.

51 Cooper, *Life as Surplus*, 163–64, 31.

52 Hoechst, *Life in and against the Odds*, 9.

53 For an incisive account of how the Indigenous women leading the Idle No More movement in Canada are demanding repayment of the unacknowledged debt owed to Indigenous communities, see Morris, "Twenty-First-Century Debt Collectors."

54 Harvey, *New Imperialism*, 147.

55 Lazzarato, *Making of the Indebted Man*, 45.

56 Lazzarato, *Making of the Indebted Man*, 55.

57 Marez, "Seeing in the Red," 265. Writing within the context of escalating levels of student debt, Marez argues that "the contemporary regime of university debt constitutes a form of racialized and gendered settler colonial capitalism based on the incorporation of disposable low-wage workers and complicity in the occupation of indigenous lands" (262).

58 For an excellent analysis of how cultural works map this contemporary landscape of debt, see McClanahan, *Dead Pledges*.

59 Spivak, *Critique of Postcolonial Reason*, 237; Joseph, *Debt to Society*, xii.

60 Wynter, "Is 'Development' a Purely Empirical Concept?," 302, emphasis in original.

61 Wynter, "Is 'Development' a Purely Empirical Concept?," 314. Wynter notes that whereas previously telic structures were articulated via theology, in particular the Judeo-Christian grand narrative of emancipation and redemption, they are now articulated via the disciplinary paradigm of economics. This disciplinary paradigm

must function not only empirically but also metaphysically, in the same manner that theology did in the earlier order.

62 Fanon, *Wretched of the Earth*, 58.

63 Federici, *Caliban and the Witch*, 17.

64 Chakravarty and Silva, "Accumulation, Dispossession, and Debt," 365.

65 See Davidson, "Warning Sounded over China's 'Debt Diplomacy.'" See also French, *China's Second Continent*.

66 Mutabaruka, "Life and Debt," track 5 on *Life Squared* (Heartbeat, 2002), compact disc. The 2001 documentary, *Life and Debt*, is directed by Stephanie Black.

67 Rajan, *Biocapital*, 14.

68 Graeber, *Debt*, 391.

69 Spillers, "Mama's Baby, Papa's Maybe," 208.

70 Hartman writes, "This is the afterlife of slavery—skewed life chances, limited access to health and education, premature death, incarceration, and impoverishment. I, too, am the afterlife of slavery." See *Lose Your Mother*, 6.

71 Hartman, *Scenes of Subjection*, 9.

72 Hartman, *Scenes of Subjection*, 131.

73 Sheller, *Island Futures*, 13.

74 Quoted in Sheller, *Island Futures*, 14.

75 Sheller, *Island Futures*, 14–15.

76 Yoneyama, "Traveling Memories, Contagious Justice," 80.

77 For an excellent analysis of this figurative debt regime in relation to the Vietnam War and the production of the figure of the indebted refugee, see Nguyen, *Gift of Freedom*.

CHAPTER 2. THE MILITARY BASE AND CAMPTOWN

1 Tōma, "Backbone," 221–22.

2 Jane Jin Kaisen, a multimedia visual artist, is a transnational and transracial adoptee who was born in Jeju and adopted by a family in Denmark. *Reiterations of Dissent* was first showcased in 2011 as part of a solo exhibition, *Dissident Translations*, in Denmark at Århus Kunstbygning. In 2016, the original five-screen installation was expanded to eight screens or channels and exhibited at the Leeum Samsung Museum of Art in Seoul, South Korea.

3 The Kuroshio Current starts off along the east coast of Luzon, Philippines; passes through Taiwan; the Ryūkyū Islands of Japan (Okinawa); the East China Sea and the Zhoushan Archipelago; Jeju Island of South Korea; and continues along the western and eastern coasts of mainland Japan. See Hyun, "Maritime and Island Culture along the Kuroshio Current," 167–70.

4 Baik, *Reencounters*, 131.

5 Gwon, "Remembering 4/3 and Resisting the Remilitarization of Jeju," 238; Baik, *Reencounters*, 31.

6 For an analysis of how Jeju's political and economic autonomy are comprised by South Korean mainland policies, see Kim, S-P., "Mainland Development Policy in an Autonomous Subnational Island Jurisdiction."

7 For analyses of protests against the construction of the Jeju naval base, see Yeo, "Realism, Critical Theory, and the Politics of Peace and Security; Gwon, "Remembering 4/3 and Resisting the Remilitarization of Jeju."

8 Baik, *Reencounters*, 142. The base has an Aegis ballistic missile defense system, twenty warships, submarines, and an American-designed missile-intercepting system.

9 Crystal Tai, "Jeju Activists Protest over Visit by Warships," *South China Morning Post*, October 14, 2018, https://www.scmp.com/news/asia/east-asia/article/2168417/jeju -jittery-us-warship-visit-reminds-islanders-dark-chapter. For coverage of a previous protest in November 2017 against the docking of the USS *Mississippi*, a nuclear-powered attack submarine, see Heo Ho-joon, "American Nuclear Submarine Enters Jeju Naval Base," *Hankyoreh*, November 24, 2017, http://english.hani.co.kr/arti /english_edition/e_international/820635.html.

10 Baik, *Reencounters*, 15.

11 Kang, *Compositional Subjects*, 201.

12 Kang, *Traffic in Asian Women*, 35, emphasis in original. Kang's formulation of "Asian women as method?" echoes yet also departs from the title of Kuan-Hsing Chen's important book, *Asia as Method: Toward Deimperialization* (2010).

13 On the "military-sexual complex," see Nagel, *Race, Ethnicity, and Sexuality*, 193. On the trafficking of sex workers, see Cheng, *On the Move for Love*.

14 Kishaba Jun's real name is Kishaba Chōjun. "Dark Flowers" was originally published in a 1955 issue of *Ryūdai bungaku* (University of the Ryūkyūs Literature), an activist student literary magazine, and was reprinted a year later in *Shin Nihon bungaku*, a national monthly publication known as well for its political radicalism. *Child of Okinawa* first appeared in a December 1971 issue of *Bungakkai* (Literary World) magazine. In 1972, it was awarded an Akutagawa Prize, one of Japan's most prestigious literary prizes. The novella was then reprinted by Bungei Shunjū press as the title work of a hardback volume of Higashi's fiction in 1972 and again in 1980 as a paperback edition. In 1983, a Japanese film loosely based on *Child of Okinawa* was released. Directed by Shinjō Taku and entitled (in English) *Okinawan Boys*, this film garnered widespread praise. "Hope" originally appeared in the June 26, 1999, issue of the *Asahi Shimbun*, a major Japanese newspaper.

15 *Silver Stallion* was first published in Seoul in 1986, then translated from Korean by the author. For a useful documentary of how US military bases in Texas, Hawai'i, Guam, Puerto Rico, Okinawa, South Korea, and the Philippines impact the lives of women, see *Living along the Fenceline* (2011), directed by Lina Hoshino and Gwyn Kirk.

16 This is the title of David Vine's introductory chapter in *The United States of War*.

17 On the guest/host metaphor, see Broudy and Simpson, "Naming and Framing in (Post)Colonial Okinawa," 81. On "structural humiliation," see Lummis, Afterword, "Defining the Situation," 281.

18 Rabson, Introduction, *Okinawa*, 9, emphasis added. The Korean War spurred the building of this vast Okinawan complex to accommodate the massive influx of US military and civilian personnel.

19 Johnson, *Sorrows of Empire*, 25.

20 Johnson, *Sorrows of Empire*, 5.

21 Quoted in Vine, *Base Nation*, 4.

22 Quoted in Johnson, *Sorrows of Empire*, 152.

23 Vine, *Base Nation*, 19, 22.

24 See Karuka, *Empire's Tracks*.

25 Quoted in Vine, *Base Nation*, 23.

26 Vine, *Base Nation*, 22–24.

27 Truman, quoted in Calder, *Embattled Garrisons*, 15.

28 Calder, *Embattled Garrisons*, 34.

29 Calder, *Embattled Garrisons*, 24. On the notable absence of US military bases in Taiwan, Chih-ming Wang argues that they are "not so much absent as displaced to Okinawa and Guam." See "Teaching American Studies in Taiwan," 389.

30 Davis, *Empire's Edge*, 48.

31 Calder, *Embattled Garrisons*, 33.

32 "Lily pads" are small bases under ten acres in size or valued at under $10 million in value. See Vine, "Lists of U.S. Military Bases Abroad, 1776–2019." According to Vine's list, the breakdown of US overseas bases and lily pads in Asia and the Pacific by country/territory is as follows: American Sāmoa—1; Cambodia—1; Guam—53; Japan—120; Johnston Atoll—1; South Korea—80; Marshall Islands—11; Northern Mariana Islands—5; Philippines—8 (all lily pads since the base closures in 1992); Singapore—2; Thailand—2; Wake Island—1.

33 Shufeldt, quoted in Kindig, "Violent Embrace."

34 Kindig, "Violent Embrace."

35 Katharine H. S. Moon writes that in Olongapo and Angeles, where the US Subic Bay Naval Base and Clark Air Force Base were respectively located until the 1992 withdrawal of US forces, virtually no industry existed except the "entertainment" business, with approximately 55,000 registered and unregistered sex workers and a total of 2,182 registered R&R establishments. Further, while US forces withdrew in 1992, their approximately fifty thousand Amerasian children were left behind, with an estimated ten thousand of them living in Olongapo. The law firm of Cotchett, Illston, and Pitre in Burlingame, California, filed a class-action suit against the US government on behalf of these Amerasian children in March 1993. See *Sex Among Allies*, 33, 35.

36 Santos, "Gathering the Dust." Santos writes, "The U.S-R.P. [Republic of the Philippines] Military Base Agreement (MBA) technically expired on 16 September 1991. This signals the termination of forty-four years of overt U.S. military presence in the country. Signed in 1947, a year after the U.S. colonial rule officially ended in the archipelago, the MBA has always been regarded as a bugbear of the supposed independent status of the Philippines" (33).

37 Calder, *Embattled Garrisons*, 12. As I noted in the Introduction, the bases at their height employed nearly seventy thousand Filipinos and thirteen thousand US military personnel. Clark Field, established in 1903, became the second-largest US airbase on the planet, while Subic Bay, in turn, grew to be the largest American naval facility outside the United States.

38 For an analysis of how the former base now operates as the Subic Bay Freeport Zone (SBFZ), conceptualized as a "global borderland," or a "spatialized unit of globaliza-

tion" characterized by foreign-local encounters and the coexistence of two or more legal systems, see Reyes, *Global Borderlands*. As Reyes relates, the SBFZ, a tourism and business destination (with complexes including a tiger zoo, a water park, tourist resorts, universities, an international high school, shipping and manufacturing facilities, an upscale mall, and three gated residential communities), is also a popular dock for foreign ships, including US military ships.

39 Simbulan, "People's Movement Responses to Evolving U.S. Military Activities in the Philippines," 174; Vine, "Lists of U.S. Military Bases Abroad, 1776–2019."

40 For an analysis of the consequences of US base closures in South Korea, including the US government's failure to abide by the "polluter pays" principle, see Kim, C. J., "Bases That Leave."

41 Sturdevant and Stoltzfus, *Let the Good Times Roll*, 79–80. Kang takes Sturdevant and Stoltzfus to task for neglecting "to take up thorny questions of their own representational motivation and practice." For Kang, their text is one among many examples of the uncritical staging of an "enforced visibility" of women in militarized sex work and sex tourism. See *Compositional Subjects*, 204, 201. Though I agree with Kang, I cite Lita's comment about debt because it is a powerful articulation of debt conceived in collective terms rather than individual.

42 Rodriguez, *Migrants for Export*, x, xii, 142, xiv. Profit is generated by workers' remittances that total millions of US dollars, and by the bureaucratic processing fees charged by migration agencies.

43 Rodriguez, *Migrants for Export*, 142.

44 According to figures from the World Bank, in the past twenty years, remittances to the Philippines as a percentage of GDP peaked at 12.7 percent in 2005, but the total amount each year in dollars has been escalating dramatically. In 2019, it was over $35 billion. See https://data.worldbank.org/indicator/BX.TRF.PWKR.CD.DT?locations =PH (accessed November 2, 2020.) According to the results of the 2019 Survey on Overseas Filipinos of the Philippine Statistics Authority, a government agency of the Philippines, the number of Overseas Filipino Workers (OFWs) is estimated to be 2.2. million. See https://psa.gov.ph/statistics/survey/labor-and-employment/survey -overseas-filipinos (accessed November 2, 2020).

45 Tadiar, *Fantasy-Production*, 50, 49.

46 Tadiar, *Fantasy-Production*, 56.

47 Moon, K. H. S., *Sex Among Allies*.

48 Kramer, "Military-Sexual Complex."

49 Perez, "Guam and Archipelagic American Studies," 98.

50 Quoted in Vine, *Base Nation*, 75. All four branches of the US military—Marines, Navy, Air Force, and Army—have bases in Okinawa. See Ames, "Crossfire Couples," 178.

51 Sturdevant, "Okinawa Then and Now," 251.

52 Ginoza, "Space of 'Militourism'"; Yoneyama, *Cold War Ruins*, 45. The "intimacies of U.S. and Japanese empires" is part of the subtitle of Ginoza's article. The full subtitle is "Intimacies of U.S. and Japanese Empires and Indigenous Sovereignty in Okinawa."

53 McCormack and Norimatsu, *Resistant Islands*. McCormack and Norimatsu make three important points. First, the reversion was less a "handing back" as the term

reversion implies and more of an actual "purchase." Second, the "return," moreover, was a "nonreturn" since the US military's occupation of Okinawa, monopoly over the most fertile agricultural lands, and control of the sea and skies continued uninterrupted. Third, "following this strange transaction in which roles of buyer and seller were reversed, Japan adopted as national policy the retention of a substantial US military presence in Okinawa. To prevent any significant reduction of US forces ever taking place, it began to pay a sum that steadily increased over the years. The price that Japan paid to *avoid* reversion thus rose steadily" (7, emphasis in original). For the "garbage dump" question, see Nashiro, "What's Going on Behind Those Blue Eyes?," 57. For an analysis of the broad multiracial and transnational coalition that formed in Okinawa against reversion to Japan (because it would merely be a continuation of Okinawa's colonized status), see Onishi, *Transpacific Antiracism*.

54 Takazato, quoted in Chibana, "Striving for Land, Sea, and Life," 142.

55 See Shibusawa, *America's Geisha Ally*.

56 Yoneyama, *Cold War Ruins*, 45.

57 McCormack and Norimatsu, *Resistant Islands*, 67, emphasis in original.

58 McCormack and Norimatsu, *Resistant Islands*, 8.

59 Tokuyama, "Collective Traumatic Memory in a Jointly-Colonized Okinawa," 192.

60 Tokuyama, "Collective Traumatic Memory in a Jointly-Colonized Okinawa," 194, emphasis in original.

61 See, for example, Chibana, "Artful Way of Making Indigenous Space" and "Striving for Land, Sea, and Life." See also Ginoza, "Dis/articulation of Ethnic Minority and Indigeneity" and "Space of 'Militourism.'" Chibana problematizes generalized uses of the term *Indigenous*, noting that there are gaps between global and local contexts. Connections and attachment to the land are strong at the intensively local village level of the microcommunity, and the Okinawan understanding of community (*shima*) is different from racialized or affiliation-based organizing found in Western settler colonial societies. Rather, since Okinawan Indigeneity is intensively local in scale, it might thus be termed "micro-indigeneity." See "Artful Way of Making Indigenous Space," 143–44.

62 Yoneyama, *Cold War Ruins*, 46.

63 Yoneyama, *Cold War Ruins*, 52.

64 In the Preface, Steve Rabson explains that in addition to the seizure of large tracts of cultivated farmland, the US Command seized control of Okinawa's infrastructure and utilities as well as the sphere of activity of Okinawans. The US military retained ultimate civil and criminal jurisdiction over everyone on the island, which "resulted in horrendous miscarriages of justice involving crimes committed by US military personnel against Okinawa residents" (xi). See Preface, *Okinawa*, ix–xiv.

65 Davinder L. Bhowmik argues that neither the rubrics of regional literature nor of minority literature provide an adequate framework for understanding prose fiction from Okinawa. See *Writing Okinawa*, 10.

66 As Annmaria M. Shimabuku writes, Koza City (previously known as Goyeku Village, then later as Okinawa City) was "encircled by the U.S. military" and "became a site of widespread sexual violence as well as an active hotbed for prostitution." See Shimabuku, *Alegal*, 55.

67 The "weird landscape" described in "Dark Flowers" is also the result of the US military's notorious "one-mile limit" policy, issued in June 1949 in response to rising rates of venereal disease. Because this policy "prohibited native structures within one mile of any dependent housing or military billet of a hundred or more soldiers in the Goyeku Village [Koza City], farmers and small businesses were cut off from their livelihood." See Shimabuku, *Alegal*, 55.

68 The Battle of Okinawa also resulted in the deaths of almost a third of the island's population, exceeding the atomic bomb casualties of Hiroshima and Nagasaki. See Bhowmik and Rabson, Introduction, *Islands of Protest*, 3.

69 Vine, *Base Nation*, 75.

70 Gillem, *America Town*, 38.

71 McCormack and Norimatsu, *Resistant Islands*, 78. See also Akibayashi and Takazato, "Okinawa."

72 Shimabuku, *Alegal*, 68. The "land confiscations were dramatic. With 'bulldozers and bayonets,' they often tricked farmers into signing documents they did not understand and burned down their houses at gunpoint."

73 Gillem, *America Town*, 238. The Japanese Diet passed the law in 1972 as part of "reversion" and secretly agreed to pay $4 million for outstanding claims against land seized for US bases. When Okinawan landowners demanded the return of their appropriated land, Japan used its Land Acquisition Law to maintain control of the land. However, in contrast to "eminent domain laws in the United States that require one-time compensation for the forced sale of private land for public use, the Japanese law allowed for continued private ownership but forced lease" (238).

74 In response to growing public sympathy for the Isahama women farmers resisting the prohibition on farming, which was announced in the summer of 1954, the Ryūkyū Legislature's special land committee, which in late 1954 had excused itself from official negotiations, "convened two sessions that were open to the public on February 5 and 8 [of 1955] to discuss their official position. Approximately sixty men and women from Isahama attended these sessions and submitted two documents for consideration: a petition signed by all residents of Isahama and a document titled the 'Women's Appeal' that articulated the position of women whose livelihoods depended on having access to farmlands." See Matsumura, "'Isahama Women Farmers' against Enclosure," 557–58.

75 Matsumura, "'Isahama Women Farmers' against Enclosure," 567.

76 Bhandar, *Colonial Lives of Property*.

77 Gillem, *America Town*, 26.

78 Hatcher, quoted in Johnson, *Sorrows of Empire*, 35.

79 2018 *Base Structure Report* of the Department of Defense, 8, https://www.acq.osd.mil/eie/BSI/BEI_Library.html (accessed June 10, 2019).

80 Gillem, *America Town*, 26, 38.

81 Gillem describes it as "a low-density suburb, exported from the homeland, replete with auto dependency, isolated uses, and low net densities." See *America Town*, xv.

82 Johnson, *Sorrows of Empire*, 23.

83 Gillem, *America Town*, 88.

84 Gillem, *America Town*, 92.

85 Raheja, *Reservation Reelism*, 13, 21.

86 Carter, "Nappy Routes and Tangled Tales," 13, 8.

87 Kajihiro, "Moananuiākea or 'American Lake'?," 132.

88 Wesley Iwao Ueunten provides these statistics: "According to 1969 statistics, 7,400 Okinawan women, or about one in every 40 to 50 women in Okinawa aged 10 to 60, were involved in prostitution. Koza, where the uprising took place, was the major site for the bar and sex industry that catered to American troops" (93). See "Rising Up from a Sea of Discontent." By the mid-1980s, predominantly Filipinas provided entertainment and sexual labor for the US military in Okinawa.

89 On the debt bondage system in Okinawa, see Sturdevant and Stoltzfus, "Disparate Threads of the Whole"; Shimabuku, *Alegal*, 91.

90 Rabson, Introduction, *Okinawa*, 17. Akibayashi and Takazato reveal that 4,790 criminal charges were brought against US military personnel between 1972 and 1995, including twelve cases of murder, 355 of robbery, and 111 of rape. These do not include the many more unreported cases, nor do they include reported and unreported cases before reversion, for which there are no official statistics. See "Okinawa," 252. For a partial list of these crimes, see http://www.uchinanchu.org/history/list_of _crimes.htm (accessed January 4, 2018).

91 Keyso, *Women of Okinawa*, 86.

92 Linda Isako Angst analyzes how the 1995 rape evoked a powerful symbolic theme of "Okinawa as sacrificed schoolgirl daughter," inciting powerful responses from Okinawan women's groups, landowners, the then governor Ota Masahide, and even the international community calling for the removal of US bases. See "Rape of a Schoolgirl," 135, 138, 140.

93 Yoneyama, *Cold War Ruins*, ix.

94 For a discussion of the author as a public intellectual, see Molasky, "Writer as Public Intellectual in Okinawa Today."

95 Bhowmik and Rabson, Introduction, *Islands of Protest*, 2.

96 Calder observes that despite strong antimilitarism among Okinawans as a collective identity as well as among media and local government, and continuous demonstrations against the overwhelming concentration of US bases on the island, "there is remarkably little transformation in the basing structure, even when political leaders agree to undertake it" (167). It is important to note that local landowners who enjoy increasing base-rental fees, which are higher than market rates, have a growing stake in the continued presence of US military bases. Moreover, given that the land has been radically transformed by the bases, these landowners realistically have few alternative uses for the land. Base landowners thus constitute a powerful interest group, well organized at the grassroots level, with local associations represented at the prefectural and national levels. Base workers as well as unions also have a vested interest in the continuing presence of the bases. See *Embattled Garrisons*, 167, 172–73.

97 The campaign was initiated in 1982 by Okinawan intellectual and activist Arasaki Moriteru and others. By the late 1980s, there were about two thousand antimilitary landlords, including "one-*tsubo*" landlords. See Inoue, *Okinawa and the U.S. Military*, 36.

98 Okinawa Women Act Against Military Violence (OWAAMV), a women's peace, human rights, and demilitarization advocacy movement, emerged. It established the first private rape crisis center in Okinawa in October 1995. Okinawan high school and college students established DOVE (De-activating Our Violent Establishment). In 1997, an international solidarity network called East-Asia-US-Puerto Rico Women's Network Against Militarism was established by feminist peace activists in San Francisco. Composed of women from Okinawa, mainland Japan, South Korea, the Philippines, the United States, Puerto Rico, and Hawai'i, the network held its first meeting in Naha, Okinawa, in 1997. Together with other feminist peace activists in different parts of the world, the women in this network have formed an analytic framework of "authentic security" that guarantees the following: an environment that sustains human and natural life; the provision of people's basic survival needs in terms of food, clothing, shelter, health, and education; respect for fundamental human dignity and cultural identities; and the protection of the human and the natural environment from avoidable harm. See Akibayashi and Takazato, "Okinawa." For a history of OWAAMW on the occasion of its 25th anniversary, see Akibayashi, "Okinawa Women Act against Military Violence."

99 Akibayashi, "Okinawa Women Act against Military Violence," 39, emphasis in original.

100 Coulthard, *Red Skin, White Masks*, 173.

101 For a classic account, see Fanon, *Black Skin, White Masks*.

102 Wolfe, "Settler Colonialism and the Elimination of the Native," 388.

103 Atwood, *Payback*, 150.

104 Atwood, *Payback*, 125.

105 Fanon, *Wretched of the Earth*, 58.

106 Bhowmik and Rabson, Introduction, *Islands of Protest*, 5. See also Ginoza, "R&R at the Intersection of US and Japanese Dual Empire," 584; Jin, "'All Okinawa' Movement."

107 Kyodo, "Okinawa Files Fresh Lawsuit to Halt U.S. Futenma Base Relocation," *Japan Times*, July 24, 2017, https://www.japantimes.co.jp/news/2017/07/24/national/crime -legal/okinawa-files-fresh-lawsuit-halt-u-s-futenma-base-relocation/#.WlBGGEtGIp8.

108 Derrida, "Force of Law."

109 Matthew M. Burke and Aya Ichihashi, "Landfill Work Begins on Controversial Futenma Relocation Facility in Okinawa," *Stars and Stripes*, December 14, 2018, https://www.stripes.com/news/landfill-work-begins-on-controversial-futenma -relocation-facility-in-okinawa-1.560610.

110 Eric Johnston, "More than 70% in Okinawa Vote No to Relocation of U.S. Futenma Base to Henoko," *Japan Times*, February 24, 2019, https://www.japantimes.co.jp /news/2019/02/24/national/politics-diplomacy/okinawa-residents-head-polls -referendum-relocation-u-s-futenma-base-henoko/#.XRF6SXt7mo0. For an analysis of the ambivalent and contradictory feelings held among Okinawans with regard to US military bases, in particular how many oppose the presence of the bases in principle but recognize the economic opportunities they provide in a stagnant local economy, see Nishiyama, "Geopolitics of Disregard."

111 Justin McCurry, "Soil to Build New US Airbase on Okinawa 'Contains Remains of War Dead,'" *Guardian*, March 22, 2021, https://www.theguardian.com/world/2021 /mar/22/okinawa-us-airbase-soil-war-dead-soldiers-japan.

112 Mei-Singh, "Geographies of Desecration."

113 Chibana, "Striving for Land, Sea, and Life," 148.

114 Chibana, "Artful Way of Making Indigenous Space," 137–38. Chibana explains that "the conceptual structure of indigeneity in Okinawa cannot be understood solely in terms of nativity versus settler colonialism. Nor is Okinawan indigeneity commensurate with '*minority minzu* (nationality)' or 'heritage residents' ideas of indigenous peoples, as articulated by other Asian states. Rather, Okinawan indigeneity hybridizes both models on an intensively local scale that might be termed *micro-indigeneity*" (142–43, emphases in original).

115 Yokota, "Okinawan (Uchinānchu) Indigenous Movement and Its Implications for Intentional/International Action," 59–60.

116 *Bloodless* was shot with eight GoPro cameras, and the images were stitched together in a costly and technologically advanced transnational postproduction process in the United States and South Korea. Quite different from a traditional film screening, VR films such as *Bloodless* are seen by donning a VR headset. As such, even if a VR film is seen in a large theater with many other viewers, it is decidedly not a collective experience in the way that a traditional filmgoing experience is. Indeed, immersion via the donning of the headset creates an individualized and isolating experience. *Bloodless* has garnered multiple awards, including the award for Best Virtual Reality Story at the 2017 Venice International Film Festival. This was the first film festival globally to create a competition category for virtual reality films, with an entire island dedicated to its newly constructed, state-of-the-art VR theaters. Soon after Venice, the Busan International Film Festival in South Korea also offered VR screenings. Other awards include Best VR Film at the 2017 Thessaloniki International Film Festival and Best VR Story at the 2017 Dubai International Film Festival. The film was also an "Official Selection" at numerous film festivals around the world, including Brazil, Australia, and Taiwan. See Doo, "Empathy without Exploitation"; Chang, "VR Trooper."

117 *Bloodless* was funded by Venta VR (a South Korean producer of VR video content), the Dankook University Graduate School of Cinematic Content in South Korea, and the University of California, Los Angeles (UCLA). Although the camptown area called "Special Tourism Zone for Foreigners" itself is not restricted to South Korean nationals, only foreign passport holders can get into the clubs and bars. Kim and her crew shot the film "guerilla style," without permits, but it was not "scandalous" insofar as they were not singling out any particular bar or store. See Chang, "VR Trooper."

118 Gina Kim, quoted in Chang, "VR Trooper."

119 Depending on the romanization, Yun's first name is variously spelled Keum Yi, Kum-i, and Geom-i.

120 Cho, *Haunting the Korean Diaspora*, 113, 118–19.

121 See Gina Kim's website: http://www.ginakimfilms.com/filmography#/bloodless -2017/ (accessed June 17, 2019).

122 See Lele, "Virtual Reality and Its Military Utility"; Rizzo et al., "Virtual Reality Goes to War."

123 Buckmaster and Yecies, "Docu-reality and Empathy in *Bloodless* (2017)."

124 Doo, "Empathy without Exploitation."

125 Tan, "Filming from a New Perspective."

126 See Chang, "VR Trooper"; Tan, "Filming from a New Perspective."

127 Wissot, "Sex Crimes and Virtual Reality."

128 The film's soundtrack was created by MarcoCo. Studios. For a detailed discussion of the film's soundscape and other elements of its form, see Buckmaster and Yecies, "Docu-reality and Empathy in *Bloodless* (2017)."

129 Gina Kim's Director's Statement, http://www.ginakimfilms.com/filmography# /bloodless-2017/ (accessed June 17, 2019, emphasis added).

130 For a useful analysis that traces the development of South Korea's regulated system of camptown sex work back to the World War II system instituted by the Japanese, see Lee, N. Y., "Construction of Military Prostitution."

131 Moon, S., *Militarized Modernity and Gendered Citizenship in South Korea.*

132 For an excellent history of US military camptown sex work in South Korea, see Moon, S., "Regulating Desire, Managing the Empire."

133 Moon, K. H. S., *Sex among Allies*, 1. Moon relates that this ongoing structure of militarized sexual labor has involved over one million Korean women employed as sex workers serving a US military clientele.

134 Lee, J-k., *Service Economies*, 127.

135 In the 1960s and 1970s, South Korea's Park Chung Hee regime, almost immediately following his coup, passed two major legal provisions actively supporting camptown sex work. The Prostitution Prevention Law *excluded* camptown sex work from the general state crackdown on sex work, and the Tourism Promotion Law designated camptowns as "special tourism districts." See Lee, J-k., *Service Economies*, 126.

136 Seungsook Moon observes that US military bases and camptowns in South Korea resemble Puerto Rico, a US colony. See "In the U.S. Army but Not Quite of It," 234.

137 Johnson, *Sorrows of Empire*, 35.

138 Lee, J-k., *Service Economies*, 2.

139 Lee, J-k., *Service Economies*, 6, 7.

140 Kim, E-S., "Itaewon as an Alien Space within the Nation-State and a Place in the Globalization Era," 53.

141 See Cho, "Diaspora of Camptown." For an important study of Korean military brides in the United States, see Yuh, *Beyond the Shadow of Camptown*.

142 Doolan, "Transpacific Camptowns," 33.

143 As Kang points out, the producers and directors of *Camp Arirang*, Diana Lee and Grace Lee, are both Korean American. In terms of *The Women Outside*, Hye Jung Park is Korean American, whereas J. T. Takaji is Japanese American. So when Kang references "Korean American," she means mainly the three Korean American documentarians. See *Compositional Subjects*, 260.

144 Kang, *Compositional Subjects*, 260. Kang quotes Marx's famous line in the *18th Brumaire of Louis Bonaparte*, "They must be represented."

145 Kang, *Compositional Subjects*, 269.

146 The plaintiffs in the case encouraged the comparison between themselves (sex workers who had been "comfort women for the US military") and "comfort women," Japan's euphemism for women conscripted in Korea and other parts of Asia into a system of forced sexual servitude for the Japanese army during World War II. See Choe, "South Korea Illegally Held Prostitutes Who Catered to G.I.s Decades Ago, Court Says."

147 Katharine H. S. Moon writes in *Sex Among Allies*,

> The "debt bondage system" is the most prominent manifestation of exploita-
> tion. A woman's debt increases each time she borrows money from the
> owner—to get medical treatment, to send money to her family, to cover an
> emergency, to bribe police officers and VD clinic workers. Most women also
> begin their work at a new club with large amounts of debt, which usually
> results from the "agency fee" and advance pay. Typically, (illegal) job place-
> ment agencies which specialize in bar and brothel prostitution place women
> in a club and charge the club owner a fee. The owner transfers the fee onto
> the new employee's "account" at usurious rates; Ms. Pak mentions one club
> owner charging 10%. Often, women ask the owners for an advance in order
> to pay off her existing debts to another club, and the cycle of debt continues.
> Owners also set up a new employee with furniture, stereo equipment, cloth-
> ing, and cosmetics—items deemed necessary for attracting GI customers.
> These costs get added to the woman's account with interest. . . . For this rea-
> son, women try to pick up as many GIs as possible night after night, and for
> this reason, women cannot leave prostitution at will. Nanhee sums up the
> debt-ridden plight: "In some American [camptown] clubs, *if you have no debt,*
> *they see to it that you incur some.* If you had no debt, you would have the choice
> of going to another club, a better club. But if the woman has debts, she can't
> leave before she pays up. Escaping from a club isn't easy to do. The women
> with a conscience stay and work [to pay off the debt]." (21–22, brackets in
> original, emphasis added)

148 Yuh, "Moved by War"; Cho, *Haunting the Korean Diaspora*. The 1965 Immigration and Nationality Act (the Hart-Celler Act) replaced immigration based on strict national origins quotas with broader hemispheric quotas. This made it possible for Koreans in the United States to sponsor multiple family members and changed anti-Asian immigration exclusion that had been in place beginning with the 1875 Page Act barring Chinese women.

149 An important example of such a social service agency for camptown sex workers is Du Rae Bang (My Sister's Place). An outreach project of the Korean Presbyte-rian Church, it opened two centers in 1986, one near Camp Stanley Army Base in Uijongbu and the other north of Seoul. Services included shelter, educational and counseling services for women, education and childcare for their children, an alternative means of making a living by opening its own bakery, and pooling money so the women could pay off their debts to club owners. See Kirk and Okazawa-Rey,

"Women Opposing U.S. Militarism in East Asia." For an analysis of how the Christian faith of Yun Ja Kim and that of other former camptown sex workers informs a "spiritual activism" that can be an alternative to war and militarism, see Pae, "Prostituted Body of War."

150 For an important analysis, see Okazawa-Rey, "Amerasian Children in GI Town."
151 Lee, J-k., *Service Economies*, 173–74.
152 See Kim, J., *Ends of Empire*; Kim, J., "Militarization."
153 Davis, *Empire's Edge*, 130.

CHAPTER 3. THE POW CAMP

1 Barrett, "Chinese Prisoners Shift Allegiance."
2 Young, "Voluntary Repatriation and Involuntary Tattooing of Korean War POWs," 152.
3 See Foot, *Substitute for Victory*.
4 Quoted in Young, *Name, Rank, and Serial Number*, 35.
5 Notable exceptions are the work of Charles S. Young and Monica Kim. See Young, "Voluntary Repatriation and Involuntary Tattooing of Korean War POWs" and *Name, Rank, and Serial Number*; Kim, M., *Interrogation Rooms of the Korean War*.
6 Young, "Voluntary Repatriation and Involuntary Tattooing of Korean War POWs," 147.
7 Baik, *Reencounters*, 15.
8 The 38th parallel was first drawn by two US military colonels on August 14, 1945, to demarcate the respective US and Soviet military occupations of the Korean Peninsula at the end of World War II. On the ground, this arbitrary dividing line did not correspond to any geographical or cultural boundary. See Kim, M., *Interrogation Rooms of the Korean War*, 6.
9 By 1952, the number of POWs peaked at 170,000, mostly on Koje Island. Of these, 21,000 were Chinese, 100,000 were North Korean, and 49,000 South Koreans (most of whom had been captured by the North Koreans earlier in the war). See Young, *Name, Rank, and Serial Number*, 33, 35, 68.
10 Darda, "Literary Afterlife of the Korean War," 88; Darda, "Introduction: Narratives of Exception in the Warfare State," 82.
11 Xiang, "Race, Tone, and Ha Jin's 'Documentary Manner,'" 75. For another analysis of Jin's "documentary manner" as exposing the slippages, limitations, and unreliability of language, see Watson, "Ha Jin's *War Trash*."
12 Young, "Voluntary Repatriation and Involuntary Tattooing of Korean War POWs," 157.
13 See Westad, *Global Cold War*; Rivero, *Myth of Development*, 138.
14 Cedric J. Robinson argues that this Manicheanism of the Cold War, the capitalism versus communism dyad, obfuscated (even as it violently suppressed) a decades-long global "race war" and masked the "transcendent and more enduring dualism": the racial order, à la Fanon, of a Manichean colonial domination. See *Black Movements in America*, 134–35.

15 On the ascendance of China, Giovanni Arrighi observes in *Adam Smith in Beijing* that "[t]he problem in US-Chinese relations at the turn of the twentieth-first [*sic*] century is no longer US commercial access to China. Rather, it is the fact that China has replaced the United States as the world's fastest-growing major economy and is seeking commercial access to the United States equal to that of other states" (277–78). Arrighi also argues that although Sinophobia has had a long-standing presence in US popular culture, "its sudden resurgence at the turn of the twenty-first century was prompted by the realization that China, rather than the United States, was emerging as the main beneficiary of the globalization project that the United States itself had sponsored in the 1980s and 1990s" (295).

16 As I related in the Introduction, in "America's Pacific Century," the October 2011 policy plan announced by the then secretary of state Hillary Clinton that the United States would "pivot" from the Middle East to the "Asia-Pacific," an "emerging" China is named as a new global reality, and the "Asia-Pacific" is identified as the United States' "real 21st century opportunity," an investment that will yield the greatest returns (63). In this global remapping of US strategic interests, Africa is also identified as holding "enormous untapped potential for economic and political development in the years ahead" (63). "America's Pacific Century" was published in the November 2011 issue of *Foreign Policy*.

17 An armistice, and not a peace treaty, was signed in 1953. The United States maintained complete wartime and peacetime operational command of the South Korean military until 1978, and under the Combined Forces Command (CFC), a majority command after 1978. Peacetime command was returned in 1994. As I relayed in Chapter 2, an agreement to return wartime command in 2012 has continually been postponed and is now scheduled to occur in 2022. See Höhn and Moon, "Politics of Gender, Sexuality, Race, and Class in the U.S. Military Empire," 16.

18 Paik, *Rightlessness*, 6. See also Kramer, "Power and Connection," 1357.

19 See Foucault, *Discipline and Punish*.

20 Darda, "Literary Afterlife of the Korean War," 83.

21 Kim, M., *Interrogation Rooms of the Korean War*, 10, 7. Kim writes, "The POW controversy of the Korean War touched off a constellation of political anxieties and ambitions because it resonated with a very basic question confronting the decolonizing world. In the post-1945 crucible of mass militarization of U.S. total warfare, the retreat of Japanese imperialism, and broad anticolonial movements across Asia, the question arose about how to configure a relationship between a state and its subject that could serve as the viable basis for a kind of national or international governance in the post-1945 world. In other words, how did one configure a person for state-building, revolution, or imperial warfare? And who would then be the agent in history that would usher in a new era of a decolonized future?" (11).

22 Schmitt, quoted in Kim, M., *Interrogation Rooms of the Korean War*, 18.

23 Kim, M., *Interrogation Rooms of the Korean War*, 5.

24 Kim, M., *Interrogation Rooms of the Korean War*, 109. Kim writes, "The Geneva Conventions of 1949 on the Treatment of Prisoners of War operated on the assumption that prisoners of war were essentially vulnerable persons and was invested in creat-

ing a normative understanding that taking a person prisoner rather than his or her life was a marker of advanced civilization" (109).

25 The camp on Koje Island, massive both in scale and population (with a total of 170,000 prisoners, US soldiers, Korean Augmentation of the US Army or KATUSA and Republic of Korea Army or ROKA members, and Korean civilian workers), would become the site of the first large-scale application of the 1949 Geneva Conventions. See Kim, M., *Interrogation Rooms of the Korean War*, 88.

26 Carruthers, *Cold War Captives*, 180.

27 Young, "Voluntary Repatriation and Involuntary Tattooing of Korean War POWs," 158. Young writes, "Notably, the tattooing was only in anticommunist compounds. In years of research, this author has never run across even a hint of pro-Communist tattoos on North Korean or Chinese Korean War POWs" (159–60).

28 Young, "Voluntary Repatriation and Involuntary Tattooing of Korean War POWs," 163.

29 Young, "Voluntary Repatriation and Involuntary Tattooing of Korean War POWs," 35.

30 Young, "Voluntary Repatriation and Involuntary Tattooing of Korean War POWs," 44.

31 Kim, M., "Empire's Babel," 4, 2; Kim, M., *Interrogation Rooms of the Korean War*, 12.

32 Young, *Name, Rank, and Serial Number*, 17.

33 Young writes, "When the psychological operation evolved into a demand that prisoners defect and not return to their families, the compounds burst into civil war." See *Name, Rank, and Serial Number*, 33. According to Rosemary Foot, in the end, 21,820 Communist POWs (out of 132,000) in UN camps opted not to repatriate, while twenty-two (out of 12,000 UN POWs) opted not to repatriate. See Foot, *Substitute for Victory*, 196–97.

34 Quoted in Young, *Name, Rank, and Serial Number*, 35.

35 Truman and Allen, quoted in Kim, M., *Interrogation Rooms of the Korean War*, 80–81.

36 Kim, M., *Interrogation Rooms of the Korean War*, 99.

37 Kim, M., *Interrogation Rooms of the Korean War*, 81.

38 Young, "Voluntary Repatriation and Involuntary Tattooing of Korean War POWs," 148.

39 Young, *Name, Rank, and Serial Number*, 37–38.

40 Kim, M., *Interrogation Rooms of the Korean War*, 18.

41 Young, *Name, Rank, and Serial Number*, 82, 103.

42 Loomis, quoted in Young, *Name, Rank, and Serial Number*, 99. For an analysis of the connection between Manifest Destiny and the POW camps of the Korean War, see Tovy, "Manifest Destiny in POW Camps."

43 Quoted in Carruthers, *Cold War Captives*, 175.

44 Carruthers, *Cold War Captives*, 175–76.

45 Carruthers, *Cold War Captives*, 178–79. See also Xiang, "Race, Tone, and Ha Jin's 'Documentary Manner,'" 77.

46 Young, *Name, Rank, and Serial Number*, 35.

47 Carruthers, *Cold War Captives*, 4. Carruthers goes on to observe that captivity became a dominant trope, an "enduring template," in American storytelling and the development of a national literature.

48 Carruthers, *Cold War Captives*, 5. Carruthers writes that during the late 1940s and 1950s, "captivity suffused American understandings of the eastern bloc and its inhabitants. . . . This threat to bodies, minds, and souls was not, however, confined to totalitarian states, nor was it exclusively a communist menace. In the 1950s, captivity served as a metaphor for a lengthening list of domestic social and psychological maladies, from the anomie of suburban housewives to the 'slave world' of drug addiction . . ." (5).

49 Elsewhere, I have discussed the Cold War "Orientalizing" of brainwashing in an analysis of the film *The Manchurian Candidate*. See Kim, J., *Ends of Empire*.

50 Monica Kim writes that the prisoners were aware of the larger international terrain within which they were embroiled and thus had to negotiate. Earlier in 1952, the International Committee of the Red Cross (ICRC) received a letter from Senior Colonel Lee Hak Ku, a Korean POW at UNC Camp #1 on Koje Island. Dated "29 December 1951," written in English, and addressed "To the Delegate of the International Committee of Red Cross," the letter begins: "I wish you are healthy and happy, on behalf of all P.O.W.s, including officers and E.M.S., who are being kept in detention by American forces at Kojedo." Although Lee was aware of the ongoing Panmunjom negotiations over the issue of POWs, he wrote to the ICRC before the conclusion of those negotiations precisely in order to protest the voluntary repatriation screening being undertaken by the US military already in the POW camp. He appealed to the humanitarian mission of the ICRC, reminding the ICRC of its responsibility to the POWs: "At the same time I hope that our request to you . . . would be fulfilled satisfactorily by you and your Committee's endeavor, whose mission is to carry out its just and sacred duties along with other humanistic problems entrusted by all the mankind of the world" (quoted in *Interrogation Rooms of the Korean War*, 177). Lee would later be elected the president of the "Korean Peoples Army and Chinese Volunteers Prisoners of War Representatives Association," the group involved in the infamous Dodd incident.

51 Kim, M., *Interrogation Rooms of the Korean War*, 179–80. The POWs involved in the Dodd incident were ultimately charged with "mutiny" by the US Army. Of the thirty-four POWs, the majority were men and three were young women. Important to note is that of the thirty-four, ten had been born in South Korea. This contradicts the US military's and media's narrative constructions of the incident as the work of "'fanatic communist North Koreans.'"

52 Kim, M., *Interrogation Rooms of the Korean War*, 186, 189.

53 Kim, M., *Interrogation Rooms of the Korean War*, 197. Ultimately, the US military stormed the compound.

54 Agamben, *Homo Sacer*, 166.

55 Agamben, *Homo Sacer*, 166–67.

56 Agamben, *Homo Sacer*, 171.

57 Young, "Voluntary Repatriation and Involuntary Tattooing of Korean War POWs," 162.

58 Young, "Voluntary Repatriation and Involuntary Tattooing of Korean War POWs," 155. Young reveals that a US Army Board of Officers who documented POW killings "produced an extraordinary log of violence. . . . The Board of Officers investigated

five hundred killings, including those by guards. Burchett and Winnington put the death toll at three thousand."

59 Agamben, *Homo Sacer*, 171

60 Agamben, *Homo Sacer*, 175

61 Agamben, *Homo Sacer*, 174.

62 Agamben, *Homo Sacer*, 166.

63 Rifkin, "Indigenizing Agamben," 117.

64 Kramer, *Blood of Government*, 152.

65 Denetdale, "Discontinuities, Remembrances, and Cultural Survival," 298.

66 Morgensen, *Spaces between Us*, 161, emphasis in original.

67 Lowe, *Intimacies of Four Continents*, 3, emphasis added.

68 See Rivero, *Myth of Development*.

69 Ha Jin's ethical injunction is complicated by a Chinese journalist's charge of plagiarism leveled against him soon after the publication of *War Trash*. This plagiarism charge was made in July 2005 by Zhang Ze-shi, chief editor of *Meijun Jizhongying* [*Personal Records in the American Prison Camps*], particularly in terms of the account of the abduction of General Dodd, fictionalized as General Bell in the novel. Ha Jin includes at the end of his novel this Author's Note with a bibliography that includes Zhang's work: "This is a work of fiction and all the main characters are fictional. Most of the events and details, however, are factual. For information on them I am indebted to the following authors and works: . . ." Rather than getting entangled in the legal and ethical issues generated by this case, Xie Xinqiu concludes that *War Trash* is a work of what Linda Hutcheon calls "historiographical metafiction." See Xie, "War Memoir as False Document," 36.

70 Foucault, *Discipline and Punish*, 31.

71 Agamben, "No to Biopolitical Tattooing," 202.

CHAPTER 4. THE UNINCORPORATED TERRITORY

1 Teaiwa, "AmneSIA," 134. Teaiwa's poem appears as part of a tribute, "Teresia Teaiwa: 'We Sweat and Cry Salt Water, So We Know That the Ocean Is Really in Our Blood,'" that appeared in the *International Feminist Journal of Politics* in 2017 after Teaiwa's passing. "AmneSIA" was originally performed by Teaiwa (with Sia Figiel) in the 2000 CD *Tereneisa* distributed by 'Elepaio Press.

2 Over the course of the second half of the twentieth century, 315 nuclear weapons tests were conducted in the Marshall Islands, Kiribati, Australia, and Maohi Nui (French Polynesia) by putatively "friendly" or colonizing powers. On October 24, 2020, the Treaty on the Prohibition of Nuclear Weapons was ratified when Honduras, the required fiftieth country, signed on. The treaty is a legally binding instrument prohibiting nuclear weapons and leading toward their total elimination. It entered into force as international law on January 22, 2021, despite opposition from the United States, China, Russia, Britain, and France, the five original nuclear powers. The Pacific Islands were prominent in the formation of the treaty and were early adopters. See Hawkins, "Now That Nuclear Weapons Are Illegal." The UN Treaty on the Prohibition of Nuclear Weapons can be found on the website of the

UN Office for Disarmament Affairs, https://www.un.org/disarmament/wmd/nuclear/tpnw/ (accessed October 26, 2020).

3 For a useful volume on archipelagic American studies and America's "imperial archipelago" that departs from continental exceptionalism, see Roberts and Stephens, *Archipelagic American Studies*.

4 A fifth to a quarter of high school graduates enter the military. See Lutz, "US Military Bases on Guam in a Global Perspective."

5 Taitano, *Inside Me an Island*, 16, emphases in original.

6 Taitano, *Inside Me an Island*, 15.

7 Quoted in Bevacqua, "Exceptional Life and Death of a Chamorro Soldier," 36.

8 Na'puti, "Archipelagic Rhetoric," 6.

9 Davis, "Repeating Islands of Resistance," 1.

10 Quoted in DeLoughrey, "Toward a Critical Ocean Studies for the Anthropocene," 25.

11 On the hypermilitarization of Guam, Lutz notes further, "Here there might have been rivals in Diego Garcia or in some areas of the continental US if the US had not forcibly removed those indigenous landowners altogether or onto the equivalent of reservations, something the US had hoped to do in Guam as far back as 1945." See "US Military Bases on Guam in Global Perspective."

12 For models of debt resistance and refusal, see the special forum on debt in the Fall 2013 issue of the *South Atlantic Quarterly*.

13 Kaplan, "Where Is Guantanamo?," 841–42. The specific legal question in *Downes v. Bidwell* (1901) concerned the issue of whether there should be tariffs on oranges shipped to New York from Puerto Rico. It revolved around the Uniformity Clause of Article I, Section 8 of the US Constitution requiring that "all Duties, Imports, and Excises shall be uniform throughout the United States."

14 Fuller, quoted in Kaplan, "Where Is Guantanamo?," 842.

15 Weiner, "Teutonic Constitutionalism," 65.

16 Thomas, "Constitution Led by the Flag," 86, emphasis in original.

17 Root, quoted in Thomas, "Constitution Led by the Flag," 86.

18 Thomas, "Constitution Led by the Flag," 86.

19 Thomas, "Constitution Led by the Flag," 84.

20 Brown, quoted in Thomas, "Constitution Led by the Flag," 86.

21 Thomas, "Constitution Led by the Flag," 88.

22 Wald, "Terms of Assimilation," 79. The *Chinese Exclusion Case* involved Chae Chan Ping, a Chinese immigrant who decided to visit his homeland of China after living and working in the United States for twelve years. Before departing, he obtained the proper permit for reentry into the United States. However, during the course of his visit to China, the United States passed the Scott Act (1888), which forbade the reentry of Chinese immigrants to the United States. This went against the Burlingame Treaty (1868) between the United States and China granting certain privileges to Chinese immigrants residing in the United States. Among other issues, Chae Chan Ping argued that the Scott Act was in violation of the Burlingame Treaty, and that the executive and legislative branches of the US government did not have the authority to violate international treaties. The US Supreme Court decided against Chae Chan Ping's reentry, thus giving birth to the plenary power doctrine grant-

ing authority to the federal government to set immigration policy and overturn international treaties. It is important to note that in his majority opinion, Justice Stephen J. Field reveals an anti-Chinese racial logic. The court's majority opinion can be found here: https://www.law.cornell.edu/supremecourt/text/130/581 (accessed May 29, 2019).

23 Bevacqua, "Exceptional Life and Death of a Chamorro Soldier," 33.

24 As Valerie Solar Woodward observes, "Overshadowed by Puerto Rico in terms of immigration visibility and population, shuffled aside in critical work about Filipinos and US colonialism, and forgotten in legal writings about island nations and citizenship that tend to focus on Hawai'i, the people of Guam are truly invisible US citizens." See "'I Guess They Didn't Want Us Asking Too Many Questions,'" 70.

25 Although Guam residents can vote in local elections and plebiscites, they cannot vote in national presidential elections outside of primaries. Guam elects a delegate, not a representative, to the US House of Representatives. A delegate's voting opportunities and political capital are severely limited. See Na'puti and Hahn, "Plebiscite Deliberations," 1.

26 Rogers, *Destiny's Landfall*, 226.

27 Although the 1950 Organic Act ended US naval control of Guam by creating the civilian Government of Guam, it provided that the governor would be "appointed by the President, by and with the advice and consent of the Senate." It was not until 1968, when the Organic Act was amended by the Guam Elective Governor Act, that the office of governor (and the newly created office of lieutenant governor) became popularly elected, as opposed to appointed, positions. Quoted in Lawson, "Territorial Governments and the Limits of Formalism," 865.

28 Rogers, *Destiny's Landfall*, 230.

29 Prior to this, the Land Acquisition Act, passed on August 2, 1946, authorized the Navy Department to acquire private land for permanent military installations on the island. See Rogers, *Destiny's Landfall*, 230, 214.

30 Hsu, "Guåhan (Guam), Literary Emergence, and the American Pacific in *Homebase* and *from unincorporated territory*," 283.

31 Quoted in DeLoughrey, "Island Studies and the US Militarism of the Pacific," 33.

32 Quoted in Rogers, *Destiny's Landfall*, 222.

33 Lawson, "Territorial Governments and the Limits of Formalism," 853. In this case, plaintiff Sakamoto and defendant Duty Free Shoppers, Limited (DFS) were competing gift merchants whose main clients were Japanese tourists purchasing gifts to take back home. These tourists expected and demanded that their gift purchases be delivered to them at the airport to avoid being inconvenienced during their vacation. Thus, the right to deliver goods sold elsewhere on the island to departing tourists at the Guam International Airport Terminal is significant to merchants competing for this important segment of tourism. Since 1975, the Guam Airport Authority (GAA), an instrumentality of the territorial Government of Guam, had directly controlled the airport terminal. "In 1978, the GAA publicly sought bids on a fifteen-year exclusive concession for the sale and delivery of gift items at the terminal. DFS demonstrated the importance of airport delivery rights by submitting a winning bid of more than $140,000,000" (863). Sakamoto then filed suit against

DFS, the GAA, and the Government of Guam, seeking to invalidate the exclusive concession granted to DFS. Sakamoto argued that the exclusive concession violated federal antitrust laws. The court ruled against Sakamoto because agencies or instrumentalities of the federal government, which would include the GAA and the Government of Guam, enjoy antitrust immunity.

34 Lawson, "Territorial Governments and the Limits of Formalism," 864.

35 Schroder, quoted in Souder-Jaffery, "Not So Perfect Union," 20.

36 Editorial introduction to Lawson, "Territorial Governments and the Limits of Formalism," 853.

37 Chamorro petitions and appeals to the US Congress seeking various forms of self-government date as far back as 1901. For a history of such ongoing efforts, see Viernes, "Won't You Please Come Back to Guam?," 105–6; Souder-Jaffery, "Not So Perfect Union," 14.

38 Quinene, *Islander's Voice*, 51.

39 Quinene, *Islander's Voice*, 61.

40 Quinene, *Islander's Voice*, vii. The Introduction is by Victoria-Lola Leon Guerrero.

41 Na'puti and Hahn, "Plebiscite Deliberations," 2–3.

42 Tydingco-Gatewood was the first female Chamorro chief judge. She was appointed by George W. Bush in 2006 to a ten-year term and renominated by Barack Obama in 2016 to another ten-year term.

43 Jasmine Stole Weiss and Jerick Sablan, "Judge: Plebiscite Law Unconstitutional; AG May Appeal," *Pacific Daily News*, March 8, 2017, https://www.guampdn.com/story /news/2017/03/08/judge-arnold-davis-plebiscite-law-unconstitutional/98888880/; Roselle Romanes and Mar-Vic Cagurangan, "Arnold 'Dave' Davis: The Outsider. Who Is This 'White Man' Who Dared to Challenge the Laws of the Island?," *Pacific Island News*, July 1, 2017, https://www.pacificislandtimes.com/single-post/2017/07 /02/Arnold-Dave-Davis-The-Outsider-Who-is-this-white-man-who-dared-to -challenge-the-laws-of-the-island; Amanda Pampuro, "Guam Argues for Native Voting Law before 9th Circuit," *Courthouse News Service*, October 11, 2018, https:// www.courthousenews.com/guam-argues-for-native-voting-law-before-9th-circuit /; Steve Limtiaco, "GovGuam Owes More Than $900K in Legal Fees for Plebiscite Case," *Pacific Daily News*, April 8, 2019, https://www.guampdn.com/story/news/local /2019/04/08/govguam-owes-more-than-900-k-legal-fees-plebiscite-case/3397840002 /; John I. Borja, "Plebiscite Law Ruling Draws Praise, Outrage," *Pacific Daily News*, March 9, 2017, https://www.guampdn.com/story/news/2017/03/09/plebiscite-law -ruling-draws-praise-outrage/98941174/; and Manny Cruz, "Plebiscite: Constitutional Law Expert Joins Guam Legal Team," *Pacific Daily News*, September 18, 2018, https:// www.guampdn.com/story/news/2018/09/18/plebiscite-constitutional-law-expert -joins-guam-legal-team/1343260002/. For the *Davis v. Guam* (2017) brief as amicus, see https://www.justice.gov/crt/case-document/file/1015166 (accessed June 8, 2019).

44 The Office of Hawaiian Affairs (OHA), a department of the state of Hawai'i with a high degree of autonomy, was established as a public trust in 1978 in response to the native Hawaiian sovereignty movement of the 1970s. Governed by a nine-member board of trustees elected to serve four-year terms, the OHA is charged with the man-

date of bettering the conditions of native Hawaiians. See Kauanui, "Multiplicity of Hawaiian Sovereignty Claims and the Struggle for Meaningful Autonomy," 287.

45 Cruz, "Plebiscite."

46 Pampuro, "Guam Argues for Native Voting Law before 9th Circuit."

47 Cruz, "Plebiscite."

48 Cruz, "Plebiscite."

49 Quoted in Gerry Partido, "Guam Loses Dave Davis Case," July 30, 2019, https:// pncguam.com/guam-loses-dave-davis-case-9th-appeals-court-upholds-injunction -against-plebiscite/.

50 The Chamorro Land Trust Commission administers approximately twenty thousand acres, amounting to 15 percent of Guam's total land area. See Mar-Vic Caguran-gan, "Judge: It's Not Race-Based, Court Favors Chamorro Land Trust Act," *Pacific Island Times*, January 5, 2019, https://www.pacificislandtimes.com/single-post/2019/01 /06/Judge-Its-not-race-based-Court-favors-Chamorro-Land-Trust-Act.

51 Steve Limtiaco, "Land Trust Faces Legal Test in Federal Court This Week," *Pacific Daily News*, November 27, 2018, https://www.guampdn.com/story/news/2018/11/27 /land-trust-faces-legal-test-federal-court-week/2121185002/; Jerick Sablan, "Federal Judge Asks Parties to Think of Possible Settlement in Chamorro Land Trust Suit," *Pacific Daily News*, November 29, 2018, https://www.guampdn.com/story/news/2018/11 /29/federal-judge-advises-other-options-chamorro-land-trust-suit/2145369002/.

52 Sablan, "Federal Judge Asks Parties to Think of Possible Settlement in Chamorro Land Trust Suit"; Haidee Eugenio Gilbert, "Court: Feds Fail to Show Chamorro Land Trust Act Is Discriminatory," *Pacific Daily News*, December 21, 2018, https:// www.guampdn.com/story/news/2018/12/21/court-feds-fail-show-chamorro-land -trust-act-discriminatory/2385252002/. For a discussion of this case and the *Davis v. Government of Guam* case within the broader context of the limitations of the existing framework of self-determination, see Kauanui, "Decolonial Self-Determination and 'No-State Solutions.'"

53 Mollway, quoted in Gilbert, "Court," emphasis added.

54 Quoted in Duane M. George, "Land Trust Lawsuit Settlement Ok'd; Legislature Must Now Act," *Pacific Daily News*, December 26, 2019, https://www.guampdn.com /news/local/land-trust-lawsuit-settlement-okd-legislature-must-now-act/article _a46817a7-9207-5fdd-8c2b-a9fc507c3cd2.html. See also Steve Limtiaco, "Land Trust Agrees to Sign Deal to Resolve Racial Disrimination Lawsuit," *Pacific Daily News*, May 23, 2020, https://www.guampdn.com/news/local/land-trust-agrees-to -sign-deal-to-resolve-racial-discrimination-lawsuit/article_9e17aafe-b1de-5490-bc85 -f931449147f1.html.

55 For an analysis of Guam as a paradigm of the military colony, one in which the law "functioned as a harbinger of militarized violence and white supremacist statecraft" (66), see Camacho, K., *Sacred Men*.

56 On "affinity poetics," see Jansen, "Writing toward Action."

57 Perez, "Guåhan, The Pacific and Decolonial Poetry," 23.

58 I echo here Hsu's reference to "poem fragments." See "Guåhan (Guam), Literary Emergence, and the American Pacific in *Homebase* and *from unincorporated territory*," 294.

59 Perez's work could also be read as "docupoetry." Joseph Harrington writes that the "new docupoetry . . . narrates history at the same time that the form of the narrative makes us aware of how we construct, perceive, and interpret history." See "Politics of Docupoetry," 67. For a useful analysis of how cultural and arts events are also forceful articulations of antimilitarist decolonization, see Na'puti and Frain, "Decolonize Oceania! Free Guåhan!"

60 Bevacqua observes that it is precisely these two things—location and ambiguous political status—that give Guam strategic value to the United States. Because of its location within just a few hours of all the major nations in Asia, the island has been used in key ways for the transportation of troops and weapons in every major US conflict in Asia since World War II. It has also been used to process refugees displaced by US wars, hosting more than 100,000 Vietnamese refugees in 1975 as part of Operation New Life. More recently, it has also hosted refugees from Burma and Kurds from Iraq. See Bevacqua, "Guam," 174–75. On Operation New Life, see also Espiritu, *Body Counts*; Lipman, *In Camps*.

61 Schlund-Vials, "'Finding' Guam," 51.

62 Coddington et al., "Embodied Possibilities, Sovereign Geographies and Island Detention," 32. In the 1990s, in response to an increasing number of asylum seekers arriving by boat to Guam from China, the US Coast Guard, Navy, and Customs and Border Protection started to intensify border patrol. The authors of this article are a team of geographers working collectively on the Island Detention Project. The project "explores why and how islands become sites of struggle over migration, entry and exclusion, detention, and migration 'management.'" (30).

63 DeLoughrey, *Routes and Roots*, 2.

64 Perez, "Transterritorial Currents and the Imperial Terripelago," 619–20, emphases in original.

65 Wolfe, "Settler Colonialism and the Elimination of the Native," 388.

66 Perez, "Transterritorial Currents and the Imperial Terripelago," 620.

67 Arnold H. Leibowitz, quoted in Perez, "Transterritorial Currents and the Imperial Terripelago," 619.

68 Lai, "Discontiguous States of America," 3.

69 As Perez details, the proposed military buildup would have included, in addition to the transfer of eight thousand marines from Okinawa to Guam, the construction of facilities to house and support them, the establishment of an Air and Missile Defense Task Force, the construction of a live firing range complex, and the creation of a deep-draft wharf in Apra Harbor to berth nuclear-powered aircraft carriers. See Perez, *from unincorporated territory [guma']*, 35. The "United States-Japan Roadmap for Realignment Implementation" agreement came with a price tag of $10.2 billion, with Japan contributing $6 billion. See Frain, "'Make America Secure,'" 224.

70 The petitions before the UN Special Political and Decolonization Committee began in October 2006. On that occasion, representatives from I Nasion CHamoru (Chamorro Nation), the Organization of People for Indigenous Rights, Guåhan Indigenous Collective, the International Peoples' Coalition against Military Pollution, the National Asian Pacific American Women's Forum, and the CHamoru Cultural Development and Research Institute voiced their concerns. Ibrahim

Gambari, UN undersecretary-general for political affairs, responded thus: "It is the goal of the United Nations to help the Chamoru people attain the basic right to self-determination, as part of its Charter and that it is also an ethical issue of great concern." Gambari then arranged a second meeting between the Chamorro and Political Affairs Bureau representatives to discuss moving Guam's decolonization process forward using a UN framework. See Viernes, "Won't You Please Come Back to Guam?," 113–14.

71 See *Filipino Primitive*, 2.

72 Goldstein, Pegues, and Vimalassery (now Karuka), "Introduction: On Colonial Unknowing."

73 On the conjoined processes of militarization and masculinization among Chamorro men in the US military, see Camacho, K., and Monnig, "Uncomfortable Fatigues," 40.

74 Perez uses brackets to indicate words and enunciations that have been typically not included or elided.

75 Camacho, K., *Cultures of Commemoration*, 29.

76 Camacho, K., *Cultures of Commemoration*, 39.

77 The song was composed by Pedro Taitingfong Rosario ("Tun Pete Siboyas") along with Hawaiian national Louie Futado. By 1942, the song had grown in popularity and was being sung across Guam by Chamorros. See Viernes, "Won't You Please Come Back to Guam?"

78 Camacho, K., *Cultures of Commemoration*, 63, brackets in original.

79 Tanji, "Japanese Wartime Occupation," 167.

80 Hartman, *Scenes of Subjection*, 130.

81 Gonzalez, *Securing Paradise*, 3.

82 Nguyen, *Gift of Freedom*, xii.

83 On the "afterlife of slavery," see Hartman, *Lose Your Mother*, 6. On the "refugee condition," see Nguyen, *Gift of Freedom*, Chapter 1.

84 Political activist groups had been primarily concerned with issues such as bilingual education, political representation, and cultural sovereignty. See Camacho, K., *Cultures of Commemoration*, 106. For an analysis of how Liberation Day is "contested even as it is commemorated," see Diaz, "Deliberating 'Liberation Day.'"

85 Rogers, *Destiny's Landfall*, 182.

86 Santos, "U.S. Return Was Reoccupation, Not Liberation," 20–21. Santos details how the United States had intelligence about Japan's pending invasion of Guam. US military personnel and their dependents were thus evacuated in October 1941. Chamorro dependents of US servicemen, however, were not on the evacuation list.

87 The National Environmental Policy Act (NEPA) of 1969 was the United States' first national environmental policy, setting a broad framework for assessing the potential environmental impact of proposed federal actions and programs, including those of the military. For the full text of the act, amended, see https://www.energy.gov/nepa /downloads/national-environmental-policy-act-1969. The Environmental Protection Agency's website on NEPA is here: https://www.epa.gov/nepa.

88 Frain, "'Make America Secure,'" 224.

89 See Bevacqua, "Guam."

90 Quoted in Camacho, L., "Resisting the Proposed Military Buildup on Guam," 186.

91 Quoted in Alexander, "Living with the Fence," 873. For an account of the lawsuit, see Camacho, L., "Resisting the Proposed Military Buildup on Guam."

92 Bevacqua, "Guam," 180. The *Enola Gay*, a B-29 bomber, became the first plane to drop an atomic bomb when the United States bombed Hiroshima, Japan, on August 6, 1945.

93 Frain, "'Make America Secure,'" 219–20.

94 Frain, "'Make America Secure,'" 222–23. On "blue washing," see Perez, "Transterritorial Currents and the Imperial Terripelago," 621.

95 On "maritime territorialism, see DeLoughrey, *Routes and Roots*, 30. On the size of US EEZs, see Frain, "'Make America Secure,'" 221.

96 Quoted in Nogues, "'With [Our] Entire Breath,'" 24. Bad press resulting from the petition helped to lead to the passage of the Organic Act in 1950.

97 See Nogues, "'With [Our] Entire Breath." Nogues cites Arturo Escobar's work on "public cyberspheres."

98 See Perez, "Facing Hawai'i's Future (Book Review)"; Perez, "Uncle Spam Wants You." For an analysis of gastrocolonialism in Perez's work, see Fresno-Calleja, "Fighting Gastrocolonialism in Indigenous Pacific Writing." For a detailed analysis of food sovereignty in the Pacific Islands, see Plahe, Hawkes, and Ponnamperuma, "Corporate Food Regime and Food Sovereignty in the Pacific Islands."

99 Francisco Delgado argues that "Guam is no longer Guam" can be interpreted less as a "statement of negation than of promise." It "presents the possibility that Chamorros can exist autonomous from their colonial relationship to the United States." See "Remade: Sovereign," 2.

100 Wolfe, "Settler Colonialism and the Elimination of the Native," 388.

EPILOGUE

1 The fifth book in Perez's *from unincorporated territory* series is scheduled to be published in 2022.

2 Perez, "Guåhan, The Pacific and Decolonial Poetry," 29.

3 The stage production credits are as follows: Peter Rockford Espiritu (director and choreographer and Oceania Dance Theatre artistic director), Igelese Ete (musical director and composer, and USP Head of Performing Arts), and Vilsoni Hereniko (producer, codirector, and story, and former director of the USP Oceania Centre for Arts, Culture, and Pacific Studies and now faculty at the University of Hawai'i, Mānoa). The European Consortium for Pacific Studies was headed at the time by Edvard Hviding of the University of Bergen, who served as the executive director.

4 Mirzoeff, "Climate Crisis Is a Debt Crisis," 832–33. Mirzoeff notes that according to Oxfam, the average US resident is the current global leader in carbon use per capita, and that the 1 percent use ten thousand times more carbon than this already-high level. What we call economic "growth" is in effect a "tool for the domination of the 99 percent" (836). The alternative to this predatory, environmentally damaging capitalist growth is not austerity. Rather, argues Mirzoeff, another world of "prosperity without growth" needs to be possible.

5 Mirzoeff, "Climate Crisis Is a Debt Crisis," 833.

6 My analysis is of the online version, which can be found here: https://video
.alexanderstreet.com/watch/moana-rua-the-rising-of-the-sea.

7 For an analysis of climate-driven noneconomic losses, see McNamara, Westoby,
and Chandra, "Exploring Climate-Driven Non-Economic Loss and Damage in the
Pacific Islands."

8 Miller, "*Moana: The Rising of the Sea* directed by Peter Rockford Espiritu (review),"
586.

9 A video of Jetñil-Kijiner's performance, along with the full text of the poem,
can be found at her website: https://www.kathyjetnilkijiner.com/united-nations
-climate-summit-opening-ceremony-my-poem-to-my-daughter/. Her recent poetry
collection critiquing nuclear testing and climate change is *Iep Jaltok: Poems from a
Marshallese Daughter*. Jaimey Hamilton Faris writes that Jetñil-Kijiner's visibility on
NGO platforms can be partly attributed to her position in the Marshall Islands (as
the daughter of Hilda Heine, the first female president of the Republic of the Marshall Islands); to her emergence as a poet and artist who publishes and exhibits in
English-language venues; and to her role as the cofounder of Jo-Jikum, a nonprofit
organization whose mission is to empower the voices of Marshallese youth seeking
climate justice. See "Sisters of Ocean and Ice," 77.

10 Diana Looser explains that the "voyaging canoe—piloted by sophisticated non-
instrument navigation techniques based on acute observation of the natural
environment—is a powerful symbol of purposeful mobility and explorative agency
in Oceania. Historically, it was the technology that enabled the determined settlement of vast reaches of the Pacific Ocean, and in the present, it has re-emerged as a
primary vehicle for community identity, collaborative synergy and global connec-
tivity." See Looser, "Symbolic *Vaka*, Sustainable Futures," 47. Looser's piece is part
of a larger article with this citation: Tammy Haili'ōpua, Sharon Mazer, and Diana
Looser, "The Vessel Will Embrace Us: Contemporary Pacific Voyaging in Oceanic
Theatre," *Performance Research* 21, no. 2 (2016): 40–49.

11 For an analysis of how climate change and the Anthropocene impact the writing of
history and history as a discipline, see Chakrabarty, "Climate of History."

12 DeLoughrey, *Allegories of the Anthropocene*, 2, emphases in original.

13 For a generative model of Indigenous climate change studies, see Whyte, "Indigenous Climate Change Studies."

14 Yamamoto, "Climate Relocation and Indigenous Culture Preservation in the Pacific
Islands," 151. The Paris Agreement was adopted by 196 parties in December 2015 and
entered into force in November 2016.

15 See Moore, "Introduction: Islands and Aquapelagos in the Anthropocene." For an
overview of how the terms *Anthropocene*, *Capitalocene*, and *Plantationocene* emerged,
see Haraway, "Anthropocene, Capitalocene, Plantationocene, Chthulucene." On
capitalism and climate change, see Chakrabarty, "Climate and Capital."

16 For a discussion of why the international community is not recognizing "climate
refugee" as a formal legal category, despite the fact that over 21.5 million people
have fled their homelands because of climate impacts, see Salem and Rosencranz,
"Climate Refugees in the Pacific."

17 Andrew Ross explains, "The concept of 'ecological debt' was first introduced by Chile's Instituto de Ecologica Politica in the lead-up to the 1992 Earth Summit in Rio de Janeiro. It was intended as a framework for discussing whether countries in the South should be responsible for repaying in full the external debts they had accumulated over the previous three decades. How did these debts to foreign creditors compare with the North's liabilities for environmental impacts from early colonization onward? Surely the South's claims as an eco-creditor were just as valid as the fiscal right of the North American and European banks to be repaid? Who owes what to whom?" See *Creditocracy and the Case for Debt Refusal*, 184–85.

18 H. Patricia Hynes, quoted in DeLoughrey, "Toward a Critical Ocean Studies for the Anthropocene," 16. The US military is exempted both from domestic carbon emission legislation as well as all major international climate agreements.

19 In addition to climate-induced migration out of low-lying Pacific Islands, we can also consider the migration into the United States from its southern border and growing levels of "eco-apartheid." See Ross, *Creditocracy and the Case for Debt Refusal*, 194.

20 For an account of Indigenous approaches to mitigating climate change, see, for example, Bryant-Tokalau, *Indigenous Pacific Approaches to Climate Change*. For analyses that center the perspectives of Pacific small island states, United States territories in the Pacific, and of small islands, respectively, on climate change, see Beyerl, Mieg, and Weber, "Comparing Perceived Effects of Climate-Related Environmental Change and Adaptation Strategies for the Pacific Small Island States of Tuvalu, Samoa, and Tonga"; Schwebel, "Climate Change Perceptions and Preparation in the United States Territories in the Pacific"; and Walshe and Stancioff, "Small Island Perspectives on Climate Change."

21 The Framework for Pacific Regionalism is "intended to support focused political conversations and settlements that address key strategic issues, including shared sovereignty, pooling of resources, and delegation of decision-making. Rather than providing a list of regional priorities, it seeks to set out a robust process through which regional priorities will be identified and implemented." See Goulding, "Marshalling a Pacific Response to Climate Change," 198.

22 The Alliance of Small Island States (AOSIS) is composed of forty-four small island states and low-lying coastal states that are very vulnerable to climate change. All fourteen Pacific Island countries are part of the coalition, with American Sāmoa and Guam having observer status. The diverse membership covers the Pacific and Indian Oceans, as well as the Caribbean Sea, but members are united by a common purpose against a common threat. See Carter, "Establishing a Pacific Voice in the Climate Change Negotiations," 211.

23 Bryant-Tokalau, *Indigenous Pacific Approaches to Climate Change*, 16.

24 Yamamoto, "Climate Relocation and Indigenous Culture Preservation in the Pacific Islands," 151.

25 Bryant-Tokalau, *Indigenous Pacific Approaches to Climate Change*, 2.

26 Faris, "Sisters of Ocean and Ice," 76. *Rise: From One Island to Another*, a video poem, is a 2018 collaboration between Jetñil-Kijiner and Aka Niviâna, an Inuk poet from Kalaallit Nunaat (Greenland). Brought together by the environmental activist

organization 350.org, Jetñil-Kijiner and Niviâna pose urgently important questions about the difference between climate mitigation and adaptation in addition to interrogating the continuities of colonialism and neocolonialism. *Rise: From One Island to Another* can be accessed here: https://350.org/rise-from-one-island-to-another /. A related project is the Pacific Climate Warriors' 350 Pacific video project *Strong Winds*. It can be accessed here: https://350.org/matagimalohifilm/.

27 Looser, "Symbolic *Vaka*, Sustainable Futures," 48. For an account of the recent history of attempts at international agreements to combat climate change, see Ross, *Creditocracy and the Case for Debt Refusal*. Examples include the following: the 1992 United Nations Framework Convention on Climate Change (UNFCCC) in Rio de Janeiro, which produced the proposal defining climate debt as comprising two parts, "emissions debt" and "adaptation debt"; the 1997 Kyoto Protocol, which outlined "common but differentiated responsibilities" between nations; the 2010 World People's Conference on Climate Change and the Rights of Mother Earth held in Cochabamba, Bolivia, which produced the "Cochabamba Declaration" asserting that the North's repayment of the climate debt had to be "the basis for a just, effective, and scientific solution to climate change"; and the more recent UNFCCC 2015 Paris Agreement among member nations to set better emissions targets.

28 Cartwright, "Images of 'Waiting Children,'" 187.

29 Sheller, "Caribbean Futures in the Offshore Anthropocene," 972.

30 Sheller, *Island Futures*, 10.

31 Sheller, *Island Futures*, 7. See also Campbell, "Islandness"; Pugh, "Relationality and Island Studies in the Anthropocene."

32 DeLoughrey, *Allegories of the Anthropocene*, 170, 184. In 2004 and 2005 alone, three films focusing specifically on Tuvalu were released: *The Disappearing of Tuvalu: Trouble in Paradise, Time and Tide,* and *Before the Flood*. These were joined by the Dutch film *King Tide: The Sinking of Tuvalu* in 2007.

33 From 1946 to 1958, the United States conducted a series of atomic and hydrogen bomb tests in the Marshall Islands. This was during a period when the Marshall Islands became a Trust Territory of the United States. Even though sovereignty came in 1979 with the establishment of the Republic of the Marshall Islands (RMI), the signing soon thereafter of a Compact of Free Association (COFA) with the United States has meant that the United States can continue to use the RMI's army garrison on Kwajalein Atoll as a missile test range until 2066, with an option to renew until 2086. In exchange, the RMI receives financial assistance from the United States. Since Kwajalein Atoll, like many atolls in the RMI, is experiencing sea-level rise, the United States has an interest in the RMI's climate mitigation and adaptation efforts. See Faris, "Sisters of Ocean and Ice," 85–86.

34 For useful analyses of recent debt refusal movements, such as Strike Debt, see McKee, "DEBT"; Caffentzis, "Reflections on the History of Debt Resistance"; Ross, *Creditocracy and the Case for Debt Refusal*; and Mirzoeff, "Climate Crisis Is a Debt Crisis."

35 Moten and Harney, "Debt and Study," 1.

Agamben, Giorgio. *Homo Sacer: Sovereign Power and Bare Life*. Stanford, CA: Stanford University Press, 1998.

Agamben, Giorgio. "No to Biopolitical Tattooing." *Communication and Critical/Cultural Studies* 5, no. 2 (2008): 201–2.

Ahn, Junghyo. *Silver Stallion: A Novel of Korea*. New York: Soho Press, 1990.

Akibayashi, Kozue. "Okinawa Women Act against Military Violence: An Island Feminism Reclaiming Dignity." *Okinawan Journal of Island Studies* 1 (2020): 37–54.

Akibayashi, Kozue, and Suzuyo Takazato. "Okinawa: Women's Struggle for Demilitarization." In Lutz, *The Bases of Empire*, 243–69.

Alexander, Ronni. "Living with the Fence: Militarization and Military Spaces on Guahan/Guam." *Gender, Place and Culture: Journal of Feminist Geography* 23, no. 6 (2016): 869–82.

Allen, Chadwick. *Trans-Indigenous: Methodologies for Global Native Literary Studies*. Minneapolis: University of Minnesota Press, 2012.

Ames, Chris. "Crossfire Couples: Marginality and Agency among Okinawan Women in Relationships with U.S. Military Men." In Höhn and Moon, *Over There*, 176–202.

Angst, Linda Isako. "The Rape of a Schoolgirl: Discourses of Power and Gendered National Identity in Okinawa." In Hein and Selden, *Islands of Discontent*, 135–57.

Arrighi, Giovanni. *Adam Smith in Beijing: Lineages of the Twenty-First Century*. London: Verso, 2007.

Arvin, Maile. *Possessing Polynesians: The Science of Settler Colonial Whiteness in Hawai'i and Oceania*. Durham, NC: Duke University Press, 2019.

Atwood, Margaret. *Payback: Debt and the Shadow Side of Wealth*. Toronto: Anansi, 2008.

Bahng, Aimee. *Migrant Futures: Decolonizing Speculation in Financial Times*. Durham, NC: Duke University Press, 2018.

Baik, Crystal Mun-hye. *Reencounters: On the Korean War and Diasporic Memory Critique*. Philadelphia: Temple University Press, 2020.

Barrett, George. "Chinese Prisoners Shift Allegiance." *New York Times*, November 20, 1951.

Bascara, Victor, Keith L. Camacho, and Elizabeth DeLoughrey. "Gender and Sexual Politics of Pacific Island Militarisation: A Call for Critical Militarisation Studies." *Intersections: Gender and Sexuality in Asia and the Pacific* 37 (March 2015). http://intersections.anu.edu.au/issue37/bascara_camacho_deloughrey.html.

Bello, Walden. "From American Lake to a People's Pacific." In *Let the Good Times Roll: Prostitution and the U.S. Military in Asia*, by Saundra Pollock Sturdevant and Brenda Stoltzfus, 14–21. New York: New Press, 1992.

Bevacqua, Michael Lujan. "The Exceptional Life and Death of a Chamorro Soldier: Tracing the Militarization of Desire in Guam, USA." In Shigematsu and Camacho, *Militarized Currents*, 33–61.

Bevacqua, Michael Lujan. "Guam: Protests at the Tip of America's Spear." *South Atlantic Quarterly* 116, no. 1 (January 2017): 174–83.

Beyerl, Katharina, Harald A. Mieg, and Eberhard Weber. "Comparing Perceived Effects of Climate-Related Environmental Change and Adaptation Strategies for the Pacific Small Island States of Tuvalu, Samoa, and Tonga." *Island Studies Journal* 13, no. 1 (2018): 25–44.

Bhandar, Brenna. *Colonial Lives of Property: Law, Land, and Racial Regimes of Ownership*. Durham, NC: Duke University Press, 2018.

Bhowmik, Davinder L. *Writing Okinawa: Narrative Acts of Identity and Resistance*. London: Routledge, 2008.

Bhowmik, Davinder L., and Steve Rabson. Introduction. *Islands of Protest*, 1–17.

Bhowmik, Davinder L., and Steve Rabson, eds. *Islands of Protest: Japanese Literature from Okinawa*. Honolulu: University of Hawai'i Press, 2016.

Bong, Joon Ho. "Audio Commentary." Disc 1. *Parasite*. Criterion Collection DVD. Directed by Bong Joon Ho. United States: Neon, 2020.

Bong, Joon Ho, dir. *Parasite*. Universal City, CA: Universal Pictures Home Entertainment, 2020. DVD, 132 minutes.

Broudy, Daniel, and Peter Simpson. "Naming and Framing in (Post)Colonial Okinawa." In Broudy, Simpson, and Arakaki, *Under Occupation*, 78–97.

Broudy, Daniel, Peter Simpson, and Makoto Arakaki, eds. *Under Occupation: Resistance and Struggle in a Militarised Asia-Pacific*. Newcastle, NE: Cambridge Scholars Publisher, 2013.

Bryant-Tokalau, Jenny. *Indigenous Pacific Approaches to Climate Change: Pacific Island Countries*. London: Palgrave Macmillan, 2018.

Buckmaster, Luke, and Brian Yecies. "Docu-reality and Empathy in *Bloodless* (2017): A Manifesto for Transnational Virtual Reality Cinema." In *Asia-Pacific Film Co-productions: Theory, Industry and Aesthetics*, edited by Dal Yong Jin and Wendy Su, 275–92. New York: Routledge, 2020.

Burnett, Christina Duffy. "The Edges of Empire and the Limits of Sovereignty: American Guano Islands." *American Quarterly* 57, no. 3 (2005): 779–803.

Burnett, Christina Duffy, and Burke Marshall, eds. *Foreign in a Domestic Sense: Puerto Rico, American Expansion, and the Constitution*. Durham, NC: Duke University Press, 2001.

Byrd, Jodi A. *The Transit of Empire: Indigenous Critiques of Colonialism*. Minneapolis: University of Minnesota Press, 2011.

Caffentzis, George. "Reflections on the History of Debt Resistance: The Case of El Barzón." *South Atlantic Quarterly* 112, no. 4 (Fall 2013): 824–40.

Calder, Kent E. *Embattled Garrisons: Comparative Base Politics and American Globalism*. Princeton, NJ: Princeton University Press, 2007.

Camacho, Keith L. *Cultures of Commemoration: The Politics of War, Memory, and History in the Mariana Islands.* Honolulu: University of Hawai'i Press, 2011.

Camacho, Keith L. *Sacred Men: Law, Torture, and Retribution in Guam.* Durham, NC: Duke University Press, 2019.

Camacho, Keith L., and Laurel A. Monnig. "Uncomfortable Fatigues: Chamorro Soldiers, Gendered Identities, and the Question of Decolonization in Guam." In Shigematsu and Camacho, *Militarized Currents*, 147–79.

Camacho, Leevin. "Resisting the Proposed Military Buildup on Guam." In Broudy, Simpson, and Arakaki, *Under Occupation*, 183–90.

Campbell, John. "Islandness: Vulnerability and Resilience in Oceania." *Shima: International Journal of Research into Island Cultures* 3, no. 1 (2009): 85–97.

Carruthers, Susan L. *Cold War Captives: Imprisonment, Escape, and Brainwashing.* Berkeley: University of California Press, 2009.

Carter, George. "Establishing a Pacific Voice in the Climate Change Negotiations." In Fry and Tarte, *The New Pacific Diplomacy*, 205–20.

Carter, Mitzi Uehara. "Nappy Routes and Tangled Tales: Critical Ethnography in a Militarised Okinawa." In Broudy, Simpson, and Arakaki, *Under Occupation*, 8–28.

Cartwright, Lisa. "Images of 'Waiting Children': Spectatorship and Pity in the Representation of the Global Social Orphan in the 1990s." In *Cultures of Transnational Adoption*, edited by Toby Alice Volkman, 185–212. Durham, NC: Duke University Press, 2005.

Chakrabarty, Dipesh. "Climate and Capital: On Conjoined Histories." *Critical Inquiry* 41 (Autumn 2014): 1–23.

Chakrabarty, Dipesh. "The Climate of History: Four Theses." *Critical Inquiry* 35 (Winter 2019): 197–222.

Chakravarty, Paula, and Denise Ferreira da Silva. "Accumulation, Dispossession, and Debt: The Racial Logic of Global Capitalism—An Introduction." In "Race, Empire, and the Crisis of the Subprime," 361–85.

Chakravarty, Paula, and Denise Ferreira da Silva, eds. "Race, Empire, and the Crisis of the Subprime." Special issue, *American Quarterly* 64, no. 3 (2012).

Chang, Kee. "VR Trooper: Gina Kim." *Anthem*, June 5, 2017. http://anthemmagazine.com/vr-trooper-gina-kim/.

Chen, Tina. "Transpacific Turns." In *Oxford Research Encyclopedia, Literature.* New York: Oxford University Press, 2020. Article published January 2020. doi: 10.1093/acrefore/9780190201098.013.782.

Cheng, Sealing. *On the Move for Love: Migrant Entertainers and the U.S. Military in South Korea.* Philadelphia: University of Pennsylvania Press, 2013.

Chibana, Megumi. "An Artful Way of Making Indigenous Space." *Verge: Studies in Global Asias* 4, no. 2 (Fall 2018): 135–62.

Chibana, Megumi. "Striving for Land, Sea, and Life: The Okinawan Demilitarization Movement." *Pacific Asia Inquiry* 4, no. 1 (Fall 2013): 136–54.

Cho, Grace M. "Diaspora of Camptown: The Forgotten War's Monstrous Family." In "The Global and the Intimate," edited by Geraldine Pratt and Victoria Rosner. Special issue, *Women's Studies Quarterly* 34, no. 1–2 (Spring–Summer 2006): 309–31.

Cho, Grace M. *Haunting the Korean Diaspora: Shame, Secrecy, and the Forgotten War*. Minneapolis: University of Minnesota Press, 2008.

Choe, Sang-Hun. "South Korea Illegally Held Prostitutes Who Catered to G.I.s Decades Ago, Court Says." *New York Times*, January 20, 2017. https://www.nytimes.com/2017/01/20/world/asia/south-korea-court-comfort-women.html#after-story-ad-4.

Clinton, Hillary. "America's Pacific Century: The Future of Geopolitics Will Be Decided in Asia, not in Afghanistan or Iraq, and the United States Should Be Right at the Center of the Action." *Foreign Policy*, no. 189 (November 2011): 56–63.

Coddington, Kate, R. Tina Catania, Jenna Loyd, Emily Mitchell-Eaton, and Alison Mountz. "Embodied Possibilities, Sovereign Geographies and Island Detention: Negotiating the 'Right to Have Rights' on Guam, Lampedusa and Christmas Island." *Shima: International Journal of Research into Island Cultures* 6, no. 2 (2012): 27–48.

Connery, Christopher L. "Pacific Rim Discourse: The U.S. Global Imaginary in the Late Cold War Years." *Boundary 2* 21, no. 1 (Spring 1994): 30–56.

Cooper, Melinda. *Life as Surplus: Biotechnology and Capitalism in the Neoliberal Era*. Seattle: University of Washington Press, 2008.

Coulthard, Glen Sean. *Red Skin, White Masks: Rejecting the Colonial Politics of Recognition*. Minneapolis: University of Minnesota Press, 2014.

Darda, Joseph. "Introduction: Narratives of Exception in the Warfare State." In "Literary Counterhistories of US Exceptionalism," edited by Joseph Darda. Special issue, *LIT: Literature Interpretation Theory* 25, no. 2 (2014): 80–87.

Darda, Joseph. "Literary Afterlife of the Korean War." *American Literature* 87, no. 1 (March 2015): 79–105.

Dargis, Manohla. "'Parasite' Review: The Lower Depths Rise with a Vengeance," review of *Parasite*, Neon. *New York Times*, October 10, 2019, updated February 10, 2020. https://www.nytimes.com/2019/10/10/movies/parasite-review.html#gateway-content.

Davidson, Helen. "Warning Sounded over China's 'Debt Diplomacy.'" *Guardian*, May 15, 2018. https://www.theguardian.com/world/2018/may/15/warning-sounded-over-chinas-debtbook-diplomacy.

Davis, Sasha. *The Empire's Edge: Militarization, Resistance, and Transcending Hegemony in the Pacific*. Athens: University of Georgia Press, 2015.

Davis, Sasha. "Repeating Islands of Resistance: Redefining Security in Militarized Landscapes." *Human Geography* 5, no. 1 (2012): 1–18.

Day, Iyko. *Alien Capital: Asian Racialization and the Logic of Settler Colonial Capitalism*. Durham, NC: Duke University Press, 2016.

Day, Iyko. "Eco-Criticism and Primitive Accumulation in Indigenous Studies." In *After Marx: Literary Criticism and the Critique of Value*, edited by Colleen Lye and Christopher Nealon. New York: Cambridge University Press, forthcoming.

Delgado, Francisco. "Remade: Sovereign: Decolonizing Guam in the Age of Environmental Anxiety." *Memory Studies* (2019): 1–13.

DeLoughrey, Elizabeth. *Allegories of the Anthropocene*. Durham, NC: Duke University Press, 2018.

DeLoughrey, Elizabeth. "Heavy Waters: Waste and Atlantic Modernity." *PMLA* 125, no. 3 (May 2010): 703–12.

DeLoughrey, Elizabeth. "Island Studies and the US Militarism of the Pacific." In Ginoza, *The Challenges of Island Studies*, 29–44.

DeLoughrey, Elizabeth. "The Myth of Isolates: Ecosystem Ecologies in the Nuclear Pacific." *Cultural Geographies* 20, no. 2 (April 2013): 167–84.

DeLoughrey, Elizabeth. *Routes and Roots: Navigating Caribbean and Pacific Island Literatures*. Manoa: University of Hawai'i Press, 2009.

DeLoughrey, Elizabeth. "Toward a Critical Ocean Studies for the Anthropocene." *English Language Notes* 57, no. 1 (April 2019): 21–36.

Denetdale, Jennifer Nez. "Discontinuities, Remembrances, and Cultural Survival: History, Diné/Navajo Memory, and the Bosque Redondo Memorial." *New Mexico Historical Review* 82, no. 3 (2007): 295–316.

Derrida, Jacques. "Force of Law: The Mystical Foundation of Authority." Translated by Mary Quaintance. *Cardozo Law Review* 11, no. 5–6 (1990): 921–1045.

Diaz, Vicente M. "Deliberating 'Liberation Day': Identity, History, Memory, and War in Guam." In Fujitani, White, and Yoneyama, *Perilous Memories*, 155–80.

Dirlik, Arif, ed. *What Is in a Rim? Critical Perspectives on the Pacific Region Idea*. Lanham, MD: Rowman & Littlefield, 1992.

Doo, Rumy. "Empathy without Exploitation." *Korea Herald*, September 15, 2017, updated October 4, 2017. http://www.koreaherald.com/view.php?ud=20170915000677.

Doolan, Yuri W. "Transpacific Camptowns: Korean Women, US Army Bases, and Military Prostitution in America." *Journal of American Ethnic History* 38, no. 4 (Summer 2019): 33–54.

Dvorak, Greg, and Miyume Tanji, eds. "Indigenous Asias." Special issue, *Amerasia Journal* 41, no. 1 (2015).

Eisenhower, Dwight D. "Farewell Address." In *Public Papers of the Presidents*, 1035–40. Washington, DC: US National Archives, 1961.

Enloe, Cynthia. *Bananas, Beaches and Bases: Making Feminist Sense of International Politics*. Berkeley: University of California Press, 1990.

Enloe, Cynthia. *Maneuvers: The International Politics of Militarizing Women's Lives*. Berkeley: University of California Press, 2000.

Espiritu, Yến Lê. *Body Counts: The Vietnam War and Militarized Refuge(es)*. Oakland: University of California Press, 2014.

Espiritu, Yến Lê. "Critical Refugee Studies and Native Pacific Studies: A Transpacific Critique." In Wang and Cho, "The Chinese Factor," 483–90.

Espiritu, Yến Lê, Lisa Lowe, and Lisa Yoneyama. "Transpacific Entanglements." In *Flashpoints for Asian American Studies*, edited by Cathy J. Schlund-Vials, 175–89. New York: Fordham University Press, 2018.

Eubanks, Charlotte, and Pasang Yangjee Sherpa, eds. "Indigeneity." Special issue, *Verge: Studies in Global Asias* 4, no. 2 (Fall 2018).

Fanon, Frantz. *Black Skin, White Masks*. New York: Grove Press, 2008.

Fanon, Frantz. *The Wretched of the Earth*. New York: Grove Press, 2004.

Faris, Jaimey Hamilton. "Sisters of Ocean and Ice: On the Hydro-feminism of Kathy Jetñil-Kijiner and Aka Niviâna's *Rise: From One Island to Another*." *Shima: International Journal of Research into Island Cultures* 13, no. 2 (2019): 76–99.

Federici, Silvia. *Caliban and the Witch: Women, the Body and Primitive Accumulation*. New York: Autonomedia, 2004.

Foot, Rosemary. *A Substitute for Victory: The Politics of Peacemaking at the Korean Armistice Talks*. Ithaca, NY: Cornell University Press, 1990.

Foucault, Michel. *Discipline and Punish: The Birth of the Prison*. New York: Vintage, 1995.

Frain, Sylvia C. "'Make America Secure': Media, Militarism, and Climate Change in the Marianas Archipelago." *Pacific Journalism Review* 24, no. 2 (2018): 218–40.

French, Howard W. *China's Second Continent: How a Million Migrants Are Building a New Empire in Africa*. New York: Knopf, 2014.

Fresno-Calleja, Paloma. "Fighting Gastrocolonialism in Indigenous Pacific Writing." *Interventions: International Journal of Postcolonial Studies* 19, no. 7 (2017): 1041–55.

Fry, Greg, and Sandra Tarte, eds. *The New Pacific Diplomacy*. Acton: Australian National University Press, 2015.

Fujikane, Candace. *Mapping Abundance for a Planetary Future: Kanaka Maoli and Critical Settler Cartographies in Hawai'i*. Durham, NC: Duke University Press, 2021.

Fujikane, Candace. "Mapping Abundance on Mauna a Wākea as a Practice of Ea." *Hūlili: Multidisciplinary Research on Hawaiian Well-Being* 11, no. 1 (2019): 23–54.

Fujitani, T., Geoffrey M. White, and Lisa Yoneyama, eds. *Perilous Memories: The Asia-Pacific War(s)*. Durham, NC: Duke University Press, 2001.

Gabilondo, Joseba. "Bong Joon Ho's *Parasite* and Post-2008 Revolts: From the Discourse of the Master to the Destituent Power of the Real." *International Journal of Zizek Studies* 14, no. 1 (2020). http://zizekstudies.org/index.php/IJZS/article/view/1158.

Gandhi, Eyvn Lê Espiritu. "Historicizing the Transpacific Settler Colonial Condition: Asian-Indigenous Relations in Shawn Wong's *Homebase* and Viet Thanh Nguyen's *The Sympathizer*." *MELUS: Society for the Study of the Multi-Ethnic Literature of the United States* 45, no. 4 (Winter 2020): 49–71.

Gillem, Mark L. *America Town: Building the Outposts of Empire*. Minneapolis: University of Minnesota Press, 2007.

Gilmore, Ruth Wilson. "Race and Globalization." In *Geographies of Global Change: Remapping the World*, edited by R. J. Johnston, Peter J. Taylor, and Michael Watts, 261–74. New York: Wiley-Blackwell, 2002.

Ginoza, Ayano, ed. *The Challenges of Island Studies*. Singapore: Springer, 2020.

Ginoza, Ayano. "Dis/articulation of Ethnic Minority and Indigeneity in the Decolonial Feminist and Independence Movements in Okinawa." *Intersections: Gender and Sexuality in Asia and the Pacific* 37 (March 2015). http://intersections.anu.edu.au/issue37/ginoza.htm.

Ginoza, Ayano. "R&R at the Intersection of US and Japanese Dual Empire: Okinawan Women and Decolonizing Militarized Heterosexuality." In "Tours of Duty and Tours of Leisure," edited by Vernadette Vicuña Gonzalez, Jana K. Lipman, and Teresia Teaiwa. Special issue, *American Quarterly* 68, no. 3 (2016): 583–91.

Ginoza, Ayano. "Space of 'Militourism': Intimacies of U.S. and Japanese Empires and Indigenous Sovereignty in Okinawa." *International Journal of Okinawan Studies* 3, no. 1 (2012): 7–23.

Goeman, Mishuana. *Mark My Words: Native Women Mapping Our Nations*. Minneapolis: University of Minnesota Press, 2013.

Goldstein, Alyosha. "Introduction: Toward a Genealogy of the U.S. Colonial Present." In *Formations of United States Colonialism*, edited by Alyosha Goldstein, 1–30. Durham, NC: Duke University Press, 2014.

Goldstein, Alyosha, Juliana Hu Pegues, and Manu Vimalassery (now Karuka). "Intro-
duction: On Colonial Unknowing." In "On Colonial Unknowing," edited by Alyosha
Goldstein, Juliana Hu Pegues, and Manu Vimalassery (now Karuka). Special issue,
Theory and Event 19, no. 4 (2016). https://muse.jhu.edu/article/633283.

Gómez-Barris, Macarena, and May Joseph. "Introduction: Coloniality and Islands."
In "Coloniality and Islands," edited by Macarena Gómez-Barris and May Joseph.
Special issue, *Shima: International Journal of Research into Island Cultures* 13, no. 2
(2019): 1–10.

González, Roberto J., Hugh Gusterson, and Gustaaf Houtman. Introduction to *Militarization: A Reader*, edited by Roberto J. González, Hugh Gusterson, and Gustaaf Houtman, 1–26. Durham, NC: Duke University Press, 2019.

Gonzalez, Vernadette Vicuña. *Securing Paradise: Tourism and Militarism in Hawai'i and the
Philippines*. Durham, NC: Duke University Press, 2013.

Gonzalez, Vernadette Vicuña. "Target/Paradise/Home/Kin: Island Orientations."
Okinawan Journal of Island Studies 1 (2020): 23–35.

Goodyear-Ka'ōpua, Noelani. *The Seeds We Planted: Portraits of a Native Hawaiian Charter
School*. Minneapolis: University of Minnesota Press, 2013.

Goodyear-Ka'ōpua, Noelani, Ikaika Hussey, and Erin Kahunawaika'ala Wright, eds. *A
Nation Rising: Hawaiian Movements for Life, Land, and Sovereignty*. Durham, NC: Duke
University Press, 2014.

Goulding, Nicollette. "Marshalling a Pacific Response to Climate Change." In Fry and
Tarte, *The New Pacific Diplomacy*, 191–204.

Graeber, David. *Debt: The First 5,000 Years*. Brooklyn, NY: Melville House, 2011.

Grydehøj, Adam, Michael Lujan Bevacqua, Megumi Chibana, Yaso Nadarajah, Aká
Simonsen, Ping Su, Renee Wright, and Sasha Davis. "Practicing Decolonial Political
Geography: Island Perspectives on Neocolonialism and the China Threat Discourse."
Political Geography 85 (March 2021). https://www.sciencedirect.com/journal/political
-geography/vol/85/suppl/C.

Gwon, Gwisook. "Remembering 4/3 and Resisting the Remilitarisation of Jeju: Building
an International Peace Movement." In Broudy, Simpson, and Arakaki, *Under Occupation*, 238–70.

Hager, Sandy Brian. *Public Debt, Inequality, and Power: The Making of a Modern Debt State*.
Oakland: University of California Press, 2016.

Hall, Lisa Kahaleole. "Which of These Things Is Not Like the Other: Hawaiians and
Other Pacific Islanders Are Not Asian Americans, and All Pacific Islanders Are Not
Hawaiian." *American Quarterly* 67, no. 3 (September 2015): 727–47.

Hanlon, David. "Losing Oceania to the Pacific and the World." *Contemporary Pacific* 29,
no. 2 (2017): 286–318.

Haraway, Donna. "Anthropocene, Capitalocene, Plantationocene, Chthulocene: Making
Kin." *Environmental Humanities* 6 (2015): 159–65.

Harrington, Joseph. "The Politics of Docupoetry." In *The News from Poems: Essays on the
21st-Century American Poetry of Engagement*, edited by Jeffrey Gray and Ann Keniston,
67–83. Ann Arbor: University of Michigan Press, 2016.

Hartman, Saidiya. *Lose Your Mother: A Journey Along the Atlantic Slave Route*. New York:
Farrar, Straus and Giroux, 2008.

Hartman, Saidiya V. *Scenes of Subjection: Terror, Slavery, and Self-Making in Nineteenth-Century America*. New York: Oxford University Press, 1997.

Harvey, David. *The New Imperialism*. Oxford: Oxford University Press, 2003.

Hau'ofa, Epeli. "Our Sea of Islands." *Contemporary Pacific* 6, no. 1 (Spring 1994): 148–61.

Hawkins, Dimity. "Now That Nuclear Weapons Are Illegal, the Pacific Demands Truth on Decades of Testing." *Guardian*, October 24, 2020. https://www.theguardian.com /world/2020/oct/25/now-that-nuclear-weapons-are-the-pacific-demands-truth-on -decades-of-testing.

Hayward, Philip. "Aquapelagos and Aquapelagic Assemblages: Towards an Integrated Study of Island Societies and Marine Environments." *Shima: International Journal of Research into Island Cultures* 6, no. 1 (2012): 1–11.

Heim, Otto. "How (not) to Globalize Oceania: Ecology and Politics in Contemporary Pacific Island Performance Arts." *Commonwealth Essays and Studies* 41, no. 1 (2018): 131–45.

Hein, Laura Elizabeth, and Mark Selden, eds. *Islands of Discontent: Okinawan Reponses to Japanese and American Power*. Lanham, MD: Rowman & Littlefield, 2003.

Henry, Marsha, and Katherine Natanel. "Militarisation as Diffusion: The Politics of Gender, Space, and the Everyday." *Gender, Place and Culture: Journal of Feminist Geography* 23, no. 6 (2016): 850–56.

Hereniko, Vilsoni, dir. *Moana Rua: The Rising of the Sea*. Suva, Fiji: University of the South Pacific, 2015. https://video.alexanderstreet.com/watch/moana-rua-the-rising-of-the-sea.

Herman, RDK. "Pacific Worlds: Indigeneity, Hybridity, and Globalization." *Verge: Studies in Global Asias* 4, no. 2 (Fall 2018): 15–24.

Higashi, Mineo. *Child of Okinawa*. In *Okinawa: Two Postwar Novellas*, translated with an introduction and afterword by Steve Rabson, 81–117. Berkeley: Institute of East Asian Studies, University of California, 1989.

Hoechst, Heidi. *Life in and against the Odds: Debts of Freedom and the Speculative Roots of U.S. Culture*. Philadelphia: Temple University Press, 2015.

Hogeland, William. *Founding Finance: How Debt, Speculation, Foreclosures, Protests, and Crackdowns Made Us a Nation*. Austin: University of Texas Press, 2012.

Höhn, Maria, and Seungsook Moon, eds. *Over There: Living with the U.S. Military Empire from World War Two to the Present*. Durham, NC: Duke University Press, 2010.

Höhn, Maria, and Seungsook Moon. "The Politics of Gender, Sexuality, Race, and Class in the U.S. Military Empire." In *Over There*, 1–36.

Hoshino, Lina, and Gwyn Kirk, dirs. *Living along the Fenceline*. Petaluma, CA: Many Threads, distributed by Third World Newsreel, 2011. DVD, 65 minutes.

Hsu, Hsuan S. "Guåhan (Guam), Literary Emergence, and the American Pacific in *Homebase* and *from unincorporated territory*." *American Literary History* 24, no. 2 (2012): 281–307.

Hudson, Michael. *Super Imperialism: The Origin and Fundamentals of U.S. World Dominance*. London: Pluto Press, 2003.

Hyun, Hyekyung. "Maritime and Island Culture along the Kuroshio Current." *Island Studies Journal* 13, no. 1 (2018): 167–70.

Inoue, Masamichi S. *Okinawa and the U.S. Military: Identity Making in the Age of Globalization*. New York: Columbia University Press, 2007.

Issar, Siddhant. "Theorising 'Racial/Colonial Primitive Accumulation': Settler Colonialism, Slavery and Racial Capitalism." *Race and Class* (April 2021): 1–28. https://doi.org/10.1177/0306396821996273.

Jansen, Anne Mai Yee. "Writing toward Action: Mapping an Affinity Poetics in Craig Santos Perez's *from unincorporated territory*." *Native American and Indigenous Studies* 6, no. 2 (Fall 2019): 3–29.

Jeon, Joseph Jonghyun. *Vicious Circuits: Korea's IMF Cinema and the End of the American Century*. Stanford, CA: Stanford University Press, 2019.

Jetñil-Kijiner, Kathy. *Iep Jaltok: Poems from a Marshallese Daughter*. Tucson: University of Arizona Press, 2017.

Jin, Ha. *War Trash: A Novel*. New York: Vintage International, 2005.

Jin, Pilsu. "The 'All Okinawa' Movement: Political and Legal Implications of the Okinawan Protest against the US Bases." *Journal of East Asia and International Law* 2 (2016): 562–75.

Johnson, Chalmers. *Blowback: The Costs and Consequences of American Empire*. New York: Metropolitan Books, 2000.

Johnson, Chalmers. *The Sorrows of Empire: Militarism, Secrecy, and the End of the Republic*. New York: Henry Holt, 2004.

Joseph, Miranda. *Debt to Society: Accounting for Life under Capitalism*. Minneapolis: University of Minnesota Press, 2014.

Kajihiro, Kyle. "Moananuiākea or 'American Lake'? Contested Histories of the US 'Pacific Pivot.'" In Broudy, Simpson, and Arakaki, *Under Occupation*, 126–60.

Kang, Laura Hyun Yi. *Compositional Subjects: Enfiguring Asian/American Women*. Durham, NC: Duke University Press, 2002.

Kang, Laura Hyun Yi. *Traffic in Asian Women*. Durham, NC: Duke University Press, 2020.

Kang, Laura Hyun Yi. "The Uses of Asianization: Figuring Crises, 1997–98 and 2007–?" In Chakravarty and Ferreira da Silva, "Race, Empire, and the Crisis of the Subprime," 411–36.

Kaplan, Amy. "Where Is Guantanamo?" *American Quarterly* 57, no. 3 (September 2005): 831–58.

Karides, Marina. "Why Island Feminism?" *Shima: International Journal of Research into Island Cultures* 11, no. 1 (2017): 30–39.

Karuka, Manu. *Empire's Tracks: Indigenous Nations, Chinese Workers, and the Transcontinental Railroad*. Oakland: University of California Press, 2019.

Kauanui, J. Kēhaulani. "Asian American Studies and the 'Pacific Question.'" In *Asian American Studies after Critical Mass*, edited by Kent A. Ono, 123–43. Malden, MA: Blackwell, 2005.

Kauanui, J. Kēhaulani. "Decolonial Self-Determination and 'No-State Solutions.'" *Humanity Journal*, July 2, 2019. http://humanityjournal.org/blog/decolonial-self-determination-and-no-state-solutions/.

Kauanui, J. Kēhaulani. "Imperial Ocean: The Pacific as a Critical Site for American Studies." In Lyons and Kāwika Tengan, "Pacific Currents," 625–36.

Kauanui, J. Kēhaulani. "The Multiplicity of Hawaiian Sovereignty Claims and the Struggle for Meaningful Autonomy." *Comparative American Studies: International Journal* 3, no. 3 (2005): 283–99.

Kelton, Stephanie. *The Deficit Myth: Modern Monetary Theory and the Birth of the People's Economy*. New York: PublicAffairs, 2020.

Keyso, Ruth Ann. *Women of Okinawa: Nine Voices from a Garrison Island*. Ithaca, NY: Cornell University Press, 2000.

Kim, Claudia J. "Bases That Leave: Consequences of US Base Closures and Realignments in South Korea." *Journal of Contemporary Asia* 48, no. 2 (2018): 339–57.

Kim, Eun-Shil. "Itaewon as an Alien Space within the Nation-State and a Place in the Globalization Era." *Korea Journal* 44, no. 3 (Autumn 2004): 34–64.

Kim, Gina, dir. *Bloodless*. Crayon Production, 2017. Virtual Reality (VR), 12 minutes.

Kim, Hyun Mee. "Work, Nation and Hypermasculinity: The 'Woman' Question in the Economic Miracle and Crisis in South Korea." *Inter-Asia Cultural Studies* 2, no. 1 (2001): 53–68.

Kim, Jinah. *Postcolonial Grief: The Afterlives of the Pacific Wars in the Americas*. Durham, NC: Duke University Press, 2019.

Kim, Jodi. *Ends of Empire: Asian American Critique and the Cold War*. Minneapolis: University of Minnesota Press, 2010.

Kim, Jodi. "Militarization." In *The Routledge Companion to Asian American and Pacific Islander Literature and Culture*, edited by Rachel C. Lee, 154–66. London: Routledge, 2014.

Kim, Monica. "Empire's Babel: US Military Interrogation Rooms of the Korean War." *History of the Present* 3, no. 1 (2013): 1–28.

Kim, Monica. *The Interrogation Rooms of the Korean War: The Untold History*. Princeton, NJ: Princeton University Press, 2019.

Kim, Seon-Pil. "Mainland Development Policy in an Autonomous Subnational Island Jurisdiction: Spatial Development and Economic Dependence in Jeju, South Korea." *Island Studies Journal* 15, no. 1 (2020): 169–84.

Kindig, Jessie. "The Violent Embrace." *Boston Review*, April 5, 2021. http://bostonreview.net/global-justice-gender-sexuality/jessie-kindig-violent-embrace.

Kirk, Gwyn, and Margo Okazawa-Rey. "Women Opposing U.S. Militarism in East Asia." *Peace Review* 16, no. 1 (2004): 59–64.

Kishaba, Jun. "Dark Flowers." In *Southern Exposure: Modern Japanese Literature from Okinawa*, translated by Steve Rabson and edited by Michael Molasky and Steve Rabson, 98–111. Honolulu: University of Hawai'i Press, 2000.

Konings, Martijn. *The Development of American Finance*. Cambridge: Cambridge University Press, 2011.

Kramer, Paul A. *The Blood of Government: Race, Empire, the United States, and the Philippines*. Chapel Hill: University of North Carolina Press, 2006.

Kramer, Paul A. "The Military-Sexual Complex: Prostitution, Disease and the Boundaries of Empire during the Philippine-American War." *Asia-Pacific Journal* 9, issue 30, no. 2 (July 20, 2011): 1–35.

Kramer, Paul A. "Power and Connection: Imperial Histories of the United States in the World." *American Historical Review* 116, no. 5 (2011): 1348–91.

LaDuke, Winona, with Sean Aaron Cruz. *The Militarization of Indian Country*. East Lansing: Michigan State University Press, 2013.

Lai, Paul. "Discontiguous States of America: The Paradox of Unincorporation in Craig Santos Perez's Poetics of Chamorro Guam." *Journal of Transnational American Studies* 3, no. 2 (2011): 1–28.

Lawson, Gary. "Territorial Governments and the Limits of Formalism." *California Law Review* 78, no. 4 (July 1990): 853–911.

Lazzarato, Maurizio. *The Making of the Indebted Man: An Essay on the Neoliberal Condition.* Los Angeles: Semiotext(e), 2012.

Le, Quynh Nhu. *Unsettled Solidarities: Asian and Indigenous Cross-Representations in the Américas.* Philadelphia: Temple University Press, 2019.

Lee, Diana S., and Grace Yoon-Kung Lee, dirs. *Camp Arirang.* Camp Arirang Productions, 1995. Videocassette (VHS), 28 minutes.

Lee, Jin-kyung. *Service Economies: Militarism, Sex Work, and Migrant Labor in South Korea.* Minneapolis: University of Minnesota Press, 2010.

Lee, Na Young. "The Construction of Military Prostitution in South Korea during the U.S. Military Rule, 1945–1948." *Feminist Studies* 33, no. 3 (Fall 2007): 453–81.

Lele, Ajey. "Virtual Reality and Its Military Utility." *Journal of Ambient Intelligence and Humanized Computing,* May 28, 2011. doi: 10.1007/s12652-011-0052-4.

Liebknecht, Karl. *Militarism and Anti-Militarism with Special Regard to the International Young Socialist Movement.* Translated by A. Sirnis. Glasgow: Karl Liebknecht, 1917.

Lim, Eng-Beng. "Living in *Parasite* Country as Asian/American." *Blarb* (blog). *Los Angeles Review of Books,* February 24, 2020. https://blog.lareviewofbooks.org/essays/living -parasite-country-asian-american/.

Lipman, Jana K. *In Camps: Vietnamese Refugees, Asylum Seekers, and Repatriates.* Oakland: University of California Press, 2020.

Lo, Marie. "Plenary Power and the Exceptionality of Igorots: Settler Imperialism and the Lewis and Clark Exposition." *Amerasia Journal* 43, no. 2 (2017): 100–121.

Lo, Marie. "Simultaneity and Solidarity in the Time of Permanent War." In "Solidarities of Nonalignment: Abolition, Decolonization, and Anticapitalism," edited by Michael J. Viola, Dean Itsuji Saranillio, Juliana Hu Pegues, and Iyko Day. Special issue, *Critical Ethnic Studies* 5, no. 1–2 (Spring 2019): 36–67.

Looser, Diana. "Symbolic *Vaka*, Sustainable Futures: Climate-Induced Migration and Oceanic Performance." *Performance Research* 21, no. 2 (2016): 46–49.

Lowe, Lisa. *The Intimacies of Four Continents.* Durham, NC: Duke University Press, 2015.

Lummis, C. Douglas. Afterword, "Defining the Situation." In Broudy, Simpson, and Arakaki, *Under Occupation,* 273–84.

Lutz, Catherine. *The Bases of Empire: The Global Struggle against U.S. Military Posts.* New York: New York University Press, 2009.

Lutz, Catherine. "The Military Normal: Feeling at Home with Counterinsurgency." In *The Counter-Counterinsurgency Manual: Or, Notes on Demilitarizing Society,* edited by Network of Concerned Anthropologists, 23–37. Chicago: Prickly Paradigm Press, 2009.

Lutz, Catherine. "US Military Bases on Guam in Global Perspective." *Asia-Pacific Journal* 8, no. 3, issue 30 (July 26, 2010). https://apjjf.org/-Catherine-Lutz/3389/article.html.

Luxemburg, Rosa. *The Accumulation of Capital.* Mansfield Centre, CT: Martino Publishing, 2015.

Luxemburg, Rosa. "The Accumulation of Capital: An Anti-Critique" In *Rosa Luxemburg: Reflections and Writings*, edited by Paul Le Blanc, 175–97. New York: Humanity Books, 1999.

Lyons, Paul, and Ty P. Kāwika Tengan, eds. "Pacific Currents." Special issue, *American Quarterly* 67, no. 3 (September 2015).

Man, Simeon. *Soldiering through Empire: Race and the Making of the Decolonizing Pacific*. Oakland: University of California Press, 2018.

Marez, Curtis. "Seeing in the Red: Looking at Student Debt." *American Quarterly* 66, no. 2 (June 2014): 261–81.

Martin, Bridget. "From Camp Town to International City: US Military Base Expansion and Local Development in Pyeongtaek, South Korea." *International Journal of Urban and Regional Research* 42, no. 6 (November 2018): 967–85.

Marx, Karl. *Capital: A Critique of Political Economy*. Vol. I. New York: Vintage Books, 1977.

Marx, Karl. "On the Jewish Question." In *The Marx-Engels Reader*. 2nd ed., edited by Robert C. Tucker, 26–52. New York: W. W. Norton, 1978.

Matsumura, Wendy. "'Isahama Women Farmers' against Enclosure: A Rejection of the Property Relation in US-Occupied Okinawa." *positions* 28, no. 3 (August 2020): 547–74.

McCall, Grant. "Nissology: A Proposal for Consideration." *Journal of the Pacific Society* 17, no. 2–3 (October 1994): 1–9.

McClanahan, Annie. *Dead Pledges: Debt, Crisis, and Twenty-First-Century Culture*. Stanford, CA: Stanford University Press, 2017.

McCormack, Gavan, and Satoko Oka Norimatsu. *Resistant Islands: Okinawa Confronts Japan and the United States*. Lanham, MD: Rowman & Littlefield, 2012.

McDougall, Brandy Nālani. "What the Island Provides: Island Sustainability and Island-Human Relationality." *Transnational American Studies* 10, no. 1 (2019): 201–8.

McKee, Yates. "D̶E̶B̶T̶: Occupy, Postcontemporary Art, and the Aesthetics of Debt Resistance." *South Atlantic Quarterly* 112, no. 4 (Fall 2013): 784–803.

McKittrick, Katherine. *Demonic Grounds: Black Women and the Cartographies of Struggle*. Minneapolis: University of Minnesota Press, 2006.

McNamara, Karen E., Ross Westoby, and Alvin Chandra. "Exploring Climate-Driven Non-Economic Loss and Damage in the Pacific Islands." *Current Opinion in Environmental Sustainability* 50 (2020): 1–11.

Medoruma, Shun. "Hope." In Bhowmik and Rabson, *Islands of Protest*, 21–24.

Mei-Singh, Laurel Turbin. "Geographies of Desecration: Race, Indigeneity, and the Militarization of Hawai'i." PhD diss., City University of New York, 2016.

Melamed, Jodi. "Racial Capitalism." *Critical Ethnic Studies* 1, no. 1 (Spring 2015): 76–85.

Miller, Kara. "*Moana: The Rising of the Sea* directed by Peter Rockford Espiritu (review)." *Contemporary Pacific* 26, no. 2 (2014): 585–87.

Mirzoeff, Nicholas. "The Climate Crisis Is a Debt Crisis." *South Atlantic Quarterly* 112, no. 4 (Fall 2013): 831–38.

Mitropoulos, Angela. *Contract and Contagion: From Biopolitics to Oikonomia*. New York: Minor Compositions, 2012.

Mok, Christine, and Aimee Bahng. "Transpacific Overtures: An Introduction." In "Transpacific Futurities: Living in the Asian Century," edited by Christine Mok and Aimee Bahng. Special issue, *Journal of Asian American Studies* 20, no. 1 (February 2017): 1–9.

Molasky, Michael. "The Writer as Public Intellectual in Okinawa Today." In Hein and Selden, *Islands of Discontent*, 161–91.

Moon, Katharine H. S. *Sex Among Allies: Military Prostitution in U.S.-Korea Relations.* New York: Columbia University Press, 1997.

Moon, Seungsook. "In the U.S. Army but Not Quite of It: Contesting the Imperial Power in a Discourse of KATUSAs." In Höhn and Moon, *Over There*, 231–57.

Moon, Seungsook. *Militarized Modernity and Gendered Citizenship in South Korea.* Durham, NC: Duke University Press, 2005.

Moon, Seungsook. "Regulating Desire, Managing the Empire: U.S. Military Prostitution in South Korea, 1945–1970." In Höhn and Moon, *Over There*, 39–77.

Moore, Amelia. "Introduction: Islands and Aquapelagos in the Anthropocene." *Shima: International Journal of Research into Island Cultures* 14, no. 2 (2020): 1–3.

Morgensen, Scott Lauria. *Spaces between Us: Queer Settler Colonialism and Indigenous Decolonization.* Minneapolis: University of Minnesota Press, 2011.

Morris, Amanda. "Twenty-First-Century Debt Collectors: Idle No More Combats a Five-Hundred-Year-Old Debt." In "Debt," edited by Rosalind Petchesky and Meena Alexander. Special issue, WSQ: *Women's Studies Quarterly* 42, no. 1–2 (Spring/Summer 2014): 244–60.

Moten, Fred, and Stefano Harney. "Debt and Study." *e-flux journal* 14 (March 2010): 1–5.

Nadarajah, Yaso, and Adam Grydehøj. "Island Studies as a Decolonial Project (Guest Editorial Introduction)." *Island Studies Journal* 11, no. 2 (2006): 437–46.

Nagel, Joane. *Race, Ethnicity, and Sexuality: Intimate Encounters, Forbidden Frontiers.* New York: Oxford University Press, 2003.

Na'puti, Tiara R. "Archipelagic Rhetoric: Remapping the Marianans and Challenging Militarization from 'A Stirring Place.'" *Communication and Critical/Cultural Studies* 16, no. 1 (2019): 4–25.

Na'puti, Tiara R., and Sylvia C. Frain. "Decolonize Oceania! Free Guåhan! Communicating Resistance at the 2016 Festival of Pacific Arts." *Amerasia Journal* 43, no. 3 (2017): 2–34.

Na'puti, Tiara R., and Allison H. Hahn. "Plebiscite Deliberations: Self-Determination and Deliberative Democracy in Guam." *Journal of Public Deliberation* 9, no. 2 (2013): 1–24.

Na'puti, Tiara R., and Michael Lujan Bevacqua. "Militarization and Resistance from Guåhan: Protecting and Defending Pågat." In Lyons and Kāwika Tengan, "Pacific Currents," 837–58.

Nashiro, Nika. "What's Going on behind Those Blue Eyes? The Military Man and His Many (Mis)perceptions." In Broudy, Simpson, and Arakaki, *Under Occupation*, 49–65.

Nebolon, Juliet. "'Life Given Straight from the Heart': Settler Militarism, Biopolitics, and Public Health in Hawai'i during World War II." *American Quarterly* 69, no. 1 (2017): 23–45.

Nguyen, Mimi Thi. *The Gift of Freedom: War, Debt, and Other Refugee Passages.* Durham, NC: Duke University Press, 2012.

Nichols, Robert. "Disaggregating Primitive Accumulation." *Radical Philosophy* 194 (2015): 18–28.

Nichols, Robert. *Theft Is Property! Dispossession and Critical Theory.* Durham, NC: Duke University Press, 2020.

Nishiyama, Hidefumi. "Geopolitics of Disregard: Living a Colonial Life in Okinawa." *Political Geography* 74 (2019): 1–9.

Nogues, Collier. "'With [Our] Entire Breath': US Military Buildup on Guåhan (Guam) and Craig Santos Perez's Literature of Resistance." *Shima: International Journal of Research into Island Cultures* 12, no. 1 (2018): 21–34.

Noh, Minjung. "Parasite as Parable: Bong Joon-Ho's Cinematic Capitalism." *CrossCurrents* 70, no. 3 (September 2020): 248–62.

Okazawa-Rey, Margo. "Amerasian Children in GI Town: A Legacy of US Militarism in South Korea." *Asian Journal of Women's Studies* 3, no. 1 (1997): 71–102.

Onishi, Yuichiro. *Transpacific Antiracism: Afro-Asian Solidarity in 20th-Century Black America, Japan, and Okinawa.* New York: New York University Press, 2013.

Pae, Keun-Joo Christine. "The Prostituted Body of War: U.S. Military Prostitution in South Korea as a Site of Spiritual Activism." In *Transformational Embodiment in Asian Religions: Subtle Bodies, Spatial Bodies,* edited by George Pati and Katherine C. Zubko, 187–205. London: Routledge, 2019.

Paik, A. Naomi. *Rightlessness: Testimony and Redress in U.S. Prison Camps since World War II.* Chapel Hill: University of North Carolina Press, 2016.

Park, Ju-Hyun. "Reading Colonialism in 'Parasite.'" *Tropics of Meta: Historiography for the Masses,* February 27, 2020. https://tropicsofmeta.com/2020/02/17/reading-colonialism-in-parasite/.

Park, K-Sue. "Money, Mortgages, and the Conquest of America." *Law and Social Inquiry* 41, no. 4 (Fall 2016): 1006–35.

Perez, Craig Santos. "Facing Hawai'i's Future." Review of *Facing Hawai'i's Future: Essential Information About GMOs,* 2nd ed., by Hawai'i SEED. *Kenyon Review,* July 10, 2013. https://kenyonreview.org/2013/07/facing-hawai%CA%BBi%CA%BBs-future-book-review/.

Perez, Craig Santos. *from unincorporated territory [guma'].* Richmond, CA: Omnidawn Publishing, 2014.

Perez, Craig Santos. *from unincorporated territory [hacha].* Kāne'ohe, HI: Tinfish Press, 2008.

Perez, Craig Santos. *from unincorporated territory [lukao].* Oakland, CA: Omnidawn Publishing, 2017.

Perez, Craig Santos. *from unincorporated territory [saina].* Richmond, CA: Omnidawn Publishing, 2010.

Perez, Craig Santos. "Guåhan, The Pacific and Decolonial Poetry." *Shima: International Journal of Research into Island Cultures* 13, no. 2 (2019): 22–29.

Perez, Craig Santos. "Guam and Archipelagic American Studies." In *Archipelagic American Studies,* edited by Brian Russell Roberts and Michelle Stephens, 97–112. Durham, NC: Duke University Press, 2017.

Perez, Craig Santos. "Transterritorial Currents and the Imperial Terripelago." In Lyons and Kāwika Tengan, "Pacific Currents," 619–24.

Perez, Craig Santos. "Uncle Spam Wants You." *Kenyon Review,* April 26, 2013. https://kenyonreview.org/2013/04/uncle-spam-wants-you/.

Plahe, Jagjit Kaur, Shona Hawkes, and Sunil Ponnamperuma. "The Corporate Food Regime and Food Sovereignty in the Pacific Islands." *Contemporary Pacific* 25, no. 2 (Fall 2013): 309–38.

Pugh, Jonathan. "Relationality and Island Studies in the Anthropocene." *Island Studies Journal* 13, no. 2 (2018): 93–110.

Quinene, Frederick B. *An Islander's Voice*. Mangilao: University of Guam Press, 2018.

Rabson, Steve. Preface and Introduction to *Okinawa: Two Postwar Novellas*, translated with an introduction and afterword by Steve Rabson, 1–30. Berkeley: Institute of East Asian Studies, University of California, Berkeley, 1989.

Raheja, Michelle H. *Reservation Reelism: Redfacing, Visual Sovereignty, and Representations of Native Americans in Film*. Lincoln: University of Nebraska Press, 2010.

Rajan, Kaushik Sunder. *Biocapital: The Constitution of Postgenomic Life*. Durham, NC: Duke University Press, 2006.

Rana, Aziz. *The Two Faces of American Freedom*. Cambridge, MA: Harvard University Press, 2010.

Randall, James E. "Island Studies Inside (and Outside) of the Academy: The State of This Interdisciplinary Field." In Ginoza, *The Challenges of Island Studies*, 45–56.

Reyes, Victoria. *Global Borderlands: Fantasy, Violence, and Empire in Subic Bay, Philippines*. Stanford, CA: Stanford University Press, 2019.

Rifkin, Mark. *Beyond Settler Time: Temporal Sovereignty and Indigenous Self-Determination*. Durham, NC: Duke University Press, 2017.

Rifkin, Mark. "Indigenizing Agamben: Rethinking Sovereignty in Light of the 'Peculiar' Status of Native Peoples." *Cultural Critique* 73 (2009): 88–124.

Rivera, Rachel, dir. *Sin City Diary*. New York: Women Make Movies, 1992. Videocassette (VHS), 29 minutes.

Rivero, Oswaldo de. *The Myth of Development: Non-Viable Economies of the 21st Century*. Translated by Claudia Encinas and Janet Herrick Encinas. London: Zed Books, 2001.

Rizzo, Albert, Thomas D. Parsons, Belinda Lange, Patrick Kenny, John G. Buckwalter, Barbara Rothbaum, JoAnn Difede, John Frazier, Brad Newman, Josh Williams, and Greg Reger. "Virtual Reality Goes to War: A Brief Review of the Future of Military Behavioral Healthcare." *Journal of Clinical Psychology in Medical Settings* 18 (2011): 176–87.

Roberts, Brian Russell, and Michelle Ann Stephens, eds. *Archipelagic American Studies*. Durham, NC: Duke University Press, 2017.

Roberts, William Clare. "What Was Primitive Accumulation? Reconstructing the Origin of a Critical Concept." *European Journal of Political Theory* (2017): 1–21.

Robinson, Cedric, J. *Black Marxism: The Making of the Black Radical Tradition*. Chapel Hill: University of North Carolina Press, 2000.

Robinson, Cedric J. *Black Movements in America*. New York: Routledge, 1997.

Rodriguez, Robyn Magalit. *Migrants for Export: How the Philippine State Brokers Labor to the World*. Minneapolis: University of Minnesota Press, 2010.

Rogers, Robert F. *Destiny's Landfall: A History of Guam*. Honolulu: University of Hawai'i Press, 1995.

Ross, Andrew. *Creditocracy and the Case for Debt Refusal*. New York: OR Books, 2013.

Sakai, Naoki, and Hyon Joo Yoo. Introduction to *The Trans-Pacific Imagination: Rethinking Boundary, Culture and Society*, edited by Naoki Sakai and Hyon Joo Yoo, 1–44. Singapore: World Scientific, 2012.

Salem, Saber, and Armin Rosencranz. "Climate Refugees in the Pacific." *Environmental Law Reporter* 50, no. 7 (2020): 10.540–45.

Santos, Aida F. "Gathering the Dust: The Bases Issue in the Philippines." In *Let the Good Times Roll: Prostitution and the U.S. Military in Asia*, by Saundra Pollock Sturdevant and Brenda Stoltzfus, 32–47. New York: New Press, 1992.

Santos, Angel. "U.S. Return Was Reoccupation, Not Liberation." *Pacific Sunday News*, July 21, 1991.

Saranillio, Dean Itsuji. *Unsustainable Empire: Alternative Histories of Hawai'i Statehood*. Durham, NC: Duke University Press, 2018.

Schlund-Vials, Cathy J. "'Finding' Guam: Distant Epistemologies and Cartographic Pedagogies." *Asian American Literature: Discourses and Pedagogies* 5 (2014): 45–60.

Schmitt, Carl. *The Nomos of the Earth in the International Law of Jus Publicum Europaeum*. Translated by G. L. Ulmen. Candor, NY: Telos Press, 2006.

Schwebel, Michael B. "Climate Change Perceptions and Preparation in the United States Territories in the Pacific: American Samoa, Guam, and the Commonwealth of the Northern Mariana Islands." *Island Studies Journal* 13, no. 1 (2018): 135–48.

See, Sarita Echavez. *The Filipino Primitive: Accumulation and Resistance in the American Museum*. New York: New York University Press, 2017.

Shapiro, Michael J. *Violent Cartographies: Mapping Cultures of War*. Minneapolis: University of Minnesota Press, 1993.

Sheller, Mimi. "Caribbean Futures in the Offshore Anthropocene: Debt, Disaster, and Duration." *Environment and Planning D: Society and Space* 36, no. 6 (2018): 971–86.

Sheller, Mimi. *Island Futures: Caribbean Survival in the Anthropocene*. Durham, NC: Duke University Press, 2020.

Shibusawa, Naoko. *America's Geisha Ally: Reimagining the Japanese Enemy*. Cambridge, MA: Harvard University Press, 2006.

Shigematsu, Setsu, and Keith L. Camacho. "Introduction: Militarized Currents, Decolonizing Futures." In *Militarized Currents*, xv–xlviii.

Shigematsu, Setsu, and Keith L. Camacho, eds. *Militarized Currents: Toward a Decolonized Future in Asia and the Pacific*. Minneapolis: University of Minnesota Press, 2010.

Shimabuku, Annmaria M. *Alegal: Biopolitics and the Unintelligibility of Okinawan Life*. New York: Fordham University Press, 2019.

Simbulan, Roland G. "People's Movement Responses to Evolving U.S. Military Activities in the Philippines." In Lutz, *The Bases of Empire*, 145–80.

Somerville, Alice Te Punga. "Searching for the Trans-Indigenous." *Verge: Studies in Global Asias* 4, no. 2 (Fall 2018): 96–105.

Son, Elizabeth. *Embodied Reckonings: "Comfort Women," Performance, and Transpacific Redress*. Ann Arbor: University of Michigan Press, 2018.

Souder-Jaffery, Laura. "A Not So Perfect Union: Federal-Territorial Relations Between the United States and Guam." In *Chamorro Self-Determination: The Right of a People*, edited by Laura Souder-Jaffery and Robert A. Underwood, 7–32. Mangilao, Guam: Chamorro Studies Association and Micronesian Area Research Center, University of Guam, July 1987.

Souder-Jaffery, Laura, and Robert A. Underwood, eds. *Chamorro Self-Determination: The Right of a People*. Mangilao, Guam: Chamorro Studies Association and Micronesian Area Research Center, University of Guam, July 1987.

Spillers, Hortense J. "Mama's Baby, Papa's Maybe: An American Grammar." Chap. 8 in *Black, White, and in Color: Essays on American Literature and Culture*. Chicago: University of Chicago Press, 2003.

Spivak, Gayatri Chakravorty. *A Critique of Postcolonial Reason: Toward a History of the Vanishing Present*. Cambridge, MA: Harvard University Press, 1999.

Streeck, Wolfgang. *Buying Time: The Delayed Crisis of Democratic Capitalism*. London: Verso, 2014.

Sturdevant, Saundra Pollock. "Okinawa Then and Now." In *Let the Good Times Roll: Prostitution and the U.S. Military in Asia*, by Saundra Pollock Sturdevant and Brenda Stoltzfus, 244–53. New York: New Press, 1992.

Sturdevant, Saundra Pollock, and Brenda Stoltzfus. "Disparate Threads of the Whole: An Interpretive Essay." In *Let the Good Times Roll: Prostitution and the U.S. Military in Asia*, by Saundra Pollock Sturdevant and Brenda Stoltzfus, 300–334. New York: New Press, 1992.

Sturdevant, Saundra Pollock, and Brenda Stoltzfus. *Let the Good Times Roll: Prostitution and the U.S. Military in Asia*. New York: New Press, 1992.

Suzuki, Erin. "And the View from the Ship: Setting Asian American Studies Asail." *Verge: Studies in Global Asias* 4, no. 2 (Fall 2018): 44–53.

Suzuki, Erin. *Ocean Passages: Navigating Pacific Islander and Asian American Literatures*. Philadelphia: Temple University Press, 2021.

Suzuki, Erin, and Aimee Bahng. "The Transpacific Subject in Asian American Culture." In *Oxford Research Encyclopedia, Literature*. New York: Oxford University Press, 2020. Article published January 2020. doi: 10.1093/acrefore/9780190201098.013.877.

Tadiar, Neferti Xina M. *Fantasy-Production: Sexual Economies and Other Philippine Consequences for the New World Order*. Hong Kong: Hong Kong University Press, 2004.

Taitano, Lehua M. *Inside Me an Island: Poems*. Cincinnati, OH: WordTech Editions, 2018.

Takagi, J. T., and Hye Jung Park, dirs. *The Women Outside: Korean Women and the U.S. Military*. New York: Third World Newsreel, 1995. Videocassette (VHS), 52 minutes.

Tan, Jared Alex. "Filming from a New Perspective: An Interview with Gina Kim." *Perspectives Film Festival*, 2018. Accessed June 17, 2019. https://www.perspectivesfilmfestival .com/filming-new-perspective-interview-gina-kim/.

Tanji, Miyume. "Japanese Wartime Occupation, War Reparation, and Guam's Chamorro Self-Determination." In Broudy, Simpson, and Arakaki, *Under Occupation*, 161–82.

Teaiwa, Teresia. "AmneSIA." In "Teresia Teaiwa: 'We Sweat and Cry Salt Water, So We Know That the Ocean Is Really in Our Blood.'" *International Feminist Journal of Politics* 19, no. 2 (2017): 133–36.

Teaiwa, Teresia. "Bleeding Boundaries: Gendered Analyses of Militarism in the Western Pacific." *Asia Pacific Viewpoint* 52, no. 1 (April 2011): 1–44.

Teaiwa, Teresia. "Island Futures and Sustainability." In *A World of Islands: An Island Studies Reader*, edited by Godfrey Baldacchino, 514. Charlottetown, PEI: Island Studies Press, 2007.

Teaiwa, Teresia. "On Analogies: Rethinking the Pacific in a Global Context." *Contemporary Pacific* 18, no. 1 (Spring 2006): 71–87.

Teaiwa, Teresia. "Reading Paul Gauguin's *Noa Noa* with Epeli Hau'ofa's *Kisses in the Nederends*: Militourism, Feminism, and the 'Polynesian' Body." In *Inside Out: Literature, Cultural Politics, and Identity in the New Pacific*, edited by Vilsoni Hereniko and Rob Wilson, 249–63. Lanham, MD: Rowman & Littlefield, 1999.

Teaiwa, Teresia K. "For or *Before* an Asia Pacific Studies Agenda? Specifying Pacific Studies." In *Remaking Area Studies: Teaching and Learning across Asia and the Pacific*, edited by Terence Wesley-Smith and Jon Gross, 110–24. Manoa: University of Hawai'i Press, 2010.

Thomas, Brook. "A Constitution Led by the Flag: The *Insular Cases* and the Metaphor of Incorporation." In Burnett and Marshall, *Foreign in a Domestic Sense*, 59–84.

Tiongson, Jr., Antonio J. "Asian American Studies, Comparative Racialization, and Settler Colonial Critique." *Journal of Asian American Studies* 22, no. 3 (October 2019): 419–43.

Tokuyama, Yukinori. "Collective Traumatic Memory in a Jointly-Colonized Okinawa." In Broudy, Simpson, and Arakaki, *Under Occupation*, 191–202.

Tōma, Hiroko. "Backbone." Translated by Steve Rabson. In Bhowmik and Rabson, *Islands of Protest*, 221–22.

Tovy, Tal. "Manifest Destiny in POW Camps: The U.S. Army Reeducation Program During the Korean War." *Historian* 73, no. 3 (Fall 2011): 503–25.

Trask, Haunani-Kay. "Settlers of Color and 'Immigrant' Hegemony: 'Locals' in Hawai'i." In *Asian Settler Colonialism: From Local Governance to the Habits of Everyday Life in Hawai'i*, edited by Candace Fujikane and Jonathan Y. Okamura, 45–65. Honolulu: University of Hawai'i Press, 2008.

Ueunten, Wesley Iwao. "Rising Up from a Sea of Discontent: The 1970 Koza Uprising in U.S.-Occupied Okinawa." In Shigematsu and Camacho, *Militarized Currents*, 91–124.

United States Department of Defense. *Base Structure Report–Fiscal Year 2018 Baseline*. https://www.acq.osd.mil/eie/BSI/BEI_Library.html.

Vagts, Alfred. *A History of Militarism: Civilian and Military*. Rev. ed. New York: Free Press, 1959.

Viernes, James Perez. "Won't You Please Come Back to Guam? Media Discourse, Military Buildup, and Chamorros in the Space Between." In *The Space Between: Negotiating Culture, Place, and Identity in the Pacific*. Occasional Paper Series 44, edited by A. Marata Tamaira, 103–18. Honolulu: Center for Pacific Islands Studies, School of Pacific and Asian Studies, University of Hawai'i at Mānoa, 2009.

Vine, David. *Base Nation: How U.S. Military Bases Abroad Harm America and the World*. New York: Metropolitan Books, 2015.

Vine, David. "Lists of U.S. Military Bases Abroad, 1776–2019." *American University Digital Research Archive*. Accessed March 2, 2021. https://dra.american.edu/islandora/object/auislandora%3A81234.

Vine, David. *The United States of War: A Global History of America's Endless Conflicts, from Columbus to the Islamic State*. Oakland: University of California Press, 2020.

Wald, Priscilla. "Terms of Assimilation: Legislating Subjectivity in the Emerging Nation." In *Cultures of United States Imperialism*, edited by Amy Kaplan and Donald E. Pease, 59–84. Durham, NC: Duke University Press, 1993.

Walshe, Rory A., and Charlotte Eloise Stancioff. "Small Island Perspectives on Climate Change." *Island Studies Journal* 13, no. 1 (2018): 13–24.

Wang, Chih-ming. "Teaching American Studies in Taiwan: Military Bases and the Paradox of Peace and Security in East Asia." *American Quarterly* 68, no. 2 (2016): 387–91.

Wang, Chih-ming, and Yu-Fang Cho, eds. "The Chinese Factor: Reorienting Global Imaginaries in American Studies." Special issue, *American Quarterly* 69, no. 3 (September 2017).

Watson, Faith C. "Ha Jin's *War Trash*: Writing War in a 'Documentary Manner.'" *Japan Studies Association Journal* 7 (2009): 115–31.

Weiner, Mark S. "Teutonic Constitutionalism: The Role of Ethno-Juridical Discourse in the Spanish-American War." In Burnett and Marshall, *Foreign in a Domestic Sense*, 48–81.

Wendt, Albert. "Towards a New Oceania." *Mana Review* 1, no. 1 (1976): 49–60.

Wesley-Smith, Terence. "Rethinking Pacific Studies Twenty Years On." *Contemporary Pacific* 28, no. 1 (2016): 153–69.

Westad, Odd Arne. *The Global Cold War: Third World Interventions and the Making of Our Times*. Cambridge: Cambridge University Press, 2005.

Whyte, Kyle. "Indigenous Climate Change Studies: Indigenizing Futures, Decolonizing the Anthropocene." *English Language Notes* 55, no. 1–2 (Fall 2017): 153–62.

Wissot, Lauren. "Sex Crimes and Virtual Reality: Best VR Storytelling of 2017, Gina Kim's *Bloodless*." *Filmmaker*, December 22, 2017. https://filmmakermagazine.com/104182 -sex-crimes-and-virtual-reality-best-vr-storytelling-of-2017-gina-kims-bloodless/# .XQq75Xt7nEh.

Wolfe, Patrick. "Settler Colonialism and the Elimination of the Native." *Journal of Genocide Research* 8, no. 4 (2006): 387–409.

Woodward, Rachel. "From Military Geography to Militarism's Geographies: Disciplinary Engagements with the Geographies of Militarism and Military Activities." *Progress in Human Geography* 29, no. 6 (2005): 718–40.

Woodward, Valerie Solar. "'I Guess They Didn't Want Us Asking Too Many Questions': Reading American Empire in Guam." *Contemporary Pacific* 25, no. 1 (2013): 67–91.

Worthy, Blythe, Steve Choe, Sangjoon Lee, Benjamin Nickl, Emma Rayward, and Lee Sung-Ae. "The Appeal of Korea: Transnational Korean Screen Culture." *Australasian Journal of American Studies* 39, no. 1 (December 2020): 149–90.

Wright, Robert E. *One Nation under Debt: Hamilton, Jefferson, and the History of What We Owe*. New York: McGraw-Hill, 2008.

Wynter, Sylvia. "Is 'Development' a Purely Empirical Concept or Also Teleological? A Perspective from 'We the Underdeveloped.'" In *Prospects for Recovery and Sustainable Development in Africa*, edited by Aguibou Y. Yansané, 299–316. Westport, CT: Greenwood Press, 1992.

Xiang, Sunny. "Race, Tone, and Ha Jin's 'Documentary Manner.'" *Comparative Literature* 70, no. 1 (2018): 72–92.

Xie, Xinqiu. "War Memoir as False Document." *Amerasia Journal* 38, no. 2 (2012): 35–42.

Yamamoto, Lilian. "Climate Relocation and Indigenous Culture Preservation in the Pacific Islands." *Georgetown Journal of International Affairs* 21 (Fall 2020): 150–57.

Yamashiro, Aiko, and Noelani Goodyear-Ka'ōpua, eds. *The Value of Hawai'i 2: Ancestral Roots, Oceanic Visions*. Honolulu: Published for the Biographical Research Center by the University of Hawai'i Press, 2014.

Yamashiro, Aiko, and Noelani Goodyear-Kaʻōpua. "We Are Islanders." In *The Value of Hawaiʻi 2: Ancestral Roots, Oceanic Visions*, edited by Aiko Yamashiro and Noelani Goodyear-Kaʻōpua, 1–8. Honolulu: Published for the Biographical Research Center by the University of Hawaiʻi Press, 2014.

Yeo, Andrew I. "Realism, Critical Theory, and the Politics of Peace and Security: Lessons from Anti-Base Protests on Jeju Island." *European Journal of International Security* 3, no. 2 (2017): 235–55.

Yokota, Ryan Masaaki. "The Okinawan (Uchinānchu) Indigenous Movement and Its Implications for Intentional/International Action." In Dvorak and Tanji, "Indigenous Asias," 55–73.

Yoneyama, Lisa. *Cold War Ruins: Transpacific Critique of American Justice and Japanese War Crimes*. Durham, NC: Duke University Press, 2016.

Yoneyama, Lisa. "Toward a Decolonial Genealogy of the Transpacific." In Wang and Cho, "The Chinese Factor," 471–82.

Yoneyama, Lisa. "Traveling Memories, Contagious Justice: Americanization of Japanese War Crimes at the End of the Post-Cold War." *Journal of Asian American Studies* 6, no. 1 (2003): 57–93.

Young, Charles S. *Name, Rank, and Serial Number: Exploiting Korean War POWs at Home and Abroad*. Oxford: Oxford University Press, 2014.

Young, Charles S. "Voluntary Repatriation and Involuntary Tattooing of Korean War POWs." In *Northeast Asia and the Legacy of Harry S. Truman: Japan, China, and the Two Koreas*, edited by James I. Matray, 145–67. Kirksville, MO: Truman State University Press, 2012.

Yuh, Ji-Yeon. *Beyond the Shadow of Camptown: Korean Military Brides in America*. New York: New York University Press, 2002.

Yuh, Ji-Yeon. "Moved by War: Migration, Diaspora, and the Korean War." *Journal of Asian American Studies* 8, no. 3 (2005): 277–91.

Zinn, Howard. "The Power and the Glory: Myths of American Exceptionalism." *Boston Review*, June 1, 2005. http://bostonreview.net/zinn-power-glory.

during, 120; end of, 120; Japan and, 79; POW camps and, 135; POW repatriation and, 127

Collins, Patricia Hill, 94

colonial cartographic violence, 140

colonialism: disaster capitalism and, 174; franchise, 46; naturalizing, 24

coloniality of climate, 182

colonial plunder, 15

colonial violence, 95

comfort women, 109

Commission on Decolonization, 149

Committee on the Murder of Yun Geum-i by American Military in Korea, 101

Commonwealth of the Northern Mariana Islands, 24

compact of mutual obligation, 49

compelled mass defection, 125

compelled repatriation, 123–24

concentration camps, 131, 134

contact economy, 42

continental imperialism, 24

contracts, 49

Cooper, Melinda, 52–54

coral reefs, 168

Coulthard, Glen, 47, 95

counterinsurgencies, Cold War and, 120

countersovereignty, 191n23

counterviolence, 95–96

COVID-19 pandemic, 37

credit-baiting, 56

critical militarisation studies, 29

crony capitalism, 10

Cuba, 70, 131, 134, 142

Cub Scouts, 6

cultural imperialism, 6

culture-systemic, 57

Darda, Joseph, 118

Dargis, Manohla, 2

"Dark Flowers" (Kishaba), 35, 67, 80–82, 85–88

Davis, Arnold, "Dave," 149, 150

Davis, Sasha, 23, 111, 141, 153

Davis v. Government of Guam, 151, 152

Day, Iyko, 22, 47

"Dear Matafele Peinam" (Jetñil-Kijiner), 176, 180

debt: affective, 9, 53; asymmetries of power and, 3; of banks, 11; consequences of

defaulting on, 9; ecological, 178, 226n17; as effect of freedom, 55–61; figurative, 10, 13, 153–66, 183; as foreclosure of freedom, 19–20, 55–61; future colonized by, 56; Haitian independence and, 60; household, 190n13; imperialism and, 19–20; national, 75–76; as necropolitical regime, 41; public, 41–49, 201n47; sovereign, 11; United States, 50–52; war and, 42–43

debt bondage, 67, 99–108; escaping, 112; sex work and, 89, 109, 110, 212n147

debt burden, 56, 57

debt ceiling, 50

debt imperialism, 35, 41, 50, 52–54, 90; resistance to, 183; temporal exception of, 161

debt incumbency, 54

debtor/creditor relationship, 55–57

debt-trap diplomacy, 57

decolonial genealogies, 30–34

decolonial political geography, 22

decolonization, 40, 120; antimilitarist, 167–68, 170; of Guam, 141; POW camps and, 117; processes of, 149

DEIS (Draft Environmental Impact Statement), 166–68, 170

Deleuze, Gilles, 56

DeLoughrey, Elizabeth, 23, 29, 157, 177, 182

demilitarization, 80, 94, 169

Democratic People's Republic of Korea (DPRK), 122, 131

Department of Defense, US (DoD), 69, 94, 168; base site count, 193n38, 195n61; energy consumption by, 178–79; formation of, 121; Guam and, 148; real property portfolio, 84

Department of Homeland Security, 118, 136

deregulation, 10

Derrida, Jacques, 97

deterritorialization, 107–8

digital uncanny, 100

disaster capitalism, 174, 182

"Discontiguous States of America" (Lai), 158

discontiguous territory, 23, 42

disembodied subjects, 146

dispossession, 41–49

docupoetry, 222n59

DoD. *See* Department of Defense, US

Dodd, Francis, 129–31

dollar, de-pegging of, 51

Rivero, Oswaldo de, 135
Roberts, William Clare, 46
Robinson, Cedric, 45
Rogers, Robert F., 146, 165
Roh Moo-hyun, 64
Root, Elihu, 144
Ryūkyū Archipelago, 79

sacrifice zones, 49, 63, 66, 141
Sakamoto v. Duty Free Shoppers, Ltd., 147, 148, 219n33
Salvation Army, 171
San Francisco Peace Treaty (1952), 79
Santos, Angel, 165, 166, 169
Schmitt, Carl, 25, 122
Scramble for Africa, 58
See, Sarita Echavez, 160
self-determination plebiscites, 149, 150
self-governing, 148
Senate Foreign Relations Committee, 70
"separate but equal" doctrine, 145
settler colonialism, 46; "astounding political creativity" and, 23-27; biopolitics of, 134; cultural imperialism and, 6; gendered nature of, 191n25; genocidal violence of, 5; land seizures of, 21; liberal multicultural, 31; as logic of elimination, 22; militarist imperialism and, 2, 16, 17; military empire and, 22; "present tenseness" of, 88; as structure of failure, 160, 189n5; territoriality and, 158
settler expansion, human interiority and, 117-29
settler garrison, 2, 4; geography of militarism and, 25; as spatial exception, 106; unincorporated territory of, 27
settler imperial failure, 16; aesthetics of, 13-15, 168
settler imperial sovereignty, 18
settler state power and sovereignty, 18
settler time, 50
sexual violence, camptowns and, 67, 99
sex work, 88-89; camptowns and, 66-67, 99, 101, 108, 109; debt bondage and, 67, 89, 109, 110, 212n147; migration and, 75; militarized, 66-67, 76, 99-112; regulation of, 105
Sheller, Mimi, 182
Shima (journal), 174
Shufeldt, Robert W., 72

sihek, 172-73
Silicon Valley, 13
Silver Stallion (Ahn), 36, 67, 103-5
Sin City Diary (documentary), 35, 67, 73, 75, 76
Skinner, Carlton, 146
slavery, 59
slicky boys, 110
social contract, 49
social hygiene clinic, 77
Société Générale, 60
SOFA (Status of Forces Agreements), 74, 91, 101, 106, 155
South Korea, 124; anti-Communist violence in, 64, 66; anti-imperialist sentiment in, 101; capitalist hierarchy in, 5; culture industry, 12; debt of banks in, 11; economic development of, 106; film industry, 190n12; household debt levels in, 190n13; Jeju Island and, 33, 34, 63-65; militarized sex work and debt bondage, 99-112; as militarized US neo-colony, 2; patriarchy in, 107; SOFAs with, 101; United States and structural feeling of, 10; United States military bases in, 30, 68; United States relationship with, 64-65; US cultural imperialism in, 6; US military presence in, 66
sovereign debt, 11
sovereignty, 122; monetary, 51; of Native Americans, 45; settler imperial, 18; United States superseding, 21
Soviet Union, 122
Spain, 133, 139, 140, 143
SPAM®, 171-72
Spanish-American War, 24, 30, 70, 74, 134, 141-43
Spanish Galleon Trade Route, 155
spatial exception, 18, 26, 66, 106, 116, 120, 133, 135, 157
Special Action Committee on Okinawa Agreement, 97
speculative nationalism, 54
Spillers, Hortense, 59
Spivak, Gayatri Chakravorty, 56
statehood: geopolitics of, 18; metapolitical authority and, 21
state of exception, 18
Status of Forces Agreements (SOFA), 74, 79, 91, 101, 106, 155